THE HOUSE OF LORDS AT WORK

ALSO PUBLISHED BY
OXFORD UNIVERSITY PRESS

Parliament and Pressure Politics
Edited by Michael Rush

The New Select Committees (2nd Edition)
Edited by Gavin Drewry

Parliamentary Questions
Edited by Mark Franklin and Philip Norton

THE HOUSE OF LORDS AT WORK

A Study based on the 1988–1989 Session

Edited by

DONALD SHELL
and
DAVID BEAMISH

for the Study of Parliament Group

CLARENDON PRESS · OXFORD
1993

Oxford University Press, Walton Street, Oxford OX2 6DP
Oxford New York Toronto
Delhi Bombay Calcutta Madras Karachi
Kuala Lumpur Singapore Hong Kong Tokyo
Nairobi Dar es Salaam Cape Town
Melbourne Auckland Madrid
and associated companies in
Berlin Ibadan

Oxford is a trade mark of Oxford University Press

Published in the United States
by Oxford University Press Inc., New York

British Library Cataloguing in Publication Data
Data available

Library of Congress Cataloging in Publication Data
The House of Lords at work: a study with particular reference to the 1988–1989 session/edited by Donald Shell and David Beamish for the Study of Parliament Group.
Includes index.
1. Great Britain. Parliament. House of Lords. 2. Great Britain—Politics and government—1979– I. Shell, Donald. II. Beamish, David. III. Study of Parliament Group.
JN623 1988a 328.4107'1—dc20 92-29010
ISBN 0–19–827762–8

Typeset by Best-set Typesetter Ltd., Hong Kong
Printed in Great Britain
on acid-free paper by
Biddles Ltd., Guildford and King's Lynn

PREFACE

This book is the outcome of work undertaken by members of the Study of Parliament Group, an organization composed of academics and officers of both Houses of Parliament which has been responsible for a number of published studies on aspects of the modern British Parliament. This is the Group's first work to be devoted exclusively to the House of Lords. When those interested in this project first met in 1987 we decided that the most useful thing to do would be to study a single session in some depth. This approach does have its limitations. No one session can be regarded as typical. But limiting ourselves to a single session does make possible a more detailed and comprehensive study than would otherwise be the case. We believe that the Appendices, and the tables (mainly in Chapter 2) based on them, contain a fuller analysis of attendance and voting than has hitherto been published.

Our purpose has been to examine what the House actually does rather than to argue about what should be done with the House. But in providing an examination of what the House does contributors have naturally also sought to evaluate its activities. It is therefore perhaps as well to stress that the contents of each chapter are the responsibility of the named authors of that chapter and not of the editors, nor indeed of the Study of Parliament Group.

We are grateful to the Nuffield Foundation for a grant which assisted with research and travel expenses. We also express our appreciation to Oxford University Press, and in particular to Henry Hardy who was in at the birth of this project, and to Tim Barton and Janet Moth who saw it through to conclusion. We regret that their patience was tried because of delayed delivery, though anyone who has attempted to orchestrate a team of a dozen contributors, all of them busy people, may well have a little sympathy with the editors in this regard. As editors we are nevertheless very grateful to all those who have contributed to this work, and who have (on the whole at least) cheerfully borne with requests for alterations from the editors. We also express our thanks to those who participated in study group discussions, but without themselves becoming contributors to this volume.

D.R.S.
D.R.B.

March 1992

CONTENTS

CONTRIBUTORS

Nicholas D. J. Baldwin, Director of Studies at Wroxton College, the British campus of Fairleigh Dickinson University, New Jersey

David Beamish, Chief Clerk, House of Lords

R. L. Borthwick, Senior Lecturer, Department of Politics, University of Leicester

Jenny Brock, freelance researcher, formerly Research Associate at Bedford College, University of London

Gavin Drewry, Professor of Social Policy and Administration, Royal Holloway and Bedford New College, University of London

Elizabeth Flood, Senior Clerk, House of Commons

Cliff Grantham, Special Adviser, Department for Education, and previously research assistant to MPs and freelance political consultant

David Jones, Librarian of the House of Lords

David Miers, Professor of Law, University of Wales College of Cardiff

Douglas Millar, Principal Clerk, House of Commons

David Natzler, Deputy Principal Clerk, House of Commons

Michael Rush, Reader in Parliamentary Government, University of Exeter

Donald Shell, Lecturer, Department of Politics, University of Bristol

1

The House of Lords in Context

Donald Shell

Discussion and argument about the House of Lords have been perennial topics for debate in Britain. Schemes for the reform or replacement of the House have abounded for at least 150 years. Its decay and eventual demise has been regularly predicted. But it has neither died nor has it (yet) been abolished. Instead the House has enjoyed over the last generation or so something of a renaissance. It has become busier, and more notice has been taken of it, especially since the arrival of television cameras in the House in 1985. And throughout the 1980s the regularity of Government defeat in the Lords contrasted with the impression of effortless dominance the Thatcher Governments generally enjoyed in the Commons. Is the House actually becoming more important in the whole business of government?

Claim and counter-claim are frequently made about the House. To some it is the epitome of wisdom, experience, and intelligence applied to public affairs. Its debates are erudite, well-informed, and therefore immensely worth while. To others it is a ridiculously lop-sided body, disproportionately full of the wealthy, the worthy, and the old, redolent with pomposity, stuffed with members whose expertise is overwhelmingly that of yesteryear. Frequently the value of its legislative work is stressed, especially its role in revising Government bills, many of which (so it is said) have received such hurried and tempestuous examination in the Commons. But others, who may have delved a little more deeply beneath the surface of the legislative process, have suggested its work of revision is primarily a formality, a mere convenience for governments, which all too often introduce ill-thought-out and badly drafted bills, which then require much alteration as they wend their way through Parliament. Some see the House as a chamber of considerable influence on public affairs; others assert its irrelevance. To some it is a benign, agreeable, if somewhat idiosyncratic body. To others it is malign, a damaging, if not pernicious, influence in a class-ridden society still holding back from a full commitment to democracy.

This book does not address such questions directly. It is not intended as another contribution to the 'mend them or end them' debate. Rather it is an attempt to examine closely the work of the House, and to analyse and evaluate this in a recent single session. This may seem a restricted aim. But the important point is that this book provides a systematic analysis of every area of activity within the House in the year 1988–9. To examine a longer period would inevitably result in considerable selectivity. Better we thought to try to be as comprehensive as possible within a single session. By so doing, a more accurate assessment of the work of the House in all its diversity and unevenness could be obtained. Hence this study. It ranges from major tussles with the Government over legislation to the largely behind-the-scenes work of select committees; from the comparatively well-publicized debates with the 'good and the great' taking part to the unnoticed discussion of obscure subjects late in the evening in a sparsely attended House. Apart from the judicial work[1] everything the House did has been examined by the authors of the chapters which follow. By this means we hope to provide a more solid basis than has hitherto been available for drawing conclusions about the role and value of the House.

But the examination of the work of the House needs to be set in a context. That is the purpose of this introductory chapter. It begins by explaining some of the more important changes which have taken place in the comparatively recent past, focusing especially upon the powers, composition, and character of the House. The functions of the House are then considered, with some indication being given of the variety of views which have been expressed about these. Finally we take a look at the House as it was in the 1988–9 session, giving particular attention to the membership of the front benches, and analysing how the time of the House was used during the session.

[1] The only area not covered by this study is the judicial work of the House; the reason for this omission is that the judicial role is now something quite distinct from the parliamentary functions of the House. On the judicial work of the House, see L. Blom-Cooper and G. Drewry, *Final Appeal: A Study of the House of Lords in its Judicial Capacity* (Oxford University Press, Oxford, 1972) and A. Paterson, *The Law Lords* (Macmillan, London, 1982).

The Changing House of Lords

The House survives in its present curious and highly anomalous form because there has never been sufficient agreement about how it should be reformed, or with what it should be replaced. The House has facilitated its own survival by demonstrating a capacity to adapt itself and its activities so as to sustain a continuing role in the whole business of parliamentary government. In so doing it typifies the character of the British Constitution.

Never in modern times has there been a crisis of sufficient severity to oblige Britain formally to enact its Constitution. If such a process had occurred then the House of Lords would surely have been replaced. For eleven years during the Cromwellian interlude the House did not meet. But this period was followed by a Restoration with the return of both monarchy and House of Lords. The relationships between the institutions of government had been decisively altered, but the institutions themselves continued, adapting gradually to new roles.

Powers restricted

The nineteenth-century franchise reforms confirmed the supremacy of the House of Commons. It was understood that a convention of the Constitution had been established precluding the House of Lords from resisting the clear will of the House of Commons. But in 1909 the Tory-dominated upper House ignored that convention and rejected the budget presented by the Liberal Government, thus precipitating a constitutional crisis, eventually to be resolved by the passage of the Parliament Act 1911. This formally limited the power of the House of Lords to interfere with legislation approved by the Commons. The majority of peers chose to acquiesce in this curtailment of their power, and through such acquiescence the survival of their House was assured.[2]

The Parliament Act replaced the absolute veto the House had formerly possessed over legislation by a suspensory veto of up to two years. Initially the House showed little inhibition in using

[2] See N. Blewett, *The Peers, the Parties and the People* (Macmillan, London, 1972).

its delaying powers. After the First World War, however, disagreement between the two Houses virtually disappeared for a generation because the Commons, like the Lords, was Tory-dominated; brief periods of minority Labour Government occurred (in 1924 and again 1929–31) but no occasion for serious conflict between the two Houses emerged.[3] When Labour did win a decisive Commons majority—in 1945—Conservative peers, under the leadership of the fifth Marquess of Salisbury, relied on the doctrine that the House accepted legislation foreshadowed in the governing party's election manifesto, while still reserving the right to make detailed amendments for reconsideration by the Commons.[4] The application of this doctrine, and the generally cautious and subdued nature of the Salisbury leadership in the House, ensured that there was little conflict between the two parts of Parliament. For their part Labour ministers increasingly acknowledged the value of the revising role of the Lords, a theme which has had growing emphasis throughout the post-war period as successive Governments of both parties have submitted ever-growing quantities of legislation to Parliament.

In 1948 talks between party leaders indicated a broad area of agreement about possible reform of the House.[5] But on the question of powers agreement could not be reached. So in place of any comprehensive reform a simple reduction in the power of the House was introduced by the Parliament Act 1949: the period of delay was cut from two years to one year. And that remains the power possessed by the House today to delay legislation. How is this power to be assessed, and how important has it been in subsequent years?

In the first place it is worth noting just what is included and

[3] On this and the whole period up to 1957, see P. A. Bromhead, *The House of Lords and Contemporary Politics* (Routledge & Kegan Paul, London, 1958).

[4] See speech by the 5th Marquess of Salisbury (Viscount Cranborne), HL Debs., 16 Aug. 1945, cols. 47–8. This drew on the view expressed by his grandfather, the 3rd Marquess, in a speech in the House on 17 June 1869 (see *Hansard*, 3rd Series, vol. CXCVII, cols. 83–4). See also C. C. Weston, 'Salisbury and the Lords, 1868–1895', *Historical Journal* 25 (1982), 103–29, repr. in *Peers, Politics and Power: The House of Lords 1603–1911*, ed. C. Jones and D. L. Jones (Hambledon Press, London, 1986).

[5] See *Agreed Statement on Conclusions of Party Leaders*, Cmd. 7380, 1948. Also B. Crick, *The Reform of Parliament* (Weidenfeld & Nicolson, London, 1964), ch. 6, esp. 128–31.

what is excluded by this power. The 1911 Act specifically exempted any legislation to prolong the life of a Parliament, that is to delay a general election beyond the stipulated five-year maximum term. The absence of an enacted Constitution has generally been taken as sufficient justification for retention of such a veto power by the second chamber. The House also retains a power of veto over all private bills and statutory instruments. The former are bills brought to Parliament by bodies such as local authorities or public corporations seeking particular powers to do things which they are not otherwise empowered to do (see Chapter 7). The Government does not take responsibility for private bills. Occasionally the Lords has rejected a bill, but only rarely has the interest of the Government been engaged; such an example was the British Transport Docks (Felixstowe) Bill, which the House rejected in 1976, much to the anger of the Labour Government. Statutory instruments were of such marginal importance in 1911 that the Parliament Act made no mention of them, an omission not rectified by the 1949 Act. The power of the House to reject such instruments was demonstrated when Conservative peers, goaded on by their former leader, Lord Salisbury, threw out the Southern Rhodesia (United Nations Sanctions) Order 1968.[6] But apart from that single display of foolish bad temper the House has taken considerable care to avoid conflict over statutory instruments, though its power in this area remains a matter with which Governments have had to reckon (see Chapter 5).

The language of the Parliament Acts is entirely in terms of bills introduced into the House of Commons, making them inapplicable to legislation introduced into the House of Lords. This is a limitation which Governments probably do well to bear in mind when determining the organization of their legislative programme; bills introduced into the House of Lords may ultimately have to be enacted in terms acceptable to that House, whereas Parliament Act procedures can be used, or at least credibly threatened, over bills introduced into the House of Commons.

[6] See Janet P. Morgan, *The House of Lords and the Labour Government 1964–1970* (Clarendon Press, Oxford, 1975).

For ordinary public legislation the period of delay fixed since 1949 at one year is measured from the date of second reading in the Commons (not from the date of disagreement between the two Houses) until the date on which the Commons passes the bill concerned in the second session. In practice this means that any delay is likely to be considerably less than one year. In 1975 the Lords failed to reach agreement with the Commons on Lords amendments to the Trade Union and Labour Relations (Amendment) Bill; the bill was reintroduced the following session under the Parliament Act procedures. In 1976 the same fate befell the Aircraft and Shipbuilding Industries Bill, which was also reintroduced the following session. Both these bills were passed without the Parliament Act procedures running their full course because soon after their introduction in the second session agreement between the Government and the House of Lords was reached. In 1989–90, however, the War Crimes Bill was rejected by the House of Lords at second reading, after it had passed all its Commons stages, and when this bill was reintroduced under Parliament Act procedures the following session, the House of Lords again rejected it outright at second reading. Following this second rejection of the bill by the upper House it proceeded without further debate in either House to royal assent. The War Crimes Act 1991 thus became the first bill to be passed under the terms of the Parliament Acts since the amending Parliament Act of 1949, and the first bill ever introduced by a Conservative Government to be passed under these procedures. The significance of this episode is considered in the concluding chapter.

In the pages that follow, very little reference is made to the powers of the House. In its day-to-day work only rarely does the question of power explicitly arise. But the possible influence of the House is a matter of continued relevance. Yet it may be unwise to divorce completely these two concepts—of power and influence—when analysing the role of the House. If influence is to be effective, it probably requires a basis in terms of power, even if it is simply the power to require the Government to seek a further vote in the Commons in order to reverse an amendment passed by the Lords. This again is a point to which we return in the conclusion.

Composition adjusted

Alongside the curtailment of the power of the House some adjustments have been made in its composition. Traditionally the House has been an aristocratic chamber, composed of peers by succession, peers by creation, and bishops. To be a peer was by definition to be a man of substance. In the twentieth century that has decisively changed.[7] The aristocracy has declined and the House of peers has become more meritocratic and less aristocratic, even a little plebeian and a good deal less plutocratic—certainly as far as the active House is concerned. In large part this change has been accomplished simply through successive Prime Ministers feeling free to recommend for the award of peerages individuals who were neither very rich nor necessarily drawn from the social circles which hitherto had monopolized the peerage. The rise of the Labour Party brought into public life many more people from ordinary backgrounds. Attlee as Prime Minister ennobled forty-four Labour Party supporters, few of whom were rich and some of whom were impecunious. Wholesale reform was of course continually in the minds of Labour politicians. A party of the Left could hardly endorse a second chamber all of whose members were *hereditary* peers (save for a few bishops and judges). But thoughts about the kind of radical surgery which might be performed on the House inhibited action aimed more modestly at modernizing the place. It therefore fell to the Conservatives to pass the only two Acts of Parliament this century which have actually altered the basis of membership of the House.

The first of these was the Life Peerages Act 1958, a simple measure long discussed but which successive governments had shied away from, either for fear of diluting the hereditary principle or for fear of strengthening a basically unreformed House of Lords.[8] The 1958 Act permitted the award of peerages which would be held for the lifetime of the recipient only; henceforth

[7] See D. Cannadine, *The Decline and Fall of the British Aristocracy* (Yale University Press, New Haven, Conn., 1990).

[8] Non-hereditary peerages had been introduced in 1876 for judges appointed to the House as Lords of Appeal in Ordinary. But this was only after considerable opposition to any dilution of the hereditary principle, and the award of life peerages had accordingly been strictly limited to this precisely defined group.

membership of the House could be accepted without heirs being threatened with the encumbrance of a peerage! Of greater moment was the fact that no limit was placed on the total of life peerages that could be awarded. Hence a considerably greater number of peerages could be created than previously without permanently adding to the nominal membership of what was already the largest legislative assembly in the world. The 1958 Act specifically allowed women as well as men to receive life peerages, and so the House at last ceased to be an exclusively male bastion. Following this measure the flow of new creations increased and attendance at the House began to improve.[9] No doubt the introduction, also in 1958, of an allowance to cover expenses peers incurred in carrying out parliamentary work further stimulated attendance. The size and scope of this allowance has steadily expanded (as is explained by Rush and Jones in Chapter 11).

If one embarrassment of the 1950s had been the low number of peers active in the work of the House, a further embarrassment was the continued nominal membership of peers who inherited their titles but had no wish to take up the responsibilities of membership of the House, or to suffer the disqualifications associated with this status. A partial relief was offered through the introduction of a peculiar Standing Order of the House in 1958 whereby peers, without abandoning any rights associated with membership of the House, could nevertheless surrender some of these rights for a time by taking 'leave of absence' from the House. The practical effect of this scheme has been marginal; it was probably of some significance initially, but its utility today seems virtually non-existent.

The Peerage Act of 1963 was, however, significant. This allowed peers by succession to renounce their peerages altogether—though renounced peerages would remain available to be assumed again by heirs. This legislation was introduced because a prominent, ambitious, and relatively youthful Labour MP (then known as Anthony Wedgwood Benn) had the misfortune to succeed to a peerage, and was thereby disqualified from continued membership of the House of Commons. Others had earlier sought some

[9] See Donald Shell, *The House of Lords*, 2nd edn. (Harvester Wheatsheaf, London, 1992).

way of remaining MPs but without success.[10] Whether because of the change in general attitudes, or because of the lengths to which Mr Wedgwood Benn was prepared to go in defying the existing law, Government and Parliament decided on this occasion to take action so as to allow those who inherited peerages to remain commoners. Though the numbers who have taken this course have been few (and fewer in the 1970s than the 1960s and none at all in the 1980s) they have included at least three leading politicians (Benn, Hogg, and Home). The passage of this Act provided further confirmation of the junior status of the House of Lords; those who had serious ambitions for the highest political offices would henceforth not only seek to become, but also take care to remain, members of the House of Commons. The same legislation admitted to the House all the holders of Scottish peerages and women who held hereditary peerages in their own right, two numerically small groups.

No further changes in the basis of membership of the House have taken place. But the arrival of life peers in relatively large numbers has been associated with change in the character of the House.

Character altered

The House had been in obvious decline in the 1950s. But this growing atrophy was arrested by the Life Peerages Act and in the period since then the House has steadily become a very much more active place. Table 1.1 illustrates and summarizes some of the changes that have taken place.

In the late 1980s the House sat more than twice as many hours as it did in the 1950s with an average daily attendance over twice as high as thirty years earlier. Sittings after 10 p.m. were virtually unknown in the 1950s but had become commonplace in the 1980s. The number of questions asked and the number of amendments made to bills had increased greatly. Select committee work—not included in Table 1.1—has also become an important element in the work of the House.

[10] See e.g. Quintin Hogg (Lord Hailsham of Saint Marylebone), *A Sparrow's Flight* (Collins, London, 1990), 262, where he tells of his attempt to divest himself of his peerage in order to remain a member of the House of Commons in 1950.

Table 1.1. *Growth in activity in the House of Lords*

	1959–60	1971–2	1981–2	1988–9
Peers on Roll	907	1,073	1,174	1,183
Peers who attended at least once	542	698	713	816
Peers who spoke at least once	283	419	503	537
Average daily attendance	136	250	284	316
Total hours House sat	450	813	930	1,077
Average length of sitting	4 hrs. 0 m.	5 hrs. 45 m.	6 hrs. 20 m.	7 hrs. 4 m.
Sittings after 10 p.m.	1	28	41	67
Number of starred questions	264	494	531	572
Number of questions for written answer	48	315	1,098	1,202
Number of amendments to Government bills	n/a	924	1,309	2,359
Number of divisions	16	171	146	189

Source: House of Lords Journal and Information Office and author's calculations.

The most immediate effect of the Life Peerages Act was to increase the strength of the Labour benches. From a couple of dozen (several too infirm for reliable service), Labour numbers expanded to over 100 during the Wilson Governments of the 1960s, and to over 150 during the 1970s. Cross-bench numbers also grew as public servants of all kinds received ennoblement. As Prime Minister in the 1960s Mr Wilson created new peers at the rate of twenty-five a year, over half of them Labour supporters. These new peers appeared to be the catalyst for changes in the attitude of the House illustrated, for example, in its support in the late 1960s for the abolition of capital punishment (a direct reversal of the view the House had held in the 1950s), and in legislation on such subjects as homosexuality and abortion.[11]

The 1960s was a decade in which institutional reform was on the parliamentary agenda. In 1968 talks were initiated by the

[11] See J. R. Vincent 'The House of Lords', *Parliamentary Affairs*, vol. XIX, No. 4 (Autumn 1966), 475–85.

Prime Minister, Harold Wilson, with other party leaders on the subject of Lords reform. These resulted in substantial agreement on reform proposals,[12] which if enacted would have resulted in the entrenchment of a new professionalism in the House. Peers by succession would have been phased out and an entirely nominated voting House of some 230 members would have emerged, with the government of the day having a plurality but not an absolute majority. The House (still the House of Lords) would probably have gained prestige initially through the removal of hereditary peers' voting rights, though peers by succession who had already taken their seats would have retained the right to attend and to speak in the House. But whether in the long run such a House—entirely the creature of prime ministerial patronage—would have been accorded legitimacy and sustained credibility is doubtful. In the event the proposed changes, though receiving overwhelming endorsement from peers themselves, failed because back-bench members on both sides of the House of Commons opposed them.[13]

The fact that peers had supported these reforms which failed because of opposition from MPs almost certainly affected the mood of the House of Lords. Throughout the 1970s the House became noticeably more assertive. The Conservatives in government after 1970 found the House very different from the one they had known prior to their loss of office in 1964.[14] The proclivity of Mr Wilson as Prime Minister in the 1960s in creating new peers ensured that the Labour Opposition in the Lords was far better placed to fight legislation in the Lords than it had ever been before. The Industrial Relations Bill, the legislative flagship of the Heath Government, was the subject of debate more protracted than had ever before occurred on any bill in the House. Labour peers seemed anxious to prove themselves in the eyes of their party in the Commons and the country. Altogether during the 1970–4 Parliament the Heath Government was defeated on 26 occasions, and most of these defeats ministers felt it imprudent or impolitic to try to reverse.

[12] See Cmnd. 3799 (1968), *House of Lords Reform*.

[13] On this attempted reform see Janet P. Morgan, *House of Lords and the Labour Government 1964–1970*.

[14] On this period see esp. Lord Windlesham, 'The House of Lords: A Study of Influence replacing Power' in *Politics in Practice* (Jonathan Cape, London, 1975).

Labour back in office from 1974 to 1979, but with an overall Commons majority only from October 1974 to April 1976, faced much greater difficulties in the Lords. What role a Tory-dominated upper House should play in a period characterized by a weak Labour Government struggling to assert its authority over truculent trades unions, austere international bankers, and a House of Commons in which it scarcely had a majority, was a perplexing question. The Government was defeated well over 300 times in the division lobbies. While the Labour Party in the Commons was irritated by the frequency of defeat in the Lords, Conservative peers were embarrassed at the ease with which such defeats could be inflicted. Securing the reversal of defeats was sometimes difficult to achieve given the Government's parlous state in the Commons. But Conservative peers gave way almost invariably when the Commons did delete Lords amendments. On two occasions, however, the Lords did delay Government legislation (as already mentioned), with the result that the Trade Union and Labour Relations (Amendment) Bill of 1975 and the Aircraft and Shipbuilding Industries Bill of 1976 were eventually passed in a form slightly different from that intended by the Government.

This was enough to cause the Labour Party at its 1977 Conference to renew its historic commitment to the abolition of the House of Lords. This decision was not, however, embodied in the party's 1979 manifesto, which instead spoke simply of removing the remaining legislative powers of the House. The Conservative leader, Mrs Thatcher, appointed a committee under Lord Home of the Hirsel (the former Conservative Prime Minister), to consider the future of the House and give her advice. This reported in 1978, making quite radical recommendations—but for reform rather than replacement.[15] In the early 1980s Mrs Thatcher came under some pressure to do something about the House. At that time it seemed reasonable to suppose that a swing of the electoral pendulum would soon see Labour back in office, possibly committed to abolition. So would it not be prudent for the Conservatives to reform the House first to

[15] Lord Home of the Hirsel, *Report of the Review Committee on the Second Chamber*, 1978, Conservative Political Centre.

enhance its acceptability? But this was not to be. A cabinet committee apparently examined the subject in the early 1980s,[16] but the Prime Minister was not interested; her priorities lay elsewhere.

Despite being the dominant party the Conservatives did not by any means enjoy a smooth ride in the Lords during the 1980s. Between 1979 and 1990 the Government was defeated 156 times in the Lords division lobbies (see Chapter 3, Table 3.6), and while most of these defeats were on relatively minor matters, many were none the less irritating to the Government and some were significant. Though she eschewed reform of the House Mrs Thatcher took good care to maintain the dominant position of the Conservative Party in the House of Lords through ensuring that the lion's share of new creations went to Conservative supporters.

The greater professionalism of the House, seen for example in the larger number of peers who work more or less full time in the chamber, and in the way Opposition parties organize their spokesmen in the House, did not lead to many changes in the procedures of the House. In 1991 the House still had no Speaker to enforce rules of order; there were no procedures for time-tabling bills; and motions to secure the closure of debate remained exceedingly rare. The committee stage of bills was with very few exceptions still taken on the floor of the House rather than off the floor in a public bill committee. In 1971 and again in 1986 the Leader of the House appointed a small group of representative peers to examine the working of the House and make recommendations for improvements. In both cases these groups circulated a questionnaire to their colleagues, but responses did not generally support significant change. Perhaps their reports were helpful in reinforcing in the minds of peers the need for collective self-discipline if extensive procedural changes were to be avoided. Debate on these reports confirmed that most peers were profoundly reluctant to see such changes introduced.

[16] See P. Hennessy 'The Other Opposition', Radio 4, 5 Nov. 1987. According to Nicholas Ridley (*My Style of Government*, Hutchinson, London, 1991, 33), reform of the House was again considered just before the 1987 election, when peers were proving particularly troublesome to the Prime Minister. But it was decided to do nothing.

The report of the 1986–7 Group is referred to at a number of points in this book.[17]

Thus the House of Lords remained in the early 1990s a legislative chamber largely unrestricted by procedural rules. In many respects it still resembled the mid-nineteenth-century House of Commons. But it remained like this only because of the relatively high degree of self-discipline exercised by peers and the role accorded to the party whips or 'usual channels' (as they are termed when this aspect of their work is under consideration) in devising timetables for bills. The House was still formally a predominantly hereditary body; in the early 1990s two-thirds of its members were there because they had inherited the right to be there. But as Nicholas Baldwin shows in Chapter 2, as far as the active membership is concerned, life peers had a slight preponderance. Hereditary peers remained numerically dominant within the Conservative Party in the House, but in the other parties they were handsomely outnumbered by their created counterparts in the form of life peers. The extent to which the voting House was different in composition from the working House—in the sense of those peers who contribute most to debates—is also a subject investigated later in this book. As well as hereditary and life peers, the House of Lords contains two ex-officio groups of members, namely bishops and senior judges. Their presence arises from now far-distant historical circumstances. But their role in the House is of some interest if only because some suggested schemes for reform have included an extension of the ex-officio principle.

The Functions of the House

In 1968 the White Paper on reform of the House of Lords suggested that the House had six main functions. These were

(*a*) the provision of a forum for full and free debate on matters of public interest;

[17] 10th Report from the Select Committee on Procedure, HL 227, 1970–1; *Report by the Group on the Working of the House*, HL 9, 1987–8; see also HL Debs., 4 Nov. 1987, cols. 988–1053.

(*b*) the revision of public bills brought from the House of Commons;
(*c*) the initiation of public legislation, including in particular those government bills which are less controversial in party political terms and private members' bills;
(*d*) the consideration of subordinate legislation;
(*e*) the scrutiny of the activities of the executive; and
(*f*) the scrutiny of private legislation.[18]

Table 1.2 shows how the House spent its time during the session under review.

It will be convenient here to consider the activities of the House under the headings 'legislative' and 'deliberative', though where to draw the line between these two is not always precisely clear and in practice the character of the proceedings under these headings may at times be not dissimilar. For example, the House sometimes debates statutory instruments under motions of a general kind (categorized as deliberative) rather than substantive motions, precisely because peers do not wish to involve the exercise of the power of veto the House still possesses in this area (see Chapter 5). The second reading debate of the Finance Bill is classified as legislative, even though the occasion is invariably taken as an opportunity for a general debate about the economic situation, with the bill then passing all its stages formally.

Legislative functions

As Table 1.2 shows, the House spends well over half its time on Government legislation, a proportion which, as Table 1.3 shows, has consistently increased during the last four Parliaments.

In Chapters 3 and 4 this major aspect of the work of the House is examined. Though all legislation must be formally approved by both Houses (and all primary legislation by the monarch as well) the actual activity of deciding what legislation to enact, of framing that legislation, and deciding its detailed content, are all matters closely controlled by Government. Influence is brought to bear upon Government by Parliament, and through Parliament by outside interests, which also exert pressure directly on

[18] *House of Lords Reform*, Cmnd. 3799, 1968, para. 8.

Table 1.2. *Allocation of time on the floor of the House of Lords, 1988–9*

Category of business	Percentage of total time	Approximate number of hours
Legislative		
Public bills	59.3	636
Lords' bills	19.8	212
Commons' bills	39.5	424
Government bills	57.0	612
Private members' bills	2.2	24
Private bills	0.8	9
Affirmative instruments	2.6	28
Other statutory instruments	0.3	3
Measures	0.3	3
Total legislative	63.3	680
Deliberative		
Starred questions	6.0	65
General debates	15.7	168
Debates on Reports from European Communities Committee	2.8	30
Debates on Reports from Science and Technology Committee	0.3	3
Statements	1.8	19
Unstarred questions	4.5	48
Total deliberative	31.1	333
Other		
(Prayers, Introductions, formal business, and adjournments during pleasure)	5.6	60
TOTAL	100.0	1,073

Sources: Calculated from *Hansard* and from figures supplied by the House of Lords Journal and Information Office.

Government. Parliament may be considered important in part because it provides the only forum in which legislation can be publicly discussed, line by line, and Government directly challenged to explain why its proposed legislation takes the form that it does. The process of parliamentary debate includes opportunity for draft legislation to be amended, but it is comparatively speaking unusual for amendments of which the Government clearly disapproves to be written into bills in either House.

While there is this similarity as regards the revising function, there are also obvious differences. Because the Commons is directly elected, and the Government of the day owes its existence to its ability to sustain a Commons majority, the lower House is the cockpit of party politics. The Government is continually under challenge there from the Opposition, which seeks to establish its claim in the eyes of the electorate to replace the Government. Most legislation is caught up in this contest of wills between Government and Opposition, but the battle tends to be concentrated each session around three or four major bills. The Opposition resists the second reading of such bills, and uses the remaining stages less for scrutiny with a view to improvement, more as a continuation of political trench warfare. The Opposition's aim is to ensure that the supposed perversity of such legislation is as clearly impressed on the public mind as possible. These few dominant bills almost invariably attract 'guillotine' motions.

But apart from proceedings on such bills it must be remembered that party politics is of the essence of the lower House. This feature is a basic determinant of the kind of scrutiny provided by the Commons. Every MP (apart from the Speaker) wears a party label, and for the vast majority securing some party advantage over their opponents, or advancing their own position within their party, are far more important than introducing so-called 'improvements' to Government legislation. It would be quite wrong to imagine that the House of Lords avoids party politics (which is most of the time clearly evident), but the party struggle is played out in more subdued tones, and personal ambition to progress within one's party is much less of a driving force. It seems reasonable to surmise that this affects the nature of the scrutiny given to legislation. For example, it has often been stated that the Lords examine bills less from a party political standpoint, more from an expert standpoint. How far this is actually the case is a further question examined below. In what ways are the proceedings in the upper House different from those in the House of Commons? Are genuinely new points raised in the House of Lords, and if so to what extent?

In so far as the latter may be the case a further question arises, namely: are the new points raised in the Lords the result of peers' own initiatives, their perceptions, expertise, assiduity, or whatever? Or are peers more accurately seen as the spokesmen for organized groups outside Parliament, who have in their own scrutiny of legislation decided on how—from their point of view—the proposed bill could be improved? Perhaps debate in the lower House serves to publicize what the Government intends to do, and—thus alerted—groups potentially affected by the legislation use the upper House to try to secure adjustments to bills.[19]

During the whole process of parliamentary debate on draft legislation ministers may change their minds. How much this is due to parliamentary pressure or indeed pressure of any kind is a matter for investigation and analysis. Certainly, parliamentary draftsmen are kept busy throughout the passage of a bill, seeking to improve the drafting, remove ambiguities, clarify the wording, and so on. Sometimes the Government decides at a relatively late stage in the process to rewrite a bill substantially, not necessarily altering the policy objectives, but choosing different means to achieve these. The House of Lords is not infrequently used for the alteration of legislation in a technical or drafting way.

The growth in time spent on Government bills is closely related to the increase in the amount of legislation submitted to Parliament by Government. This subject was debated in the Lords in January 1990. The Labour Chief Whip, Lord Ponsonby of Shulbrede, gave some figures indicating the legislative inflation that had occurred:

> During a five-year period in the late 1940s, under a reforming and vigorous Labour Government, there were fewer than a thousand pages of legislation each year. During the 1950s the number of pages started to creep up past the thousand mark. In the 1960s it increased to around 1,500 pages a year. During the 1970s the average was 1,874 pages of legislation a year. When we move into the 1980s we find that up to 1986 the figure was 2,540 pages of legislation a year. At that point the format of government bills changed so that it is difficult to make a comparison with later years.[20]

[19] See Nicholas Baldwin, 'The House of Lords' in *Parliament and Pressure Politics*, ed. Michael Rush (Clarendon Press, Oxford, 1990).

[20] HL Debs., 31 Jan. 1990, cols. 382–407; for Lord Ponsonby's remarks see col. 398.

Earlier in the same debate Lord Rippon of Hexham, formerly a Conservative cabinet minister, quoted with heavy irony from a pamphlet Sir Geoffrey Howe had written in 1977 entitled *Too Much Law* in which he had said: 'We are doubling the statute law once in every fifteen years. It should be the first duty of Parliament to resist the temptation to add any more. We must make fewer laws and the laws fewer.' It is because the Thatcher Governments of the 1980s so signally failed to do what the Thatcher Opposition of the 1970s declared to be so highly desirable that the burden of legislative scrutiny has become so great.

But it is not only the quantity of legislation that has increased; its quality on first submission to Parliament appears to have declined. At least, the Government itself finds it necessary to introduce a great many more amendments to its own bills than formerly. One way of illustrating this is to calculate the average number of amendments made by the House of Lords to bills per sitting day throughout a session. For the 1970–4 Parliament the average was between six and seven amendments per sitting day; for 1974–9 the figure had risen to slightly over nine; by 1987–90 it had climbed to sixteen! And such figures conceal the acute pressure felt towards the end of the session. As is shown in Chapter 3, during the spillover period (that is, the time between the return of the House after the summer recess and the end of the session) in autumn 1989, Government amendments to bills were being passed at the rate of just under one a minute. Does such enforced haste make a mockery of any notion of genuine scrutiny of amendments? How well does the House fulfil its revising role? These are questions addressed in Chapters 3 and 4.

So far we have been thinking of primary legislation introduced by the Government. Secondary or delegated legislation has greatly increased in recent decades. The growth in the volume, the scope, and the significance of delegated legislation has been a matter of heightened concern within both Houses. Such concern is aggravated by the fact that statutory instruments cannot be amended except in very rare cases; they must be either accepted or rejected. Furthermore, scrutiny is limited to a single debate in each House, rather than the various stages through which all primary legislation goes. Since 1973 a joint select committee has existed to examine statutory instruments (replacing earlier separate committees in both Houses). How significant is the contribution of peers to the work of this committee? And how valuable are debates on the floor of the House on statutory instruments which can in any case be debated in the Commons? These are questions tackled by Robert Borthwick in Chapter 5.

Though Government dominates the legislative process in both Houses, opportunities exist for private members to introduce bills. Table 1.2 indicates that the House spent only just over 2 per cent of its time on private members' bills during the session. The proportion of time given to this category of business in the upper House has been lower in the 1987 Parliament than for many years past, averaging in the first three sessions (1987–90) 2½ per cent, as opposed to over 5 per cent in 1983–7, over 6 per cent in 1979–83, and almost 7 per cent in 1974–9. Does this reduction in time spent indicate a more marginal role for the House of Lords? In the 1960s, when the so-called 'permissive society' legislation was enacted, the House of Lords gained a reputation for tackling issues for which governments had no wish to take responsibility, and which MPs felt inhibited about introducing for reasons of electoral calculation.[21] Has this role of introducing legislation, especially on subjects which the Commons is hesitant to tackle, been of any continuing importance? Because the procedural restrictions which curtail the role of the Commons in debating private members' bills do not have a parallel in the Lords, is the House able to debate some bills more carefully than the Commons? Does the House provide a forum for stalking-horses for private enterprise initiatives from parliamentarians? Or is the fall in the time spent by the Lords on private members' bills a recognition of realism in regard to the extreme difficulties of getting such legislation through the Commons? These and other related questions are discussed by David Natzler and Douglas Millar in Chapter 6.

So far we have been considering public legislation. But private legislation is not to be ignored, even though it has become gradually less important throughout this century. Just as the powers of the House remain coequal with the Commons in regard to private bills, so the burden of scrutinizing such legis-

[21] See P. Richards, *Parliament and Conscience* (Allen & Unwin, London, 1970).

lation has traditionally been shared equally with the Commons. This is an area which has recently been the subject of an extensive review by a joint select committee.[22] The significance of the contribution made by the House of Lords can be evaluated from the careful attention given to this subject in Chapter 7.

The scope of the legislative role of the House has been outlined here, and some indication given of the kind of questions which may be asked about it. A precise analysis of this work is developed later in this volume. But whether or not the House should have such a role thrust upon it; whether in practice its activity simply excuses the Commons and the Government from more fundamental reform of the legislative procedure; whether, without the legislative long-stop provided by the Lords, Governments would be obliged to curtail their legislative ambitions to the advantage of the community generally; these are among the questions taken up again in the conclusion.

The Deliberative Role

Parliament has traditionally been a place where people 'parley'; it has been a place for talk, the purpose of which is to subject Government to scrutiny and oblige ministers to offer public explanations for the decisions Government has taken. The House of Lords, like the Commons, affords opportunity for question and debate on any aspect of the Government's stewardship. But the nature of the Government's responsibility to the upper House is different from its responsibility to the lower. For while the Commons has the power to censure ministers, and ultimately to effect the removal of the Government from office, the upper House cannot even aspire to exercise such sanctions.

Have increased legislative demands diminished the time available in the House for non-legislative debate? Table 1.3 shows that over each of the last four Parliaments the proportion of time spent on deliberation has diminished as the proportion of time spent on legislation has increased. However, when account is taken of the longer hours the House has sat in recent years it

[22] Report from the Joint Committee on Private Bill Procedure, HL Paper 97 (HC 625), 1987–8. See also Cm. 1110.

Table 1.3. *Time spent on legislative and deliberative work, 1974–90*

	Average percentage of time		Average no. of hours per session	
	Legislation	Deliberation	Legislation	Deliberation
1974–8	53.4	43.2	444	336
1979–82	57.9	37.5	598	393
1983–6	58.7	37.1	690	435
1987–91	61.8	33.2	679	358

Notes: This table excludes the final session of each Parliament. In all the above Parliaments the final session was foreshortened because of early dissolution. This distorts the pattern of business in the Lords where work on legislation is always heavier later in the session. Excluding the final session also facilitates comparison with the 1987–91 period. For categories of business treated as 'legislative' and 'deliberative' see Table 1.2.

Sources: Calculated from figures supplied by the House of Lords Journal and Information Office.

can be seen that the actual time spent on deliberative work has not declined so sharply.

It is not decline in time spent on debates and questions, but the sharply increased time spent on legislation, which stands out. Added to this is the fact that the House has spent increasing time on select committee work in the 1970s and 1980s, the bulk of which may reasonably be thought of as deliberative rather than legislative.

In Chapter 8 Robert Borthwick analyses the procedures available on the floor of the House and the use made of these. Opinions about the value of this activity vary sharply. If the aim is taken as being the provision of a forum for the expression of opinion which may influence Government or public, then it is difficult to provide objective assessment of such influence. When the Bryce Conference reported in 1918 it drew particular attention to the role of the Lords in debating issues which the Commons was unable to debate because of its preoccupations elsewhere. International affairs was no doubt very much in mind. To what extent the House of Lords actually does provide a forum for debating issues undebated in the Commons is a matter discussed in this book.

The 1968 White Paper on House of Lords Reform[23] drew attention to ways in which the House could develop its activities on its own initiative. One of these concerned the work of select committees, and the last twenty years has indeed seen a considerable growth in this area in the Lords as well as in the Commons. *Ad hoc* committees have been established, sometimes to examine legislation (almost always private members' bills), and sometimes to consider topics. Some of these committees have gained wide attention; others not so. Some have borne fruit in legislation.[24] In 1974 the European Communities Committee was established and this rapidly developed into an important part of the work of the House, complementing in its manner of work a parallel Commons committee. When in 1979 the Commons decided to abandon its twelve-year-old Science and Technology select committee, the Lords stepped in and established a committee to ensure some continued parliamentary scrutiny. The select committee work of the House is examined in Chapters 9 and 10.

Such were the major areas of activity of the House in the late 1980s. Whether it should have these functions, whether some should be added or others subtracted, is not a question addressed directly in the chapters which follow. But it is a subject to which we return in the concluding chapter. Meanwhile, before an analysis of the membership of the House is given in Chapter 2, some elucidation of the role of parties within the House is provided in the concluding section of this chapter.

Political Parties in the House

Though the House of Lords is less party-dominated than the Commons, parties remained of great importance in most of the work carried out by the upper House. The impact of parties has been moderated by the fact that the House is not elected and by the presence of a sizeable group of non-party peers on the cross-benches of the House. The fact that the Conservative Party has always been dominant has also in its way blunted the competitive

[23] *House of Lords Reform*, Cmnd. 3799, 1968. See esp. App. 2.
[24] See below, Ch. 10, n. 4; also Shell, *House of Lords*, 236–40.

Table 1.4. *Changing party strength in the House of Lords*

Session		Conservative	Labour	Liberal/ Alliance	Cross-bench/ Independent
1967–8	Attending	314	113	37	215
	Regular	125	95	19	52
1975–6	Attending	292	149	30	281
	Regular	141	104	24	60
1984–5	Attending	376	122	76	245
	Regular	168	91	51	68
1988–9	Attending	393	108	71	241
	Regular	185	86	49	63

Note: Attending: all who attended on one or more days during the session. Regular: all who attended on one-third or more of the days during the session.

Sources: Calculated from information supplied by the House of Lords Journal and Information Office. See also Cmnd. 3799, 1968, p. 5; and HL Paper 9 (1987–8), Tables 1 and 2.

element between parties in the House. Reference has already been made to the growth in the size of the Labour Party following the Life Peerages Act. Table 1.4 shows how party strength in the House has altered since the 1960s. What is notable is that Labour Party numbers, after rising throughout the 1960s and 1970s, declined again in the 1980s. In the early part of the decade that was largely because of the defection of Labour supporters to the Social Democratic Party. In the later part of the decade the fall had more to do with the failure of the Prime Minister to recommend as many new Labour peers as there were losses from the Labour benches through infirmity, old age, and death. By the commencement of the session under review here the Labour Party in the Lords was feeling starved of new recruits.

As Table 1.4 shows, the only group to grow in size in the House in the late 1980s was the already preponderant Conservative Party. Between the time Mrs Thatcher entered Downing Street in 1979 and November 1988, 182 new life peers had been created, but these (including Mr Callaghan's resignation honours list) included only 49 Labour supporters, compared with 78 Conservatives. During the 1988–9 session the usual New Year and Queen's Birthday honours lists were published, but of the six new peers named two were Conservative and four cross-bench. Two further creations during the year were politician/lawyers, one Conservative and one Labour.

From time to time special lists of 'working peers' have been issued, quite distinct from the twice yearly honours lists. No such list was issued during this session, though one had been in February 1987 and another was in April 1990. In these lists, upon which Labour relied heavily for new recruits, Mrs Thatcher always ensured that there were more Conservative names than Labour names. In the regular honours lists, for which the Labour Party leadership declined to make nominations, there were only five newly created peers who took the Labour whip in the eleven years from 1979 to 1990. And very few of those who inherit peerages take the Labour whip. The failure to secure a more satisfying representation for the Opposition party in the House is a point to which we return in the concluding chapter.

The Labour peers were noticeably aggrieved at all this. Lord Stoddart of Swindon initiated a debate suggesting that the House itself take action through amending its own standing orders to restrict the right to vote to peers who attended on a stipulated minimum number of days.[25] The possible effects of such a change are referred to in various places in this volume, in particular by Nicholas Baldwin in Chapter 2.

The Labour leader in the Lords since 1982 had been Lord Cledwyn of Penrhos, formerly Cledwyn Hughes MP and Secretary of State for Wales. He led a team of thirty peers who acted as party spokesmen. Many of them, like Lord Cledwyn himself, were elderly; he was seventy-two in 1988, and twelve other members of the Labour front bench were over seventy. All except the Chief Whip, Lord Ponsonby of Shulbrede, were life peers; Lord Ponsonby was the third holder of a barony, and at fifty-eight was one of the younger occupants of the Opposition front bench (though sadly he died in 1990). All told, twelve of the thirty were former MPs. The remainder had varied backgrounds as academics, lawyers, trade unionists, local council leaders, and businessmen.

[25] HL Debs., 8 Dec. 1988, cols. 719–51.

The Social and Liberal Democrats[26] were led by Lord Jenkins of Hillhead, formerly Roy Jenkins, who as an MP had been both Labour Chancellor of the Exchequer and Home Secretary, before serving as President of the Commission of the European Communities. Baroness Seear, the former Liberal Party leader in the House, served as deputy leader of the merged former Alliance parties. Baroness Stedman led those peers who remained outside this group as Social Democrats (SDP); she had for a time been a junior minister in the Lords when Labour was in office in the 1970s. While the Social and Liberal Democrats had an official front-bench team of some seventeen spokesmen, the SDP peers simply announced areas of interest, with every member of the party in the House having his or her interests stated.

The Conservative peers were led by Lord Belstead, who had become Leader of the House when Viscount Whitelaw resigned in January 1988. But he certainly had not inherited the authority that his predecessor had enjoyed in the Government. And with Lord Whitelaw's departure not a single member of the Government front bench in the Lords had direct experience as a member of the House of Commons, a situation without any recent precedent. This dearth among members of the Government front bench of former Commons experience contrasted both with the Opposition front benches and with the Government back benches, the latter by this time bristling with former Commons ministers, not least those who had departed from successive Thatcher Governments.

At the beginning of the 1988–9 session there were two other cabinet ministers in the House besides Lord Belstead. These were the Lord Chancellor, Lord Mackay of Clashfern, and Lord Young of Graffham, Secretary of State for Trade and Industry, who had entered the House in 1985. There were also five ministers of state and five parliamentary under-secretaries, as well as the Lord Advocate, a Scottish Law Officer. The Chief Whip was Lord Denham (who had occupied that office continuously since Mrs Thatcher came to power in 1979); he was assisted by the

[26] The Liberal Party and the Social Democratic Party had merged in summer 1988 to form the Social and Liberal Democrats. Initially they were often known as Democrats, but in Oct. 1989 the party decided to use the name Liberal Democrats. The abbreviation 'Dem.' is used in this book.

Deputy Chief Whip, Viscount Davidson, and five other whips. Because there have never in recent decades been enough ministers to speak for all departments in the Lords, the whips act as spokesmen—unlike their silent counterparts in the Commons. At the commencement of the 1988–9 session there were five departments without direct ministerial representation in the House; these were Employment, Education, Health, the Treasury, and the Welsh Office. As Table 1.5 shows, Lords in Waiting (junior whips) also acted as assistant spokesmen in departments with ministers, and ministers themselves spoke on behalf of other departments besides those in which they held office. During the 1988–9 session the total serving on the Government front bench varied from twenty to twenty-two, with a major ministerial reshuffle taking place in July 1989, and some other changes at different times. All told twenty-seven different individuals held office on the Government front bench during the session. Table 1.5 sets out the details.

Former experience of the House of Commons was represented on the front bench from January 1989 when Lord Fraser of Carmyllie was appointed Lord Advocate in place of Lord Cameron of Lochbroom, who resigned from the Government. Lord Fraser had been an MP from 1979 until he lost his seat in the 1987 election; at that time he had been Solicitor-General for Scotland, a post he continued to hold (though outside Parliament) until his appointment as Lord Advocate and simultaneous entry to the Lords. Further extensive changes took place in July when four Lords ministers left the Government, including Lord Young of Graffham, whose departure brought the number of cabinet ministers in the Lords down to two, lower than it had ever before been in any Conservative Government. The three others to leave in July were Lord Lyell (who had served in the Government since 1979), Lord Glenarthur (who had joined the Government in 1982), and the Earl of Dundee (who had accepted office first in 1986). Baroness Hooper also left the Government in July, apparently refusing a sideways move from Energy to Social Security.[27] At the same time Lord Trafford was appointed to the Government at the Department of Health, but he died in

[27] See *The Times*, 28 Sept. 1989.

Table 1.5. *The Government front bench in the House of Lords, 1988–9*

Peer and Office	Departments	Changes
L. Mackay of Clashfern Lord Chancellor	Lord Chancellor Legal Affairs	—
L. Belstead Lord Privy Seal	Leader of the House Civil Service	—
L. Young of Graffham Secretary of State for Trade & Industry	Trade & Industry Employment Treasury	Resigned 25 July 1989
L. Cameron of Lochbroom Lord Advocate	Legal Affairs (Scotland)	Resigned 4 Jan. 1989
L. Fraser of Carmyllie Lord Advocate	Legal Affairs (Scotland)	Appointed 4 Jan. 1989
E. Ferrers Minister of State, Home Office	Deputy Leader Home Office	—
L. Trefgarne Minister of State, Defence Procurement	Defence Foreign Affairs Employment Wales	Appointed Minister of State, Trade & Industry 25 July 1989
L. Glenarthur Minister of State, Foreign & Commonwealth	Foreign Affairs Defence	Resigned 25 July 1989
E. Caithness Minister of State, Department of the Environment	Environment Arts (Heritage)	Appointed Paymaster-General 25 July 1989
L. Lyell Under-Secretary, Northern Ireland	Northern Ireland	Resigned 25 July 1989
L. Sanderson of Bowden Minister of State, Scottish Office	Scotland	—
B. Trumpington Under-Secretary, Agriculture, Fisheries & Food	Agriculture Home Office Arts	Promoted Minister of State 25 July 1989

L. Skelmersdale Under-Secretary, Health & Social Security	Social Security Employment	Appointed U-S Northern Ireland 25 July 1989
L. Brabazon of Tara Under-Secretary, Transport	Transport Treasury	Appointed Minister of State FCO 25 July 1989
B. Hooper Under-Secretary, Education & Science	Energy Education Foreign Affairs	Resigned 25 July 1989; appointed U-S Health 28 Sept. 1989
L. Trafford Minister of State, Health	Health	Appointed 25 July 1989; died 16 Sept. 1989
L. Denham Captain, Gentlemen at Arms	Chief Whip	—
V. Davidson Captain, Yeomen of the Guard	Deputy Chief Whip Education Transport	—
V. Long Lord in Waiting	Defence Northern Ireland Foreign Affairs	—
L. Hesketh Lord in Waiting	Health Environment	Appointed U-S Environment Feb. 1989
E. Dundee Lord in Waiting	Scotland Employment Energy Home Office Agriculture	Resigned 25 July 1989
L. Strathclyde Lord in Waiting	Trade & Industry Treasury Scotland	Appointed U-S Employment 25 July 1989
E. Arran Lord in Waiting	Health Social Security Environment	—
L. Henley Lord in Waiting	Health	Appointed February 1989; appointed U-S DSS 25 July 1989

Table 1.5. *(contd.)*

Peer and Office	Departments	Changes
V. Ullswater Lord in Waiting	Energy Transport Home Office Trade & Industry	Appointed July 1989
L. Reay Lord in Waiting	Environment Defence Foreign Affairs	Appointed Aug. 1989
E. Strathmore & Kinghorne Lord in Waiting	Employment Agriculture Scotland Treasury	Appointed Aug. 1989

September and Baroness Hooper then returned to the Government to take junior ministerial office at Health.

The usual route to ministerial office in the Lords is via service in the whips' office. During the session three Lords in Waiting were promoted (see Table 1.5) and one peer, Lord Henley, who joined the Government for the first time as a junior whip early in the session, was quickly promoted in July to take the post at Social Security which Baroness Hooper had declined. The other newcomers to the Government in the whips' office were first Lord Reay, a fifty-two-year-old peer who had entered the House twenty-six years earlier and for a number of years had been an active member of the Liberal benches; second, Viscount Ullswater, a forty-seven-year-old peer who had succeeded his great-grandfather (a former Speaker of the Commons) at the age of seven; and third, the Earl of Strathmore and Kinghorne, a thirty-one-year-old great-nephew of the Queen Mother, who had inherited his peerage the previous year, and who at the time of his appointment had yet to make his maiden speech in the House. The *Financial Times* commented that the 'task of finding suitable people [to join the front bench in the Lords] was harder than ever'.[28]

The Conservatives still relied heavily on peers by succession;

[28] *Financial Times*, 4 Aug. 1989.

of the twenty-seven peers listed in Table 1.5, eighteen were hereditary and only nine were life peers. Many were young, certainly in House of Lords terms, where some of the most youthful faces in the House were seen on the Government front bench, the average age of which was just below forty-nine. For any Conservative who happens to inherit a peerage, ministerial office and rapid promotion is much more likely in the Lords than it is in the Commons. Lord Strathclyde was promoted Under-Secretary of State at Employment in July 1989 at the age of twenty-nine, and it is inconceivable that someone like Lord Strathmore, if he had just entered the House of Commons and had yet to make his maiden speech, would be given office. Perhaps one reason for the Government having this difficulty concerns the salaries paid to ministers in the Lords. That point is analysed by Michael Rush and David Jones in Chapter 11, and again it is something we come back to in the conclusion.

The 1988–9 Session

No session can be considered to be completely normal. But the 1988–9 session was not obviously unusual in any way. It was a normal-length session (22 November 1988 to 16 November 1989). It was neither immediately after an election, nor was it in the run-up period to an election. It followed the eighteen-month-long 1987–8 session, the first after a general election, with its high proportion of manifesto bills. At the end of the 1988–9 session the next election was possibly as close as eighteen months, possibly as distant as two and a half years. This session was at the mid-point of the Parliament.

At the beginning of the 1987 Parliament the Leader of the Lords, Viscount Whitelaw, had spoken of the importance of the Government taking due notice of the upper House and the likelihood of serious defeats for the Government's legislative programme in the Lords.[29] He did this against the background of a House which in the previous Parliament had increasingly become an irritant to the Government. In the Commons between 1983 and 1987 the Government had enjoyed an overwhelming

[29] *Independent*, 9 Oct. 1987; also P. Hennessy, 'The Other Opposition'.

majority. The Labour Party had been in disarray, and it was not only peers who spoke of the extra responsibilities placed upon their House as the 'other Opposition' to the Thatcher Government. Whitelaw had been sent to the Lords in 1983 in order to smooth the way for government legislation in the increasingly troublesome House. In the event his time as Leader seemed only to see the difficulties increase; the Conservatives' big majority in the House of Commons and Labour's returning credibility as the Opposition party were also responsible for this. After making his remarks about the likelihood of serious defeats in October 1987, he offered a partial retraction, though perhaps what he had said had the effect desired in impressing on Conservative peers the Government's need for their regular presence and support. He then fell ill in December and resigned in January 1988.

The first session of the new Parliament was not as difficult for the Government as he—and many others—seemed to have expected. A substantial Tory rebellion in the Lords on the community charge legislation resulted in a total of 501 peers voting in a division on an amendment designed to 'band' the charge (or 'poll tax') according to the ability of people to pay, an amendment proposed by the former chairman of the 1922 Committee, Lord Chelwood (formerly Sir Tufton Beamish), but successfully resisted by the Government. The Government did go down to defeat in the House over its proposal to introduce charges for eye tests and increases in dental charges but, despite considerable support for the Lords' decisions on the Conservative back benches in the Commons, the Government managed to overturn these defeats (though its majority sank to only eight on the eye-tests issue).[30]

During the long post-election 1987–8 session it seemed as if the Government's attitude to the House was hardening. Had the Prime Minister concluded that reaching a compromise with their Lordships only seemed to encourage further rebellion? What then of 1988–9? It is that session which is the focal point of all the chapters which follow.

[30] On this and other developments pertaining to the House see Shell, *House of Lords*.

2

The Membership of the House

Nicholas D. J. Baldwin

Introduction

This chapter examines, on the basis of the 1988–9 session, the questions: who are the members of the House of Lords, and who are the active members, those who take part in its work? When considering the membership of the House of Lords, and members' participation in the work of the House, it is misleading to treat the House as a uniform body, for it consists of a large and diverse membership, and its nature can vary from day to day, indeed even from hour to hour. So although it is necessary to start with a formal statement of the various categories which together form the membership of the House, it is then necessary to look rather deeper in order to obtain a clear picture of what can be termed the 'active' House.

Categories of Membership

The House of Lords is the oldest of all British institutions, reaching back beyond the Norman Conquest, beyond King Alfred, into the shadowy regions of Teutonic antiquity. Indeed, by the accession of the Tudor dynasty Parliament was already clearly divided into two Houses. In one—the Lords—sat the king's officials, counsellors and judges, the magnates summoned to Parliament in their personal capacity as 'peers of the realm', and the great ecclesiastics, archbishops, bishops, and abbots. In total there was a membership of approximately 100, of whom a majority were from the Church. During the reign of Henry VIII, as a result of the suppression of the monasteries, the House of Lords became for the first time a predominantly secular body.

Today the membership of the House of Lords is still divided between ecclesiastical and lay members, formally described as 'lords spiritual' and 'lords temporal'. The lords spiritual (referred to in this chapter as 'bishops') are the Archbishops of Canterbury and York, the Bishops of London, Durham, and Winchester, and the twenty-one most senior among the other diocesan bishops of the Church of England. They cease to be members of the House when they leave office, and are thus the only members who do not hold their seats for life. The lords temporal are the peers of England, of Scotland, of Great Britain, and of the United Kingdom (but not of Ireland). All peers of these types who are aged twenty-one or over, are not bankrupt, have not been convicted of treason (until pardon or completion of sentence), and are of British, Commonwealth, or Irish nationality, are entitled to a seat in the House of Lords.

A further distinction can be made between hereditary and non-hereditary peers. Hereditary peers are those whose title can be transferred from one generation to another. Within this category it is helpful to separate those—the vast majority—whose title is held by virtue of inheritance and those who are hereditary peers of the first creation. In this chapter, those who have succeeded to their titles will be termed 'hereditary peers', while those who have had a hereditary title bestowed upon them will be termed 'created hereditary peers'. Most hereditary peerages pass through the male line only, though certain older peerages can pass through the female line in default of a male heir, and special provision has been made for a few more recently created peerages (for example, that of Earl Mountbatten of Burma) to pass through the female line, normally for one generation only. Only since the passing of the Peerage Act 1963 have women holders of hereditary peerages been able to sit in the House of Lords.

Non-hereditary peers are those whose title is limited to the lifetime of the title-holder. They fall into two categories, those created under the Appellate Jurisdiction Act 1876 (as amended) and those created under the Life Peerages Act 1958. The Appellate Jurisdiction Act 1876 provided for the introduction of a limited number of Lords of Appeal in Ordinary, judges appointed by the Crown to take part in the hearing and determination of appeals to the House of Lords. Those concerned are created peers for life. A number of other peers, not created under the Appellate Jurisdiction Act, have none the less held high judicial office and are accordingly entitled to sit judicially.

Table 2.1. *Composition of the House of Lords at the beginning and end of the 1988–9 session*

Peerage category	Beginning of session		End of session	
	No.	%	No.	%
Hereditary peers (male)	738	62.3	744	62.9
Hereditary peers (female)	20	1.7	20	1.7
Created hereditary peers (all male)	25	2.1	20	1.7
Life peers (male)	309	26.1	308	26.0
Life peers (female)	45	3.8	45	3.8
Law lords (all male)	22	1.8	20	1.7
Bishops (all male)	26	2.2	26	2.2
TOTAL	1,185	100.0	1,183	100.0

The term 'law lord' may be used to refer to this wider group, but in this chapter it is used to refer exclusively to those created peers under the Appellate Jurisdiction Act.

The Life Peerages Act 1958 enabled individuals, men and women, to have peerages for life conferred upon them. For the first time it enabled women to sit in the House of Lords. In this chapter, those created peers under the Life Peerages Act will be termed 'life peers'.

Having made these formal distinctions, the total membership of the House can be presented as shown in Table 2.1.

From this it is apparent that the membership of the House is predominantly male, with the sixty-five females accounting for only 5.5 per cent. It is also similarly apparent that there is a significant preponderance of hereditary over non-hereditary members, hereditary peers by succession accounting for 64.0 per cent (758) at the beginning of the session. The session witnessed a significant decline—20 per cent—in the number of lords who had themselves been created a hereditary peer, five of the twenty-five holders of such titles which were in existence at the beginning of the session dying during the session. This may be explained by the fact that after 1965 no new hereditary peerages were created until 1983, and only four were created between then and 1989;[1] thus the created hereditary peers nearly all received their peerages many years ago. In all, forty members of the House (3.4 per cent) either died, or in the case of bishops retired, during the session, while thirty-eight members (3.2 per cent) either succeeded to a hereditary title, were themselves awarded a peerage during the course of the session, or entered the House as a bishop.

As the only category of membership to change significantly during the session was the comparatively small category of created hereditary peers, in the remainder of this chapter figures relating to the composition of the House will be based on the composition at the beginning of the session.

The total membership of the House—1,185 at the beginning of the 1988–9 session— is misleadingly large, because there are two categories of member who are in practice unable to take part. First, there are those who do not seek a writ of summons to the House. Writs of summons are issued by the Crown, and go automatically to those on whom peerages are conferred. Peers succeeding to their titles must, however, apply for a writ of summons and prove their entitlement thereto. At the beginning of the 1988–9 session there were eighty-four peers not in receipt of a writ of summons. It is reasonable to assume that the majority of these had simply taken no steps to apply for a writ, though three were ineligible because under the age of twenty-one. Peers who are in receipt of a writ of summons but who do not expect to be able to attend the House may apply for leave of absence, which is granted for the duration of a Parliament. Peers on leave of absence are expected not to attend the House until their leave of absence has been terminated, which requires a month's notice. At the beginning of the 1988–9 session there were 169 peers on leave of absence. Thus the total number of members eligible to participate at the beginning of the 1988–9 session was 932. A further thirty-three lords became eligible to attend in the course of the session, making 965 lords altogether who were eligible to attend during at least part of the session.

[1] Viscounts Whitelaw and Tonypandy (1983), the Earl of Stockton (1984), and the Duke of York (1986).

Table 2.2. *The occupational background of peers in the early 1980s*

Category	% of peerage category		Total	
	hereditary	created/ appointed	No.	%
Worker				
Worker	1.4	8.8	47	4.0
Full-time trade union official	—	4.9	20	1.7
Professional				
Accountant/economist	1.9	2.4	25	2.1
Advertising/public relations	2.6	1.5	26	2.2
Civil Service/Diplomatic Service	6.2	16.1	114	9.7
Engineer	1.6	3.2	25	2.1
Journalist/author	6.0	7.8	78	6.6
Legal (judge/barrister/solicitor)	5.9	18.3	120	10.2
Medical (doctor/dentist)	0.6	3.4	19	1.6
Military—regular	20.3	6.1	181	15.4
Teaching/academics	3.4	18.8	103	8.7
Business				
Landowner/farmer	60.3	14.6	523	44.4
Financial (banking/insurance)	11.6	7.8	121	10.3
Industrialist/service industry	15.6	21.5	208	17.7
Manufacturing/retail	4.6	5.1	56	4.7
Publishing/printing	3.1	2.9	36	3.1
Miscellaneous				
The Arts/entertainment	5.1	3.4	53	4.5
Public service/administration	14.2	58.0	347	29.4
Political service	3.0	34.9	166	14.1

Source: Unpublished Ph.D. thesis by the writer, University of Exeter.

Background of Peers

Table 2.2 outlines the occupational background of peers as found in the early 1980s. Certainly there are considerable difficulties in seeking to categorize peers in this way—not least of all because some peers have had, or indeed still have, more than one occupation—but the overall picture portrayed in the table is undoubtedly indicative of the character of the combined membership of the House, and the balances indicated are likely to

Table 2.3. *Political affiliation and peerage category at the beginning of the 1988–9 session*

Party/group	Created hereditary	Hereditary by succession	Life peers	Law lords	Total	%
Conservative	9	319	105		433	46.5
Labour	1	11	101		113	12.1
Social and Liberal Democrat	1	28	27		56	56.0
Social Democrat		9	14		23	2.5
Cross-bench	7	127	86	20	240	25.8
Other	2	31	6	2	41	4.4
Bishops					26	2.8
TOTAL	20	525	339	22	932	100.0

reflect the approximate position found during the 1988–9 session. The effect of this—participation of members based on their experience—will be considered later.

Political Affiliation of Peers

The balance of support for the various political parties or groupings at the beginning of the 1988–9 session, among the 932 lords eligible to take part, was as shown in Table 2.3. The figures are of those in receipt of the 'whip' circulated to party members each week when the House is sitting. The term 'cross-bench' is, for the purposes of the table and elsewhere in this chapter, used to describe those peers who are not formally aligned with any political party but who belong to an unofficial group which meets each week with a convenor, Baroness Hylton-Foster, in the chair, to discuss forthcoming business. These members receive a so-called 'unlined whip', with information about future business but no request for attendance for divisions as included in a party whip. Peers listed as 'other' may also sit on the cross-benches, though some sit elsewhere (for example, Lord Alport, sitting on the Conservative benches as an independent Conservative, and

Lord Fitt, sitting on the Labour benches though not taking the Labour whip).

By far the largest political grouping was the Conservative Party, accounting for 46.2 per cent of eligible members at the beginning of the session.

Table 2.3 includes a cross-tabulation of political affiliation by peerage category. This shows that there is a marked contrast among the parties in the balance of hereditary peers on the one hand and life peers and created hereditary peers on the other. The percentage of hereditary peers was 74 among Conservative peers, 50 among Social and Liberal Democrat peers, and 10 among Labour peers. Perhaps the starkest contrast is that between the numbers of hereditary peers taking the Conservative and Labour whips—319 and eleven respectively.

Attendance

The figures just given make no allowance for the fact that the degree to which members take part in the work of the House varies widely. This is shown in Table 2.4, recording attendances by the 965 lords who were eligible to attend during the session. There were 153 sitting days during the session, but lords who were eligible to attend for only part of the session have been categorized by reference to the number of sittings which they were eligible to attend. A full attendance record is given in Appendix C.

The average attendance on each sitting day was 316, though this figure masks differences between days of the week: the average attendance on the nine Fridays when the House sat during the session was 177, while on the thirty-seven Tuesdays it was 354.

The reasons for non-attendance are varied, including age or illness, lack of either time or interest, and distaste for the institution itself. The reasons for attending sittings of the House are similarly varied, peers attending because of a sense of duty or responsibility, out of interest and enjoyment, or even out of a sense of habit. Primarily the reasons why some peers attend sittings of the House more frequently than others are the same as, or at least similar to, those reasons given by peers who do not

Table 2.4. *Levels of attendance during the 1988–9 session*

Sittings attended	No.	% of eligible lords	Total days attended
None	149	15.4	
Rare (0% $< n \leqslant$ 5%)	159	16.5	502
Infrequent (5% $< n \leqslant$ 33⅓%)	274	28.4	6,566
Frequent (33⅓% $< n \leqslant$ 66⅔%)	155	16.1	11,520
Regular (66⅔% $< n \leqslant$ 100%)	228	23.6	29,811
TOTAL	965	100.0	48,399

attend at all, namely age, illness, lack of time, job not permitting political involvement, and lack of interest.

There is an additional factor to be taken into account, namely the financial aspect of attendance at sittings. Members of the House are not paid a salary, nor do they receive a daily attendance fee. Rather, the position—as explained in more detail in Chapter 11—is that there is an expense allowance, the purpose of which is to enable lords to reclaim a reimbursement, within defined limits, of certain of the expenses they incur in attending sittings of the House, or of committees of the House. It is undoubtedly the case that the availability of the reimbursement of expenses has encouraged members to attend, and to do so more regularly than they would otherwise have been able to do.

As Table 2.4 shows, the level of attendance during the session varied widely. For the purpose of this study those peers who attended 5 per cent of sittings or fewer are categorized as 'rare' attenders, those who attended more than 5 per cent but not more than 33⅓ per cent as 'infrequent' attenders, those who attended more than 33⅓ per cent and not more than 66⅔ per cent as 'frequent' attenders, and those who attended more often as 'regular' attenders.[2] It can be seen that some 60 per cent of the peers present on an average day would be regular attenders.

[2] The 5% and 33⅓% thresholds correspond to those used in the 1968 White Paper 'House of Lords Reform' (Cmnd. 3799), where lords are described in para. 11 as attending 'rarely' (up to 5%), 'from time to time' (more than 5% and up to 33⅓%), or 'reasonably often' (more than 33⅓%). The same thresholds are used in Table 2.6 (p. 50) of *The House of Lords*, by Donald Shell (Harvester

A breakdown of attendance by frequency of attendance, peerage type, and party is given later in this chapter in Table 2.12; a similar breakdown of members attending on an average day is given in Table 2.13.

Participation

Attendance statistics do not by any means give a complete picture of the participation of members in the work of the House. By no means all those who attend sittings of the House participate in debate; and conversely members who attend sittings less often may be active on select committees. Attendance at meetings of committees cannot be satisfactorily measured, as comprehensive statistics are not available,[3] but it is clear from anecdotal evidence that a significant number of members play a full part in committee work and comparatively little part on the floor of the House.

An approximate indication of levels of participation in proceedings in the House can be obtained by a count of interventions as recorded in the index to the Official Report (*Hansard*).[4] Interventions on the same item of business on the same day are counted only once. The asking and answering of written questions are (because they cannot be distinguished in the index) also treated as interventions. The approach has limitations—for example, a brief supplementary question is treated the same as several hours' frequent speaking on a committee stage of a bill—but nevertheless may be helpful in distinguishing the more active from the less active participants in the business of the House. A complete record of lords' interventions forms a column in Appendix C. Table 2.5 gives a breakdown by party, and Table 2.6 a breakdown by attendance levels.

Wheatsheaf, London, 2nd edn. 1992). The Appendix to *Social Trends 21* (HMSO, London, 1991), 223, gives a figure for 'the working House' based on a criterion of 'those Lords who attend at least 1 sitting day in 3'.

[3] But see Ch. 9 for some data on attendance at meetings of the European Communities Committee and its subcommittees.

[4] This approach was used by Donald Shell in analyses of the 1984–5 and 1989–90 sessions respectively in the 1st and 2nd edns. of his book, *The House of Lords*, Table 2.7.

Table 2.5. *Lords intervening in debate during the 1988–9 session, broken down by party*

Level of attendance	No. of interventions during the session					
	0	1 to 10	11 to 50	51 or more	Total 1 or more	Total no. of interventions
Conservative	149	149	61	33	243	5,404
Labour	21	26	41	20	87	3,151
Social and Liberal Democrat	8	13	20	8	41	1,167
Social Democrat	6	10	5	2	17	425
Cross-bench	76	99	24	4	127	1,094
Other	12	2	1	1	4	95
Bishops	8	17	1		18	51
TOTAL	280	316	153	68	537	11,387

Note: The total number of lords (817) appearing in this table and Table 2.6 is one greater than the number attending during the session because it includes Lord Melchett, who asked a written question but did not attend. Changes of party after the beginning of the session have been ignored.

Voting

Another form of participation is measured by the voting record of lords attending the House. An analysis of each division is given in Appendix B, and a complete list of lords' voting records in Appendix C. There were a total of 189 divisions during the 1988–9 session, in which a total of 31,834 votes were cast and in which 684 lords voted at least once. Thus 132 lords attended during the session but never voted. Table 2.7 gives a breakdown of voting by attendance levels. It is confined to voting in divisions on Government bills—186 out of the total of 189. The three divisions which have been excluded were all on private members' bills. As in the case of attendance statistics, lords who were eligible to attend for only part of the session have been categorized by reference to the number of divisions in which they were eligible to take part.

Table 2.7 shows that only fifty-nine lords voted in over two-thirds of divisions on Government bills, whereas 200 voted at

Table 2.6. *Lords intervening in debate during the 1988–9 session, broken down by level of attendance*

Level of attendance	No. of interventions during the session				
	0	1 to 10	11 to 50	51 or more	Total 1 or more
Rare (⩽5%)	126	32	2	0	33
Infrequent (5% < n ⩽ 33⅓%)	110	150	14	0	164
Frequent (33⅓% < n ⩽ 66⅔%)	20	74	53	8	135
Regular (66⅔% < n ⩽ 100%)	24	60	84	60	204
TOTAL	280	316	153	68	537

Table 2.7. *Voting in divisions on Government bills during the 1988–9 session, broken down by level of attendance*

Level of attendance	Percentage of divisions voted in					Total votes cast
	0	⩽5	5 to 33⅓	33⅓ to 66⅔	Over 66⅔	
Rare (⩽5%)	91	68	0	0	0	258
Infrequent (5% < n ⩽ 33⅓%)	36	123	111	4	0	3,387
Frequent (33⅓% < n ⩽ 66⅔%)	3	6	99	44	3	7,466
Regular (66⅔% < n ⩽ 100%)	2	3	52	115	56	20,522
TOTAL	132	200	262	163	59	31,633

least once but in not more than 5 per cent of divisions. A modest but significant number of lords attended regularly or frequently but voted infrequently, rarely, or not at all. There is little sign of lords attending only in order to vote—only three lords voting more than two-thirds of the time but attending not more than two-thirds of the time—but this in part reflects the fact that divisions took place on eighty out of 153 days and were possible

Table 2.8. *Voting in all divisions, broken down by peerage type*

Type	Lords voting	Votes cast	Mean	Median	Pro-Govt.	Anti-Govt.
Hereditary peers	369	15,154	41.1	22	11,984	3,066
All others	315	16,680	53.0	43	6,963	9,620
Created hereditary peers	13	550	42.3	31	356	192
Life peers	283	16,065	56.8	46	6,573	9,397
Law lords	3	28	9.3	5	20	8
Bishops	16	37	2.3	2	14	23
TOTAL	684	31,834	46.5	31	18,947	12,686

Table 2.9. *Voting in divisions on Government bills, broken down by party*

Party	Lords voting	Votes cast	Mean	Median
Conservative	366	17,233	47.0	31
Labour	100	7,725	76.6	77
Social and Liberal Democrat	51	2,967	59.4	59
Social Democrat	19	726	41.5	42
Cross-bench	128	2,807	22.0	8
Other	7	138	19.7	15
Bishops	16	37	2.3	2
TOTAL	684	31,633	46.2	31

Note: The figures in the second column total 687 because of double counting of three peers who changed party during the session (Viscount Hanworth, Lord Thomson of Monifieth, and Lord Young of Dartington).

(and therefore two- or three-line whips were imposed) on a substantial number of other days when in the event no divisions took place.

Table 2.8 gives a breakdown by peerage type of voting during the session. Table 2.9 gives a similar breakdown by party, but confined to divisions on Government bills.

It is often observed that party discipline cannot be enforced in the Lords because effective sanctions do not exist. But it is worth noting that party cohesion in the division lobbies is in fact remarkably high, with a distinctive difference between the behaviour of Labour and Conservative peers in this respect. Thus during the 1988–9 session dissent among Labour peers was limited to two Labour peers who cast a total of four pro-Government votes. Dissent among Conservative peers was rather more common. A total of eighty-nine Conservative peers voted against the Government at least once. Of these, however, forty-nine dissented on only one occasion, so that only 10.9 per cent (forty out of 366) of Conservatives who voted during the session voted against their party on more than a single occasion. Of these, thirteen—3.6 per cent of all Conservatives who voted—voted against their party in more than 10 per cent of the divisions in which they voted. One Conservative peer, Lord Boston, voted against the Government on the only occasion on which he voted during the session, while the maximum number of anti-Government votes recorded by a Conservative member was 11 by Baroness Elliot of Harwood and Lord Milverton.

Dissent among members of the Social and Liberal Democrats and Social Democratic Party is harder to measure because the party line is not always easily identified. What can easily be measured is the extent to which members of these parties voted in both lobbies in a division. In the case of the Social and Liberal Democrats there were six divisions in which this occurred. In five of these there was only a single member in one lobby as opposed to between eight and fourteen in the other; in the remaining case the split was five to two. In the case of the Social Democratic Party there were two divisions in which party members voted in both lobbies, the split being seven to two and two to one.

The Composition of the 'Working' and 'Voting' House

The fact that there is a considerable numerical difference not just between the total possible membership and the actually achieved day-to-day membership, but between the composition of the membership which is engaged in questions on the floor of the House and those members who take part in divisions—a difference between the so-called 'working' and 'voting' House—has given rise to the belief in the existence of backwoodsmen, peers who seldom attend, or have never attended, sittings of the House, but who nevertheless could do so at the 'drop of a hat', or at least at the crack of a whip. The perceived existence of many such peers has given rise to the concept of the 'menace of the backwoodsmen', the idea that large numbers of inactive peers can be summoned down to the House by the whips and whipped through the lobbies in a division, thereby having a decisive influence on the outcome of that division. At the same time the belief has developed that such individuals are certainly conservative, and more likely reactionary, in their outlook, hence providing the Conservative Party leadership with an almost limitless reservoir of support upon which they can call. Thus the perceived 'menace' is one directed at radical opinion—it would be the radical point of view which would be 'swamped' by these backwoodsmen in the division lobbies. In short it is said that whereas the Conservative Party may indeed be vulnerable in the working House, at the end of debates it is the votes that count, and in the voting House the position is very different. As one writer puts it:

> Only when the Lords votes does the Conservatives' inbuilt advantage reveal itself: a reserve army of mainly hereditary peers—the so-called 'backwoodsmen'—who attend irregularly but come up to London in large numbers when required by the Tory whips.[5]

The phrase 'backwoodsmen' is not normally a term of endearment, it being applied in general to peers who are thought to be out of touch with the political situation at the time and basically unaware of public matters, but who emerge from obscurity chiefly to protect their own wealth and privileges, in order to vote in a division in the House of Lords, and then return to the obscurity whence they came. As so much has been said about the existence of backwoodsmen and the 'menace' they pose, it is useful to attempt to discover what meaning the concept has, and to attempt to ascertain whether it has any real influence on the course of events; whether there is in effect a difference between the 'working' and the 'voting' House.

Analysis of all votes cast in divisions shows that in no case during the 1988–9 session would the result of a division have

[5] Andrew Adonis, *Parliament Today* (Manchester University Press, Manchester, 1990), 159.

been altered by eliminating those votes cast by rare attenders—members attending not more than 5 per cent of sittings. Between them rare attenders cast only 163 votes, 0.5 per cent of the total. That is not to say that rare attenders did not occasionally turn out in much greater force than usual. Appendix A shows that, while the mean attendance by rare attenders was 3.3 per day, on 4 May 1989 there were twenty-one rare attenders present, and on 7 November 1989 there were nineteen. These were the only two days in the session when total attendance exceeded 400, and there was clearly heavy whipping. If the votes cast by lords attending not more than 10 per cent of sittings had been discounted, then one division, on an amendment to the Companies Bill [HL], would have had a different outcome—it would have been a Government defeat (89 votes to 90) instead of a Government victory (94 votes to 90). Only six divisions would have had a different outcome if the votes of members attending a third of sittings or fewer had been discounted. Five of these were Government victories which would have been Government defeats, but the sixth was a Government defeat on an amendment to the Water Bill. The division took place at 11 p.m. and the Government was defeated by 62 votes to 53, with eight Conservative peers voting against the Government. Without the votes of those attending a third of sittings or fewer, the result would have been 51 votes on each side—eleven of those voting against the Government (including five of the eight Conservative peers) would have been excluded, but only two of those voting for the Government.

It is apparent that the concept of there being a difference between the working and voting House affects only a very limited number of divisions—on which occasions anyway other factors come into play, factors which will be discussed later.

A further point which is often cited is that the votes of the cross-benchers are more often than not cast in support of the Conservatives. Taking the session in question it can be seen that of the 2,807 votes cast by cross-benchers in divisions on Government bills, 1,771, or 61.0 per cent, were indeed pro-Government votes. Nevertheless, it should be noted that the cross-benchers never in fact saved the Government from defeat. In only two divisions—one on the Electricity Bill and one on the Social Security Bill—would there have been a different outcome if the votes of cross-benchers had been excluded, and both of these divisions were in fact Government defeats. In other words, although the majority of cross-bench votes were pro-Government, the Government would have won more divisions if no cross-benchers had voted.

The net effect of cross-bench voting in all 189 divisions varied from 29 votes (on the Prevention of Terrorism Bill, when all twenty-nine cross-benchers who voted supported the Government) to zero, with a mean of 6.8 and a median of 6. In four cases the net effect was twenty or more, in a further forty-eight cases ten or more. The total number of cross-bench votes in divisions ranged from 36 (in a division on the Water Bill) to 1, with a mean of 15.0 and a median of 14.

The Active and Inactive Membership of the House

Having established that a large section of the eligible membership of the House of Lords chooses for various reasons either not to attend sittings of the House or to attend only occasionally, it is necessary to turn from the consideration of the whole membership to a study of the active and inactive elements in order to obtain a clearer picture of the House of Lords during the 1988–9 session.

An analysis of inactive and active peers by peerage category and political affiliation for the 1988–9 session is provided in Tables 2.10 and 2.11. In order to make possible a fair comparison between inactive and active members of the House, a 'snapshot' has been taken of the membership at the beginning of the 1988–9 session, distinguishing those who did not attend during the session from those who did.

From Table 2.10 it is clear that the vast majority of peers who do not attend the sittings of the House—85.8 per cent (333)—are hereditary peers. Indeed, 43.9 per cent of all hereditary peers did not attend any of the sittings of the House during the session. This is in marked contrast to the 11.3 per cent of life peers who, likewise, did not attend any of the sittings of the House during the period. Clearly, with regard to attendance, there is a considerable difference between members of the peerage who owe their position to hereditary succession and those who have either

Table 2.10. *Analysis of lords as at the beginning of the 1988–9 session not attending during the session*

	Hereditary		Created hereditary	Life peers		Law lords	Bishops	Total
	M	F		M	F			
Conservative	48	1		2	2			53
Labour	1			4	2			7
Social and Liberal Democrat	5			2				7
Social Democrat								0
Cross-bench	27	1	5	12		2		47
Other	24		2	2				28
Bishops							1	1
On leave of absence	143	3	5	10	4			165
Without writs	76	4						80
TOTAL	324	9	10	32	8	4	1	388

Table 2.11. *Analysis of lords as at the beginning of the 1988–9 session attending during the session*

	Hereditary		Created hereditary	Life peers		Law lords	Bishops	Total
	M	F		M	F			
Conservative	269	4	9	89	13			384
Labour	10		1	80	15			106
Social and Liberal Democrat	23		1	23	2			49
Social Democrat	9			12	2			23
Cross-bench	95	7	2	69	5	18		196
Other	8		2	4				14
Bishops							25	25
TOTAL	414	11	15	277	37	18	25	797

been ennobled themselves or owe their position to being either a law lord or an archbishop or bishop. (The position with regard to those who have themselves been created hereditary peers is not straightforward. Owing to the fact that only four new hereditary titles have been created since 1965 the age and health of the individuals concerned is a major contributing factor.) There is also a difference with regard to attendance and non-attendance between male and female members of the peerage: 26.2 per cent of female members did not attend, as against 33.1 per cent of male members. This difference is, however, explained by the smaller proportion of hereditary peers among female members of the House. If one compares male with female hereditary peers, and male with female life peers, there is no distinction of note: 43.9 per cent of male hereditary peers and 45.0 per cent of female hereditary peers are inactive, and 10.4 per cent of male life peers and 17.8 per cent of female life peers are inactive.[6] This serves to underline the clear, and fundamental, distinction between those who have succeeded to titles and those who have themselves been given peerages for life.

With regard to party or group affiliation, a substantial majority (67.9 per cent) of those who did not attend sittings of the House during the session were without writs of summons or on leave of absence, and thus in practice not in a position to take a party whip. Of the remainder among non-attenders, 45.8 per cent (49 out of 107) were declared supporters of the Conservative Party. In fact, 12.1 per cent of peers taking the Conservative whip did not attend at any point during the session. This is comparable with the equivalent figure of 12.5 per cent (7 out of 56) for the Social and Liberal Democrats, but contrasts with figures of 6.2 per cent (7 out of 113) for the Labour Party and no non-attenders among the 23 Social Democrats.

It is necessary to look at those peers who do attend, taking account of the frequency of attendance to see whether or not a similar pattern is found. The basic 'raw data' is provided in Table 2.12. Unlike Table 2.11, the table includes all those who attended the House during the 1988–9 session, whether or not they were members at the beginning of the session.

[6] These findings are in line with those of Gavin Drewry and Jenny Brock in their 1983 study 'The Impact of Women on the House of Lords' (Centre for the Study of Public Policy, University of Strathclyde).

It is clear from Table 2.12 that the pattern remains the same. In particular, members who are life peers are more active than members who owe their seat to the workings of the hereditary principle. Only 23.5 per cent (102) of attending hereditary peers are regular attenders, and only a further 14.7 per cent (64) are frequent attenders. These figures contrast with the comparable figures for life peers: amongst their ranks those who are classified as regular attenders account for 37.5 per cent (121), while those classified as frequent attenders account for a further 26.0 per cent (84). Hence in general the life peers are much the more regular attenders. In contrast, when those members whose attendance is classified as rare are looked at, it can be seen that 25.6 per cent (111) of attending hereditary peers fall into this category. This is in marked contrast to the position found amongst life peers, where only 10.5 per cent (34) of attenders are rare attenders. From amongst the ranks of active hereditary peers, 36.2 per cent (157) are infrequent attenders, while the figure for life peers stands at 26.0 per cent (81).

Thus the figures for both rare and infrequent attenders show the opposite pattern to those for regular and frequent attenders—active hereditary peers are proportionately more likely to be rare or infrequent attenders, and in absolute terms account for a substantial majority of these categories.

The figures also show a contrast between different parties, to a large extent reflecting their differing proportions of hereditary and other peers. No fewer than 60.7 per cent (65) of attenders taking the Labour whip were regular attenders, as against 24.7 per cent (97) of Conservatives. For the Social and Liberal Democrats and the Social Democratic Party the figures were between these, 40.8 per cent (20) and 30.4 per cent (7) respectively. Only 7.5 per cent (8) of Labour attenders were rare attenders, as against 18.1 per cent (71) of Conservatives. In this category the Social and Liberal Democrats (6.1 per cent) were similar to the Labour Party and the Social Democratic Party (17.4 per cent) similar to the Conservative Party; but in both cases the numbers—3 and 4 respectively—are too small to draw firm conclusions.

If political affiliation is looked at in conjunction with peerage category, a number of factors are underlined. For example, it can be seen that while 29.9 per cent (32) of attending Conservative

Table 2.12. *Lords attending the House of Lords during the 1988–9 session: analysis by frequency of attendance and peerage type*

A. Rare attenders (up to 5% of sittings)

Party	Peerage category					Total	% of attenders in party
	Hereditary	Created hereditary	Life peers	Law lords	Bishops		
Conservative	63	1	7	0		71	18.1
Labour	2	0	6	0		8	7.5
Social and Liberal Democrat	3	0	0	0		3	6.1
Social Democratic Party	2	0	2	0		4	17.4
Cross-bench	36	0	18	4		58	28.6
Other	5	2	1	0		8	50.0
Bishops					7	7	26.9
TOTAL	111	3	34	4	7	159	19.5
% of rare attenders	69.8	1.9	21.4	2.5	4.4	100.0	
% of all attenders in peerage category	25.6	20.0	10.5	22.2	26.9	19.5	

B. Infrequent attenders (over 5% and up to 33⅓% of sittings)

Party	Peerage category					Total	% of attenders in party
	Hereditary	Created hereditary	Life peers	Law lords	Bishops		
Conservative	105	3	29	0		137	34.9
Labour	1	0	10	0		11	10.3
Social and Liberal Democrat	6	0	3	0		9	18.4
Social Democratic Party	3	0	5	0		8	34.8
Cross-bench	38	1	36	11		86	42.4
Other	4	0	1	0		5	31.3
Bishops					18	18	69.2
TOTAL	157	4	84	11	18	274	33.6
% of infrequent attenders	57.3	1.5	30.7	4.0	6.6	100.0	
% of all attenders in peerage category	36.2	26.7	26.0	61.1	69.2	33.6	

C. Frequent attenders (over 33⅓% and up to 66⅔% of sittings)

Party	Peerage category					Total	% of attenders in party
	Hereditary	Created hereditary	Life peers	Law lords	Bishops		
Conservative	45	3	39	0		87	22.2
Labour	3	0	20	0		23	21.5
Social and Liberal Democrat	6	0	11	0		17	34.7
Social Democratic Party	1	0	3	0		4	17.4
Cross-bench	9	1	10	2		22	10.8
Other	0	0	1	0		1	6.3
Bishops					1	1	3.8
TOTAL	64	4	84	2	1	155	19.0
% of frequent attenders	41.3	2.6	54.2	1.3	0.6	100.0	
% of all attenders in peerage category	14.7	26.7	26.0	11.1	3.8	19.0	

D. Regular attenders (over 66⅔% of sittings)

Party	Peerage category					Total	% of attenders in party
	Hereditary	Created hereditary	Life peers	Law lords	Bishops		
Conservative	63	2	32	0		97	24.7
Labour	4	1	60	0		65	60.7
Social and Liberal Democrat	8	1	11	0		20	40.8
Social Democratic Party	3	0	4	0		7	30.4
Cross-bench	24	0	12	1		37	18.2
Other	0	0	2	0		2	12.5
Bishops					0	0	0.0
TOTAL	102	4	121	1	0	228	27.9
% of regular attenders	44.7	1.8	53.1	0.4	0.0	100.0	
% of all attenders in peerage category	23.5	26.7	37.5	5.6	0.0	27.9	

life peers were classified as regular attenders, the same was true of 62.5 per cent (60) of attending life peers from the Labour benches, and of 44.0 per cent (11) of attending Social and Liberal Democrat life peers. While only 22.8 per cent (63) of attending hereditary peers who were members of the Conservative Party were regular attenders, the same could be said of 40 per cent (4) of attending hereditary peers who were members of the Labour Party and 34.8 per cent (8) of attending hereditary Social and Liberal Democrat peers.

Clearly there was a considerable difference between the total possible membership of the House of Lords during the 1988–9 session and what could be termed the actual active membership, namely between those individuals who as a body constitute the membership of the House of Lords and those who are involved when it is acting as a legislative chamber, as participants in the legislative process. (This is not, of course, a characteristic only of the session in question.) What can be termed the 'active' or 'participating' House is certainly not a microcosm of the whole House; indeed, there are marked differences with regard to the political balance and the balance between the various peerage categories. These differences are highlighted when the total eligible membership (Table 2.3) is contrasted with the active membership on what can be termed the average day during the session, as outlined in Table 2.13.

The most significant difference is the alteration in the ratio that existed between members who have themselves been created peers for life and those whose membership is derived from the functioning of the hereditary principle. Amongst the overall eligible membership hereditary peers formed a majority. Even if those members who have themselves been created hereditary peers are not included within the total, the remaining hereditary element accounted for 56.3 per cent. However, in the 'average' active House life peers themselves were in a majority, albeit only just, accounting for 50.3 per cent of attendance. If one adds created hereditary peers together with law lords and bishops to this, the non-hereditary by succession element accounted for 53.9 per cent of the membership of the average active House as against 43.7 per cent of the total eligible membership.

Table 2.13. *Political affiliation and peerage category on an average day during the 1988–9 session*

Party	Peerage category: Hereditary	Created hereditary	Life peers	Law lords	Bishops	Total	% of total attendance
Conservative	93	3	51			147	46.6
Labour	6	1	63			70	22.1
Social and Liberal Democrat	11	1	15			27	8.5
Social Democratic Party	4		6			10	3.2
Cross-bench	32	1	21	3		57	18.0
Other	0	0	3			3	1.0
Bishops					2	2	0.7
TOTAL	146	6	159	3	2	316	100.0
% of total attendance	46.1	1.9	50.3	1.0	0.7	100.0	

Note: Figures are based on total attendances recorded during the 1988–9 session, divided by the number of sitting days (153). 0 indicates a figure of less than 0.5, while a blank indicates no attendances by the category in question. Apparent discrepancies in totals and percentages are the result of rounding.

Twentieth-century Developments in the Membership of the House of Lords

During the constitutional conflict between the Lords and Commons in the early years of the twentieth century, Winston Churchill described the House of Lords as 'a one-sided, hereditary, unpurged, unrepresentative, irresponsible, absentee'[7] and as 'filled with old doddering peers, cute financial magnates, clever wire-pullers, big brewers with bulbous noses. All the enemies of progress are there—weaklings, sleek, smug, comfortable, self-important individuals',[8] while Lloyd George described hereditary

[7] Cited in Robert Rhodes James (ed.), *Churchill Speaks* (Windward, London, 1981), 10.

[8] Ibid.

peers as 'Dug out of the cellars of the House of Lords . . . stuff bottled in the Dark Ages . . . not fit to drink . . . cobwebby, dusty, muddy, sour.'[9] The peerage is indeed an ancient order, with the premier barony of England (de Ros) dating back to 1264. Nevertheless, most of the hereditary titles in existence today are of a comparatively recent historical creation. In addition to this, the innovation in 1958 of peerages for life proved to be an ingenious method whereby new life was breathed into an ancient institution, and has had a significant effect on the House. Although today the 'popular' image of the House of Lords may indeed be of a place full of landed aristocrats up from their country estates, mainstream politicians of a bygone age, wealthy patrons of party funds, friends of former Prime Ministers, and titled fugitives from the pages of P. G. Wodehouse, to portray the membership in such terms would be inaccurate. The addition of a large number of life peers, although not fundamentally altering the nature of the composition of the House (as, for example, direct elections would have done) has undoubtedly enriched it by bringing in members of more varied backgrounds and experiences. Since the passage of the Life Peerages Act 1958 the House of Lords has acquired newly ennobled bankers, engineers, diplomats, lawyers, businessmen, economists, trade unionists, military commanders, politicians, academics, educationalists, scientists, administrators, and senior civil servants on a scale unprecedented before the passage of the Act. As a result of this blend of hereditary and life peers, the House has members with very considerable knowledge of almost every aspect of life. Because of this it has become the custom for these experts—or at any rate people with considerable knowledge—to attend and speak on their specialized subjects, often leading to a very high level of debate. As shown in Chapter 8 it is difficult, although certainly not impossible, to find a topic for debate on which there is not at least one peer, and more often than not several peers, who is either a recognized authority or at least has considerable practical knowledge, and today any major debate in the House is likely to include speeches from experts.

[9] Cited in Ian Gilmour, *The Body Politic* (Hutchinson, London, 1969), 297.

The Political Balance of the House of Lords

Returning to the difference between the total membership and the average membership, there were major differences, again in terms of balance, between the party or group affiliations of active members on the average day and that found amongst the total membership. The most notable—and indeed noticeable—difference is the proportionate increase in support for the Labour Party. Although peers who were in receipt of the Labour whip accounted for only 13.1 per cent of the total number of members attending during the session, they accounted for 22.1 per cent of the average active membership, an increase of nearly 70 per cent.

By far the largest political grouping amongst the average active membership, as would be expected, consists of members who are in receipt of the Conservative whip: 46.6 per cent, certainly by far and away the party or grouping with the largest level of support, although not in a position of majority.

In recognizing that there are a considerable number of members who are not affiliated to any political party and that there is a significant difference between the total possible membership and the actual achieved day-to-day membership, one goes a long way to understanding why considerable confusion surrounds the issue of the political balance to be found within the House of Lords.

A significant part of this confusion is of course the existence of the cross-benchers, the increasingly large number of peers who choose not to associate themselves with one or other of the political parties. Indeed, it cannot be said with any certainty, save for a very small number where an educated guess could be made, whether these individuals would vote for or against any particular clause or motion. To a very great extent it is genuinely the case that one cannot predict how individuals from the cross-benches will cast their votes. Hence it is evident that a large number of 'jokers' have been, and are being, shuffled into the Lords political pack.

Furthermore, also to be found occupying the cross-benches are the law lords. Although these peers are not in any way forbidden to take part in the ordinary work of the House, there is undoubtedly not only a convention against their becoming involved with any political party but also one preventing them from participating in partisan political controversy. Such restraint does not of course prevent law lords from speaking out on the legal aspects of politically controversial topics, nor indeed from participating in the divisions which take place in the House. Hence, although few in number, the law lords are part of the equation and therefore have to be taken into account by those trying to judge the likely outcome of any division, not least of all because of the influence they can have upon other members. Their presence within the Chamber serves to heighten the confusion.

In addition to the non-party members who actually sit on the cross-benches, there are the lords spiritual, the twenty-six 'representatives' of the Church of England. Irrespective of the position in the past when bishops would, on the whole, consider themselves under obligation to support the government under whom they had been raised to their position, today bishops tend not to become involved in partisan political controversy. Rather, they tend to see it as being their duty to scrutinize matters under debate in the light of the Christian faith, forming and expressing the Christian conscience on some of the major problems of the day. In doing this they certainly do not vote together as a block.[10] None the less, because they are able to attend and vote the confusion over the political balance in the Lords is only increased.

An additional part of the equation is the fact that there are a number of other peers—some who although they have no connection with any of the four political parties are none the less not in receipt of the cross-bench notification of business and some about whom information regarding party allegiance is not known—whose attendance in any great number is either non-existent or, at the very most, rare. The fact that they could and indeed in some instances do attend the House only adds to the confusion.

The outcome of any division depends upon the number of members voting as well as the way in which they cast their votes. These basic factors themselves depend upon a number of

[10] During the 1988–9 session the bishops cast a total of only 37 votes, 23 anti-Government, and 14 pro-Government (see Table 2.9). On one occasion bishops voted in both lobbies (one in each).

variables, such as the subject under discussion, the advocacy of certain individuals, the day of the week, and the hour of the day. Any exposition of the political complexion of the House of Lords is invalidated unless it takes into account these factors. When they are taken into account, it becames apparent that the complete Conservative control evident in 1945, indeed evident into the 1960s, has disappeared; gone are the days when a Conservative Government need have no fear of defeat in the Lords. Indeed, the Lords have in recent years been a source of embarrassment, an irritant, and obstruction to the Conservative Government—as is shown by the more than 150 defeats inflicted upon the Conservative Government in the division lobbies of the House of Lords since 1979. (During the 1988–9 session the House defeated the Government on twelve occasions, out of 186 divisions in which the Government took a stand.) Today, although an overall Conservative majority is perceived by many to exist, in practice the Conservative Party lacks an automatic majority over all other groups combined, and, more especially, among active peers is in a minority—albeit only just—relative to them. As Lord Denham, Government Chief Whip from 1979 to 1991, has pointed out:

> However you calculate it, the Conservative Party has no overall majority in [the House of Lords]. When it does not get Cross-Bench support or when some [Conservatives] withhold their support, Her Majesty's Government are very much at risk.[11]

Indeed, as a Labour peer who has served as leader of his party in the Lords has said, the position is not one of Conservative dominance, but rather one in which:

> A Conservative Government, because of its numerical position in relation to the Labour Party, has a greater degree of control over events than does a Labour Government. It cannot, however, when acting alone, 'impose' its will upon the House.[12]

Similarly, and as another senior figure from the Labour benches has explained:

> In point of fact the Tory majority over Labour is not all that impor-

[11] HL Debs., 26 Apr. 1984, col. 149. See also HL Debs., 17 May 1984, col. 1506.

[12] Former Labour Leader of the House—confidential to author.

tant—after all, the whole Chamber has voted many times for Labour motions and amendments according to conscience. There is no ego, no constituency, no power-push to persuade the Lords to vote in any way they don't want to. They are *very* independent.[13]

Indeed, time and again the members of the House of Lords have demonstrated their freedom to speak and vote on the merits of proposals as they see them. This being the case, the true position today, as one of the bishops explained it, is that:

The House of Lords has a mind of its own, and no single party can rely unreservedly on its support.[14]

[13] Labour life peer—confidential to author.
[14] Bishop—confidential to author.

3

Government Legislation: An Overview

Gavin Drewry and Jenny Brock

Legislative business looms very large in the working life of the House of Lords. As the introductory chapter indicates, the House spends more than half its time considering public bills, the overwhelming preponderance of its attention being directed at Government bills. Approximately one-third of this time is spent on measures that originate in the Lords, the remainder on Commons bills. Interviews with peers, carried out for the purposes of this study,[1] confirmed that peers themselves regard legislative scrutiny as the most important function of the House of Lords (with scrutiny of European Community business coming a fairly close second).

Peers who were interviewed generally agreed that the main contribution of the House to the legislative process is to provide an opportunity for ministerial second thoughts about bills; many of them also felt that there had been something of a renaissance in the legislative significance of the Lords in recent years, attributable, so they thought, to the size of the Government's Commons majority, which meant that more scope for critical scrutiny and constructive (or destructive) amendment tended to be left to the other House. Most peers interviewed—even those who were critical, for instance, of the hereditary membership of the House, or who had unkind things to say about the calibre of the Government front bench—felt that the House was generally doing 'a good job'.

This chapter examines the work of the House of Lords on Government bills in the 1988–9 session. It is complemented by the next chapter, which examines eight specific 'case-study' bills.

What is the legislative role of the House? Does it really do 'a

[1] A total of 30 interviews were carried out, on a strictly non-attributable basis, in July 1989 with 21 peers, with several party research workers in the Lords, and with Officers of the House.

good job'? We hope in these two chapters to throw useful light on—if not provide definitive answers to—questions such as these.

Public Bill Procedure in the House of Lords

Detailed accounts of legislative procedure in the Lords can be found elsewhere,[2] but it is appropriate to note here, very briefly, a few procedural peculiarities, some illustrative examples of which will be encountered later, in this and other chapters.

Broadly speaking, public bill procedure in the Lords is similar to that of the Commons, but there are differences—some of them enshrined in the Standing Orders, others having a less formal status. Thus, although second reading debates in the two Houses give MPs and peers respectively the chance to discuss the broad principles of a bill, in the Lords, unlike the Commons, it is almost unheard of in modern times for the Opposition to divide the House at the end of the second reading debate with a view to securing the outright rejection of a Government bill.[3]

Clause-by-clause consideration of a bill at committee stage in the Commons normally takes place in standing committee, but almost all bills in the Lords are considered in committee of the whole House. The conventions concerning the grouping of amendments at committee stage are discussed later in this chapter. For most financial bills, the Lords committee stage is negatived following the second reading, and the remaining stages can be taken forthwith, without further debate. Bills that have been considered at committee stage by select committee (very rare nowadays with Government bills, apart from occasional hybrid bills) or by a joint committee of the two Houses (the normal procedure for consolidation bills) are recommitted to a committee of the whole House—unless the select committee or

[2] E.g. Donald Shell, *The House of Lords*, 2nd edn. (Harvester Wheatsheaf, London, 1992), 133–9; Erskine May, *Parliamentary Practice*, 21st edn. (Butterworths, London, 1989), 443–61.

[3] The War Crimes Bill was rejected at second reading on 4 June 1990 and 30 Apr. 1991, but, although this was a Government bill, no party whips were applied. While accepting the second reading of a bill, the Opposition may divide the House on a non-fatal amendment, e.g. expressing regret at the contents of a bill.

the joint committee has recommended that the bill should not proceed. Other bills can be recommitted, wholly or in part, to a committee of the whole House at any time between committee stage and third reading, on the following grounds, identified by Erskine May:

> when it is desirable that there should be the freedom of debate possible on a committee stage to give further detailed consideration to a bill or certain parts of it; for instance when substantial amendments are tabled too late in the committee stage to enable them to be properly considered; or after the committee stage; or where there is extensive redrafting. This procedure reserves to the report stage its proper function as an opportunity to review and perfect the bill as amended in committee.[4]

During the session under review the only bill to be recommitted was the Companies Bill.

A bill is reported from committee to the House, following which the third reading, unlike the corresponding stage in the Commons, gives further opportunity for amendment. And when amendments are moved at third reading, the House considers a further motion 'that the bill do now pass'—usually the occasion for a few brief speeches from those who have been most involved in the earlier debates on the bill.

Because no one parliamentary session can be viewed in isolation, we offer some general observations about recent trends and patterns in public legislation and about the recent history of public bill scrutiny in the House of Lords, before turning specifically to the 1988–9 session.

The House under Pressure

One general point to be borne very much in mind in this and other contexts is that the volume of business transacted by the House of Lords has grown dramatically in recent years, and shows no obvious signs of diminishing. This increase, combined with the growth in the number of active peers, has put increasing pressure on the time of the House.

The Group on the Working of the House (whose report was published in July 1987) concluded that the increased pressure

[4] Erskine May, *Parl. Practice*, 457.

was mainly attributable to 'the amount of public legislation considered, the time taken to do so, and the number of amendments made'.[5] The tabulated evidence on which this conclusion was based is reproduced here as Table 3.1, updated to include comparable statistics for subsequent sessions.

This pressure is aggravated by the uneven flow of legislative business: since most major bills are first introduced in the Commons this tends to produce an end-of-session logjam in the Lords. Although there is no formal guillotine in the Lords, the build-up of work later in the session, with regular late sittings and insufficient time for consideration of last-minute amendments, can be very intense. Peers now usually return to Westminster after the summer recess before MPs in order to clear the backlog.[6] But even so the time available can be too short (from the draftsman's point of view, as well as that of legislators) for the job to be done properly. Ironically, during the 1988–9 autumn overspill (which lasted a full six weeks) peers were under particular pressure because of the need to consider the major new additions to bills which had started early in the session in their own House.

Pressure of business also means that there is not always sufficient time between successive stages to allow for consultation and preparation of amendments. In 1977 the House of Lords accepted recommendations from its Select Committee on Procedure for minimum intervals between successive stages of bills. Table 3.2 indicates when these intervals were breached during the 1988–9 session.

The breach of these recommended intervals not only places strains on peers involved, but also impairs the capacity of the House to fulfil its revising role effectively.

Opposition peers interviewed thought that the effectiveness of the House was limited by the sheer volume of legislation—though the main concern was the quality of the legislation rather than its quantity. The Group on the Working of the House also expressed concern that, where possible, reasonable notice should be given for consideration of Commons amendments. Without

[5] *Report by the Group on the Working of the House*, HL Paper 9, 1987–8, para. 5.

[6] In the 1988–9 session the Lords returned on Monday 9 Oct., the Commons on Tuesday 17 Oct. The Lords sat during the Conservative Party Conference. See App. A for a complete list of sittings during the session.

Table 3.1. *Lords proceedings on public bills, 1976–91*

	1976–7	1977–8	1978–9	1979–80	1980–1	1981–2	1982–3	1983–4	1984–5	1985–6	1986–7	1987–8	1988–9	1989–90	1990–91
Commons bills															
Government (excluding money/supply bills)															
Bills reaching HL	15	29	23	46	31	29	28	32	31	29	16	26	17	18	27
Bills amended	11	11	8	18	14	8	3	15	13	15	7	16	10	12	9
Amendments	81	525	842	971	418	842	52	1,117	854	2,167	539	1,967	1,540	1,674	544
Rejected	19	157	0	0	1	0	0	6	36	4	0	21	17	0	25
Accepted (%)	76	70			99			99	96	99		99	99		95
Private Members'															
Bills reaching HL	10	8	3	10	10	8	10	11	17	17	12	12	9	12	20
Bills amended	6	4	2	3	5	2	0	3	4	3	1	5	5	4	4
Amendments	175	71	39	6	49	39	0	46	33	133	8	47	19	39	24
Lords bills															
Government (excluding consolidation bills)															
Bills introduced	11	22	9	11	12	10	11	14	12	16	14	9	12	8	10
Bills amended	6	8	5	7	8	5	9	11	8	9	6	6	6	6	6
Amendments	821	356	467	307	940	467	429	456	652	265	388	1,019	816	852	1,012
Private Members'															
Bills introduced	21	8	13	22	23	25	21	19	17	13	10	7	8	10	8
Bills amended	8	5	6	5	9	6	5	8	5	8	3	3	2	5	2
Amendments	213	125	101	35	53	101	22	161	61	86	11	30	23	49	5
Government defeats (HL & HC bills)															
Defeats	22	73	7	14	17	7	4	19	16	22	3	17	12	20	17
Nos. of bills concerned	11	7	3	6	8	5	3	10	10	11	2	9	6	10	7
Divisions (not necessarily on legislation)	45	96	21	303	184	146	89	237	145	250	80	279	189	186	104

Sources: Report by the Group on the Working of the House (HL Paper 9, Session 1987–8), Para. 5 and Table VI: Pt. 2; House of Lords Public Bill Office Sessional Statistics; House of Lords Journal and Information Office.

Table 3.2. *Breaches of recommended minimum intervals between stages of bills*

1st reading–2nd reading 2 weekends	2nd reading–committee 14 days	Committee–report 14 days[a]
	Children (13 days)	
Continental Shelf (4 days, no weekend)		
	Dock Work (11 days)	Dock Work (8 days)
Elected Authorities (Northern Ireland) (9 days, 1 weekend)		
		Electricity (10 days)
	Fair Employment (Northern Ireland) (13 days)	Fair Employment (Northern Ireland) (6 days)
Human Organ Transplants (9 days, 1 weekend)		
		Law of Property (Miscellaneous Provisions) (7 days)
		Local Government and Housing (8 days)
Pesticides (Fees and Enforcement) (7 days, 1 weekend)		
Representation of the People (3 days, no weekend)		
		Transport (Scotland) (8 days)

[a] 'for bills of considerable length and complexity'.
Note: The recommended minimum interval of 3 sitting days between report and third reading was not breached during the 1988–9 session.

sufficient notice, adequate time is not available for the tabling of amendments to the amendments, or amendments in lieu, unless manuscript amendments (which are not encouraged under present rules of practice) are tabled. Without time for proper consideration, the Lords may have to let what they consider to be an unsatisfactory Commons amendment be accepted by default, rather than risk confrontation with the Commons, or the loss of the bill in question.[7]

There is on the other hand pressure on the Government later in the session to acquiesce in amendments—and concessions may be made in order to complete the final stages before the end of the session.

Many bills, and not only those that are primarily financial, go through their later stages in the Lords on the nod—without being examined in committee—simply because no amendments are tabled. Even fewer bills are considered on report and fewer still at third reading. In any event, the Commons spends more time in aggregate than the Lords on almost all bills including those first introduced in the upper House (see Table 3.3).

The amount of time given to most individual bills in the Lords is quite short. A disproportionate amount of time is taken up by a small number of particularly controversial or complex bills. In the 1988–9 session, one-third of the time spent on primary legislation was taken by the three longest bills (excluding the Finance Bill), and well over half of the time was taken by just six bills.

Legislative Business in 1987–8

The 1988–9 session, the focal point of this chapter, and of the study as a whole, was the second session of a Parliament which commenced after the 1987 general election. A few comments about the 1987–8 session are necessary, to set the following session in its context.

The session 1987–8 was not only unusually long, running from the opening of the new Parliament in June 1987 until November

[7] *Report by the Group on the Working of the House*, para. 42.

Table 3.3. *Government bills considered by the House of Lords during the 1988–9 session*

	Type	Pages intro. HL	Pages intro. HC	Pages enacted	HL 2nd rdg.	HL 3rd rdg. and passing	HL amdts.	HC 2nd rdg.	HC 3rd rdg.	HC amdts.	Total time HL hrs. m.	Total time HC hrs. m.	Total time hrs. m.
Government bills introduced in the House of Lords (excluding consolidation bills)													
Antarctic Minerals [HL]		11	11	11	20 Apr.	8 June	0	4 July	17 July	0	1:15	11:58	13:13
Atomic Energy [HL]		6	6	6	13 Dec.	13 Feb.	2	13 Apr.	22 May	0	2:07	8:17	10:24
Brunei (Appeals) [HL]		2	2	2	18 Apr.	8 June	0	11 July	30 Oct.	0	0:12	0:17	0:29
Children [HL]	G	121	124	218	6 Dec.	16 Mar.	187	27 Apr.	27 Oct.	463	65:01	59:24	124:25
Civil Aviation (Air Navigation Charges) [HL]		1	1	1	22 Dec.	30 Jan.	0	2 Mar.	22 May	0	0:19	0:42	1:01
Companies [HL]	G	207	240	332	16 Jan.	27 Apr.	488	3 May	26 Oct.	531	69:29	56:59	121:11
Continental Shelf [HL]		1	1	1	21 July	21 July	0	26 July	26 July	0	0:05	0:03	0:08
Football Spectators [HL]	G	19	21	28	2 Feb.	16 June	79	27 June	30 Oct.	101	40:17	64:30	104:47
Law of Property (Miscellaneous Provisions) [HL]		5	5	6	24 Jan.	27 Feb.	7	10 Apr.	26 July	0	0:53	0:38	1:31
National Maritime Museum [HL]		2	2	2	19 Jan.	6 Feb.	0	2 Mar.	22 May	0	0:36	1:24	2:00

Police Officers (Central Service) [HL]	3	3	3	2 Mar.	24 Apr.	0	4 May	14 June	0	0:23	0:38	1:01
Road Traffic (Driver Licensing and Information Systems) [HL]	40	43	56	15 Dec.	16 Mar.	53	13 Apr.	4 July	25	11:37	9:20	20:57
TOTAL (12 bills)	418	459	666			816			1,120	197:26	214:10	411:36
Consolidation bills introduced in the House of Lords												
Extradition [HL]	34	34	34	29 June	19 July	0	26 July	26 July	0	0:02	0:21	0:23
Opticians [HL]	32	32	32	17 July	2 Nov.	3	9 Nov.	9 Nov.	0	0:30	0:03	0:33
Prisons (Scotland) [HL]	26	25	25	4 May	22 May	0	9 Nov.	9 Nov.	0	0:01	0:03	0:04
Statute Law Repeals [HL]	43	43	44	13 June	12 July	0	9 Nov.	9 Nov.	0	0:05	0:03	0:08
TOTAL (4 bills)	135	134	135			3			0	0:38	0:30	1:08

Table 3.3. *(contd.)*

	Type	Pages intro. HC	Pages intro. HL	Pages enacted	HC 2nd rdg.	HC 3rd rdg.	HL 2nd rdg.	HL 3rd rdg. and passing	HL amdts. (1)	HL amdts. (2)	Total time HC hrs. m.	Total time HL hrs. m.	Total time hrs. m.
Government bills brought from the House of Commons													
Consolidated Fund	MS	1		1	19 Dec.	19 Dec.	20 Dec.	20 Dec.	0	0	0:01	0:00	0:01
Consolidated Fund (No. 2)	MS	1		1	13 Mar.	13 Mar.	14 Mar.	14 Mar.	0	0	0:01	0:00	0:01
Consolidated Fund (Appropriation)	MS	47		47	27 July	27 July	27 July	27 July	0	0	0:01	0:00	0:01
Dock Work	G	12	12	12	17 Apr.	24 May	9 June	3 July	0	0	58:58	13:19	72:17
Elected Authorities (Northern Ireland)		13	13	13	5 Dec.	26 Jan.	9 Feb.	13 Mar.	0	0	21:23	8:14	29:37
Electricity		139	149	164	12 Dec.	10 Apr.	25 Apr.	18 July	196	182	155:40	65:53	211:02
Employment	G	38	41	48	11 Jan.	6 June	14 July	2 Nov.	33	33	67:57	25:31	93:28
Fair Employment (Northern Ireland)		46	54	56	31 Jan.	25 May	28 June	20 July	91	81	48:54	15:31	64:25
Finance	MS	250	277	275	25 Apr.	12 July	25 July	25 July	0	0	80:13	3:03	83:16
Human Organ Transplants		3	4	4	22 May	6 July	19 July	25 July	0	0	5:40	1:03	6:43
Local Government and Housing	G	180	223	322	14 Feb.	21 June	4 July	1 Nov.	702	604	131:56	85:52	207:14
Official Secrets	G	14	14	14	21 Dec.	22 Feb.	9 Mar.	24 Apr.	10	10	46:00	22:08	67:00
Pesticides (Fees and Enforcement)		3	3	3	2 Mar.	19 June	27 June	25 July	0	0	1:33	0:08	1:41

Petroleum Royalties (Relief) and Continental Shelf		4	4	4	30 Nov.	15 Dec.	17 Jan.	6 Feb.	0	0	2:20	0:53	3:13
Prevention of Terrorism (Temporary Provisions)	G	64	65	72	6 Dec.	30 Jan.	13 Feb.	13 Mar.	34	29	66:27	7:44	74:11
Representation of the People		4	4	4	29 June	5 July	13 July	25 July	0	0	4:29	0:31	5:00
Security Service		8	8	8	15 Dec.	23 Jan.	27 Feb.	27 Apr.	0	0	15:56	9:59	25:55
Self-Governing Schools etc. (Scotland)	G	70	78	81	6 Mar.	20 June	21 July	6 Nov.	96	94	121:01	16:07	137:08
Social Security		60	81	81	10 Jan.	26 Apr.	25 May	17 July	3	3	93:40	28:26	122:06
Transport (Scotland)		9	9	10	14 Dec.	20 Feb.	23 Mar.	17 July	4	4	43:44	2:12	45:56
Water	G	343	388	419	7 Dec.	4 Apr.	17 Apr.	27 June	371	341	158:43	107:19	256:03
TOTAL (21 bills)		1,309	1,427	1,639					1,540	1,381	1,135:13	413:45	1,548:58

Notes: Privilege amendments, and amendments made by the Joint Committee on Consolidation Bills, are not recorded.
In the 'Type' column, G = bill guillotined in Commons, M = certified money bill, S = supply bill.
For Lords bills, HL amdts. gives the sum of amendments at each stage, HC amdts. the number of amendments returned from the Commons.
For Commons bills, HL amdts. (1) gives the sum of amendments at each stage, HL amdts. (2) the number of amendments returned to the Commons.
Case-study bills discussed in Ch. 4 are shown in bold.

1988, but was also peculiarly burdensome in legislative terms. The Government was anxious to get several controversial bills on to the statute book before the summer recess. Two bills in particular—Local Government Finance (the bill which introduced the community charge in England and Wales) and Education Reform—were especially long and controversial, and were guillotined in the Commons, meaning that major parts of these bills arrived in the Lords having undergone truncated scrutiny by the other House.

The Copyright, Designs and Patents Bill, destined to be amended heavily in both Houses, was introduced in the Lords, which at least helped to spread the unusually heavy burdens imposed on the House during this session. The House spent twelve days on this bill, and made the exceptionally large total of 561 amendments.

The increase in the political support staff employed by the opposition parties probably also contributed to the considerable increase in the number of non-Government amendments tabled in the 1987–8 session, a point referred to below; the length of session and thus size of programme were also undoubtedly factors.

Thus the baseline from which our assessment of the 1988–9 session is made was set at a very high level by the record figures for 1987–8, when 3,071 amendments were made (excluding privilege amendments, amendments off the floor of the House, and amendments to Commons amendments). This total was the largest on record. Three-quarters of the amendments were accounted for by just five bills: Education Reform (632); Copyright, Designs and Patents (561); Local Government Finance (520); Housing (308); and Criminal Justice (261), a further illustration of the fact that the limelight—in terms of political controversiality, media attention, and academic analysis—tends to fall disproportionately on a few bills.

The Legislative Programme in the 1988–9 Session: The Pressure Sustained

In the 1988–9 session the Queen's speech (on 22 November 1988) was later than it had been in any year since 1976 and it

Table 3.4. *Government legislation, session 1988–9*

	Ordinary bills		Consolidated Fund bills	Consolidation bills	Total
	Commons	Lords			
Total	18	12	3	4	37
In Queen's speech	12	4	—	—	16
Average length (pages enacted)[a]	88.3	55.5	16.3	33.8	

[a] The average length of the 8 case-study bills considered in the next chapter was 143.7 pages.

signalled a further heavy programme of legislative business. Additional bills were added to the sixteen 'programme bills' originally promised in the speech. Four of the sixteen programme bills—Road Traffic (Driver Licensing and Information Systems), Football Spectators, Companies, and Children—began in the Lords: all are included among the case-studies in the next chapter. The session ended with thirty-seven Government bills having received the royal assent, four of these being consolidation measures. A breakdown is shown at Table 3.4—which also indicates the relative lengths of different kinds of Government bill, measured by the number of pages as enacted.

Although this was the lowest number of bills passed in any ordinary-length session since the war, it included some that by virtue of their great complexity or contentiousness—or both—were bound to have a long and difficult passage.

This led to a crowded timetable. Commons debate on ten Government bills was curtailed by timetable motions (the corresponding figure for the preceding session was six). Details are given in Table 3.5.

It is sometimes suggested that guillotine motions have important implications for the revising role of the House of Lords. Peers often claim that their House gives particular attention to those bills, and sections of bills, upon which debate in the Commons has been curtailed by the guillotine. However, some observers have pointed to the converse tendency for debate in the Lords to be truncated when peers do not have the benefit of Commons debate to draw upon. Six of the bills listed below are

Table 3.5. *Use of the guillotine in the House of Commons, session 1988–9*

Bill	Stages guillotined
Children	report, 3rd reading
Companies	report, 3rd reading
Dock Work	committee, report, 3rd reading
Employment	Lords amendments
Football Spectators	committee, report, 3rd reading
Local Government and Housing	Lords amendments
Official Secrets	committee, report, 3rd reading, Lords amendments
Prevention of Terrorism (Temporary Provisions)	committee, report, 3rd reading
Self-Governing Schools, etc. (Scotland)	committee, report, 3rd reading, Lords amendments
Water	committee, report, 3rd reading, Lords amendments

discussed in detail in the next chapter. It would seem from this discussion that the application of the guillotine in the Commons was not on its own a major determinant of the focus of debate in the Lords. Other factors seem more important in deciding on what sections of a bill the House spends its time: such factors include the role of outside groups in bringing forward amendments, the activities of groups well represented in the House such as those speaking for the disabled or for environmental concerns, and the Opposition's assessment of which clauses they particularly wish to undermine. In practice various considerations overlap, and disentangling the effect of any one of these, such as the use of the guillotine in the Commons, is difficult to do with any precision. It is, however, worth noting that on the Official Secrets Bill the Lords actually spent less time than the Commons on those clauses guillotined in the lower House, with two of the principal clauses affected by the guillotine not being debated at all in the upper House. On the Water Bill both Houses gave most time to the earlier parts of this guillotined bill.

There were during the 1988–9 session certainly frequent complaints (mainly but not entirely from Opposition members) in both Houses regarding the quality of legislation. Bills, it was said, were increasingly being brought before Parliament that were ill-thought-out, incomplete, and poorly drafted. Lord Williams of Elvel (Labour), speaking on the Companies Bill, said he was tired of the House being used as a 'legislative sausage machine'.[8]

From a different standpoint, Viscount Whitelaw, talking to a Westminster press gallery lunch at the beginning of the 1989–90 session, warned of the danger of producing low-quality Acts of Parliament by supplementing the programme bills in the Queen's speech with additional 'instant legislation'.[9] Referring to the legislative events of the preceding session, Lord Whitelaw said the problem was not the properly prepared Queen's speech programme of bills but the demand for instant legislation following a serious event, with ministers being deemed failures if they did not promise a new bill. The result was a hastily produced bill, heavily amended to correct its mistakes.

The other danger, he said, arose from Government departments squeezing a small bill into the Queen's speech: 'they say it is just two or three little clauses and . . . it immediately turns out that the process is not nearly as simple as was promised. It leads to ill-informed and ill-prepared new clauses and amendments which . . . then have to be amended again.'[10]

While peers on all sides like to be seen as playing an active part in the legislative process—and the extent to which they amend legislation is an index of this—both Opposition and Government back-bench peers, among those interviewed for this study, deplored the very large number of amendments being made in both Houses, which they felt reflected badly on the original drafting of legislation. This was generally attributed to the sheer volume of legislation.

Amendments as an Indicator of 'Impact'

'In considering amendments moved to a bill,' writes Griffith, 'what is important is their relative effect on the bill, not their number.'[11] A simple quantitative assessment gives the same

[8] HL Debs., 7 Nov. 1989, col. 548.
[9] *Guardian*, 23 Nov. 1989. [10] Ibid.
[11] J. A. G. Griffith, *Parliamentary Scrutiny of Government Bills* (Allen & Unwin, London, 1974), 14.

weight to a minor drafting amendment as to a major alteration to the intention of a bill.

Shell notes that the raw statistics showing the total number of amendments made fail to distinguish between amendments of greatly differing importance:

> Some can be described as 'purely drafting' amendments, which means they involve no intention to alter, in any way, the substance or impact of the bill, but simply seek to clarify its wording. Some are 'technical' amendments which are intended to improve the bill by making its impact more precise; others are 'substantive' amendments which may concede important points without altering the basic purpose of the bill; while still others can be described as 'wrecking' amendments because they do change the basic nature of the bill, and may indeed result in the whole bill having to be abandoned.[12]

However, any classification of amendments as to their degree of significance will be subjective: what one person sees as a purely technical amendment, another may regard as a substantive change (though legislators themselves often agree across the floor of the House about such descriptions of significance). Griffith addresses this problem of subjectivity by giving a fairly full account of those amendments which he has designated as more, or less, substantive, so that the meaning of terms like 'substantial' or 'important' becomes clearer. There is still of course the underlying assumption in his analysis that all those amendments (the majority) not thus subjected to qualitative analysis are 'trivial, drafting or wholly consequential' amendments—but this approach nevertheless seems preferable to either a simple totalling of amendments or a spuriously precise ranking system.

According to researchers employed by the Labour Party and the Social and Liberal Democrats, interviewed for this study, many Commons amendments are poorly drafted. Some of them thought that this could be attributable, in the case of Government amendments, to the worrying phenomenon of 'legislating as you go along', which places impossible burdens on the professional skills of Parliamentary Counsel. Opposition amendments are often intended to probe or to expose rather than to change the letter of the law, and thus do not need to be 'well drafted' in technical or legal terms.

In framing amendments in the Lords, although the broad party line is generally followed, rather more consideration is given to what is politically feasible—and what is likely to command the broadest support.

What then of Lords amendments in the session under review?

Lords Amendments in 1988–9

As Table 3.3 shows, fewer than half the thirty-seven Government bills introduced during the session were amended in the Lords. Four of the twenty not amended were supply bills, including three Consolidated Fund bills, which are not amendable in the Lords; three were consolidation bills. These statistics are consistent with those recorded by Shell in respect of earlier sessions.[13] His study also showed that most bills which are not amended in the Lords are not amended in the Commons either, or undergo very slight amendment there—underlining the point made earlier, that Government bills vary enormously in their controversiality and complexity. Of the fourteen Government bills (excluding Consolidated Fund and consolidation bills) not amended in the Lords, twelve were not amended in the Commons either.

Seventeen Government bills were amended by the Lords during the session, the total number of amendments being 2,359. Details may be found in Table 3.3. Just five bills accounted for 82.4 per cent of all Lords amendments: 702 amendments to the Local Government and Housing Bill, 488 to the Companies Bill, 371 to the Water Bill, 196 to the Electricity Bill, and 187 to the Children Bill. No other bill was subjected to more than 100 amendments during the session. All five of these bills were major programme bills—signalled as such by inclusion in the Queen's speech.

Grouping of Amendments

Amendments may all be debated since there is no selection of amendments as there is in the Commons. But, by agreement

[13] Ibid., 143–4.

related amendments are often debated together in an informal grouping. The Report by the Group on the Working of the House described current practice and identified some shortcomings:

> The present system [of informal and non-binding grouping of amendments] is operated by the Government Whips' Office and proposed groupings are suggested by the department concerned. They are usually discussed with the opposition spokesmen and, if possible, with other Peers who have tabled amendments to the bill. The difficulty is timing—the proposed groupings are based on the Marshalled List of amendments, which is usually printed only in the morning, a few hours before the debate takes place. This gives little time for the requisite consultations between 11.00 a.m. and 1.30 p.m. The weak point in the system is the hurry in which it has to take place, preventing consultation with some interested parties. Our evidence did suggest that, despite efforts by the Government Whips' Office, the system is not as widely understood as is desirable and does not work as smoothly as it might.[14]

The Report went on to recommend a number of improvements, for instance that copies of proposed groupings should be made available in the Printed Paper Office and at the desks in the Prince's Chamber and the Peers' Lobby, and that peers who have tabled amendments should be advised to consult the Government whips' office between 11 a.m. and 1.30 p.m. to discuss proposed groupings.

Sources of, and Responses to, Amendments

The names of up to four peers may be put down as sponsors of an amendment (or five if the peer in charge of a bill chooses to add his name). It is not uncommon for these sponsors to include peers from more than one party. Thus on the eight case-study bills discussed in detail in the next chapter, a large number of amendments were jointly sponsored by the Opposition and Social and Liberal Democrat front benches and in a significant number of cases there was sponsorship from all sides of the House (see Table 4.2).

Shell points out that 'close observers of the House of Lords suggest that, in recent years, much more careful consideration

[14] *Report by the Group on the Working of the House*, para. 30.

has been given to the question of amendment sponsorship, with important amendments being drafted in such a way as to secure cross-party support, reflected in the names of sponsoring peers.'[15] This subject is discussed further in relation to the case-study bills considered in Chapter 4.

The listed sponsors of an amendment do not, however, necessarily reveal its true origins, especially in respect of Government amendments (the majority). In Shell's words, 'Not infrequently these are put down by the Government as concessions in direct response to criticisms made at earlier stages of a bill's passage, sometimes even as a result of a defeat the Government has suffered, after which it brings forward amendments to clarify the change it has been forced to accept.'[16]

Nicholas Baldwin found that nearly half the amendments moved in the Lords to Government bills between 1970 and 1983 were moved by Government spokesmen, but he also found that the proportion of these which were actually initiated by the Government was something under three-quarters, the remainder being Government responses to undertakings given at earlier stages or as the direct result of an undertaking given to an interest group.[17]

If the Government spokesman undertakes to 'look again' then he can certainly expect to be challenged at a later stage in the bill's proceedings to explain the outcome of such re-examination of a point (if the outcome is not clear from Government amendments that have been tabled). Peers (like MPs) frequently regard such a promise to look again as their highest realistic aspiration in moving an amendment. If it is not granted, they may force a division, but if such a division is lost then the Government's position will have received a considerable measure of reinforcement. For their part, ministers will often resist pressure to look again because they do not want to leave the door open for further discussions either inside or outside Parliament. If a minister does promise to look again, but it later becomes apparent that this has not been done other than in a perfunctory way, then the minister can expect criticism. Suspicion that an undertaking has been given casually, either without sufficient thought or merely to give the minister temporary respite from his critics, is regarded as a

[15] Shell, *House of Lords*, 137. [16] Ibid., 149. [17] Cited in ibid.

breach of parliamentary etiquette (see Chapter 4). A stronger form of undertaking—breach of which would be regarded much more seriously—is one definitely to bring forward amendments at a later stage.

According to Shell, a considerable number of Government amendments to bills in the Lords are the result of undertakings given during the bill's passage through the Commons.[18] However, in Griffith's study of the 1968–9 and 1970–1 sessions, this happened only rarely—which led him to the view that this seemed to be a much less important function of the second chamber than is generally supposed.[19] The Government may of course choose to keep some concessions up their sleeve to use later as instruments of political trade.

One important factor to be noted is the growing use of party research staff. In the past, the official Opposition in the House of Lords has had only one researcher to co-ordinate Opposition amendments. The Top Salaries Review Body, however, recommended[20] that the Opposition should have an allocation of funds sufficient to provide eight to ten researchers, with limited provision for other opposition parties. The official Opposition in the Lords had, at the beginning of the session under review, three full-time researchers and were hoping to recruit a fourth. The Social and Liberal Democrats retained a second full-time research worker. It has already been noted that the exceptionally large number of non-Government amendments tabled in 1987–8 had resulted directly from this increase in research staff and is therefore part of a general trend rather than a flash in the pan.

Amendments moved by opposition spokesmen, by Government back-benchers, and by cross-bench peers often originate with outside interest groups (see below). But pressure groups may take a while to organize themselves in respect of a bill, and this plays a major part in determining when and where amendments are tabled.

[18] Ibid.

[19] Griffith, *Parl. Scrutiny*, 231.

[20] Report No. 24, 'Review of Parliamentary Allowances', Apr. 1987 (Cm. 131–I), para. 67.

Repetition

To what extent are the same amendments raised at different stages in the Lords? Though the Companion to the Standing Orders emphasizes the undesirability of repeating at length at report stage arguments already fully deployed in committee, and amendments already fully debated and decided may not be retabled at third reading, in practice very similar amendments are often debated at successive stages.

Certainly, in the debates on the case-study bills, discussed in the next chapter, repetition occurred. Nevertheless, according to the Group on the Working of the House, although there was concern over the repetitious moving of amendments, the majority of peers believed that in a revising House some repeat amendments were justified, in that arguments can develop as legislation moves through successive stages, particularly when ministers are persuaded by debate to reconsider some aspect of a bill or to give further information. It was recognized, in any case, that low attendance can cause an unrepresentative vote at one stage.[21]

Outcome

It is not surprising to discover, as Griffith found in his analysis of the sessions 1968–9 and 1970–1, that virtually all amendments moved by ministers are agreed whereas the success rate for all other sponsors is much lower.[22]

Griffith noted that, for the sessions he studied, the success rate of Government back-bench and Opposition MPs in securing amendments to bills was lower than that for non-ministers in the Lords. He contended that:

> when all allowance has been made for the dangers of using such statistics, the difference is not only considerable but also confirms the impression given by reading the debates in the Lords: that Ministers in the Lords are more willing to accept amendments than they are in the Commons. Partly this may be because the details of a House of Commons bill are much more settled and firm by the time it arrives in committee in the Lords so that the effect of amendments can be clearly seen. But partly it

[21] *Report by the Group on the Working of the House*, para. 32.
[22] Griffith, *Parl. Scrutiny*, 209.

may be because the less contentious, less partisan, atmosphere in the Lords makes amendments moved by those who are not Ministers more likely to be accepted.[23]

Shell has observed—on the basis of an analysis of the periods 1974–7 (with Labour in office) and 1979–83 (the early sessions of the Thatcher era)—that:

> The proportion of Lords' amendments accepted or rejected by the Commons has varied greatly according to whether the Conservative or Labour Party has been in office . . . One may generalise by saying that when Labour has been in office, it has experienced frequent defeat in the Lords and therefore, as a matter of routine, seeks the cancellation of large numbers of Lords' amendments in the Commons . . . When the Conservatives are in office comparatively few amendments are carried in the House against the Government's wishes, though when this does happen, a Conservative Government is much more hesitant about simply asking the Commons to reverse such amendments. This is because their acceptance by the Lords has frequently depended on support by some Conservative peers, if not on substantial cross-bench support, and may well have been foreshadowed by rebellion in the Commons as well.[24]

Therefore, Shell says, 'the pressure to compromise can be considerable'. However, as noted elsewhere in this chapter, and in the next, the 1988–9 session, with a Conservative Government buttressed by a large Commons majority, a willingness to compromise, let alone to bow meekly to Lords defeats, was conspicuous by its absence—even when such defeats stemmed from all-party initiatives.

We turn now to divisions—the outcome of which provides the acid test of a Government's theoretical capacity to impose its will upon Parliament. In the Commons, of course, the outcome of that test is usually a foregone conclusion. In the non-elected Chamber, however, the Government whips have far less cause for complacency—though the consequences of comparatively commonplace embarrassments in the division lobbies of the Lords are, on the face of it, far less serious than those arising from the rare event of defeat in the Commons.

[23] Ibid. 231.
[24] Shell, *House of Lords*, 146–8.

Divisions

All the 189 divisions which took place during the 1988–9 session related to proceedings on bills, and all but three were on Government bills. An analysis of each division appears in Appendix B. A breakdown by party of votes cast in divisions on Government bills is given in Table 2.9. The general picture is one of hereditary peers, cross-bench peers, and rare attenders all tending to support the Government; but of the votes of the last two categories never actually saving the Government from defeat. Two Labour and eighty-nine Conservative peers cast votes against their party's whip, a total of four and 223 dissenting votes respectively. Four of the twelve Government defeats would have been averted if all Conservative peers who voted had voted for the Government. The impact of peers deliberately abstaining or staying away from a vote is, of course, impossible to measure.

The 'payroll vote'—that is, voting by Government ministers—accounted for 3,251 votes on Government bills, 18.9 per cent of the total of Conservative votes. Twenty divisions would have resulted in Government defeats but for the payroll vote.

Holders of peerages created by Mrs Thatcher (including one second holder, the Earl of Stockton) cast 9,032 votes in divisions on Government bills, 28.6 per cent of the total—4,589 for the Government, 4,443 against. In the three divisions where they affected the outcome, their votes turned what would otherwise have been Government victories into defeats. Thus although the overall effect of the Thatcher creations was to sustain rather than undermine Conservative dominance in the House, it is interesting to note that in terms of their voting record their effect was the reverse.

Voting—Tactics and Strategies

The timing of divisions can be crucial: 5 p.m. is regarded as an Opposition deadline, as after that the 'City' vote comes in to support the Government. Time-related analysis of divisions in 1988–9 does tend to confirm that, on the whole, Conservative votes hold up better later in the day.

According to one interview respondent, the Government

has recently revived the old tactic of filibustering, using Tory stalwarts such as Lords Boyd-Carpenter and Harmar-Nicholls to keep things going in the afternoon until the 'City' vote comes in. It is also claimed that on important issues the Government sometimes summons up the support of 'backwoodsmen': both tactics were said to have been used to help secure the passage of the Electricity Bill.

For their part, the Opposition parties may sometimes deploy subterfuge in order to defeat the usual Government majority—in particular, using the strategy of the 'ambush': this term has rather an imprecise meaning, but may generally be taken to refer to any occasion when the Government whip is caught unawares by the Opposition parties covertly mustering larger numbers of voters than would normally be expected. This usually takes place fairly late in the evening (Government supporters tend to categorize divisions called after 9.00 p.m. as ambushes) but where, as on the political donations amendment to the Companies Bill,[25] there was an organized early Monday vote with few Opposition speeches, this might also qualify as an ambush. The EEC amendment on the Water Bill was a classic late-evening ambush (see Chapter 4).

Another device is to put down a last-minute manuscript amendment which takes the Government unawares. This was successfully used by the Opposition to achieve a Government defeat on the Electricity Bill.

Most peers interviewed were fairly open about the use of ambushes, last-minute manuscript amendments, and filibustering, which they saw on the whole as part and parcel of the day-to-day rough and tumble of politics, though it seems that the use of last-minute manuscript amendments as a device to defeat the Government is generally frowned upon.

Whipping

Each Thursday while the House is sitting a document (the whip) is prepared by the party whips' offices and sent to party members indicating the timetable for the coming week and noting expected

[25] For details see Ch. 4.

divisions with appropriate underlining. The whip may be supplemented by a statement indicating its degree of importance.

One important difference between the two Houses in this context lies in the fact that, in the Lords, unlike the Commons, the committee stage of nearly all bills is taken on the floor of the House. Thus, to quote Shell:

> While in the Commons party whips can take steps to exclude backbenchers whose contributions might be unwelcome, in the Lords no such opportunity is afforded. Lords whips never know who may turn up at committee stage, and even if the proceedings tend to be dominated by a few peers, divisions are much less predictable than in Commons Standing Committees.[26]

It is in any case a long-recognized truth that party discipline in the Lords is very much more relaxed, and whipping is less effective, than in the Commons. Peers, of course, do not face the hurdle of re-election, contemplation of which helps to concentrate the minds of MPs (sometimes with the prompting of their whips) on where their loyalties, and their self-interests, ultimately lie. Thus, to quote one respondent, a Government whip: 'whipping in the Lords carries no real sanction and bringing people in at the last minute is difficult—but whips need to be seen to be doing their best.'

And, to quote Lord Harmar-Nicholls, speaking on the Football Spectators Bill:

> I should like to explain to noble friends who are not as fully acquainted with parliamentary procedure as some of us who have been at it for 39 to 40 years, that the Whip is not an instruction how to vote. The Whip is for the Government of the day, very properly, to indicate how important they think is the measure under discussion. Once we have obeyed their Whip and attended, so recognising the importance of the debate, it is for us as individuals—in the light of the arguments, and in the light of the facts—to say how we use our attendance.[27]

A Conservative party three-line whip can produce over 200 Conservative peers but Lord Denham, the then Chief Whip, was very reluctant to use it other than in exceptional circumstances, arguing that more intensive use would, in the long run, be counter-productive. As Shell has put it, 'one cannot put excessive

[26] Shell, *House of Lords*, 136.
[27] HL Debs., 20 Feb. 1989, col. 417.

pressure on volunteers, or else they may cease to be volunteers'.[28] However, the Government does use what the whips euphemistically describe as 'stern whipping' to stop threatened Tory revolts. Government whips have also experimented with rotas of peers that they call in on certain days. In the 1988–9 session the attendance statistics show that the Government whipping was strongest on 4 May and on 7 November—the only two days when more than 400 peers attended (see Appendix A).

The Labour party used a three-line whip much more frequently, but the response did not seem to be particularly good, judging by the attendance statistics. This may partly have been a function of the high average age of Labour peers but perhaps also a consequence of the rather indiscriminate use of the three-line whip. Social and Liberal Democrat peers appear to have been more responsive to three-line whips, perhaps because they were used more sparingly, though according to interview respondents, the Social and Liberal Democrats often work hard to bring their peers in to vote, phoning round where necessary.

Government Defeats

The success or otherwise of a whipping system—as viewed from all sides of the House—can be seen in the incidence of Government defeats. Appendix B shows that in 1988–9 there was a total of twelve Government defeats, all in divisions on amendments. This conforms to the average under the Thatcher administration overall, though the figure is somewhat lower than during her second Parliament when the House of Lords gained its reputation as the 'real opposition' (see Table 3.6).

It is clear that, by 1988–9, Mrs Thatcher had very negative feelings towards the House of Lords, which she saw as a significant hindrance to the Government's legislative ambitions. One interview respondent said that at the beginning of the session Lord Denham was told by the Prime Minister that she did not want any Government defeats in the Lords, and the expectation was that the Government would be much more ruthless than in the past in reversing any that did slip through.

[28] Shell, *House of Lords*, 95.

Table 3.6. *Government defeats in the House of Lords, 1979–91*

Session	Government defeats	of which on amendments to or clauses of bills
1979–80[a]	15	14
1980–1	18	17
1981–2	7	7
1982–3[b]	5	3
1983–4[a]	20	19
1984–5	17	16
1985–6	22	22
1986–7[b]	3	3
1987–8[a]	17	17
1988–9	12	12
1989–90	20	19
1990–1	17	16

[a] long session
[b] short session

The ultimate fate of amendments passed in the Lords during the session against the will of the Government was as follows: four survived substantially intact; compromise was reached on three; and in five cases the Lords amendment was overturned without concession. The corresponding figures for the 1987–8 session were: nine survived intact; compromise was reached on four; and four were reversed without concession.

Amendments won by political stratagem, such as the Opposition ambush on the Companies Bill (see above, and Chapter 4), were overturned without much hesitation. But on amendments that had been sponsored by Government back-benchers and cross-benchers, and had attracted support from all parts of the House, the risk of further defeats in either or both Houses proved apparently to be a significant inhibiting factor. In such cases a compromise was usually offered, albeit sometimes one that from the original sponsors' point of view was more anodyne than effective. Most Government defeats in 1988–9 related to the case-study bills, examined in the next chapter. It is, however, important to note that there were certainly occasions when the Government avoided likely defeat by granting concessions.

Thus on the Water Bill (see Chapter 4) all-party concern over the authority to be given to the private companies to disconnect defaulting customers was headed off by the Government's agreement to revisions to the disconnection code that would oblige the companies to seek a county court order before taking action to disconnect. This issue had also been raised in the Commons. On the same bill the Government, after initial resistance, also bowed on third reading to strong all-party pressures within the Lords, backed by external lobbying from the Royal Society for the Protection of Birds and other environmental interest groups, to extend the environmental controls on the disposal of land to Sites of Special Scientific Interest. This was, however, at the cost of withdrawing the discretionary power to designate any other areas for protection.

Party Researchers

We have already noted the likelihood that the exceptionally large number of non-Government amendments tabled in the 1987–8 session was a direct result of the increase in research staff employed by the non-Government parties. The function of the political researchers is to provide a very modest counterweight to the huge advantage in terms of information and advice available to ministers through the civil service—particularly, though not exclusively, in relation to legislation and, so far as Labour (but not Social and Liberal Democrat) researchers are concerned, for front-benchers rather than back-benchers. Some of the Opposition and Social and Liberal Democrat researchers interviewed for this study said that they found the Government machine overwhelming—and they regarded it as particularly unfair that ministers alone have immediate back-up available in the House during debate.

Amendments are normally drafted by peers or by pressure groups before they get to the political researchers working for Opposition parties in the House. The clerks sometimes help the peers with the drafting of amendments.

It seems that the increase in the number of research workers has produced a quite definite change in the way in which their work is carried out, from a situation in which a single and extremely hard-pressed researcher dealt principally with fairly urgent requests for information, with little or no help from other research sources, to one in which a team of workers, though busy, nevertheless has sufficient capacity to enable them to approach their work in a more considered and co-ordinated fashion than hitherto and, in particular, to liaise with and draw upon the resources of colleagues both in the House of Commons and at party headquarters. Briefings are supplied by both these sources, and the researchers also attend team meetings in the Commons.

This 'multiplier' effect is also felt in the links with pressure groups; the research workers interviewed believed that, if there had been an increase in the number of Opposition amendments, this was not so much a function of their increased numbers as of their ability to maintain better lines of communication with these outside groups which are an important source of amendments.[29] Nevertheless, the research workers are still generally too busy to do much more than hand over a set of briefing papers on most bills; more positive initiatives on their part are precluded by lack of time.

A researcher employed by the Social and Liberal Democrats explained that the Commons researchers cannot really help because they are too busy with their own work, though it might sometimes be suggested that the Lords researchers look at the Commons file on a bill. In fact the Commons Social and Liberal Democrat researchers did offer help with the Electricity Bill.

The first report of the House of Lords Offices Committee in the 1989–90 session (published in December 1989) recommended that Opposition requests for on-the-spot back-up in the Chamber be met on an experimental basis by allowing them to use the Clerks' box (opposite the civil servants' box) for up to three advisers (two for the Opposition and one for the Social and Liberal Democrats) during the committee and report stages of bills. According to Opposition party researchers the idea for this originally came from the Labour front-bencher Lord McIntosh of

[29] On the increased use made of the House of Lords by outside groups, see N. Baldwin, 'The House of Lords', esp. 158–65, in M. Rush (ed.) *Parliament and Pressure Politics* (Clarendon Press, Oxford,1990).

Haringey. The recommendation was implemented, on a provisional footing, after Christmas 1989. The Opposition used the box for their own party researchers, but the intention was also that the Opposition front benches would be able to draw directly on the expertise of specialist interest groups who could provide some counterbalance to the Government's departmental advisers. Thus in the 1989–90 session the Consumers' Association, the National Consumer Council, and the Association of Municipal Authorities all used this new facility to advise on the Food Safety Bill; and the Bar Council, the Law Society, and various consumer groups contributed advice on the Courts and Legal Services Bill.

There were one or two teething problems, such as difficulties in getting doorkeepers to pass notes, and advisers not fully understanding House protocol. Also, on at least one occasion, an interest group, although willing to provide a brief, was not prepared to advise from the box on the grounds that this would indicate too explicit an identification with the Opposition. Nevertheless the arrangement seems generally to have worked well and, although still stressing the relative paucity of their own resources *vis-à-vis* the Government, the Opposition parties seemed to welcome it as a modest step in the right direction.

Spokesmen

The arrangements by which each department is spoken for in the House of Lords from the Government front bench have been described in Chapter 1. It is questionable whether the Government is sufficiently well represented in the Lords. As the business of the House has become more onerous and arguably of greater importance, increasingly pointed questions have been asked, inside the House and outside, about the calibre of the Government front bench. The situation in 1988–9 was particularly problematical, for reasons discussed earlier. From the Government's point of view a weak-looking front bench may aggravate problems faced in managing the House. From the House's point of view the fact that few Lords ministers carry much weight in Government may be seen as undermining the reputation of the House, and such a perception may tend to add to peers' frustrations.

On the basis both of general observation and of the expressed perceptions of non-Government respondents interviewed for this study, a picture emerges of a Government front bench whose calibre was held in low esteem. This was regarded by interview respondents as one of the biggest problems faced by the Lords. This seems no longer to provoke anger as much as apathy. In the face of mechanically recited briefs and blatant stonewalling, many peers seemed to have lost heart. The problem is exacerbated by the fact that many non-Government peers manifestly are experts in their various specialisms.

Opposition comments about the poor performance and unpreparedness of ministers were particularly evident in the proceedings on the Football Spectators Bill (see Chapter 4). Thus, to quote Lord Graham of Edmonton, referring in debate to the Earl of Arran:

> I do not believe that the Minister will alter what he has said. I do not think that he has the power or authority to do so. The sad aspect that Members must reflect upon is that on these bills the Minister comes into the Chamber with a brief and is unable or unwilling in the face of prepared arguments to consider what we are saying. Not to concede, but to consider. That is very offensive.[30]

And:

> The noble Earl must do more homework on his briefs before he speaks to the Committee. He has now contradicted himself within the space of 30 seconds . . . The noble Earl does his department no good at all by giving conflicting answers.[31]

Lord Harris of Greenwich, the Social and Liberal Democrat spokesman, was also deeply critical of the minister:

> I had to say a few perhaps slightly harsh things about some of his colleagues only because they appeared at the time to be incapable of answering any of the questions addressed to them. I believe that a certain level of competence is necessary for Ministers of the Crown.[32]

By contrast peers on all sides of the House acknowledged that the Opposition front bench was relatively strong in terms of experience, but among Opposition peers themselves there was concern about the lack of new blood on their front bench.

[30] HL Debs., 7 Mar. 1989, col. 1454.
[31] Ibid., col. 1458.
[32] Ibid., 14 Mar. 1989, col. 199.

There was some feeling among Opposition peers that Commons shadow ministers did not consult with colleagues in the Lords as much as they should. Some Labour spokesmen in the Commons—including those concerned with education, local government, and energy—were said to have regular weekly meetings with their counterparts in the Lords, but other shadow ministers apparently did not. House of Lords Opposition spokesmen, respondents said, were always keen to consult, but this attitude was by no means always reciprocated by their colleagues in the Commons. Liaison between the Social and Liberal Democrats in the Lords and the Commons seemed better, probably because the party is so much smaller; and there are indications that the party's researcher may have played a positive part in this. Labour front-benchers were inclined to consider themselves very much as an integral part of the bipartisan usual channels, and to operate through and as members of what they regarded and valued as an established two-party system.

House of Lords versus Government

In recent years, against the background of a large Government majority in the Commons and the personal dominance of Mrs Thatcher, the Lords have come to be popularly regarded both inside and outside the House as the 'conscience' of the Government, perhaps even as the 'real' opposition.

Thus, in a debate on a private member's bill on political honours in the Commons, Neil Hamilton MP (Conservative) argued that 'It would be a shame indeed to abolish the only real opposition to the Government in this country today, which is in the House of Lords.'[33]

Shell has argued that, for a period, this view merited some credence: 'the role of the Lords in getting particular changes made to bills shows that this has grown significantly in recent years. By 1987 the impact of the Upper House in amending the actual content of bills was widely recognised to be greater than that of the House of Commons.'[34] In general, during the 1983–7

[33] Ibid., 7 June 1989, col. 244.
[34] Shell, *House of Lords*, 1st edn. (Philip Allan, London, 1988), 151.

Parliament there was probably a good case for saying that the Lords did prove itself more effective than the Commons in securing changes to Government legislation. Television coverage of the Lords may also have contributed to the heightened profile of the Lords—perhaps at the expense of an untelevised House of Commons, as some MPs remarked[35]—during the period. However, as already noted, the 1987 election marked a distinct hardening of the Government's line towards obstruction by the Lords.

Opposition peers interviewed expressed awareness of the Prime Minister's hostility to the House but there was also some feeling that this reflected a more general sentiment in the Commons. Respondents felt that ministers in the Commons, now and in past administrations, both Conservative and Labour, had never had a very high opinion of the House of Lords and that, indeed, the Commons as a whole is far from over-fond of the other House.

In a debate on peers' voting rights,[36] Lord McNair (Social and Liberal Democrat) claimed that, on unpopular issues, like the poll tax, National Health Service charges for eye tests and dental treatment, and water privatization, the press have encouraged an image of the Lords as 'the seventh cavalry poised to snatch victory out of the jaws of defeat'; but, he said, in practice the Government's capacity to pack the House and bulldoze measures through belied that image.

Certainly the dominant impression during this session was one of Government obduracy in the face of any attempt—by Opposition, cross-bench, or Conservative back-bench peers—to amend legislation. This view was forcefully expressed by Lord Mishcon during proceedings on the Official Secrets Bill:

> We have reached a situation where, first, all amendments, unless they be moved from the Government Benches, are unreasonable and therefore should not be allowed. The second stage is that, while they are quite reasonable, it is nevertheless appropriate not to agree with them. The third stage has now been reached; they are perfectly reasonable but they are unnecessary. I wonder what further classification will be used from the Benches opposite in order to ensure that not one word of the bill is altered and that not all the combined thinking of the Opposition in your

[35] See for instance HC Debs., 6 Feb. 1989, col. 672.
[36] HL Debs., 8 Dec. 1988, col. 726.

Lordships' House will ever penetrate through the Government's very substantial armour.[37]

And, further:

I am only sorry that there now appears to be a habit in government to take it for granted that it is a display of ministerial strength to resist every conceivable amendment that one can and that it is a triumph for the Government when they take through a measure almost completely unamended, if not completely unamended. It is not a triumph for democracy if that happens, nor is it a triumph for this House in its capacity as a revising Chamber.[38]

On the Official Secrets Bill (discussed in Chapter 4), opposition in the Lords was generally less vehement than it had been in the Commons—something that may have stemmed from the fact that in the earlier part of the session the self-perceived ability of Opposition peers to 'win the argument but never the vote' had apparently generated something approaching a general spirit of apathy. Subsequent Government defeats on the Water Bill (also discussed in Chapter 4), combined with opinion poll results suggestive of growing Government unpopularity, appeared to bring some improvement in the morale of non-Government peers; at least by the time the bulk of the interviews for this study were conducted, their mood had become somewhat more buoyant.

Even during the earlier part of the session, the conception of the House of Lords as constituting a vital last-ditch defence against the Government juggernaut persisted, especially when the guillotine was used in the Commons. This point was made in both Houses during the debates on the Official Secrets Bill (see Chapter 4). Thus, in implicit contradiction of the remarks by Lord Mishcon, cited earlier, Earl Ferrers went out of his way, in his winding-up speech on the third reading of the bill, to defend the Government's stance in the Lords:

The Bill has been . . . changed in a number of respects in your Lordships' House. Your Lordships proposed changes and, having heard the arguments, the Government have responded. That is not the attitude of a Government who are not prepared to listen. I know that some of your

[37] Ibid., 3 Apr. 1989, col. 990.
[38] Ibid., 24 Apr. 1989, col. 1095.

Lordships would have wished us to respond more often and with perhaps more abandon. But, I make no apologies for having sought to persuade your Lordships otherwise.[39]

One factor that remains to be considered is how far the House of Lords is inhibited by express and implied constitutional constraints. Arguably, Commons financial privilege can be invoked on almost every contentious issue between the two Houses. In non-financial matters, the Lords theoretically can confront the Commons without offending constitutional protocol. However, according to Opposition party peers and researchers interviewed for this study, this 'right' to confront is inhibited both by peers' own self-consciousness regarding the 'undemocratic' nature of the House and by the Government's use of 'spurious constitutional arguments' to intimidate peers.

Thus a senior Government front-bencher in the Lords, talking about the need to maintain the constitutional position between the Lords and Commons, said that the Government would use a three-line whip if the Lords threatened to send an amendment back after it had been rejected by the Commons. One senior Opposition spokesman agreed that there was some feeling in the Lords that sending back amendments to the Commons for a second time is not really compatible with the role of the Lords, but that as far as the Opposition was concerned, the final decision about the line to be taken on this depended on the issue. A Social and Liberal Democrat spokesman, however, thought that arguments regarding what the House can and cannot do constitutionally are overstated, especially regarding the propriety of reinstating amendments; but this argument evidently does weigh with cross-benchers and with Government back-benchers.

One respondent, a party researcher, told us that cross-benchers are particularly susceptible to the argument that insisting on an amendment deleted by the Commons is 'unconstitutional'. And the same respondent claimed that the Government whips reputedly guard against the possibility of backwoodsmen being swayed by debate by putting up grandees, like Viscount Whitelaw, to argue against the Lords 'damaging its reputation' by 'going too far'.

[39] Ibid., col. 1087.

Secondary Legislation

The oft-heard complaint that Parliament cannot properly carry out its role of legislative scrutiny, because so much detailed provision is nowadays left to secondary legislation, was repeated by some of the respondents interviewed for this study. This was certainly an issue in the Football Spectators Bill—which was described as 'an empty shell'. Some of the amendments tabled were directed at persuading the minister to divulge some of the details of the proposed scheme (see Chapter 4). Similar concern was expressed in the context of the Children Bill. And on the Companies Bill Lord Williams of Elvel observed at second reading: 'a number of clauses have been inserted into the Bill which allow the Government to change the resulting Act by statutory instrument, if they find that they do not like it. Examples of this phenomenon occur in Clauses 18, 24, 108, 122 and 125.'[40]

There were on this bill a number of divisions on amendments that were essentially on the question of whether or not primary legislation should be amended by secondary legislation: the Social and Liberal Democrat spokesman Lord Lloyd of Kilgerran also highlighted this growing tendency, which, he said, greatly diminished parliamentary control.[41]

A leading Government spokesman, when asked in interview about such criticisms of delegated legislation, opined that it was a matter of balance: such critics would not like it if there was too much detail in bills.

With this general overview of Government legislation, we turn in the following chapter to case-studies of eight specific bills. Chapter 5 takes up the discussion of secondary legislation.

[40] Ibid., 16 Jan. 1989, col. 15.

[41] Ibid., col. 19.

4

Government Legislation: Case-Studies

David Miers and Jenny Brock

Introduction

Assessing the impact that the House has on Government legislation is not an easy matter. Though their significance is open to interpretation, it is generally agreed that one of the better indicators of impact is the outcome of amendments tabled in respect of Government bills, in particular, those of non-Government origin. While the mere counting of the number of amendments made to a bill says nothing, for example, of their qualitative importance nor of the degree to which they represented Government policy, analysis has to begin with some reckonable data. These have been given in the previous chapter. Our purpose here is to examine in greater depth the work of the House in respect of a limited but representative sample of bills.

This chapter therefore focuses on the origins, content, and outcome of Lords amendments made to eight Government bills during the 1988–9 session. The principal focus will be on non-Government amendments, which can be defined as amendments put down otherwise than in the name of a minister. The eight bills (listed in Table 4.1) include an equal number introduced in each House. Bills were chosen which could prima facie be regarded as items of major policy (Football Spectators, Official Secrets, and Water), as minor policy (Companies, Transport (Scotland), and Prevention of Terrorism (Temporary Provisions)), or as instances of essentially legal-administrative arrangements (Children and Road Traffic (Driver Licensing and Information Systems)). In addition, we sought variety in departmental origins, subject categorization, length, debating time, and the use of the guillotine in the Commons. Some bills assumed greater significance as a consequence of a Government defeat in the Lords (Companies, Football Spectators, Water) or of substantial Government amendment there (Companies). In each

Table 4.1. *Case-study bills*

Children Bill [HL]
Companies Bill [HL]
Football Spectators Bill [HL]
Official Secrets Bill
Prevention of Terrorism (Temporary Provisions) Bill
Road Traffic (Driver Licensing and Information Systems) Bill [HL]
Transport (Scotland) Bill
Water Bill

case, an analysis was made of the debates accompanying each stage, and of the outcome of amendments moved. Interviews were conducted, in particular with peers active in proceedings on these bills and with parliamentary staff and lobbyists.

An Overview of the Eight Case-Study Bills

The Children Bill was a major, largely non-controversial and certainly non-party, piece of legislation sponsored by the Lord Chancellor's Department. Its material origins were many, its introduction having been preceded by a number of departmental and other inquiries, a consultation paper from the Lord Chancellor's Department on aspects of care proceedings, and media attention to instances of child abuse.[1] The bill was given an enthusiastic welcome in the Lords, the Government being congratulated on all sides for its readiness (declared by Government spokesmen in both Houses) to consult both within and without Parliament as part of its efforts to resolve areas upon which it remained undecided.

By contrast, the Companies Bill, the second of the Queen's speech measures introduced in the Lords, was critically received.

[1] See 'Children in Care', 2nd Report from the House of Commons Social Services Committee 1983–4, HC 360; 'Review of Child Care Law: report to ministers of an interdepartmental working party' (HMSO, 1985); 'The Law on Child Care and Family Services', Cm. 62, Jan. 1987; Law Commission Report on Custody and Guardianship, HC 594, 1987–8; Report of the Inquiry into Child Abuse in Cleveland 1987 (Chairman, Lord Justice Butler-Sloss), Cm. 412.

Sponsored by the Department of Trade and Industry, its objects were to give effect to two European Community Directives, on company accounts and auditors, and to introduce a variety of other unconnected measures on companies' internal regulation. Greeted as a 'glorified Lancashire hotpot',[2] it was not so much that the bill failed to deal with a number of other issues which the Opposition considered more pressing, but that the Department had so signally failed to think through what it wanted, which provoked more hostility. This was prompted first by the Government moving a large number of amendments on the first day of committee, and secondly by the fact that when it returned from the Commons (having left the Lords with 488 amendments) the bill came with a further 180 pages of text, much of it entirely new and some of the Commons amendments (531 in all) thirteen, sixteen, and even twenty-four pages long. The Companies Bill also provided one of the few (twelve) instances in 1988–9 in which the Government suffered a defeat on a Lords amendment.

If, by virtue of their relatively technical nature dealing with matters not of acute political controversy, the Children and Companies Bills might be considered typical examples of bills suitable for introduction in the Lords, the same cannot be said of the Football Spectators Bill. Representing the Government's legislative response to the problem of football-associated hooliganism, this bill proved very much more difficult to manage than the Home Office (or the Department of the Environment, whose minister took responsibility for the bill in the Lords) had expected, the more so as a result of the unforeseen events at Hillsborough football ground in April 1989 (when ninety-five football spectators were crushed to death) which coincided with the committee stage. The Opposition's explanation for the introduction of the bill in the Lords was that the Government hoped thereby to secure a less controversial Commons passage after the football season was over. It may be that some peers resented what they took to be the Government's disdainful attitude about the strength of their opposition. Largely owing to some confusion as to the effect of an amendment designed to delay the introduction of the membership card scheme, the Government also suffered a defeat in the Lords on this bill.

[2] Lord Williams of Elvel, HL Debs., 16 Jan. 1989, col. 14.

Introduced in the Commons, the Official Secrets Bill sought to replace the much-criticized Official Secrets Act 1911 with a regime more clearly distinguishing between the authorized and unauthorized disclosure of official information. In general the Lords accepted the Government's case, though particular criticism was made of the failure to include a public interest defence. In this respect, like the Security Service Bill and, to a lesser extent, the Football Spectators Bill, the bill presented a classic example of the conflict between the desire to secure on the one hand individual freedom and on the other collective security. Otherwise, the Lords made comparatively little effort to amend the bill, the most acrimonious exchanges concerning what some peers regarded as the Government's intransigence in the use of the guillotine in the Commons.

The Prevention of Terrorism (Temporary Provisions) Bill excited little interest in the Lords. Its main objects were to extend police powers of arrest and detention of persons suspected of terrorist offences, and to give powers to trace and to obtain the forfeiture of funds used in terrorist offences. Where the Lords were critical (principally of the Home Office's failure to provide a permanent answer to a decision of the European Court of Human Rights), they were so in a more restrained manner than the Commons. This was typical of their response in other cases; even where, like the Lords, the Commons were in broad agreement with a bill's objectives, criticisms were usually more strongly expressed than in the Lords, and the more so where MPs disagreed with them.

A short, non-party measure, the Road Traffic (Driver Licensing and Information Systems) Bill may be regarded as a paradigm of what has traditionally been considered a House of Lords bill. In part based on a Report of the Lords Select Committee on Science and Technology dealing with electronic information and guidance systems for motorists, and in part giving effect to a European Community Directive requiring the introduction of a single driving-licence document replacing the existing additional Public Service Vehicle and Heavy Goods Vehicle licences, its passage through the House was characterized by good-humoured exchanges and mutual congratulation on a job well done.

The Transport (Scotland) Bill, whose object was to privatize the Scottish Bus Group, prompted furious exchanges in the Commons but caused scarcely a ripple in the Lords.

By contrast, the other instance of the Government's privatization programme, the Water Bill, proved much more widely controversial, and there was a widespread expectation that the Lords would embarrass the Government on a number of its provisions. Their disquiet was reflected not merely at second reading but in the eight days (sixty hours) of the committee stage and in two defeats for the Government. As well as being highly controversial, this was also a technically complex bill to which 341 amendments were made. As with the Children Bill, though changes were made during the bill's passage through the House, it is difficult to say to what extent the concessions made, in particular on environmental issues, were pre-planned by the Government.

Table 3.3 gives a summary of the stages of Government bills considered by the Lords in the 1988–9 session. The eight case-study bills are shown in bold type.

The Use of Amendments as Indicators of the Impact of the House

As Table 3.3 shows, in 1988–9 thirty-seven Government bills were considered by the Lords (twenty-one brought from the Commons and sixteen introduced in the Lords, of which four were consolidation bills). A total of 2,359 amendments were made to seventeen bills (ten Commons and seven Lords bills (one consolidation)), and none to the other twenty.

So far as amendments to bills are concerned, 'what is important is their relative effect on the bill, not their number'.[3] Elaborating Shell's analysis, we may differentiate amendments according to the degree to which they imply a change in Government policy:[4]

(1) pure drafting changes;

(2) a clarification in the application of the bill to a particular case for which it has made provision, but involving no change of policy in that case;

[3] J. A. G. Griffith, *Parliamentary Scrutiny of Government Bills* (Allen & Unwin, London, 1974), 14.

[4] Donald Shell, *The House of Lords*, 2nd edn. (Harvester Wheatsheaf, London, 1992), 148–9.

(3) an extension or restriction in the application of the bill to a class of case for which it has made provision, and involving a change of policy in the particular case now included or excluded;

(4) an extension in the application of the bill to a particular case or class of case for which it has not made provision. This failure may be attributable to one of three causes: (*a*) the Government had not foreseen the case; or (*b*) the Government had foreseen the case but had made no provision for it, either because it did not consider it desirable as a matter of policy to do so, or because, though desirable, it was not possible to draft a satisfactory provision or it thought that it would involve implementation costs that it was not prepared to incur; or (*c*) the Government had not given itself time even to consider the application of the bill to this case.

In any of these instances, amendment involves a policy choice on the part of the Government.

Though it is attractive to measure success in terms of the degree to which the Government has now adopted a different policy, one obvious difficulty with an analysis of this kind is that it fails to take into account the degree to which the amendments had already secured Government agreement. As Griffith observed: 'The direct impact of the House of Lords on Government bills is seen first when amendments are successfully moved on a division against the Government's wish; secondly, when non-ministerial amendments are agreed to without a division; and, thirdly, when ministers move amendments in response to points made.'[5] Thus, for every one of the four effects outlined above (even drafting amendments can be controversial) the following outcomes are possible:

(1) the Government accepts the amendment (or the prospect of it) having had first (or second) thoughts, agreeing to it without a division or bringing it forward (with or without qualification) itself; or

(2) the amendment is carried against its wishes and, having had first (or second) thoughts, the Goverment (*a*) accepts the policy of the amendment; or (*b*) accepts the amendment because the cost to the management of the legislative programme of the

[5] Griffith, *Parl. Scrutiny*, 212.

effort to reverse it is too high; or (*c*) reverses the amendment at a later stage or in the Commons.

Sponsorship and the outcome of amendments

Table 4.2 shows the total numbers of amendments tabled and moved at all the Lords stages of all eight case-study bills, followed by the outcome at each stage, and the effect of any reversal in the Commons, according to sponsorship. The results of this quantitative analysis confirm, first, that a substantial proportion (918 out of 1,965, 47 per cent) of non-Government amendments are tabled but are not moved. Many are tabled with no intention on the part of their sponsors that they be moved, but that they be used to test, to question, to seek assurances from, or sometimes to obstruct the Government, or—perhaps most often—because they are part of a group of amendments of which only the first is moved. By contrast, the Government moved virtually the entirety of the amendments it tabled (1,164 out of 1,166). Secondly, whereas the total number moved on these eight bills was roughly equally divided between Government (1,164) and non-Government (1,047) amendments, both the number and the proportion of Government amendments that were made (1,161 or 99.7 per cent—three amendments to the Companies Bill were withdrawn) far exceed those made in consequence of non-Government sponsorship (sixty-five or 6.2 per cent). These results are very much in line with earlier studies on the outcome of amendments.

The figures for the non-Government amendments moved in respect of each of the case-study bills are given in Table 4.3.

Four of the non-ministerial amendments to the case-study bills were successfully moved in division against the Government, and thus represent an unwanted change (albeit temporary in three instances) to its policy. The first Government defeat of the 1988–9 session was on an amendment to the Companies Bill moved by the Opposition in committee. It was sponsored by Lord Williams of Elvel and was supported by the Social and Liberal Democrats, by the Social Democratic Party, and by Lord Morris, a Government back-bencher and the sole Conservative rebel in the division. The amendment sought to impose a requirement on the directors of public companies to obtain their shareholders' consent at an

Table 4.2. *Amendments moved to case-study bills in the House of Lords*

Sponsorship	Tabled (all stages)	Moved (all stages)	Committee		Report		3rd reading		Rej. by HC*
			Div	N/div	Div	N/div	Div	N/div	
Government	1,166	1,164	—	511[a] 3[w]	2[a]	462[a]	1[a]	185[a]	1
Labour	874	447	2[a] 18[n]	6[a] 261[w]	14[n]	18[a] 108[w]	1[n]	1[a] 1[n] 17[w]	2
Social and Liberal Democrat	221	120	2[n]	82[w]	1[n]	4[a] 26[w]	1[n]	4[w]	—
Social Democrat	1	—	—	—	—	—	—	—	—
Government back-bench	242	151	2[n]	97[w]	—	7[a] 1[n] 39[w]	— —	1[a] 4[w]	—
Cross-bench	93	57	1[n]	38[w]	—	2[a] 14[w]	—	2[w]	—
Two or more opposition parties	254	124	10[n]	5[a] 60[w]	4[n]	1[a] 42[w]	2[n]	—	1

Opposition and cross-bench	56	35	4[n]	1[a] 10[w]	2[n]	12[w]	2[n]	4[w]	—
Opposition and Government back-bench	54	30	—	1[a] 14[w]	1[n]	8[w]	1[n]	5[w]	—
Opposition and cross-bench and Government back-bench	85	47	1[a]	4[a] 16[w]	4[n]	8[a] 1[n] 6[w]	1[a] 5[w]	1[a]	2
Cross-bench and Government back-bench	86	36	1[n]	1[a] 17[w]	—	12[w]	—	5[w]	—
TOTALS	3,131	2,211	3[a] 38[n]	529[a] 598[w]	2[a] 26[n]	502[a] 2[n] 267[w]	2[a] 7[n]	188[a] 1[n] 46[w]	6

* i.e. disagreed to with a reason or with amendments in lieu
Notes: [a] = agreed to, [n] = negatived, [w] = withdrawn; opposition = one or more opposition parties

Table 4.3. *Amendments to case-study bills*

Bill	Amendments moved	Amendments agreed	Percentage agreed
Children [HL]	250	4	1.6
Companies [HL]	222	8	3.6
Football Spectators [HL]	84	17	20.0
Official Secrets	26	—	—
Prevention of Terrorism (Temporary Provisions)	9	—	—
Road Traffic (Driver Licensing and Information Systems) [HL]	38	1	2.6
Transport (Scotland)	3	—	—
Water	415	35	8.4
TOTALS	1,407	65	6.2

annual general meeting prior to the company making donations to political parties, and was carried (106–93). The explanation for the defeat was attributed to careful organization by the combined opposition in moving a division on a Monday when there were (discounting the cross-benchers) fewer Conservative (eighty, with Lord Morris supporting the amendment) than other peers (ninety-four) in the House. The absence of the senior responsible minister, Lord Young of Graffham, was also considered to have contributed to the Government being caught off-guard. However, due to a procedural error, only a paving amendment was passed, and though a substantive amendment was agreed to at report stage, Lord Young made it clear that it was the Government's intention to reverse it in the Commons. This was achieved, after a lengthy debate, in standing committee. When the Lords came to consider the Commons amendments, heavy Government whipping ensured that the Opposition attempt to reinstate this provision was defeated.[6]

[6] Committee amendment 1, HL Debs., 30 Jan. 1989, cols. 876–85; report amendment 40, HL Debs., 20 Mar. 1989, col. 512; HC Debs., Standing Committee D, 16 May 1989, cols. 6–40; HL Debs., 7 Nov. 1989, cols. 551–73.

A second defeat for the Government followed the division on a cross-party committee amendment to the Football Spectators Bill. This provided for the phasing in of the national membership scheme, and was moved by Lord Harmar-Nicholls (Conservative) and co-sponsored by Lord Graham of Edmonton (Labour) and Lord Mellish (independent). The amendment was unacceptable to the Government, who considered the universal implementation of the scheme to be essential to its integrity, but it was carried (124–121).[7] In the event, there was some confusion as to the effect of the amendment, which its sponsors claimed gave the Football Membership Authority (FMA) discretion to phase in the scheme, but which in fact made it non-optional. Thus, immediately after the vote, while indicating its intention to reverse the outcome, the Government was content to explain the defection by the thirteen of its back-benchers who cross-voted as being attributable to their misunderstanding of the amendment rather than to their opposition to the bill's policy. However, on the second day of committee, and in a more conciliatory mood, the Government announced that it would discuss some new amendments with the opposition parties in an attempt to give clearer effect to their intentions. These were moved at report, but nevertheless retained the scheme's integrity by giving power to the Secretary of State to reject any phasing recommendation made by the FMA.[8]

Much was expected of the Lords debates on the Water Bill, which took place against growing public concern about pollution of the seas and the rivers and, more generally, about the impact of industrial processes upon the environment. Over half of the non-ministerial amendments made to the case-study bills were made to this bill, and the Government suffered two further defeats on divisions. In committee, the Government brought forward an amendment to establish a framework for compliance with a European Community Directive on standards of drinking-water (see Chapter 9), but the Opposition (Lord McIntosh of Haringey), unconvinced of the Government's commitment, moved an amendment requiring compliance by 1993, which, in

[7] HL Debs., 20 Feb. 1989, cols. 398–419.

[8] The indefinite postponement of the scheme was announced the following Jan. (see HL Debs., 29 Jan. 1990, col. 21).

a House containing only forty-one Conservative peers, all of whom voted with the Government, was carried by a substantial margin (81–47). However, like the amendment to the Football Spectators Bill, this also misfired, as it both contradicted the Directive, which required immediate compliance, and cut across the negotiations between the Government and the Commission concerning a timetable for compliance before 1993. In its objections to the amendment the Government received support from an unexpected quarter— the Friends of the Earth—who described the Opposition amendment as well-motivated but ill-conceived. The amendment was reversed in the Commons, and when the bill returned to the Lords, Lord McIntosh made a further attempt to force the issue, moving a new clause which would require an investment plan to be produced with a timetable for compliance (involving consultation with the European Commission) before the flotation of the private water companies. In a fuller House, and after a forceful display by the Government and its supporters, who regarded it at worst as a wrecking amendment and at best as an attempt to delay flotation, the amendment was rejected by 168 votes to 114.[9]

A second environmental issue that exercised the Lords concerned the powers of the water companies. A cross-party amendment moved at third reading by the Earl of Radnor (Conservative), whose co-sponsors were Lord Carter (Labour), Lord Addington (Social and Liberal Democrat), and Lord Monson (cross-bench), to alter the rules concerning access by the water companies to private land to lay pipes was carried by 62 to 53, with eight Conservative peers cross-voting.[10] This was another example of an 'ambush' by an alliance of Opposition peers,[11] but unlike its response in the other cases, the Government substituted amendments in lieu which both the Lords and the original sponsors agreed on consideration of Commons amendments to be an acceptable compromise.

Of the sixty-one amendments moved by non-ministerial peers on the case-study bills and agreed to without a division, thirty-five were consequential on Government defeats or on

[9] Committee amendment 287A, HL Debs., 15 May 1989, cols. 1000–7; HC Debs., 3 July 1989, cols. 123–6; HL Debs., 6 July 1989, cols. 1278–96.

[10] Third reading amendment 126, HL Debs., 27 June 1989, cols. 698–706.

[11] See above, Ch. 3.

other accepted amendments, and four of the other agreed non-ministerial amendments were stated to be drafting amendments. A brief account of each of the other twenty-two non-ministerial amendments is given below.

On the Children Bill, there were two such amendments, both in committee. The effect of the first, moved by Lord Banks (Social and Liberal Democrat) and sponsored by him, Lord Meston (Social and Liberal Democrat), and Lord Kilmarnock (Social Democrat), was to permit a child who is the subject of a contact order to stay with as well as visit the person gaining contact. This was a minor amendment accepted by the Government as a clarification of the definition of a contact order.[12] The second, an Opposition amendment moved by Baroness David (sponsored by Lord Irvine of Lairg), deleted a subsection requiring the agreement of the Secretary of State to the making of rules of court under the Act. This was also a relatively minor amendment accepted by the Government.[13]

There were three Opposition amendments to the Companies Bill moved successfully without division, two in committee and one on report. The first, moved by Lord Williams of Elvel, underlined the requirement on directors to give a true and fair view of the state of affairs of a company in its annual accounts. The Government's view was that this was not strictly necessary but it was willing to accept it.[14] The other committee amendment provided for the registration of non-monetary as well as monetary obligations. The Government was happy to accept this.[15] On report Lord Williams moved a third amendment requiring holding companies to ensure that group accounts met the requirements of the Act. The Government was happy to accept this amendment as a 'modest but important improvement to company law'.[16]

Three non-ministerial alterations were made to the Football Spectators Bill without division, including the modified version of the phasing amendment moved on report. In committee an Opposition and Social and Liberal Democrat amendment to

[12] Committee amendment 25, HL Debs., 19 Dec. 1988, cols. 1217–18.
[13] Committee amendment 224, HL Debs., 23 Jan. 1989, col. 556.
[14] Committee amendment 14, HL Debs., 30 Jan. 1989, cols. 909–10.
[15] Committee amendment 272Z, HL Debs., 14 Feb. 1989, col. 139.
[16] Report amendment 1, HL Debs., 20 Mar. 1989, cols. 461–4.

provide for the exemption of designated groups from the national membership scheme was accepted by the Government. In effect this made a discretionary provision into a mandatory one.[17] Another amendment, jointly sponsored by the Opposition and Social and Liberal Democrat peers, to lessen the burden of proof on a person to show why he should be exempted from the requirement to report when a designated match is being played overseas, was also accepted.[18]

On the Road Traffic Bill an amendment to enable a maximum limit to be set on charges for the compulsory training of motor cyclists was successfully moved by Lord Carmichael of Kelvingrove (Labour), jointly sponsored by Lord Underhill (Labour) and Lord Lucas of Chilworth (Conservative, and a former junior minister in the 1980s).[19]

The greatest number of alterations of non-ministerial origin were made to the Water Bill, one in committee, ten on report, and two on third reading. The first of these was an amendment moved by Lord Carter (Labour), supported by Lord Allen of Abbeydale (cross-bench), to remove some wording offensive to people with disabilities from the bill. This was accepted by the Government, with apologies.[20]

Three amendments were successfully moved by the Opposition. On report Lord McIntosh of Haringey moved an amendment to strengthen the provisions relating to the conservation of sites of archaeological, architectural, or historical interest. A similar amendment had been moved in committee, and the one agreed had subsequently been drafted by the Government's draftsmen.[21] A second Opposition amendment effected the removal of a provision enabling the Secretary of State to direct the exclusion from the register of the Director-General of Water Services of any information that might be against the commercial interests of any person, as opposed to the public interest. A similar amendment had been moved in committee; at this stage it was accepted and commended by the Government.[22] A third Opposition

[17] Committee amendment 45, HL Debs., 7 Mar. 1989, cols. 1386–99.
[18] Committee amendment 81, HL Debs., 14 Mar. 1989, col. 216.
[19] Committee amendment 15, HL Debs., 24 Jan. 1989, cols. 642–3.
[20] Committee amendment 13, HL Debs., 2 May 1989, cols. 102–3.
[21] Report amendment 56, HL Debs., 8 June 1989, col. 996.
[22] Report amendment 108, HL Debs., 12 June 1989, col. 1149.

amendment, which had been discussed briefly in committee, extended the prohibition on charging for water for fire-fighting to include that taken for fire-fighting training.[23]

Government back-benchers were responsible for a number of changes to the bill. The Earl of Radnor successfully moved an amendment on report providing that members of the National Rivers Authority should not be eligible for membership of the regional rivers advisory committees. A similar amendment had been moved in committee but had been withdrawn.[24] He also successfully moved an amendment applying the same restriction to membership of fishery advisory committees.[25] Lord Elliott of Morpeth successfully moved an amendment to enable a court to order an award of compensation if it finds that the interests of a minority of shareholders have been unfairly prejudiced in the conversion of a statutory water company to a public limited company. The object of this amendment, which was similar to one moved in committee, was to reduce the chances of a minority blocking the conversion process.[26] Lord Stanley of Alderley successfully moved two amendments, one providing for notification to farmers in nitrate-sensitive areas,[27] the second designed to protect the interests of rural customers. Amendments similar to this had been moved in committee and on report, that which was successful being the result of negotiations between Lord Stanley and the parliamentary adviser to the National Farmers' Union on the one hand, and the Earl of Caithness (the minister responsible for the bill) and his officials on the other. It did not, however, go as far as the Opposition wanted.[28]

Cross-benchers successfully moved two amendments, both on report. The Earl of Shannon's amendment required sewerage undertakers to provide for the disposal of trade effluent. This was similar to an amendment that had been moved in committee, Government officials subsequently assisting with its redrafting.[29] Lord Greenway sponsored an amendment to strengthen the environmental code of practice by making it subject to the

[23] Report amendment 122, ibid., col. 1255.
[24] Report amendment 13, HL Debs., 6 June 1989, cols. 793–4.
[25] Report amendment 135, HL Debs., 13 June 1989, col. 1330.
[26] Report amendment 121, HL Debs., 12 June 1989, col. 1254.
[27] Report amendment 130BA, HL Debs., 13 June 1989, cols. 1312–13.
[28] Third reading amendment 2, HL Debs., 27 June 1989, cols. 607–11.
[29] Report amendment 110, HL Debs., 12 June 1989, cols. 1211–14.

negative resolution procedure. This had already been raised in committee and the Government, having had second thoughts, had by the report stage decided to support the amendment.[30]

The variety and choice of, and factors affecting, sponsorship

As Table 4.2 shows, the Opposition are, on most bills, the most active grouping after the Government. The exceptions were the Football Spectators Bill, on which they mainly worked in tandem with the Social and Liberal Democrats, and the Official Secrets Bill, where they were allied with the Social and Liberal Democrats and with Lord Hemingford (cross-bench).

The Social and Liberal Democrats made a smaller but significant contribution to the amending process, sometimes operating on their own, sometimes with the Opposition, or with cross-bench or Government back-bench peers. On the Children, Companies, and Water Bills there were a large number of amendments co-sponsored by the Opposition and Social and Liberal Democrats, but more where they operated independently. On none of the case-study bills were there any amendments sponsored by the Social Democratic Party alone. There were a few, very few, occasions when a Social Democrat peer put his name to an amendment together with peers from other sections of the House, for example, Lord Kilmarnock on the Children Bill.

As discussed above, the names of up to four peers may be put down as sponsors to an amendment (or five if the peer in charge of a bill chooses to add his name). In the case-study bills, in addition to the co-sponsorship between the Opposition and the Social and Liberal Democrat front benches noted above, there was sponsorship from all sides of the House on a number of amendments. Table 4.4 shows the proportion of non-ministerial amendments moved on which at least one of the sponsors was either a cross-bench peer or a Conservative back-bencher, and in the last column the total proportion of non-ministerial amendments sponsored by either cross-benchers or Government back-benchers.

These figures in turn prompt a consideration of the factors that

[30] Report amendment 89, HL Debs., 8 June 1989, col. 1042.

Table 4.4. *Sponsorship of non-Government amendments to case-study bills*

Bill	Amendments moved	Government back-bench (%)	Cross-bench (%)	Cross-bench and/or Govt back-bench (%)
Children	243	28.8	27.5	35.3
Companies	223	10.3	10.7	20.1
Football Spectators	84	17.8	32.0	33.3
Official Secrets	26	23.0	42.3	61.5
Prevention of Terrorism (Temporary Provisions)	9	0.0	11.1	11.1
Road Traffic (Driver Licensing and Information Systems)	38	44.7	0.0	44.7
Transport (Scotland)	0	0.0	0.0	0.0
Water	415	31.8	11.3	39.5

influence the choice and management of cross-party support for non-ministerial amendments. The first, and most obvious, reason why a sponsor seeks cross-party support is to win the vote should the issue come to a division. In pursuit of this objective, peers may be prepared to co-sponsor amendments with others for whom, in party terms, they otherwise have little sympathy. Lord Graham of Edmonton (Labour), for example, co-sponsored the amendment to the Water Bill concerning the water companies' powers to lay pipes across private land which was moved by the Earl of Radnor (Conservative) and on which the Government was defeated on a division. Lord Graham's view was that if by such alliances the Opposition could defeat or discomfort the Government, it was quite in order to form them.

A second reason is to give a more powerful signal to the Government about the strength of feeling in the House than would otherwise be the case if sponsorship emanated from one source only. A particularly interesting example of this was the sponsorship by Lord Harmar-Nicholls (Conservative) of the amendment to the Football Spectators Bill which sought to phase in the scheme. Lord Harmar-Nicholls was in fact initially concerned to protect his party from possible embarrassment on one of the wrecking amendments which he had heard that some of the unofficial opposition co-ordinating committee were planning. Accordingly, though he had some doubts about the bill, he suggested the phasing-in amendment in the expectation that, as the amendment would itself be more likely to attract cross-party support, the committee would prefer it to an amendment that was bound to lose and would cause some difficulties in the House. He also expected that, as a back-bencher sponsoring an amendment against his own Government, he would, in line with past practice, be approached by the minister or a whip with a view to reaching a compromise. When he was not, he himself took the initiative, urging the Government that there was every chance of its being defeated should he press the amendment, and suggesting that it make some concession to his position. The Government failed to respond, and narrowly lost the vote (124–121). Implicit in Lord Harmar-Nicholls's reasons for moving the amendment was an element of protest against what he perceived to be a growing indifference in the Government's attitude to its own supporters in the Lords.

However, effective sponsorship of amendments is not only a question of the breadth of support in the House, but also of the source of that support. Interviews conducted with peers confirmed that, from the Opposition's standpoint, it is first of all the cross-benchers who are perceived to make a difference. This perception is, for some, based on the notion that since, in the absence of its making a special effort, the Government enjoys an everyday working majority of about twenty to thirty, having a cross-bencher as a sponsor may convince other cross-benchers to support the amendment. Although they have in practice tended to vote with the Government (60.8 per cent of votes cast by them in 1988–9), cross-benchers owe it no allegiance, and therefore their vote is seen as being open to persuasion.

If voting by cross-benchers may make a difference only rarely, their sponsorship is nevertheless seen to be valuable in that it encourages other peers to come and listen to the debate, rather than simply turning up to vote according to party affiliation.[31] Their influence appears more potent, however, when it is employed in conjunction with sponsorship by a Government back-bencher. Although a number of the Opposition peers who were interviewed spoke of winning the cross-benchers' vote, it is clear from Table 4.2 that, in the case of the eight bills, it was only when they acted with this second group that there was any marked correlation between cross-bench sponsorship of an amendment and the likelihood of its being agreed to. On their own, opposition parties enjoyed success rates when moving amendments of between 3.3 per cent (Social and Liberal Democrat) and 6.0 per cent (Labour), while two opposition parties acting in concert had a success rate of 4.8 per cent. Where cross-benchers and Government back-benchers acted separately in concert with one or more opposition parties, the success rate was around 2.8 per cent and 3.3 per cent, and when cross-benchers and Government back-benchers only acted together, the rate was also 3.3 per cent. But where they acted together with one or more opposition parties, the rate was 31.9 per cent; of the forty-seven amendments moved by this combination, thirteen

[31] See e.g. Lord Mishcon's advice to Lord Mottistone at the Report stage of the Children Bill concerning the wisdom of leading the House to a division, HL Debs., 6 Feb. 1989, col. 1327.

of the fifteen successful amendments were agreed to without a division.

Thus a key factor in terms of proportionate degrees of success appears to be joint sponsorship by cross-benchers and Government back-benchers in conjunction with one or more opposition parties. Both Lord Denham, the Conservative Chief Whip, and the Earl of Caithness, Minister of State at the Department of the Environment, confirmed in interview that the Government takes the views of its back-benchers and of the cross-benchers seriously, more so perhaps than those of the Opposition, for whom opposition is a duty as much as a matter of argument about policy. Moreover, Lord Denham thought that the Government would be far more chary about reversing a defeat in the Commons in which these two groups had been instrumental than a defeat which had been brought about only by the opposition parties. The ultimate outcome of the twelve defeats provides some support for this proposition. Eight of the twelve were amendments sponsored by Government back-benchers and cross-benchers, as well as by Opposition peers. Of these eight, four were substantially accepted, and on two a compromise was reached, while only two were reversed outright. Of the four defeats which resulted from divisions on amendments sponsored solely by Opposition peers, three were rejected outright while a compromise was reached on the fourth.

There are, of course, some factors that might discourage a peer from seeking cross-party support for his amendment. From the standpoint of the opposition parties, the value of Government back-benchers must be tempered by the recognition that they may be reluctant to press an amendment to a vote. From the Government back-bencher's standpoint, it might be better not to have co-sponsorship from the opposition parties as they may well alienate other non-aligned peers. Lord Harmar-Nicholls (Conservative), for example, expressed disappointment (in interview) that his co-sponsor on the phasing-in amendment to the Football Spectators Bill, Lord Graham of Edmonton (Labour), used the debate upon the amendment to make party points.

This in turn raises the more general question how cross-party sponsorship is managed, in particular where cross-benchers and Government back-benchers, who are not generally represented at meetings set up by opposition parties to co-ordinate their strategy within the House on a bill, are involved. It appears that, apart from the usual negotiations between the two main opposition parties, cross-party sponsorship depends partly on informal soundings and partly on the liaising work of interest groups, the role of which was described by an Opposition front-bencher in interview as 'a cement'.

Repetition of amendments

As might be expected, a number of amendments moved in the Lords repeat or are broadly similar to those moved at an earlier stage or in the Commons. In the case of the Official Secrets Bill, for example, efforts were made in both Houses to introduce a public interest defence,[32] to make the test of harm in clause 2 more onerous for the prosecution by requiring proof of 'serious' injury or damage to the interests of the nation,[33] and to remove from clause 3 breaches of foreign confidence.[34] All of these were negatived on division. Similarly, unsuccessful Commons amendments to the Water Bill were repeated in the Lords, for example, to extend the remit of the National Rivers Authority,[35] and to ensure that existing rights and concessionary agreements on access to land currently owned by the water authorities would be transferred to the private companies.[36]

A particularly interesting pair of amendments to the Water Bill were those, moved in the Commons by the Opposition and in the Lords by Conservative back-benchers, which called in question the acceptability of the privatization of water supply. In the Commons, this was a straightforward wrecking amendment, seeking to remove Part II of the bill (that is, the Part that dealt with privatization), and was comfortably defeated. In the Lords, Lord Nugent of Guildford (Conservative), a former chairman of the National Water Council, moved an amendment, perhaps reflecting the less overt party political aspect to the Lords proceedings, which sought to substitute statutory water companies

[32] HL Debs., 3 Apr. 1989, cols. 906–34.
[33] Ibid., cols. 948–59.
[34] HL Debs., 4 Apr. 1989, cols. 1019–33.
[35] HL Debs., 2 May 1989, cols. 9–43.
[36] HL Debs., 8 May 1989, cols. 474–9.

for the private companies. Though this substitution would limit the dividend that would be payable, Lord Nugent denied that his was a wrecking amendment since it did not challenge privatization as such; the statutory companies would still, as the Government intended, have access to the money markets. Nevertheless, the Government took the matter very seriously, using an exceptionally strong whip. Its view was that the amendment, if carried, would mean both that the Lords would return a skeleton bill to the Commons and that they would thereby deprive themselves of the opportunity to debate substantial sections of Part II. The amendment was defeated by 208 votes to 112.[37] Among the eight other Conservative back-benchers who defected was the former Foreign Secretary Lord Pym, who argued that the bill as it stood could bring discredit on the Government's entire privatization programme. From the cross-benches the Earl of Halsbury also supported the amendment, arguing that 'constant reference to market forces as a remedy for everything under the sun' was evidence of 'creeping philistinism'.[38] The amendment was not moved again in the Lords.

In respect of those case-study bills introduced in the Lords and amended there, repetition of amendments was common. On the Road Traffic (Driver Licensing and Information Systems) Bill two sets of amendments were moved at all three stages, committee, report, and third reading; these were, first, amendments to prevent residential streets being used as 'rat-runs' by regular commuters seeking to avoid congestion on major routes, and secondly, amendments to enable local authorities to have access to Autoguide information. These were moved on each occasion by Lord Underhill (Labour), President of the Association of Metropolitan Authorities. On the former issue, the amendment moved in committee sought to require the Secretary of State to consult local authorities about the results of the trials to be conducted by him concerning road use by drivers having access to Autoguide, and was withdrawn on an assurance by the minister, Lord Brabazon of Tara, that they would be. However, with no explicit requirement being introduced by the Government on report, Lord Underhill moved an amendment to that effect. This was resisted on the ground that an undesirable additional

[37] HL Debs., 4 May 1989, cols. 265–99. [38] Ibid., col. 272.

layer of bureaucracy would be created in the management of the Autoguide system, which would also have a commercially deleterious effect upon those firms tendering to provide the system. Lord Underhill withdrew the amendment, but moved a new amendment at third reading designed to produce the same effect, but without the additional bureaucracy. This too he withdrew on the understanding that the local authorities would be consulted on the issue of 'rat-runs' in the meetings of the working party to be established by the Secretary of State.[39]

On an assurance that the minister would look at the question of local authority access to Autoguide information, Lord Underhill withdrew his committee amendment, but moved an amendment on report intended to provide a statutory stimulus to any arrangements for the provision of information that were to be agreed. This was withdrawn on assurances by the minister that local authorities would be given access, and at third reading Lord Underhill indicated that he was satisfied that this matter too would be dealt with by the Secretary of State's working party.[40]

On the Children Bill the House divided on the same amendment (to oblige local authorities to support young people who have left their care) both in committee and on report, the Government winning the former division very narrowly, 110–114. The amendment was moved by Baroness David (Labour), and was strongly supported by a number of Conservative back-benchers, including Baroness Faithfull (who co-sponsored the amendment), Lord Mottistone, and Lord Campbell of Alloway. In the event not all of these voted for it, but three Conservative back-benchers did cross-vote, Lord Campbell, Earl Kitchener, and Baroness Macleod of Borve. Owing to the strength of feeling expressed in a deputation to the House by local agencies concerned with homeless young people, Baroness David was unwilling to accept the Lord Chancellor's suggestion that she withdraw the similar amendment she moved on report, and on this occasion Baroness Faithfull did vote against the Government,

[39] Committee amendment 41, HL Debs., 24 Jan. 1989, cols. 670–3; report amendment 16, HL Debs., 9 Feb. 1989, cols. 1696–1704; third reading amendment 4, HL Debs., 16 Mar. 1989, cols. 428–33.

[40] Committee amendment 46, HL Debs., 24 Jan. 1989, cols. 678–81; report amendment 19, HL Debs., 9 Feb. 1989, cols. 1704–8; HL Debs., 16 Mar. 1989, cols. 428–33.

with one other Conservative back-bencher, Baroness Elliot of Harwood. However, on this division the Government majority was more comfortable, 112–128, largely owing to an increase in the number of Conservative peers present in the House (121 as against 104).[41]

A number of amendments which were debated at great length in committee on the Football Spectators Bill were tabled again on report. In the case of the amendment defeated in committee by six votes, to exempt 'female persons' from the bill (the words were chosen to meet the objection that if 'women' was used, men would dress up as women in order to avoid having to join the membership scheme, and prompted Lord Mishcon to describe the proceedings as Alice in Football Land), repetition gave rise to a discussion on report on the procedural propriety of this practice. Lord Stoddart of Swindon (Labour), who moved both amendments, argued that the subsequent amendment, which exempted 'women and unaccompanied children', though raising the same arguments of substance, was nevertheless a different amendment. This view was not shared by the House, and following the invocation by Lord Hesketh of the Companion to the Standing Orders, Lord Stoddart withdrew the amendment.[42]

Beside the propriety or utility of repetition, the question arises, what relationship, if any, is there between repetition or duplication of amendments and their outcome? No unambiguous indications emerge from the case-study bills. Certainly some amendments may be moved repeatedly because the level of support they command both inside and outside the House, and possibly some indication of flexibility on the part of the Government, augurs well but, on the other hand, many of those amendments that are raised repeatedly in both Houses are those on which there is the most profound disagreement and which the Government is determined to resist. Even if a statistically significant correlation between repetition and final agreement could be shown, which is unlikely, this would not demonstrate a causal relationship *per se*.

[41] Committee amendment 101, HL Debs., 17 Jan. 1989, cols. 135–48; report amendment 52, HL Debs., 7 Feb. 1989, cols. 1454–67.

[42] Committee amendment 53C, HL Debs., 14 Mar. 1989, cols. 96–107; report amendment 29, HL Debs., 10 Apr. 1989, cols. 85–9.

Ministerial undertakings

The primary focus of our discussion so far has been non-ministerial amendments, in particular those moved in respect of the eight case-study bills. The listed sponsors of an amendment do not, however, necessarily reveal its true origins—especially in respect of Government amendments, which as we saw earlier constitute by far the greatest number that are made to Government bills, and as noted above not infrequently represent concessions made by the Government in direct response to criticisms made at earlier stages.

Amendments of this kind are clearly of importance when attempting to assess the impact of the House upon Government legislation. Two possibilities arise in response to a non-ministerial amendment moved in respect of a bill originating in the Lords: the Government amendment is moved at a later stage, or is moved when the bill is in the Commons. The third possibility is that Government amendments are made in the Lords in response to undertakings given in respect of Commons bills, but with all three possibilities it is often far from easy to trace a clear causal relationship between an initial non-ministerial amendment and a subsequent Government amendment, even where it apparently seeks to deal with what concerned its sponsors, since other factors may in the meantime have convinced the Government of the wisdom of moving its own amendment. It may genuinely be reacting to sustained lobbying or, more manipulatively, have been holding some concessions in readiness to disarm predicted opposition. If it is not possible to be precise about the origin of all amendments, some of those made to the case-study bills can fairly unambiguously be traced to Government undertakings given at an earlier stage. The following discussion illustrates this.

On the Children Bill a large number of minor and technical amendments were moved in the Lords in response to points made at earlier stages. On more substantive issues the Government also brought forward its own amendments meeting points raised at earlier stages. These included: that court welfare reports might be prepared by persons other than local authority officials, for example, an officer in the NSPCC;[43] that local authorities

[43] Report amendment 5, HL Debs., 6 Feb. 1989, cols. 1329–30.

should be empowered to prevent non-physical as well as physical abuse;[44] and that the Secretary of State should be required to keep under review the adequacy of child-care training.[45] There was also some concession on the desire for the establishment of a proper complaints procedure in respect of local authority care functions, the right to complain itself being made clearer.[46] The concern that had been expressed in committee about the Secretary of State's powers under clause 15(4) was met by two Government amendments made at third reading: one of these removed the Secretary of State's power to repeal by order any of a local authority's duties under Part I of Schedule 2;[47] the second placed his remaining order making powers under the clause subject to affirmative instead of negative resolution procedure.[48] In addition, non-ministerial amendments designed to strengthen the rights of relatives other than parents, particularly grandparents, were partly met by a Government amendment allowing them to make representations in respect of children in care,[49] and a further amendment at third reading met some of the concern that local authorities should take steps to avoid the need for children within their area to be placed in secure accommodation.[50]

A good many issues raised in the Lords were eventually addressed in the Commons. However, because of the Lord Chancellor's willingness to consider most points put to him (to a degree unusual for senior ministers), and also because of the continuous activities of several interest groups, it is difficult to be precise about the distinctive importance of Lords proceedings in respect of points first raised in the upper House.

In respect of the Companies Bill there were a few specific undertakings to bring amendments forward at a later stage, for example to specify the retention of the Registrar's certificate as conclusive evidence of the date of delivery of particulars, a point raised in committee and partially met on report.[51] Some points

[44] Report amendment 70, HL Debs., 7 Feb. 1989, cols. 1489–90.
[45] Report amendment 124D, HL Debs., 16 Feb. 1989, cols. 344–5.
[46] Report amendment 61, HL Debs., 7 July 1989, cols. 344–5.
[47] Third reading amendment 10, HL Debs., 16 Mar. 1989, cols. 346–52.
[48] Third reading amendment 58, ibid., cols. 410–13.
[49] Third reading amendment 30, ibid., cols. 384–5.
[50] Third reading amendment 61, ibid., col. 414.
[51] Report amendment 139C, agreed to on a division, HL Debs., 6 Apr. 1989, cols. 1209–16.

raised by Lord Benson (cross-bench) were also taken on board by the Government, but many other complex points were taken away for consideration or reconsideration by the Government without any clear undertakings being given. Also, some of the issues that were raised were still being examined outside Parliament (for example the consultations on the Dearing proposals on accounting standards) with a view to producing amendments. Some later Government amendments certainly touched on these proposals, which were discussed at length in the Lords, but it is difficult to say whether the views expressed in the Lords had any influence at all on the final outcome.

On the Football Spectators Bill a large number of promises were made by the Government in the Lords both in committee and on report to look at matters again. For example, in committee Lord Hesketh, speaking from the Government dispatch-box, undertook to bring forward amendments to clarify the composition and powers of the Football Membership Authority (FMA); though not going as far as the Opposition wanted, these were moved on report.[52] The Government also brought forward an amendment to meet the demand that the FMA produce an annual report.[53] Another issue that attracted lengthy debate in committee concerned the creation of categories of persons, such as club guests and the disabled, who would be exempt from the scheme. The Government's promise to bring forward amendments was fulfilled on report, and indeed went further by extending exemption to accompanied children under ten, and by allowing the FMA to specify other exemptions for special cases like Wembley.[54] Agreements to look at the question of what charges would be imposed for bringing appeals against disqualification and to consider the possibility of an appeal against a court's declaration that an offence is 'relevant' for the purposes of disqualification were met on report.[55] The Government also

[52] Committee amendment 15, HL Debs., 20 Feb. 1989, cols. 480–6; report amendments 7, 9, 12–15, 17–19, and 21, HL Debs., 10 Apr. 1989, cols. 57–68; report amendment 58, HL Debs., 13 Apr. 1989, col. 467.

[53] Report amendment 7, HL Debs., 10 Apr. 1989, cols. 57–9.

[54] HL Debs., 7 Mar. 1989, cols. 1394–5, 1401, 1408, and 1438; report amendments 25, 27, 39, HL Debs., 10 Apr. 1989, cols. 60–105 and 115; report amendment 46, HL Debs., 14 Apr. 1989, col. 433.

[55] HL Debs., 14 Mar. 1989, cols. 152 and 1170; report amendments 43–5 and 69, HL Debs., 13 Apr. 1989, cols. 433 and 475–6.

brought forward amendments at third reading in response to three earlier undertakings: first, to increase the period required for notification that an offence was to be declared relevant from three to five days,[56] secondly, to limit aspects of the FMA's discretionary powers,[57] and thirdly, to make the Secretary of State's approval of the scheme subject to negative resolution procedure.[58]

Amendments were made in the Commons following discussions with the Association of Chief Police Officers, first to meet a concern which, following the events at Hillsborough football ground in April 1989 became more real, that the requirements of the scheme should be suspended in an emergency,[59] and secondly, to regulate the use of police as reporting agencies.[60]

On the other hand, there were also undertakings and agreements to consider points that apparently did not produce any positive results. For example, an undertaking to consider the question of protecting members of the scheme from disclosure of personal information was given in committee and repeated on report,[61] but nothing was done, and no further explanation was given. Another undertaking concerning the unauthorized confiscation of membership cards by stewards,[62] and a third, to consult upon an amendment to exempt Welsh clubs, likewise came to naught.

Some peers expressed suspicions that the Government was, in these instances, misusing offers to consider or consult on amendments in order to avoid difficulties in debate. For example, Lord Brooks of Tremorfa was persuaded to withdraw his committee amendment (No. 2) exempting Welsh clubs, following an assurance from Lord Hesketh (prompted by a hasty note from Lord Denham) that the Government would, without commit-

[56] HL Debs., 13 Apr. 1989, cols. 476–8; third reading amendment 19, HL Debs., 16 June 1989, col. 1688.

[57] HL Debs., 14 Mar. 1989, col. 108; repeated on report, HL Debs., 10 Apr. 1989, cols. 109–12; third reading amendments 12–13, HL Debs., 16 June 1989, col. 1685.

[58] Report amendment 4, HL Debs., 10 Apr. 1989, cols. 34–43; third reading amendments 1 and 3–10, HL Debs., 16 June 1989, cols. 1674–5 and 1677–8.

[59] Committee amendment 73, HL Debs., 14 Mar. 1989, col. 199.

[60] Committee amendment 75, ibid., cols. 208–9.

[61] Committee amendment 62, ibid., cols. 156–7; HL Debs., 10 Apr. 1989, col. 117; HL Debs., 13 Apr. 1989, cols. 436–7.

[62] HL Debs., 14 Mar. 1989, col. 165.

ment, take the matter away for consultation. In the event, the only consultation with the Welsh Football Association (WFA), the three Welsh clubs, and the police that did take place was a meeting that had been arranged prior to the committee stage of the bill. This was held at the invitation of the Secretary of State for Wales, but was confined to the question of the implementation of the scheme in Wales, and did not address the issue of principle raised by the amendment. Lord Brooks's suspicions that this was consultation in name only were based on a letter sent to him by the Secretary of the WFA, who indicated that, when the matter of Lord Hesketh's promise was raised, 'the meeting was informed that the Government's majority in the House of Commons was sufficient to pass the bill and that other matters were quite irrelevant and would be to waste time spent more constructively.' Despite Lord Hesketh's denial that there had been no consultation, Lord Graham of Edmonton (Labour) was also critical of what he described as a con trick designed to save the Government from the possibility of further embarrassment, Lord Brooks's amendment following immediately upon the division on amendment 1 on which the Government had been defeated. On report Lord Brooks forced a division which was comfortably won by the Government.[63]

On the Official Secrets Bill the Government gave three undertakings to look again at points raised in committee. All were met by Government amendments. The first, upon which there was general support in the House, provided for a notification under clause 1 to lapse after four, instead of five, years unless renewed or previously terminated, if deemed fit by the minister.[64] The second involved the substitution of the word 'endangers' for 'jeopardizes' in respect of the harm tests for defence and international relations,[65] while the third was a drafting amendment of clause 8(6).[66]

A fourth Government undertaking was made at third reading,

[63] HL Debs., 20 Feb. 1989, cols. 420–6; HL Debs., 10 Apr. 1989, cols. 16–28, col. 17.

[64] HL Debs., 3 Apr. 1989, cols. 989–92; report amendments 6 and 7, HL Debs., 18 Apr. 1989, col. 738.

[65] HL Debs., 4 Apr. 1989, cols. 1033–41; report amendments 9 and 13, HL Debs., 18 Apr. 1989, cols. 738–9 and 743.

[66] HL Debs., 4 Apr. 1989, cols. 1053–61; report amendments 20–3, HL Debs., 18 Apr. 1989, col. 745.

to write to Lord Renton about an amendment which he had moved. This led to an unusual adjournment. Because this was a Commons bill, there could, after this stage, be no further opportunity for the Lords to consider amendments, and, on the motion that the bill do now pass, the House adjourned during pleasure for thirty minutes. During this time the merits and procedural implications of Lord Renton's amendment (if meritorious) were considered. The matter was perhaps more unusual still, for, contrary to what was implied by the other peers who spoke after the adjournment, Lord Renton had indeed raised the matter at an earlier stage, when the bill was on report. On that occasion he had withdrawn the amendment following an assurance from the Government spokesman, Earl Ferrers, that he would write to him. Evidently Lord Renton considered that the subsequent letter did not meet the point, but was again prepared to withdraw the amendment on Earl Ferrers's undertaking to draw the Secretary of State's attention to the issue he had raised.[67]

There were no undertakings given on the Transport (Scotland) Bill and, as previously noted, very little modification in the Lords of the Prevention of Terrorism (Temporary Provisions) Bill. The Government did bring forward amendments there concerning the criteria governing the taking of fingerprints from persons detained under the Act, in response to undertakings given in standing committee in the Commons.[68]

On the Road Traffic (Driver Licensing and Information Systems) Bill an undertaking was given in committee to consider an amendment to authorize a person to drive public-service vehicles after having passed the appropriate test, but while still waiting for the licence and the badge to be sent from the traffic commissioners. There was subsequently a meeting on this attended by Lord Teviot (a former bus-driver) and the Earl of Shrewsbury, Government back-benchers who had together sponsored the amendment, the minister (Lord Brabazon of Tara), and interested parties from the bus industry and the tendering authorities. On report the minister stated that the

[67] Report amendment 10, HL Debs., 18 Apr. 1989, cols. 739–42; HL Debs., 24 Apr. 1989, cols. 1077–1106.

[68] Third reading amendments 8, 11, 25, and 26, HL Debs., 7 Mar. 1989, cols. 1376–7.

Government was prepared to accept the amendment in principle but that there were drafting defects and other points that needed changing. He undertook to introduce a redrafted version at third reading, which he did.[69] In committee, the Government agreed to consider amendments to provide special exemptions from training requirements for cyclists[70] and to prevent the use of Autoguide as a means of invading personal privacy.[71] Both matters were dealt with by Government amendments brought forward on report. The Government also introduced an amendment in response to a point made in committee that under clause 10(8)(e) the Secretary of State's powers to regulate charges could extend to services that were not part of Autoguide, for example, membership fees of the Automobile Association.[72]

In the Lords the Government tabled a number of amendments to meet peers' and MPs' concerns about the impact of the Water Bill on the environment. In particular, undertakings were given in both Houses to look at the question of providing long-term protection for countryside areas of special environmental value. These were met in the Lords on report by amendments and by a new clause to protect land sold by a water company. All such sales were to be made subject to the Secretary of State's consent, while land in the National Parks, in the Norfolk Broads, and in Areas of Outstanding Natural Beauty were to be offered first to conservation bodies. In addition, the Secretary of State was given powers to impose covenants for the future protection of any land sold. The new clause was generally welcomed, but there was criticism of the omission of Sites of Special Scientific Interest. A number of all-party amendments were tabled to remedy this. These were initially resisted by the minister, but in the face of strong pressure within the House and from such groups as the Royal Society for the Protection of Birds, the Government conceded the point at third reading, though its price was to

[69] HL Debs., 24, Jan. 1989, col. 617; report amendment 2, HL Debs., 9 Feb. 1989, cols. 1673–6; third reading amendment 1, HL Debs., 16 Mar. 1989, cols. 426–8.

[70] HL Debs., 24 Jan. 1989, col. 646; report amendments 7–11 and 14, HL Debs., 9 Feb. 1989, cols. 1690–2 and 1695.

[71] HL Debs., 24 Jan. 1989, col. 680; report amendments 22–3, HL Debs., 9 Feb. 1989, col. 1711.

[72] HL Debs., 24 Jan. 1989, cols. 683–4; report amendment 20, HL Debs., 9 Feb. 1989, col. 1708.

withdraw the discretionary power to designate new areas for such protection.[73]

Other issues on which undertakings were given included discriminatory charges to customers in rural areas, charges for connecting to new developments, and the collection of unpaid charges from subsequent occupiers. The first was met by an all-party amendment that was moved at third reading by Lord Stanley of Alderley and earlier approved by the Government.[74] The second was met in committee when the minister, in moving a Government amendment, accepted an amendment tabled in the names of three Conservative peers, Lords Jenkin of Roding, Elliott of Morpeth, and Nugent of Guildford. The Government's concession here was in response to an undertaking given in the Commons, but it had been clearly signalled a week earlier in the written answer given by the minister (the Earl of Caithness) to a question concerning the issue that had been put by Lord Kimball.[75] The third undertaking concerned the Government's original proposal that a supplier of water could, where an existing occupier had defaulted on the payment of his water charges, in some instances recover the deficit from any subsequent occupier of the same premises. In response to the 'persuasive' arguments of Lord McIntosh of Haringey, a Labour peer active on the bill, and two Conservative peers, Lords Renton and Trafford, the Government agreed to discuss the matter further. At third reading the minister indicated that the Government now agreed that the clause was defective, and brought forward a new clause which was welcomed by those concerned.[76]

The Impact of the Lords on the Case-Study Bills

As we have seen, in both theoretical and practical terms, 'revision' subsumes a number of possibilities, broadly speaking

[73] Report amendment 140, HL Debs., 13 June 1989, cols. 1336–53; third reading amendment 81, HL Debs., 27 June 1989, cols. 672–84.

[74] Third reading amendment 2, HL Debs., 27 June 1989, cols. 607–11.

[75] Committee amendment 350A (Government amendment 345AB), HL Debs., 22 May 1989, cols. 56–7; written answer (Earl of Caithness), HL Debs., 15 May 1989, col. 913.

[76] Report amendment 113A, HL Debs., 12 June 1989, cols. 1231–3; third reading amendment 33, HL Debs., 27 June 1989, cols. 649–52.

drafting and technical amendments, amendments designed to realize more effectively the original intention of the legislation, and substantive amendments which reflect a more significant change of policy in the particular case. The major part of the revising process in the Lords, quantitatively speaking, is a tidying-up process, that is, making drafting and technical changes, but the Lords also made a number of genuine substantive adjustments to the case-study bills, many of them minor but others involving quite significant departures from their original intentions. Before making some more general remarks by way of conclusion, we give a summary of the main impact of the Lords on the eight bills.

The Children Bill was a complex piece of legislation; it included fifty pages of Schedules, and the debates on it were protracted, extending over five days in committee and three days on report. Judged simply in terms of the number of amendments made, the impact of the House does not appear to have been very great. A total of 187 were agreed, but only thirty or so of these arose from concerns first expressed in the House and few related to the major substantive issues debated. The overall structure and content of the bill was unchanged when it left the Lords. Nevertheless it was generally thought by those participating that some significant improvements had been made. Further, as the Lord Chancellor commented on third reading, many of the amendments put forward that were not successful would inform progress in the Commons and in secondary legislation. The number of amendments that were to be met by regulations was, however, regarded as something of a mixed blessing by most of the peers who had proposed them. When the bill left the House there had also been a failure to resolve some important issues, for example concerning child assessment orders.

As can be seen in Table 3.3, the Commons spent almost as many hours debating this bill as had the Lords. It came back to the upper House with a very large number of amendments, 463 in all, running to 136 pages and virtually doubling the length of the bill. While some of the changes were straightforward responses to matters already discussed in the Lords, and others were minor drafting amendments, much of the material was entirely new. Thus the clauses relating to the jurisdiction and procedure of the courts in matters concerning children were, when they left the Lords, fifteen and eight lines long respectively. When the bill returned from the Commons, they had been replaced by a massive new clause which extended over six pages. This, and similar large-scale amendments, prompted some sharp criticism in the Lords. With so much being added to the bill after it had completed its Lords stages, peers felt that their House had been insulted; they were also angry because so little time was available for them to give proper consideration to the substantial changes made in the Commons. The Deputy Leader of the Social and Liberal Democrats, Baroness Seear, complained bitterly that the Government's handling of this bill 'treats your Lordships' House with not even something approaching contempt but with actual contempt. It makes an absolute mockery of the whole proceedings when we are given this amount of material at this stage and no opportunity of going through it.'[77] There was actually less dissatisfaction over what finally went into the bill than had been feared, but the way the Government had managed the parliamentary passage of the bill begged the question why these important provisions were left to the last minute, and why they were not available when the bill was first presented in the Lords, or at least during its Lords stages. When the Commons amendments were considered the Lord Chancellor did express regret that the bill had left the House in an incomplete state, but in response to Baroness Seear's complaint, and in support of what had happened, he argued that it was better at least to achieve things this way than not at all.[78]

The Companies Bill was also detailed and technically complex, and there was cross-party agreement when it had completed its passage in the Lords that it had been improved. But in the Commons it was largely rewritten. The amendments comprised 100 pages of text, much of it new. As we note below, this was a matter of considerable criticism in the Lords.

As has already been noted, for the Government the Football Spectators Bill proved to be far more troublesome in the Lords than had been expected. The popular view after the committee stage was that rebellious peers, including Conservative backbenchers, had run a successful campaign and won significant amendments to the bill. Certainly the Opposition peers expressed

[77] HL Debs., 8 Nov. 1989, col. 842. [78] Ibid., cols. 844–5.

themselves as being quite satisfied with what they had achieved. An alternative view was that the Government had made only minor concessions in order to palliate opposition and that it had not been deflected from realizing its primary intention, namely to introduce a clear membership scheme. For example, despite the concession on phasing in, the Secretary of State retained the last word. Similarly, other Lords amendments did not substantively alter the proposed scheme as such, though they did pressure the Government into making the details of its implementation more explicit and in some minor respects 'softened' its application.

There were no major changes to the Official Secrets Bill in the Lords. Of the ten amendments made, two were technical or drafting changes that were not discussed; the other eight were Government responses to undertakings, all of which were agreed to be minor matters. In the Commons the substitution in clauses 2 and 3 of 'endanger' for 'jeopardize' was regarded by some MPs as making the test of harm more substantial and thus the amendment more significant, but the Government's view was that the substituted word would simply make the test more intelligible to juries.

It was agreed at third reading, amongst mutual compliments and thanks, that the debates on the Road Traffic (Driver Licensing and Information Systems) Bill had been constructive and that valuable improvements to the bill had been made, both to the original provisions and in the introduction of new clauses. The Government was particularly accommodating in respect of the concern that had been expressed regarding the delay for PSV drivers between passing the test and being authorized to drive. Although this problem would be resolved anyway with the commencement of the new licensing system in 1991, it produced an amendment to bridge the gap even though this entailed some quite lengthy and complicated drafting. The Opposition-initiated amendment to avoid the 'tracking' of individual drivers was, said Lord Brabazon of Tara, 'a very important point, which but for the noble Lord, Lord Underhill [the Labour front-bench spokesman on Transport], might have gone unnoticed.'[79]

The impact of the Lords on the Prevention of Terrorism

[79] Third reading amendments 1, 2, 5–11, and 13–17, HL Debs., 16 Mar. 1989, cols. 426–8 and 433–7.

(Temporary Provisions) Bill was minimal, being confined to technical and drafting improvements. No amendments were made to the Transport (Scotland) Bill.

The Lords spent 100 hours over fourteen days debating the Water Bill, at 416 pages one of the longest bills ever to be enacted. Many of the 341 amendments made in the Lords were technical or were intended to improve the organizational structure of the bill; for the rest, many were Government responses to arguments which had support on all sides of the House. Despite its unpopularity, it was generally agreed, even by those who opposed the whole principle of privatization, that the bill had been improved by the Lords. The environmental lobby both inside and outside the House in particular produced some substantive changes. These included major amendments making disposals of water-industry land subject to environmental controls; an Opposition amendment to make the environmental code of practice applicable to the National Rivers Authority, which the Government accepted; and an amendment moved by Lord Greenway (cross-bench) making the code subject to parliamentary approval by means of negative resolution procedure. Other principal changes gave protection for rural customers against discriminatory charges and exempted the fire services from charges for water used for the purpose of training or equipment testing.

As with the Children Bill it was difficult to say, especially in respect of the concessions on environmental issues, how much these owed to the arguments of peers, particularly on the Government's own benches, and how much to pressure exerted directly on the Government by the interest groups outside Parliament. It was probably a complementary process. We should bear in mind also the view of *The Times*'s parliamentary correspondent, Sheila Gunn, that the Government had some concessions in mind that it could keep until there was a revolt in the Lords, so that it would appear to be listening. In the event, the view within Government circles as expressed in interview was that the impact of the Lords on the bill was much less than expected; its passage, though lengthy, was relatively easy.

Concluding Remarks

Of the eight case-study bills, the Lords made amendments to five of them. The impact of Lords debates varied very substantially, as we have seen. In some cases the effect of non-ministerial amendments was direct, in the sense that their substance was agreed by the Government, with or without qualification. This happened in respect of some sixty-five amendments. In other cases amendments were withdrawn in return for an undertaking either to 'look again' or to bring forward amendments subsequently. As already explained, it is difficult to be exact about the numbers, but over thirty-five Government amendments can be fairly unambiguously traced to such undertakings. These thirty-five or so must have been considered by the Government as necessary or desirable improvements. In other cases the undertaking to 'look again' resulted in no change being made, despite the criticisms expressed by peers.

It is also relevant to any assessment of the impact of the House that in some instances where the Lords did achieve such improvements, the Government had, at an early stage, indicated its willingness to listen to peers' suggestions. Thus, in the case of the Road Traffic (Driver Licensing and Information Systems) Bill, the minister, Lord Brabazon of Tara, described the proceedings as being 'in the best traditions of this House' and continued: 'At first we were not convinced that any amendments were necessary. My noble friends rapidly convinced us that their arguments inside and outside the House were what can best be described as vigorous. I am delighted to have been able to bring forward amendments to meet their concerns.'[80] Likewise the Children Bill appears as a paradigm of a Lords bill. 'Expert' peers worked hard and when the bill left the Lords the Lord Chancellor underlined how helpful their Lordships had been in their strongly held, though non-partisan, views. His sentiments were shared by a number of others; Baroness Seear, for instance, spoke of the bill's progress through the House as a prime example of the Lords at its best and of the wisdom of introducing such bills there (though as we have already noted, she and other peers were to express their regret that they were denied the opportunity

[80] HL Debs., 16 Mar. 1989, col. 436.

properly to consider many further substantial changes introduced by the Commons).

However, on two major issues, both of which had attracted repeated criticism throughout the 1980s, there was less than harmony. First, it had become commonplace to refer to the Government's tendency to 'legislate as you go'.[81] Whereas amendments brought about in consequence of debate are properly regarded as the desirable outcome of the legislative process, the tabling of large numbers of amendments embodying material wholly new to the bill suggests that the department concerned has not fully addressed or settled its policy. Such a practice is a matter of criticism. It is also one thing, as with the Children Bill, to make an effort to deal with difficult issues while recognizing the measure's limitations and welcoming assistance, but quite another, as with the Companies Bill, not to have essayed an answer at all. On this latter bill Lord Williams of Elvel deplored the fact that it was clearly an example of rushed, ill-considered legislation which would result in 'large shoals' of Government amendments. Such a state of affairs arose, he said,

> where the department may know that it wants something but is not entirely clear exactly what it is or how it can be formulated into legislation. Nothing is put in the Bill when it is originally published but an announcement is made that certain parts of the legislation are not yet available and will at some unspecified time be made available in the form of government amendments. As the Secretary of State said, that is the case in respect of the *ultra vires* provisions which will come later. The Bill to which your Lordships are today being invited to give a Second Reading is therefore incomplete. It will be completed when the Government have got their act together.
>
> I hope I reflect the general view of the House when I say that this situation is, to put it at its mildest, far from satisfactory. The Government should make up their mind what it is they want and then put forward the legislation designed to achieve their objective. It is fair enough that the original Bill should be amended as the result of parliamentary debate. But the Government should not waste our time by asking us to debate what are only tentative suggestions. Nor should they be allowed to make it all up as they go along.[82]

[81] See e.g. the *Report by the Group on the Working of the House* (HL Paper 9, 1987–8), para. 99.

[82] HL Debs., 16 Jan. 1989, col. 15.

This complaint was repeatedly voiced, at the end of the first and fourth days in committee,[83] and, during report, when Part V of the bill was recommitted to a committee of the whole House in order to enable the new provisions relating to *ultra vires* to be discussed under committee procedure. This produced a lengthy confrontation between Lord Wedderburn of Charlton for the Opposition and Lord Fraser of Carmyllie for the Government on some complex legal issues, but no changes in the Government's position.[84]

Amendments based on DTI consultations on the Dearing Report on the making of accountancy standards and proposed amendments to the Financial Services Act 1986 did not appear until the bill reached the Commons. When it returned to the Lords, the Government took the unprecedented step of setting aside three days for the consideration of Commons amendments, and also ensured that a clear week elapsed between the completion of Commons amendments and their consideration in the Lords. Lord Belstead's efforts to convince the Lords that the large number of new amendments was a healthy indication that Parliament was doing its job were not, however, wholly successful.[85]

The second contentious issue centred on what a number of peers perceived to be the Government's insistence upon getting its way, despite the cogency of the arguments presented in support of their amendments. This was reflected, for example, in the reasoned amendments that were moved at third reading on both the Football Spectators Bill and the Water Bill. In the former case, Lord Graham of Edmonton took the opportunity to regret the Government's insistence on going ahead with the bill without waiting for the publication of Lord Justice Taylor's Report on the Hillsborough disaster (in the event the Report did not address the question of identity cards, though it did make clear its rejection of the Government's membership scheme, which was indefinitely postponed in early 1990). In the case of the Water Bill, the amendment regretted that completion of the bill was sought 'in the absence of adequate information in respect

[83] HL Debs., 30 Jan. 1989, cols. 976–7; 21 Feb. 1989, cols. 517–18.

[84] HL Debs., 6 Apr. 1989, cols. 1232–54 and 1264–90; 11 Apr. 1989, cols. 131–236.

[85] HL Debs., 7 Nov. 1989, cols. 548–9, 695–6.

of the terms of appointment of water and sewerage undertakers; the likely terms of the flotation and the sale of securities; the basis upon which prices to consumers will be set; the final terms of the code of practice on environmental and recreational matters; the detailed requirements in respect of quality of drinking-water and river water, and the relevant timetables for compliance.'[86]

However, the most acrimonious exchanges occurred on the Official Secrets Bill. In the first place, the fact that ministers initially set a Friday (17 March) for the second reading in the Lords was taken by the bill's critics to be an attempt to limit detailed consideration, but it was the Government's use of the guillotine in the Commons that prompted the most vitriolic observations. In part these underlined one of the traditional justifications for the Lords: to act as a check upon the indiscriminate exercise of a Commons majority. Thus Lord Mishcon, the Labour Opposition spokesman, claimed at second reading, 'If ever a Bill justified the existence of a reviewing chamber it is this Official Secrets Bill.'[87] The Government's intransigence was a matter of comment both in the Commons and in the Lords;[88] even on those clauses of the bill guillotined in the Commons, the Government appeared to show considerable unwillingness to reconsider its proposals during the Lords stages. This underlines the difficulty faced by the House on major legislation when it is confronted by a determined or, depending on your point of view, obdurate Government. The remarks made on this bill by the front-bench spokesmen that are quoted in Chapter 3 underline the point that the extent to which the House of Lords is perceived to have a significant impact depends essentially on the standpoint of the observer.

[86] HL Debs., 27 June 1989, col. 585.

[87] HL Debs., 9 Mar. 1989, col. 1610.

[88] HC Debs., 16 Feb. 1989, col. 606; HC Debs., 22 Feb. 1989, col. 1091; HC Debs., 2 May 1989, col. 131; HL Debs., 9 Mar. 1989, cols. 1614–16; HL Debs., 3 Apr. 1989, col. 907.

5

Delegated Legislation

R. L. Borthwick

Delegated or secondary legislation is an inescapable feature of modern States but one which poses considerable problems for parliamentary bodies. The problems of scrutiny and control in this area are arguably even greater than for primary legislation.

Part of the problem is volume, part timing, and part the complexity of what is contained in the variety of creatures gathered in the delegated legislation zoo. Some delegated legislation requires a positive decision from Parliament before it becomes operative, that is it needs an affirmative resolution from each House. Some comes into effect unless a negative resolution (a prayer) is passed by either House to annul the proposed legislation. Some instruments, dealing with taxation and public expenditure, are subject to affirmative or negative resolution of the Commons alone. Others permit of no action by Parliament, being laid before it purely for information, while yet others may come into effect without going anywhere near Parliament.

Delegated legislation appears in a number of forms: for example, Orders in Council, statutory instruments, regulations, and a variety of what has come to be called quasi-legislation such as codes of practice and circulars from government departments.

Although their number may not have increased in recent years, statutory instruments have grown longer and more complex. The number produced each year is around 2,000 but, as a former chairman of the Joint Committee on Statutory Instruments pointed out in 1989, 'In 1955, in the bound volume, the instruments ran to 3,240 pages; by 1965, that had almost doubled to 6,435 pages and, by 1988, it was up to 9,048 pages.'[1] Andrew Bennett went on to point out that many instruments were now 100 pages or more. They cover an enormous variety of subjects:

[1] Mr Andrew F. Bennett, Third Commonwealth Conference on Delegated Legislation, Record of Proceedings (HMSO, 1989), 32.

commencement orders, the powers of ministers in relation to local authorities, powers to set detailed standards in a variety of fields, as well as virtually the whole of the legislation relating to Northern Ireland. Moreover they are concerned not just with detail but increasingly with matters of policy. To quote Andrew Bennett again: 'I believe that some statutory instruments have stopped being about the nuts and bolts of things and have gone on to become more a matter of designing the car.'[2]

Certain characteristics of delegated legislation are worth emphasizing. First, unlike primary legislation, delegated legislation, if debated at all, goes through only a single stage in each House. A second related point is that no opportunity exists in either House for delegated legislation to be amended; it is either accepted or rejected. Third, a Joint Select Committee (analysed below) consisting of an equal number of MPs and peers exists to scrutinize all delegated legislation. Fourth, apart from those items relating to finance which are dealt with only by the Commons, delegated legislation is an area where, formally at least, the powers of the House of Lords remain on a par with those of the Commons.

However, as Shell points out, peers are loath to push their power to the limit: 'Never has a prayer against a negative instrument been carried, and only once has the House rejected an affirmative instrument.'[3] To avoid politically damaging conflicts with the government of the day, peers have developed techniques which allow them to express an opinion without going so far as to reject instruments that come before them.[4]

It is convenient to deal with the House's activities in relation to delegated legislation under two broad categories: proceedings on the floor of the House, primarily the consideration of affirmative and negative resolutions, and the work done off the floor by the Lords members of the Joint Committee on Statutory In-

[2] Ibid., 33.

[3] Donald Shell, *The House of Lords*, 2nd edn. (Harvester Wheatsheaf, London, 1992), 218. The one rejection had serious consequences: while the instrument in question, the Southern Rhodesia (United Nations Sanctions) Order 1968, was not significantly affected, being approved when put to the House again, the temerity shown by the Lords proved fatal to the inter-party talks being held at that time on reform of the Lords.

[4] See Shell, *House of Lords*, 219.

Table 5.1. *Delegated legislation, 1988–9*

Category	No.	Time taken in Lords (hrs. m.)	Time taken *on these items only* in Commons (hrs. m.)
Affirmative resolutions	120	28:33	68:52 (41:38 on floor and 27:14 in standing committee)
Prayers	3	3:15	8:21
Measures	1	3:18	1:30[a]

[a] Plus a further 11 minutes on a division.

struments. This committee is not concerned with the policy implications of delegated legislation but purely with its technical merits.

Before considering how the Lords dealt with delegated legislation on the floor of the House in the 1988–9 session, it may be useful to set out the volume of material dealt with and the time it occupied. Table 5.1 indicates that the bulk of the House's work on delegated legislation was under the affirmative procedure. Prayers were relatively few in number and there was only one Church of England Measure.

As Table 5.1 shows, the Commons spent more than twice the time spent by the Lords on the 120 affirmative instruments considered in both Houses. The Commons dealt also with affirmative instruments that did not concern the Lords, spending a further nineteen hours on these on the floor, and additional time in standing committee. Of the 120 affirmative instruments dealt with by both Houses, eighty-seven were dealt with first in the Commons, six were considered in both Houses on the same day, and only twenty-seven taken first in the Lords.

There were only three debates in the Lords during the session on prayers to reject statutory instruments (though one of these covered fifteen instruments), but the Commons held sixteen debates on prayers on the floor as well as other debates in standing committees. In all, the Commons spent over twenty-seven hours debating prayers on the floor of the House, the Lords just over three hours.

Affirmative Resolutions

Debates on affirmative resolutions in the Lords are a fairly regular feature of proceedings. Such debates are often held during the so-called 'dinner break' when the House interrupts its business; fifty-one were taken in that way during 1988–9. Only once during the 1988–9 session did the House discuss delegated legislation after midnight. Unlike the Commons, however, all debates on delegated legislation are held on the floor of the Chamber. Some indication of the number of instruments subject to the affirmative resolution procedure dealt with by the Lords in 1988–9 is given in Table 5.2. Although a considerable number of resolutions are considered, in most cases matters are dispatched very expeditiously. Of the 120 considered, only twenty occupied thirty minutes or more of the House's time. However, the House frequently debates instruments on related topics together and then approves them separately at the end of the debate. This means that some instruments are dealt with formally but have in fact been the subject of debate; to that extent the number of instruments shown in the table as taking a minute or less is somewhat misleading. All but one of the forty-five instruments that took a minute or less were taken formally but all but two of these had been debated with other, related, instruments.[5] Although only one in six of the instruments requiring approval by the House was debated for as long as thirty minutes, those debates accounted for three-fifths of the time that the Lords spent on affirmative resolutions. In fifty-six other cases there was at least some brief debate. In such cases there was the opportunity for questions to be asked or a view to be registered. Overall, in seventy-six cases there was at least some small input from the Opposition front bench; in twenty-six of those cases the only contributors were the minister and his Opposition counterpart. In thirty of the remaining fifty debates, only one other peer spoke. In the other twenty debates the number of additional speakers varied between two and six.

The one debate which had the distinction of having six con-

[5] The marginal exception is an order on Northern Ireland where *Hansard* records the debate as lasting only one minute, although three peers made brief contributions.

Table 5.2. *Affirmative resolutions considered in House of Lords, 1988–9*

Time taken	No.	Total time occupied	
		hrs. m.	%
1 minute or less	45	0:26	1.5
2–9 minutes	23	2:14	7.8
10–29 minutes	32	8:35	30.0
30–59 minutes	13	8:50	30.9
1 hour or more	7	8:28	29.7
TOTAL	120	28:33	99.9

tributors, other than the minister and Opposition front-bench spokesman, was on an order amending the 1988 Merchant Shipping Act and was interesting because it raised some wider issues. This order was necessitated by an interim judgment from the European Court of Justice requiring the suspension of parts of the 1988 Merchant Shipping Act which related to the nationality requirements of certain British shipping vessels and which the Court had held were discriminatory. The minister moving the order, Viscount Davidson, indicated that the Government felt obliged to give effect to the Court's judgment. Not surprisingly this issue raised the hackles of those who disliked the European Community and all its doings. Lord Stoddart of Swindon intervened to ask the minister, 'whether it was not intolerable that a court sitting in a foreign land could instruct the British Parliament to alter an Act of Parliament'.[6] The response was that this was a possibility we had accepted on joining the Community. Most speakers were sympathetic to the Government's efforts to argue against the European Commission's case in the Court while accepting the need to comply with the judgment.

Of the eight longest debates on affirmative resolutions during the session (seven of at least an hour in length and another lasting fifty-nine minutes) five dealt with Northern Ireland.

[6] HL Debs., 25 Oct. 1989, col. 1451.

That is a much higher proportion than Northern Ireland orders represented as a proportion of the total (twenty-five out of 120). The length of the Northern Ireland debates reflected the absence of primary legislation dealing with the province; it did not reflect the presence of Ulster Unionist peers, because there were no such peers. Several of these longer debates were on items that made an annual appearance on the House's programme and could be said to have been embarked on with a certain weariness by peers.

Among these annual occasions are the various instruments needed to provide Northern Ireland with money. In March 1989 the Lords debated the Appropriation (NI) Order under which supplementary estimates for the province were approved as well as the vote-on-account for the forthcoming financial year. The debate was opened by Lord Lyell, who set out in some detail the financial provisions contained in the Order. He was followed by Lord Prys-Davies, for the Opposition, who argued that the instrument should have been discussed by the directly elected representatives of the people of Northern Ireland: 'I fear that the best we can do in your Lordships' House is to raise a number of issues.'[7] This he proceeded to do. After three other peers, including Lord Fitt, the former Social Democratic and Labour MP for Belfast West, had spoken, Lord Lyell replied with a series of detailed answers to the points raised.

The impression conveyed by the debate is of serious and careful coverage of the issues, as well as a general consideration of the problems of Northern Ireland. This raises an interesting point of contrast between the way the House deals with 'mainland' and Northern Ireland money. As regards the former, Consolidated Fund Bills go through the Lords on the nod, whereas in the Commons they provide a wide-ranging opportunity for debate. In the case of money for Northern Ireland the Lords seem to follow the Commons pattern of using the occasion to debate general issues with none of the constraints that normally apply where the granting of money is concerned.

Two days later the House debated Northern Ireland again when Regulations and an Order extending the Emergency Provisions Acts were considered. On this occasion the Opposition

[7] HL Debs., 13 Mar. 1989, col. 54.

were more critical of the Government's policies. Lord Graham of Edmonton argued that the Government had not done enough to find a political solution to the problems of Northern Ireland, though he indicated that the Opposition would not seek to divide the House. Lord Bonham-Carter for the Social and Liberal Democrats revealed a certain weariness in beginning his speech: 'It is with some melancholy, I suppose, that I join in this annual ritual.'[8] He supported the renewal of the provisions, as did Lord Fitt, who argued that criticism of the Government for not doing more to find a political solution was unfair. At the end Lord Lyell replied to what he described, with perhaps a little hyperbole, as 'a fascinating debate'.

The air of inevitability about the cycle of Northern Ireland delegated legislation was remarked upon also in June when the Order extending the provisions of the 1974 Northern Ireland Act was debated. This Order was necessary to extend direct rule for a further year, and in moving it Lord Lyell observed that this was the fifteenth occasion on which the House had been asked to do this. The House debated this Order for over an hour and then moved straight on to a further hour and a quarter on an Appropriation Order for Northern Ireland.

Two other debates on affirmative resolutions are worth mentioning. One dealt with a code of recommendations for the welfare of goats, farmed deer, and sheep. Here was a topic which revealed the expertise of some members of the House. Lady Kinloss was able to praise her daughter's success as a goat-keeper, while Viscount Massereene and Ferrard made no attempt to hide his expertise: 'I have written on this subject, and with due respect I know a lot about it.'[9] Lord Houghton of Sowerby spoke as a long-time campaigner for animal welfare. Lord Northfield pointed to a number of what he regarded as loopholes in the codes and went on: 'However, this Chamber and the other place has no opportunity to amend and put right these loopholes. That is a ridiculous way for Parliament to proceed.'[10] He went on to suggest that a better procedure would be for such matters to be examined by a committee in the same way as was done with European secondary legislation. However, he was not optimistic

[8] HL Debs., 15 Mar. 1989, col. 311.
[9] HL Debs., 23 Feb. 1989, col. 819.
[10] Ibid., col. 825.

that this would be done: 'I have made this point before and have almost given up making it because the House does not like to listen to reforms of procedure of that sort.'[11]

In May 1989 the House debated an order extending the existing arrangements for the starting and ending of summer time. Viscount Mountgarret moved an amendment to leave out the entire wording and replace it with a statement that the House declined to proceed further until a Home Office document on the subject had been issued. He objected to making arrangements for three years ahead rather than one, thereby pre-empting the contents of the Home Office paper. The debate lasted only thirty-seven minutes, but that was sufficient for seven peers to speak and for Lord Mountgarret to make a brief final speech withdrawing his amendment. This was the only occasion during the session on which an amendment was moved to a motion to approve an affirmative order.

Occasionally an affirmative resolution which looks relatively uncontroversial can produce an impassioned speech from a backbencher. Two orders which were taken together in April 1989 are a case in point. One raised the permitted maximum that could be spent by candidates in United Kingdom or European elections while the other raised the deposit for candidates in European elections. In both cases the increases were broadly in line with inflation and the matter had been agreed beforehand by the two main parties. This did not prevent Lord Houghton of Sowerby from speaking at length against what he described as 'a shocking proposal to put before the House during the supper break'.[12] He argued that the proposed increase in deposits was unfair to small parties, especially the Green Party, and that the issue was too important to be dealt with during the supper break. In a debate lasting forty-two minutes, Lord Houghton spoke for thirty-five minutes.

Under the Standing Orders of the Lords, debates on affirmative resolutions are not held until the instrument in question has been reported on by the Joint Committee on Statutory Instruments. In that respect the procedure of the Lords was described by the chairman of the Joint Committee (himself a

[11] Ibid.
[12] HL Debs., 6 Apr. 1989, col. 1255.

member of the Commons) as better than that of the Commons.[13] It is true that the Lords Standing Order can, by agreement of the House, be dispensed with if necessary, but it never was during the 1988–9 session.

On a great many affirmative resolutions during the session, debate was not only brief but extremely courteous. Often the Opposition expressed themselves as in agreement with the instruments in question. Sometimes there were a few polite questions and the questioners often appeared grateful for the clarifications which were offered. Ministerial replies were full of promises to write to peers to clear up details, sometimes coupled with a degree of uncertainty on the part of the ministerial respondent: 'Should I not be correct in this instance I will, as he suggests, write to him.'[14]

Occasionally, however, even lordly courtesies cannot disguise the depth of dissatisfaction with a Government response. On an order relating to the Monopolies and Mergers Commission, Lord Williams of Elvel said that it was only the convention that draft orders were not divided against that prevented him from taking such action. He went on to warn the minister: 'if this draft is put into final form and promulgated as such I intend to move amendments to the Companies Bill to nullify the two provisions that the statutory instrument sets out.'[15]

Having looked at the way the Lords dealt with affirmative resolutions during 1988–9 and before turning to negative resolutions, we should examine briefly a subspecies of affirmative instruments known as hybrid instruments.

Hybrid Instruments

While in most respects the two Houses have similar procedures for the scrutiny of delegated legislation, the concept of a 'hybrid instrument' is unique to the Lords. It thus provides the basis for a distinctive Lords contribution to the scrutiny of certain instruments.

[13] Third Commonwealth Conference, Proceedings, 4.
[14] HL Debs., 6 Feb. 1989, col. 1379.
[15] HL Debs., 26 Feb. 1989, col. 853.

The term 'hybrid' is borrowed from the public bill procedure of both Houses, in which a 'hybrid bill' is a public bill which is considered to affect specific private or local interests, and which is accordingly subject in certain respects to private bill procedure, in particular the procedure whereby petitioners against a bill may be heard by a select committee.

Similarly, House of Lords Private Business Standing Order 216 provides that the Chairman of Committees may report that an affirmative instrument 'is such that, apart from the provisions of the Act authorising it to be made, it would require to be enacted by a Private or Hybrid Bill'. Such an instrument is known as a hybrid instrument. Within fourteen days after the report of the Chairman of Committees is laid before the House, petitions may be deposited against a hybrid instrument. Such petitions are considered by the Hybrid Instruments Committee. The Committee decides whether a petitioner has *locus standi* and if so whether there ought to be a further inquiry by a select committee into all or any of the matters complained of. No motion to approve a hybrid instrument may be moved until the special procedures applying to such an instrument have been completed.[16]

During the 1988–9 session seventeen[17] affirmative instruments were reported by the Chairman of Committees as being hybrid. A further two instruments reported as hybrid in the previous session were considered during the session.

Seventeen of the nineteen hybrid instruments related to Urban Development Corporations. The first two such instruments to be considered concerned the Bristol Development Corporation. One of these had been laid during the 1987–8 session; its purpose was to set up an Urban Development Corporation covering an area of 1,050 acres to the south-east of the centre of Bristol. It was opposed by Bristol City Council in a petition which was referred to a select committee in the 1987–8 session. The committee began its inquiry on 11 October 1988 and sat for nine days to hear evidence and submissions, and on a further two days to consider its report. The committee also visited Bristol. The

[16] Certain exceptions to these general provisions are set out in Private Business Standing Orders 216 and 216A.

[17] The Magistrates' Courts (Remands in Custody) Order 1989 was withdrawn and a new instrument with the same title was laid. The two versions were both reported as hybrid but have not been counted separately.

committee's report, of sixty-two paragraphs, made in November 1988,[18] recommended that the principle of an Urban Development Corporation for the area should be accepted, but that four sites originally proposed for designation, about 140 acres in all, should be excluded. The Government accepted the committee's recommendations and accordingly on 12 December 1988 laid an amending order to give effect to the changes proposed by the committee. This order too was declared hybrid, but on 13 December 1988 the House agreed without debate to a motion to dispense with hybrid instrument procedure, so as to enable the committee's recommendations to be put into effect without delay.[19] Both orders were approved in the course of a dinner-hour debate of just under forty minutes on 19 December 1988.[20]

The other fifteen hybrid instruments relating to Urban Development Corporations were all similar in kind, having as their purpose the vesting in Urban Development Corporations of land owned by other public bodies. Eleven of them, none of which had been petitioned against, were approved together in a quarter-hour debate beginning in the early hours of 12 July 1989. The only speakers—perhaps not surprisingly in view of the time—were the minister (the Earl of Arran, a Lord in Waiting) and the Opposition spokesman (Lord Graham of Edmonton).[21] Another three similar instruments were approved together on 27 July 1989 in a ten-minute debate in which the same two Lords were again the only speakers.[22] This time one of the instruments, the Black Country Development Corporation (Vesting of Land) (British Railways Board) Order 1989, had been the subject of a petition by the British Railways Board. But the petition was said to have been 'quickly withdrawn following further negotiations between the corporation and British Rail'.[23]

The last of the hybrid instruments relating to Urban Development Corporations, the London Docklands Development Corporation (Vesting of Land) (London Borough of Southwark)

[18] HL Paper 113, session 1987–8.
[19] HL Debs., 13 Dec. 1988, cols. 827–8.
[20] HL Debs., 19 Dec. 1988, cols. 1187–96.
[21] HL Debs., 11 July 1989, cols. 244–9.
[22] HL Debs., 27 July 1989, cols. 1634–7. The debate began just after 4 p.m. on a day (the last before the summer recess) on which the House sat at 11 a.m.
[23] The Earl of Arran, HL Debs., 27 July 1989, col. 1634.

Order 1989, was laid on 14 June 1989 but its consideration by the House was not completed during the 1988–9 session. It was the subject of a petition from the London Borough of Southwark, and the Hybrid Instruments Committee reported that the petition disclosed substantial grounds of complaint and that 'there ought to be a further inquiry by a Select Committee into the matters complained of'.[24] On the penultimate day of the session the House accordingly agreed that the Order should be referred to a select committee.[25] In the event no select committee was ever appointed. On 1 March 1990 the House agreed to a motion moved by the Chairman of Committees to refer the matter back to the Hybrid Instruments Committee.[26] On 20 March 1990 the Committee reported that there should not now be a further inquiry by a select committee, as the main ground of the petition—that the Order pre-empted a public inquiry to be held in connection with a planning appeal—had in the meantime been dealt with by the completion of the appeal proceedings.[27] The Order was approved on 22 May 1990.[28]

The other two hybrid instruments considered during the 1988–9 session were the Laganside Development (Northern Ireland) Order 1988 (laid during the 1987–8 session) and the Magistrates' Courts (Remands in Custody) Order 1989.

The first of these had as its purpose the establishment, and the granting of powers to, a new authority, the Laganside Corporation, to 'promote and market development opportunities for the riverside area of Belfast known as Laganside'.[29] The Order was the subject of petitions from two groups, but the Hybrid Instruments Committee decided that neither had a *locus standi*;[30] hence the Order was not considered by a select committee. It was approved on 21 February 1989 after a forty-minute debate.[31]

The purpose of the Magistrates' Courts Order was to introduce

[24] 2nd Report from the Hybrid Instruments Committee, 24 July 1989 (HL Paper 79), agreed to by the House on 9 Nov. 1989 (HL Debs., col. 948).
[25] HL Debs., 15 Nov. 1989, col. 1319.
[26] HL Debs., cols. 833–4.
[27] 1st Report from the Hybrid Instruments Committee, Session 1989–90 (HL Paper 42).
[28] HL Debs., cols. 827–30.
[29] Lord Lyell, HL Debs., 21 Feb. 1989, col. 591.
[30] HL Journals, vol. 222, 62 (20 Dec. 1988).
[31] HL Debs., 21 Feb. 1989, cols. 591–600.

provision for extended remands in custody (twenty-eight days instead of eight) on an experimental basis in certain areas. Its hybridity arose from the fact that it applied only to certain named localities. However, no petitions were presented against it. Nevertheless, when it was debated the Opposition spokesman, Lord Mishcon, stated that only convention prevented the Opposition dividing the House against it.[32]

It is difficult to assess the value of the hybrid instrument procedure on the basis of the limited number of instances described above. But it is noteworthy that in one case—that of the Bristol Corporation orders—the proceedings in the House of Lords led to a change in the Government's proposals. That is more than can be said for any other affirmative instrument which came before the House during the session.

Prayers

During the session 1988–9 there were only three motions moved for the annulment of delegated legislation. In each case the debate took place during the 'dinner break' of approximately one hour around 7 p.m. In two cases the debates were accommodated comfortably within this period but in the third the debate overran the scheduled slot by some forty minutes.

In each case the prayer was moved by an Opposition peer and the aim was very largely to secure a short debate on the topic rather than to achieve specific concessions. In all three cases the topics were of considerable political visibility: the national curriculum debate in education, the consequences of water privatization, and the introduction of new contracts for doctors and pharmacists.

Of the three debates, that dealing with the national science curriculum was the shortest and best humoured. The prayer was moved by Lord Peston, an Opposition front-bencher and a professor of economics, who was at pains to indicate at the outset that he had no intention of pushing the issue to a vote and that there was much in both the science order and that dealing with mathematics of which he approved. His criticisms were a mixture

[32] HL Debs., 5 June 1989, col. 652.

of the specific, for example, that in the maths order 'there is a reference to vector notation but no reference at all to matrices',[33] and the more general, for example, that the science curriculum did not prescribe a sufficiently high standard, that it was insufficiently theoretical and so on. In addition there were more general worries about the shortage of science teachers and the lack of up-to-date textbooks. Lord Peston was worried too about procedures: 'Let us suppose that during a debate such as this, one or other noble Member by some miracle makes a good point about the curriculum . . . it is not obvious how the curriculum can be modified.'[34] Apart from the minister who replied to the motion, the only other speaker was Earl Russell, a Social and Liberal Democrat peer and a professor of history, who generally welcomed the new curriculum but had reservations about the pace of implementation and about the shortage of science teachers.

The reply for the Government was as courteous as the rest of the debate appears to have been. Viscount Davidson used some of the standard responses of ministers in such debates, for example, that he would reply by letter to some of Lord Peston's detailed points after he had studied the Hansard report of the debate, and that matters would be kept under review. He even went so far as to answer a question which Lord Peston had not asked but which before the debate he had said that he was going to ask. 'I have a feeling he forgot.'[35] This concerned the date for publication of the national curriculum proposals for English. Here as elsewhere, the debate was probably useful in getting a number of points on to the public record. When the debate ended with the withdrawal of the prayer, it had lasted just forty-six minutes.

The next prayer was moved in July when fifteen sets of regulations were the subject of a combined motion. They dealt with various aspects of the implementation of water privatization and covered such controversial matters as the code of practice on environmental and recreational matters, the quality of drinking-water, and the various timetables for compliance. In moving the motion for annulment, Lord McIntosh of Haringey indicated that

[33] HL Debs., 2 May 1989, col. 79.
[34] Ibid., col. 82. [35] Ibid., col. 89.

he did not propose to make a long speech on the contents of the regulations though 'if I did so we could readily fill up not only the dinner hour but also the rest of the evening's business'.[36] Rather his concern was a procedural one and a follow-up to his having, unusually, moved a reasoned amendment at the third reading stage of the Water Bill. Essentially his complaint was that the fifteen orders in question had not been available in final draft form when the Bill was going through the House: 'However, the moment that the Bill received the Royal Assent, 15 orders were placed by the Secretary of State covering the very matters to which I referred in my reasoned amendment.'[37] That meant, Lord McIntosh argued, that the Bill was 'in very material aspects a hollow Bill: it provides for regulations but does not tell the House what they will be'.[38] Moreover, as he went on to argue, some of the regulations were now being prayed against only because the Bill had been amended in the Lords so as to make certain regulations subject to the negative procedure.

Lord McIntosh was followed by Lord Shaughnessy, a member of the Joint Committee on Statutory Instruments, who in a very brief speech endorsed Lord McIntosh's criticisms and went on to say: 'It is extraordinary that with legislation of this magnitude and importance, the regulations should have been found by our committee to be defective in at least three instances.'[39] Three other peers spoke before the Earl of Caithness replied for the Government. All three were critical of the regulations either on procedural grounds or on points of detail. Lord Caithness did his best to defend the Government's position, suggesting that their record was better than Labour's had been when they were in office. He acknowledged the Joint Committee's criticisms and indicated that amended regulations would be brought forward to three of the fifteen instruments. Lord Shaughnessy intervened in the speech to suggest that pushing through the orders so quickly had resulted in anomalies.

Lord McIntosh in withdrawing his motion emphasized that he did so because the orders had already been approved by the Commons: 'it is an established procedure of this House, . . . that we do not seek to divide on a Motion to annul orders that have

[36] HL Debs., 24 July 1989, col. 1195.
[37] Ibid. [38] Ibid., col. 1196. [39] Ibid., col. 1199.

already been approved by another place.'[40] He lamented the fact that the orders had to be accepted or rejected as a whole, without any possibility of amendment. He suggested that virtually none of the criticisms which had been made had been answered and went on: 'It is a pity that the minister thought fit to reply to the serious criticisms that have been made of the form and content of the regulations in the way that he did. It is not worthy of him or of the House.'[41]

This debate lasted forty-nine minutes and seven peers spoke. On the next prayer, moved just before the end of the session in November, nine peers spoke in a debate lasting exactly 100 minutes. The topic on this occasion was the new contracts proposed for, or (as the critics would put it) being imposed on, doctors and pharmacists. The debate was interesting not only because, as already noted, it lasted longer than the business managers expected but because, apart from the minister's speech, all who spoke were critical of the changes.

Lord Ennals, who moved the motion to annul the order in question, began by asking the minister the disconcerting question whether the order contained drafting errors. The minister was clearly unprepared for this, 'I confess the noble Lord has taken me somewhat by surprise.'[42] As in the prayer on the national curriculum it was made clear at the outset that there would be no division at the end of the debate. The reason for the debate, Lord Ennals suggested, was that the Opposition 'felt that it would be wrong to allow the regulations to go through your Lordships' House without critical comment on the Government's handling of the nation's general practitioners.'[43] He had a number of criticisms, notably that the new contracts had been imposed on doctors against their wishes, that this had been done crudely by the Secretary of State, and that public money had been spent by the Government to publicize their side of the argument. Others who spoke echoed these criticisms or had other points of detail about which they were unhappy. One reason for the absence of support for the Government's position was alluded to in Lord Ennals's closing remarks when he pointed out that there had been only one Conservative back-bench peer present during the debate.

[40] Ibid., col. 1206. [41] Ibid., col. 1208.
[42] HL Debs., 9 Nov. 1989, col. 1022. [43] Ibid.

Baroness Hooper was the somewhat lonely minister whose job it was to defend the Government's conduct in this matter. She denied any knowledge of the alleged drafting errors and proceeded to defend the Government's conduct in a speech lasting almost twenty minutes. One has the impression that the temperature never rose in this debate as high as it did in the debate on the water privatization orders. More heat was certainly generated when the House considered a Church of England Measure.

Measures

Under the Church of England Assembly (Powers) Act 1919 secondary legislation known as Measures requires the approval of both Houses of Parliament. Such items appear as constitutional oddities but they can arouse great interest and passion in the upper House. Of the delegated legislation considered by the Lords during 1988–9, none created so much interest as the Clergy (Ordination) Measure which was debated for over three hours in July 1989. This was twice as long as the longest debate on an affirmative or a negative motion. Moreover, the number of peers participating, twenty-two, was far more than in the most popular affirmative motion debate (eight peers) or debate on a prayer (nine peers).

The motion to approve the Measure was moved by the Archbishop of Canterbury, who set out its aim: 'to permit a variation, in exceptional circumstances, to the general rule that no person may be ordained who has married a divorcee or has himself or herself been married after a divorce in the lifetime of a previous partner'.[44] He pointed out that the measure had been approved by all three Houses of the General Synod (the Church's own parliament) by what he described as 'substantial majorities'.

The opposition to the Measure was led by the Earl of Lauderdale who moved an amendment to adjourn the debate until the anomaly between the position of candidates for ordination and those already ordained had been corrected 'to ensure that no beneficed clergyman who is divorced, or has married a divorcee while a former partner of either is living, may continue to minister'.[45]

[44] HL Debs., 3 July 1989, col. 1012.

[45] Ibid., col. 1016.

The Earl put a quite different interpretation on the level of support for the Measure in the Synod, suggesting it fell short of the two-thirds majority which he felt was required. He pointed out that the Ecclesiastical Committee (a body composed of fifteen peers and fifteen MPs) had passed the Measure by only a single vote, ten to nine with one abstention. At the heart of his impassioned speech was a plea 'not to ignore the laity' and to have a priesthood who commanded respect.

The next speaker, Lord Bridge of Harwich, a serving law lord, had given advice to the Ecclesiastical Committee. He pronounced himself happy with the Measure and suggested the idea of turning the clock back implied by the amendment 'would be wholly unacceptable to public opinion, either in the Church of England or in the country at large'.[46] He went on to argue that it would be wrong for the House to block a measure which was concerned with theology and doctrine if it had been properly passed by the Church's own elected body. This last point was echoed by a number of others who spoke. Lord Nugent of Guildford, for example, thought the two sides of the argument evenly balanced, but went on: 'It seems to me that the decision in this case should lie within the judgment of the General Synod and that we in Parliament ought not to argue it all over again.'[47]

Other speakers for the most part supported approval of the Measure. Lord Hailsham of Saint Marylebone, for example, described Lord Lauderdale's amendment as 'utterly misguided'. The Marquess of Salisbury, on the other hand, supported the amendment because he thought the Measure's effect would be a lowering of general standards among the clergy. Lord Soper supported the Archbishop of Canterbury, arguing that 'The House does not of necessity possess the expertise and experience which would be required to make a formal and final judgment on a moral issue.'[48]

Some peers confessed themselves unhappy with the main motion but unable to support the amendment. Viscount Caldecote (who chaired the committee which in 1990 advised the Prime Minister on the appointment of the Archbishop of Canterbury) was in that position; he said he would listen carefully to the

[46] Ibid., col. 1022. [47] Ibid., col. 1032. [48] Ibid., col. 1030.

winding-up speeches before deciding how to vote. The Earl of Halsbury's solution to the same dilemma was to suggest both motion and amendment be withdrawn. Lord Halsbury reflected also another strand in the debate, that of the simple churchgoer confused by, and suspicious of, the leaders of the Church. He confessed that he had been pressed by Lord Lauderdale to participate in the debate, but had been reluctant because 'I felt sure that most of the legalistic arguments would be above my head. Having listened to them, I find that they are.'[49]

Several of those who spoke were Lords members of the Ecclesiastical Committee. One of these, Lord Robertson of Oakridge, explained why he would not vote against the Measure, though he had done so in the Committee. He did not believe it was his place to challenge the Synod on matters of doctrine, and his earlier opposition had been purely procedural, because at that time there were no guidelines available on how the two Archbishops would exercise the discretion given to them in the Measure.

The Government did not take a position and the concluding speeches came instead from the same peers who had opened the debate: the Archbishop of Canterbury and Lord Lauderdale. Apart from the Archbishop only one other bishop spoke.

At the end of the debate, Lord Lauderdale withdrew his amendment, while taking some pleasure in the amount of interest created by the debate: 'The best part of 100 Peers have listened to the debate. There are about seventy Peers in the Chamber at this moment, and this at nine o'clock at night for what was expected to go through on the nod in the dinner hour.'[50] The chief lesson which emerged from the debate, he suggested, was that the episcopate should pay more attention to what he called 'the inarticulate, stupid, slow-on-the-uptake Back-Bench pew men'.[51] Clearly the topic was one which had aroused a great deal of interest and provided a debate of considerable impact.

When the Measure was debated in the Commons two weeks later it was rejected 51–45. The debate began just after 2 a.m. and ended just after 3.30 a.m. In moving approval of the Measure, the Second Church Estates Commissioner, Michael Alison, referred several times to the Lords debate, notably to the speeches of the Bishop of Guildford and the Archbishop of Canterbury.

[49] Ibid., col. 1041. [50] Ibid., col. 1053. [51] Ibid., col. 1054.

The outcome of the Commons vote raised questions about the appropriateness of a group of MPs deciding on a theological matter for the Church of England and about the arbitrariness of fifty-one MPs deciding it at 3.30 in the morning. By comparison, the self-restraint of the Lords appears rather more defensible. The Measure was eventually approved by the Commons in the following session on 20 February 1990.

Joint Committee on Statutory Instruments

So far our consideration of delegated legislation has been concerned largely with its treatment on the floor of the Lords. More numerous than the instruments discussed in the Chamber are those considered by the Joint Committee on Statutory Instruments. Perhaps the very nature of its work means that it has acquired the reputation of being a worthy but unexciting committee, so that even its own chairman could say: 'The Joint Committee on Statutory Instruments is one of the more obscure, completely unglamorous, but very important Committees for which Members make sacrifices.'[52] Continuing in this self-depreciating way, he went on to describe the work of his committee as 'extremely drab'.[53]

The Committee is of relatively recent origin, dating only from 1973. Prior to that the Lords and Commons each had their own select committees. The Joint Committee consists of seven members from each House, by convention chaired by an Opposition MP.

The Joint Committee has power to deal with almost all orders or instruments that are laid before Parliament under the affirmative or negative procedures, as well as those not requiring any parliamentary action and those not required to be laid before Parliament at all. The only exceptions, apart from those financial instruments that are considered only by the Commons, are certain Orders in Council (or draft orders) made under the Northern Ireland Act 1974 and Church of England Measures.

The Joint Committee is concerned with technicalities and not with the merits of an instrument or the policy behind it. As we

[52] Third Commonwealth Conference, Proceedings, 2. [53] Ibid. 3.

Table 5.3. *Delegated legislation considered by the Joint Committee, 1988–9*

Procedure applicable	No.
Instruments requiring affirmative approval	130 (includes draft instruments)
Instruments subject to negative procedure	868 (includes draft instruments)
General Instruments (laid before Parliament)	50
General Instruments (not laid before Parliament)	253
Special Procedure Orders	5
TOTAL	1,306

Source: House of Commons Sessional Returns 1988–9, House, Committees of the Whole House, Standing Committees and Select Committees, HC 110 (1989–90).

have seen, debates in the House do concern themselves with such matters. Among the grounds on which the Joint Committee is empowered to draw the attention of the two Houses to an instrument are that 'it imposes a charge on the public revenues . . . ; it is made in pursuance of any enactment containing specific provisions excluding it from challenge in the courts . . . ; it purports to have retrospective effect . . . ; there appears to have been unjustifiable delay in its publication . . . ; that there appears to be a doubt about whether it is *intra vires* or that it appears to make some unusual or unexpected use of the powers conferred by the statute under which it is made; that for any special reason its form or purport calls for elucidation; that its drafting appears to be defective; or on any other ground which does not impinge on its merits or on the policy behind it.'[54]

As Table 5.3 indicates, the Joint Committee considered a substantial volume of delegated legislation during the 1988–9 session. The Committee met on thirty-one occasions during the session: in effect, every Tuesday afternoon at 4.15 p.m. when the House was sitting (except on Budget day). After each meeting it

[54] The terms of reference are set out in Minutes of Proceedings of the Joint Committee on Statutory Instruments, 1988–89, HL 10 (of 1989–90), 2.

Table 5.4. *Grounds on which instruments reported by Joint Committee, 1988–9*

Ground[a]	No.
Drafting appears to be defective	57
Form or purport calls for elucidation	36
Doubt concerning vires	29
Other grounds	15
TOTALS	137

[a] An instrument may be reported on more than one ground.

Source: House of Commons Sessional Returns 1988–9, House, Committees of the Whole House, Standing Committees and Select Committees, HC 110 (1989–90).

issued a report drawing the attention of both parent Houses to instruments which it felt gave grounds for concern. Of the instruments which it examined, only a fairly small proportion were the subject of such reports. The grounds on which it drew attention to instruments are summarized in Table 5.4. Those reports are made to both Houses and it is then up to each House to decide what use to make of them.

In their work the Joint Committee have the assistance of two individuals: the Counsel to the Chairman of Committees in the House of Lords (since 1977 Mr D. Rippengal) and the Counsel to Mr Speaker (since 1985, Mr H. Knorpel). During the session in question the former looked after affirmative procedure instruments and the latter those amenable to the negative procedure.[55] A great deal of the work of the Joint Committee is dependent on the prior work of these two individuals. As the Chairman put it, 'Mr Rippengal and Mr Knorpel report to us and the Committee decides what is reported to Parliament.'[56]

One might expect the Lords members of the Joint Committee who lack some of the pressures of work experienced by Commons members to be more assiduous in their attendance. At least as far as 1988–9 was concerned this was not the case. As Table 5.5 indicates, the attendance by peers at the Joint Committee was less good than that of MPs.

[55] Third Commonwealth Conference, Proceedings, 3. [56] Ibid.

Table 5.5. *Attendance at meetings of Joint Committee, 1988–9*

Lords members	No.	Commons members	No.
Lord Airedale	25	Richard Alexander	26
Baroness Blatch	13	Rosie Barnes	0
Lord Boston of Faversham	18	Andrew Bennett	21
Lord Brooks of Tremorfa	26	William Cash	10
Lord Cullen of Ashbourne	11	Bob Cryer	25
Viscount Dilhorne	0	Timothy Kirkhope	26
Lord Shaughnessy	22	David Martin	17
TOTAL	115		125

Source: Minutes of Proceedings of the Joint Committee on Statutory Instruments, Session 1988–89 (HL Paper 10 (1989–90); HC 637 (1988–9)). The figures for MPs' attendances differ slightly from those given in the House of Commons Return of Committee attendances.

The figures indicate that attendance patterns among the peers vary considerably: three were fairly regular attenders, three attended moderately well, while one peer failed to attend a single meeting. In one sense attendance is not crucial: 'In general party differences do not arise in the Joint Committee.' Moreover, 'No votes are taken, because discussion continues until agreement is reached.'[57] Nevertheless it appears from the figures in Table 5.5 as though the bulk of the Committee's work is done by only half its members, if one defines those who attended at least two-thirds of the meetings as the core of the work-force.[58]

The Committee's terms of reference require 'that, before reporting that the special attention of the House be drawn to any instrument, the Committee do afford to any Government department concerned the opportunity of furnishing orally or in writing to them or to any subcommittee of the Committee such explanations as the department think fit'.[59] (It is relevant here to note that whereas primary legislation is drafted by parliamentary counsel, statutory instruments are drafted by departmental lawyers.) The Joint Committee does the bulk of its work on the

[57] Ibid.

[58] As with all parliamentary committtees, attendance records must be treated with caution. Some members attend for the whole of a meeting, others for little longer than is necessary to have the clerk record them as present.

basis of written evidence; during the 1988–9 session it received 318 written memoranda, all from Government departments.

At only four of its meetings in 1988–9 was oral evidence taken, in each case from civil servants. On the first of these occasions, officials from the Health and Safety Executive were questioned about the Control of Substances Hazardous to Health (COSHH) Regulations and the Quarries (Explosives) Regulations. In April 1989 officials from the Department of the Environment were questioned about Air Quality Standards Regulations, while civil servants from the Department of Transport faced questions on Civil Aviation Regulations. In June officials from the Treasury and the Home Office were asked about regulations dealing with returning officers' expenses; while in July it was the Department of the Environment again to answer on regulations following the privatization of water. The questioning tends to be brisk and businesslike with little of the elaborate courtesies which are apparent with evidence given at some other parliamentary committees.

The fact that oral evidence is called for is itself an indication that the Committee are not happy over some aspects of the regulations in question. On the COSHH regulations a good deal of the questioning was concerned with whether the new regulations were more permissive than some parts of earlier acts that they replaced. Sometimes the Committee has quick success: on the Water Supply and Reorganization Regulations the civil servants were frank in their acknowledgement of errors. On a regulation dealing with standards of service to the customer, the witness accepted that following representations from the Committee amending regulations would be introduced; while the next question relating to the transfer of pensions rights was met by the admission that the intention was not reflected accurately in the regulation. When the Chairman then asked, 'So you are embarking on further amendments?' the reply was 'I am afraid we are, yes.'[60]

At each session of oral evidence the questioning was relatively brief: over the four occasions eight orders were dealt with and

[59] Minutes of Proceedings of the Joint Committee on Statutory Instruments (HL 10), 3.

[60] Joint Committee on Statutory Instruments, Minutes of Evidence, 18 July 1989 (HL 74), Q. 50.

Table 5.6. *Questions by members of the Joint Committee at evidence-taking*

Member	No.
Bob Cryer	60
Andrew Bennett	28
William Cash	18
Robert Alexander	10
Timothy Kirkhope	7
Lord Airedale	5
Lord Boston of Faversham	1
TOTAL	129

only 129 questions in all were asked. The questioning was very much dominated by the MP in the chair, who over the four sessions of evidence taking was responsible for seventy-one of the 129 questions asked, or 55 per cent of the total. The distribution of questions is set out in Table 5.6. These figures indicate that only half the members of the Joint Committee actually asked questions at the evidence-taking sessions. Of the questioners only two were peers and between them they accounted for only six questions or less than 5 per cent of those asked.

Primary v. Secondary Legislation

There are three main issues which arise from the way in which primary legislation is framed but which it is worth mentioning briefly here because they have an impact on delegated legislation. First is the tendency of Governments to produce what they would call framework bills but what one of their critics was quoted in the previous chapter as calling 'empty shell' bills. Second is the argument about whether the subsequent fleshing out of such skeletal legislation should be subject to affirmative or negative procedures or indeed to any parliamentary procedures at all. The third area of concern is the tendency of governments to include what are known as 'Henry VIII' clauses in primary legislation, that is clauses which permit primary legislation to be amended by subsequent secondary legislation.

The concern about the tendency to produce legislation in which a great deal of the detail was left to be filled in later has already been referred to in the previous two chapters. Nowhere was this more apparent than in the case of the ill-fated Football Spectators Bill where the crucial elements of the scheme were not in the bill at all. A similar accusation, it will be recalled, was made against the Children Bill. There is an obvious conflict here between the understandable desire not to overload primary legislation with too much detail and the danger that such legislation will be meaningless if all the crucial detail is left to be filled in later.

That danger is exacerbated by the recognition that such details may be subject to only limited parliamentary scrutiny. In part this arises from the obvious difficulty Parliament has in coping with delegated legislation; in part also because such legislation, if it is subject to some parliamentary process, can only be accepted or rejected and not amended.

This leads to the second concern outlined above, namely that there is a tendency for Governments to pitch the level of scrutiny lower than may be desirable. The tendency for departments to avoid the affirmative procedure if they can was confirmed in a discussion at the Third Commonwealth Conference on Delegated Legislation by Mr Rippengal. Speaking of his previous work in Government departments he said: 'I have had some experience at the production end of Acts of Parliament, and it was that if there was any doubt about what procedure to go for as between affirmative and negative, the Departments rather naturally went for the negative and waited to see how matters developed.'[61]

As is pointed out in the previous chapter, this issue arose on a number of bills during the 1988–9 session. The Children Bill was amended at third reading to make certain powers exercised by the Secretary of State subject to the affirmative procedure rather than the negative procedure. On the Football Spectators Bill there was quite a long debate on the point. Lord Harris of Greenwich moved an amendment at the report stage to make orders made under the bill subject to the same procedure. Lord Boyd-Carpenter argued that this was inappropriate since some would be important and others not: 'The suggestion that every

[61] Third Commonwealth Conference, Proceedings, 58.

one should be put in the affirmative procedure and have to come before both Houses of Parliament quite frankly appals me.'[62] He went on to suggest that in practice the affirmative procedure in the Lords was not much more effective than the negative procedure since 'It is a convention of this House that in general we do not reject affirmative resolutions carried by another place, any more than we tend to accept Prayers for the negative annulment of orders subject to that procedure.'[63] Lord Hesketh indicated that the Government would be unhappy with having the affirmative procedure prescribed, partly because that would increase the likelihood that such orders would be subject to hybridity procedures. As we have seen, if invoked, these could lead to delays. The minister suggested that the Government would accept an amendment to make the orders open to annulment; this promise was sufficient for Lord Harris to withdraw his amendment, and, as described in the previous chapter, this change was made at third reading.

One might expect those items of delegated legislation requiring positive approval from Parliament before they become effective to be the most important. In practice the relationship between importance and type of parliamentary treatment is not always so logical. It is possible to find what appear to be important matters being subject merely to annulment by Parliament or even requiring no parliamentary action at all. Of particular concern here is the tendency of Governments to give themselves powers to amend primary legislation by statutory instrument. On the Children Bill, for example, such powers were described by Lord Simon of Glaisdale (sometime President of the Family Division of the High Court and a former Conservative MP and minister) as 'a constitutional outrage'.[64] Similar powers were complained about on the Companies Bill and the Water Bill.

The issue was discussed also at the Commonwealth Conference on Delegated Legislation. The chairman of the Joint Committee on Statutory Instruments, Bob Cryer MP, pointed out to that gathering that 'in the past 18 months there [have] been 23 primary Acts of Parliament which granted powers to Ministers to change those Acts of Parliament—some of them not even by

[62] HL Debs., 10 Apr. 1989, col. 37.
[63] Ibid.
[64] HL Debs., 20 Dec. 1988, col. 1295.

affirmative resolution approving the instrument itself'.[65] Among those facing questions was one of the legal advisers at the Department of Education and Science, who had perhaps rashly confessed to being responsible for the drafting of the Education Reform Act 1988. Mr Cryer challenged him directly: 'Why did he allow powers to be given to the Secretary of State in the bill to amend that legislation without even the formality of laying an instrument before Parliament?'[66] This state of affairs was criticized also by Mr Knorpel who suggested it might be right to give the Secretary of State powers to amend the legislation, 'but it cannot be reasonable that he should be able to exercise such a power and not have to put his instrument in front of Parliament so that at least it knew what he had done even if there was nothing it could do about it except pass an Act of Parliament to undo it if it did not like it.'[67]

One of the complainants on the Companies Bill about the practice of making primary legislation amendable by secondary legislation was Lord Rippon of Hexham. In the following session he raised the issue in a debate in the Lords. He suggested that a select committee be established to examine bills before they were considered in Parliament and to report on whether they included such types of delegation. During the debate there was a great deal of sympathy for Lord Rippon's complaints. There was considerable agreement that there was little the House could do on delegated legislation. As Lord Diamond put it, 'this House has no control whatever on delegated legislation; negative resolutions mean nothing and affirmative resolutions, for all practical purposes, mean even less than that.'[68] The House of Lords is evidently at something of a loss to know how to cope with this problem.

Conclusion

The issues raised in the debate initiated by Lord Rippon and discussed in the previous section highlight one of the central

[65] Third Commonwealth Conference, Proceedings, 3.
[66] Ibid., 57. [67] Ibid.
[68] HL Debs., 14 Feb. 1990, col. 1414.

dilemmas for the House of Lords as far as delegated legislation is concerned. That dilemma is essentially the choice between accepting that a great deal of the detail cannot be put into primary legislation and will therefore have to be put into secondary legislation where providing adequate scrutiny of it will pose great problems; or demanding that more be put in primary legislation, in which case the burden of that may become intolerable for a House which tries to do a great deal on the floor of the Chamber. In addition, of course, more primary legislation would be needed if fewer details could be changed by statutory instrument.

Part of the problem for the Lords is that politically they are circumscribed in matters of delegated legislation. Although they are formally the equal of the Commons in this area, in practice as we have seen convention is sufficiently strong that there is little that the House can do to block such legislation directly. It is of course possible that more may be achieved indirectly, that, as Shell points out,[69] Governments may be persuaded to have second thoughts. Certainly it is useful that the House can debate, albeit usually briefly, a variety of orders. However as we have seen, most of the time that means that a few questions are answered, a few points clarified, though that may have value in that those answers are then part of the public record.

It is also possible that attempts to amend primary legislation, although unsuccessful, may have an effect on the content of delegated legislation. A hint of that is contained in the remarks of the Lord Chancellor on the third reading of the Children Bill, noted in the previous chapter. It is of course true that in many areas the Lords contains experts and, as Shell notes, those who draft statutory instruments in departments must be aware of the possibility of critical scrutiny in the Lords.

The Joint Committee on Statutory Instruments, as we have seen, beavers diligently at the technicalities of delegated legislation. Such work is undoubtedly worthy, unglamorous, and moderately useful. Perhaps the same could be said for the work of the House of Lords as a whole in this area.

[69] Shell, *House of Lords*, 219.

6

Private Members' Bills

David Natzler and Douglas Millar

Introduction

In this chapter we examine private members' bills in the House of Lords in the 1988–9 session, both those originally introduced in the Lords and those passed by the Commons and sent to the Lords. Table 6.1 suggests that the session was not entirely typical as regards the number of Commons private members' bills reaching the Lords. The session seems to have been more or less typical of recent sessions as regards the number, content, and ultimate fate of private members' bills introduced in the Lords. As Table 6.2 illustrates, the number of such bills introduced has been dropping sharply, and with it the number—although not the proportion—subsequently receiving royal assent. Within this decline, the most significant element is the substantial reduction over the past decade in the number of Lords private members' bills defeated on second reading in the Lords, withdrawn, or not proceeded with. Peers would seem to be pursuing the other opportunities open to them to procure a debate on a particular issue and a Government response, whether by unstarred question or balloted motions, possibly because of the increasing pressure of other business.

The recent fall in the volume of private members' bills introduced in the Lords is less surprising if set in a historical context. Following a relatively active period in the 1920s and 1930s, Bromhead wrote in 1958:

> The past generation has seen a big change in the habits of the Lords regarding the introduction of private members' bills. If we go back only a little way, to the years just before 1939, we find that unofficial peers' bills were fairly numerous—there were generally a dozen or more in each session—and occupied a fair amount of the House's time. . . . The time spent in debating the private members' bills on second reading greatly exceeded the corresponding time spent on the Government's

Table 6.1. *Private members' bills brought from the House of Commons to the House of Lords, 1980–91*

Session	Brought from Commons	Not passed by Lords	Lords amendments not agreed to by Commons	Received royal assent
1980–1	10			10
1981–2	8			8
1982–3	10	2		8
1983–4	11			11
1984–5	17			17
1985–6	17			17
1986–7	12	1		11
1987–8	12	1		11
1988–9	*9*	*1*		*8*
1989–90	12		2	10
1990–1	20	1		19

Sources: House of Lords Public Bill Office sessional statistics; House of Commons sessional returns.

Table 6.2. *Private members' bills introduced in the House of Lords, 1980–91*

Session	Introduced	Not passed by Lords	Passed by Lord but not by Commons	Received royal assent
1980–1	23	15	3	5
1981–2	25	18	5	2
1982–3	21	15	4	2
1983–4	19	8	9	2
1984–5	17	10	3	4
1985–6	13	6	3	4
1986–7	10	4	2	4
1987–8	7	3	2	2
1988–9	*8*	*3*	*4*	*1*
1989–90	10	3	6	1
1990–1	8	1	6	1

Sources: House of Lords Public Bill Office sessional statistics; House of Commons sessional returns.

Lords' bills. Since 1945, however, bills of this type have almost entirely disappeared, and in the whole of the past ten years their total number has hardly exceeded a dozen.[1]

There followed a revival of such bills, culminating in the significant part played by private members' bills introduced in the Lords in the so-called 'permissive society' legislation in the 1966–70 Parliament. It may none the less be worth while to seek some explanation for the relatively modest use made by backbench peers of their unfettered right of legislative initiative, and, conversely, for the decisions made by some peers to pursue legislative remedies even where there is little or no chance of their bill being enacted.

Any member of the House of Lords may present a bill without notice. The first reading is moved immediately on presentation, and is normally agreed to 'without discussion or dissent'.[2] The bill is then immediately printed. There is no formal rationing of the time available for subsequent stages; a peer can therefore reasonably expect that time will be found not only for a second reading of a bill, but also for subsequent stages if it receives a second reading. Unless the bill is unusually controversial[3] it is relatively easy to pass the bill through its remaining stages and have it sent to the Commons. This can even apply when the Government is doubtful about, or openly hostile to, the bill's provisions, since ministers can rely on the effects of the Commons timetable to ensure that a bill passed by the Lords is blocked in the Commons. A single objection after the moment of interruption will normally suffice, thus obviating the risk of forcing a division in the Lords. Most Lords private members' bills which are enacted are therefore what Shell has defined as 'minor measures enjoying the benevolent neutrality (if not open support) of government': fewer are 'significant changes in areas of law where parties traditionally fear to tread'.[4]

That only minimally controversial measures are likely to be

[1] P. A. Bromhead, *The House of Lords and Contemporary Politics* (Routledge & Kegan Paul, London, 1958), 200–1.

[2] Erskine May, *Parliamentary Practice*, 21st edn. (Butterworths, London, 1989), 444.

[3] As e.g. in the case of the Unborn Children (Protection) Bill [HL], discussed below.

[4] Donald Shell, *The House of Lords*, 2nd edn. (Harvester Wheatsheaf, London, 1992), 151.

enacted does not discourage peers from introducing controversial private members' bills. This is, of course, because enactment is far from being the sole purpose of introducing a private member's bill and attempting to pass it through the Lords. Bromhead suggested three possible motives: (*a*) the use of discussion of a bill in the Lords to promote a situation in which an unopposed second reading may be obtained in the Commons; (*b*) giving a measure a trial run, to discover the nature of objection and the attitude of Government; or (*c*) to persuade the Government itself to adopt a measure either immediately or in future legislation.[5] There have been a number of recent examples in all of these categories. A further motive may be the desire of a peer to have a select committee on a certain subject: since 1970, six select committees have been set up by the Lords to examine private members' bills,[6] several of which were followed by successful legislation. Reference to a select committee was for example suggested during debate on the Junior Hospital Doctors (Regulation of Hours) Bill. The introduction of private members' legislation in the Lords can also be used as part of a wider public campaign on a particular issue, where the intention is public education rather than the persuasion of ministers.

In the remainder of this chapter, we briefly describe the timetable and procedures governing private members' bills in the House of Lords, and go on to look at the private members' bills considered by the House during the 1988–9 session. Finally, we make some general observations on Government responses to debates on private members' bills, the role of pressure groups, the reasons for the introduction of private members' bills, and participation in debate.

Timetable

There is no fixed timetable for the consideration of private members' bills in the Lords, nor a particular day or time on which the stages of private members' bills are taken. All are subject to the general provisions which govern the timetabling of

[5] Bromhead, *House of Lords and Contemporary Politics*, 199–200.
[6] See Ch. 10, n. 2. See also Shell, *House of Lords*, 236–40.

business in the House. As a matter of routine, the second reading debate on a private member's bill is often scheduled for a Wednesday evening, but other times and days are found, particularly towards the end of the session, and further stages of such bills are fitted in as convenient. The one firm conclusion is that a private member's bill in the Lords will not normally fail for lack of time for debate.

In contrast to the flexibility of the Lords procedure, proceedings on private members' bills in the Commons follow a much more rigid pattern. The time for private members' legislation in the Commons is structured in accordance with the provisions of Standing Order No. 13,[7] as applied each session by an Order passed by the House soon after the Opening of Parliament.[8] In effect, some twelve (or from session 1989–90 thirteen) Friday sittings are set aside for private members' bills in the Commons and, to make progress, a bill must be considered in that limited time. In the 1988–9 session, second readings of bills took priority on six Fridays between 27 January and 3 March. Bills which had progressed beyond second reading took priority on the six remaining days. Five days for remaining stages were scheduled between 7 April and 5 May, while on 7 July bills which had passed through both Houses, but to which amendments had been made in the Lords, were taken.

The operation of the Commons timetable allows the bills introduced by MPs successful in the ballot to pre-empt the bulk of the time available in the Commons. It effectively precludes bills introduced in the Lords from making progress after they have been sent to the Commons unless they receive a second reading without debate, so that only such bills as are wholly uncontroversial can expect to be passed into law.

The rigidity of the procedures in the Commons also has a number of effects on the way in which Commons private members' bills are dealt with in the House of Lords. First, in practice, all proceedings on bills of any controversy are concentrated between the beginning of April and the end of June: that is, after the timetable in the Commons has allowed bills to complete all their stages there and before the final day in the Commons when any amendments made by the Lords can be considered.

[7] House of Commons SO No. 13 (Arrangement of Public Business).
[8] HC Debs., 24 Nov. 1988, col. 240.

Second, the strict limitation on the time available in the Commons has the effect that it is most unlikely that a bill which is fiercely opposed will be able to complete all its stages in that House. Thus it is probable that the bills which do reach the Lords have general support and are serious candidates for the statute book. The House of Lords, therefore, must undertake its revising role in the expectation that the bills will become law, but also do so within the time constraints described.

The Procedures

The House of Lords procedures governing private members' bills are broadly the same as those governing other public legislation introduced into the Lords. If a bill passes all its stages it is sent to the Commons. The peer in charge of the bill will normally have arranged for a member sympathetic to his cause to 'take up' the bill—that is, to take charge of it, and name a day for second reading. When he does so, by informing the Clerks at the Table of his intentions, the bill is deemed to have been read the first time and is ordered to be printed, and the member will name a day for second reading.[9]

A bill which has passed through all its stages in the Commons (second reading, committee, report, and third reading) is sent from the Commons to the Lords, whereupon it is customarily read the first time and ordered to be printed. The bill must then wait to be taken up by a peer. Any peer may seek to take up a bill; the member who introduced the bill in the Commons normally arranges for a peer sympathetic to the aims of the bill to take charge of it. It may be several days before a peer signifies that he wishes to take charge of a bill and nominate a day for second reading.[10] In practice the peer in charge will seek the agreement of the Government's business managers to the bill being set down for second reading on a particular day.

Since the procedure for passage of all public bills, whether Government or private members', is the same, a private

[9] House of Commons SO No. 58(3).

[10] Under House of Lords SO No. 47, if 12 sitting days elapse between the receipt of a bill from the Commons and notice of second reading being given, the bill may not be further proceeded with except after 8 days' notice of the second reading; see also Erskine May, *Parl. Practice*, 446.

member's bill must pass through all the necessary stages, second reading, committee, report, and third reading. The assumption of the Government business managers is that any bill reaching the Lords after passing through the Commons must be found time within the effective period so that any amendments can be dealt with and the bill receive royal assent before the end of the session. This assumption is borne out by the fact that, since 1958, only ten Commons bills have failed to complete all stages in the Lords and seven of these fell when a general election was called.[11]

Commons Private Members' Bills in the House of Lords in Session 1988–9

In session 1988–9, 137 private members' bills were introduced into the Commons (though only ninety-seven of these were printed). Of them, nine were passed by that House and were sent to, and taken up in, the House of Lords. They are listed in Table 6.3.

How far the exigencies of the Commons timetable control the fortunes of Commons bills can be seen from an analysis of their origins: of the nine, six were ballot bills (presented after the member in charge had won a place in the ballot which gives priority to twenty members to present their bills and to have the first option on the time available for debate). The other three were bills presented subsequently, one of which was presented shortly after the ballot. Only two of them, including the Licensing Amendment (Scotland) Bill, which failed to complete all of its stages in the Lords, were presented much later in the session.

In all, the nine bills were debated for a little more than ten hours in the Lords; almost half of that time was spent on proceedings on the Licensing Amendment (Scotland) Bill, which failed to complete its passage. Six and three-quarter hours were spent on second readings, while the remaining stages lasted less than three and a half hours. By contrast, the time spent in the Commons was much greater, despite the fact that bills which pass the Commons without debate are subject to at least some debate

[11] HC Debs., 12 July 1988, col. 97 (written answers).

Table 6.3. *Private members' bills brought from the House of Commons to the House of Lords in session 1988–9*

	Date intro. HC	No. in ballot	Final stage completed	Pages intro. HC	Pages intro. HL	Pages enacted	HL amdts.	Total time floor of HC (hrs. m.)	Total time HC Stg. Cttee. (hrs. m.)	Total time HL (hrs. m.)
Common Land (Rectification of Registers)	20 Feb.		Royal assent	2	2	2	7	0:49		0:47
Control of Pollution (Amendment)	21 Dec.	5	Royal assent	11	10	10	0	3:43	1:43	1:18
Control of Smoke Pollution	21 Dec.	16	Royal assent	1	1	2	2	4:42		0:33
Dangerous Dogs	4 July		Royal assent	3	3	3	0	0:00		0:39
Disabled Persons (Northern Ireland)	21 Dec.	11	Royal assent	12	12	12	0	1:04	1:06	0:58
Hearing Aid Council (Amendment)	21 Dec.	9	Royal assent	2	3	3	0	3:10	1:25	0:40
International Parliamentary Organisations (Registration)	21 Dec.	19	Royal assent	2	2	2	5	0:31		0:19
Licensing Amendment (Scotland)	26 Apr.		Committee HL	2	2		4	0:00	1:43	4:04
Parking	21 Dec.	18	Royal assent	6	7	8	1	5:16	1:15	0:54
TOTAL (9 bills)				41	42	42	19	19:15	7:12	10:12

Note: HL amdts. gives the sum of amendments at each stage. In the cases of bills returned to the Commons, the number of amendments returned was identical.

in the Lords. For example, the Dangerous Dogs Bill passed purely formally through the House of Commons, but was debated for thirty-nine minutes in the House of Lords. In addition to fifteen and a half hours of debate on the floor of the House of Commons, just over seven hours was also spent in discussing five of the bills in standing committee. Nearly three and three-quarter further hours were spent, on 7 July 1989, discussing Lords amendments to four of the bills.

That no more than ten hours of time was spent on consideration of Commons private members' bills represented a considerable bonus to the Lords business managers. In other sessions the amount of time required for the consideration of Commons bills was substantially greater. In session 1984–5, for example, more than thirty hours were taken up by the examination of the seventeen Commons bills, all of which passed into law. The amount of time required for debate of Commons bills is demand-led, depending on the number and complexity of bills passed by the Commons. The limited amount of time required to be devoted to this category of business represented a particularly significant saving in time because it was made at the busiest period of the session when progress had to be made with the major bills in the Government's legislative programme.

We discuss below the proceedings on two of the nine bills.

Control of Pollution (Amendment) Bill

The Control of Pollution (Amendment) Bill was introduced in the Commons by the member who came fifth in the ballot, Ms Joan Ruddock, a Labour member. Her bill sought to prevent illegal dumping of waste or 'fly-tipping' on unlicensed sites by requiring waste-carriers to register with the local authority. As it was the fifth bill presented in the session (at the same time as the other ballot bills) the member in charge was able to set her bill down for second reading on the fifth Friday set aside for private members' bills, 24 February. After some three hours' debate the bill was given an unopposed second reading and was committed to Standing Committee C. In the standing committee, the bill was substantially redrafted with the support of the Government and passed through its remaining stages in the House on 28 April without further amendment in only forty-six minutes.

In the Lords the passage of the bill was quicker and even less controversial. The bill was given an unopposed second reading after only forty-one minutes' debate on 25 May, immediately before the House rose for the spring bank holiday recess. In committee of the whole House, only one amendment was tabled. This was from the peer in charge of the bill, Lord Gregson, a Labour life peer. The amendment sought to give power to local authorities to refuse to register a waste-carrier unless the carrier could demonstrate technical competence and financial soundness. After a debate of half an hour, on the advice of the Parliamentary Under-Secretary of State, Department of the Environment, Lord Hesketh, the amendment was defeated on a division by 45 votes to 41.[12] It is interesting to note that the debate centred entirely on the merits of the amendment, and considerations of Lords competence or of the parliamentary timetable were not raised. The remainder of the committee stage and the remaining stages were taken purely formally.

Licensing Amendment (Scotland) Bill

The Licensing Amendment (Scotland) Bill sought to control the sale of alcohol for consumption off the premises by imposing restrictions on the conditions under which shops such as supermarkets could sell drink. The bill did not have any debate on the floor of the Commons at all. Its only substantive consideration was in the Second Scottish Standing Committee where the bill was debated for almost one and three-quarter hours and was amended. The bill was presented under Standing Order No. 58 by Mr James Hood, a Labour back-bencher, on 26 April, given a second reading without debate on 28 April, and read the third time on the nod on 9 June. At this stage, the bill clearly had Government support and was welcomed by the minister in the standing committee.[13] The only questioning of the provisions of the bill came from two English Conservative members, who put forward some of the arguments advanced by the Retail Consortium which finally led to the inconclusive proceedings in the Lords.[14]

[12] HL Debs., 14 June 1989, cols. 1477–85.
[13] Official Report, Second Scottish Standing Committee, 10 May 1989, col. 11.
[14] Ibid., cols. 3–26.

In the Lords, the bill was taken up by Lord Stallard, a Labour life peer and former MP. There was insufficient time for the bill to complete all of its stages before the end of June so that any amendments could be dealt with by the Commons on 7 July, the last opportunity to do so. Perhaps for that reason, no attempt was made to rush consideration of the bill; second reading in the Lords was not scheduled until 11 July. Despite the fact that the second reading debate began at 10.20 p.m. it continued for over two hours.[15] It soon became apparent that there would be considerable opposition to the bill even though the Government had been in support of it in the Commons. Using arguments put forward by the Scottish Consumer Council and the Retail Consortium, a number of peers pressed to limit the scope of the restrictions contained in the bill. The critics even complained of the fact that the bill had not been debated on the floor of the Commons.[16]

By the time that the bill reached its committee stage on 21 July, a substantial number of amendments had been tabled for consideration. At several points in the proceedings, it was recognized that if any amendment were made, that would be the end of the bill for that session. Indeed peers complained, notably in the speech of Lord Campbell of Croy,[17] that they were faced with a situation of all or nothing. The Government spokesman, the Lord Advocate, Lord Fraser of Carmyllie, admitted in the debate on amendment No. 2 that 'if this amendment is pressed, the bill falls, whatever may be the particular virtues of the amendment'.[18]

After a division, with only fifty-eight peers voting, the amendment was carried by 38 votes to 20. The remaining amendments were rapidly disposed of, three more being made, one after a division, and the bill was reported with amendments. No attempt was made to proceed subsequently with remaining stages because there was no time remaining in the Commons timetable for Lords amendments to be considered and so the bill was effectively killed.

[15] HL Debs., 11 July 1989, cols. 209–39.
[16] See e.g. the speech of Lord Lucas of Chilworth, ibid., col. 215.
[17] HL Debs., 21 July 1989, cols. 1081–2.
[18] Ibid., col. 1093.

Lords Private Members' Bills in Session 1988–9

Eight private members' bills originated in the House of Lords during the 1988–9 session. They are listed in Table 6.4. The Lords devoted approximately fourteen hours to consideration of these bills, mostly to three bills—the Junior Hospital Doctors (Regulation of Hours Bill), the Schizophrenia After-Care Bill, and the Unborn Children (Protection) Bill—described hereinafter and for that reason as the 'major' bills. The analysis below of the bills introduced is intended to give some idea of the variety of purposes served by Lords private members' bills.

Junior Hospital Doctors (Regulation of Hours) Bill: raising an important question

The Lords private member's bill which probably attracted the most public attention was the Junior Hospital Doctors (Regulation of Hours) Bill, introduced by Lord Rea on 15 December 1988 and the subject of a three-and-a-quarter-hour second reading debate in the evening of Wednesday 25 January 1989. In the course of the month before the second reading debate, there was a series of public protests by junior doctors, ranging from demonstrations outside hospitals to numerous letters to the press.

The second reading debate, in which fifteen peers in addition to the minister and the bill's sponsor participated, revealed a consensus that some action was desirable to reduce the hours worked by junior doctors, but some doubts amongst experienced medical professionals as to the appropriateness of legislation in achieving this. Lord Trafford, a transplant consultant and former Conservative MP, was one influential voice raised against the use of legislation for the purpose proposed, while praising Lord Rea—himself a practising doctor—for having raised 'an important question'.[19] For the Government, Lord Hesketh expressed 'grave reservations' on the effect which would be produced by statutory limitation on hours worked.[20]

[19] HL Debs., 25 Jan. 1989, col. 781. Lord Trafford was subsequently appointed Minister of State in the Department of Health in July 1989, but died in Sept. 1989.

[20] Ibid., col. 812.

Table 6.4. *Private members' bills introduced in the House of Lords in session 1988–9*

	Date intro. HL.	Final stage completed	Pages intro. HL	Pages intro. HC	Pages enacted	HL amdts.	Total time HL (hrs. m.)
Employment (Age Limits) [HL]	2 Mar.	passed by HL	2			0	0:50
Junior Hospital Doctors (Regulation of Hours) [HL]	15 Dec.	1st reading HC	2	2		0	3:29
Licensing (Amendment) [HL]	4 Mar.	Royal assent	1	1	1	1	0:22
Protection of Privacy (No. 2) [HL]	16 Feb.	1st reading HL	4				0:00
Religious Prosecutions (Abolition) (No. 2) [HL]	6 July	1st reading HL	1				0:00
Schizophrenia After-Care [HL]	9 Mar.	1st reading HC	6	7		22	4:11
Trade Union Act 1984 (Amendment) [HL]	11 Oct.	passed by HL	1			0	1:15
Unborn Children (Protection) [HL]	1 Feb.	2nd reading HL	3				3:49
TOTAL (8 bills)			20	8	1	23	13:56

Notes: Privilege amendments are not recorded. HL amdts. gives the sum of amendments at each stage. None of the bills was discussed at all in the House of Commons.

Several peers supported the idea of committing the bill to a select committee, which would have provided the opportunity for a detailed study of the problem as a whole. Lord Rea agreed to give the idea 'very serious thought' and to 'inquire into the possibility through the usual channels'.[21] It is not clear how far the possibility of a select committee was pursued. There was at the time already one 'special' select committee, on Murder and Life Imprisonment,[22] and there may have been difficulties about establishing another major one. The Earl of Halsbury suggested in the course of debate that there was a 'Select Committee bottleneck . . . caused by a lack of clerks and rooms'.[23] Given that the issue had already been examined by a number of bodies over the years, it may well have seemed preferable to Lord Rea to proceed with the bill as far as possible, and oblige the Government to be seen to block it in the Commons.[24]

The bill received an unopposed second reading. On 2 March 1989, it received its third reading and was passed, no amendments having been put down for its committee stage. It was taken up in the Commons by Mr Terry Davis, a former Labour frontbench spokesman on health, who on 15 February 1989 had introduced an identical bill under the ten-minute rule. Although it was put down for second reading on a number of Fridays, it was objected to on every occasion.

The bill can perhaps best be seen as having been part of a process of raising public awareness of the issue of the hours worked by junior doctors, in which both the Medical Practitioners Union and the British Medical Association Hospital Junior Staff Committee played a part.[25] While it must have been well understood by those involved that the bill stood little or no chance of reaching the statute book, dealing with an issue to which legislation is not necessarily appropriate, its passage was presumably intended to persuade the Government of the urgency of taking some action on a problem which has been recognized for many years and which has been the subject of numerous reports, inquiries, and initiatives.

[21] Ibid., col. 814.
[22] See Ch. 10.
[23] HL Debs., 25 Jan. 1989, col. 805.
[24] Interview with Lord Rea.
[25] Interview with Lord Rea; also HC Debs., 15 Feb. 1989, col. 331.

Schizophrenia After-Care Bill: 'providing a model'[26]

Lord Mottistone, a Conservative hereditary peer and Chairman of SANE, a schizophrenia charity, introduced the Schizophrenia After-Care Bill on 9 March 1989. It was debated on second reading for two hours and forty minutes on Wednesday 12 April, following a five-hour debate on higher education. The bill, which had been drafted by Graham Pitt, a retired solicitor, on behalf of the National Schizophrenia Fellowship,[27] sought to lay a statutory duty on local and health authorities to provide after-care for schizophrenics discharged from hospital. Sixteen peers in addition to the sponsor and minister spoke in the debate. Most supported the bill, and used the occasion to raise a number of wider issues connected with community care of the mentally ill in general, and schizophrenics in particular. Several regretted that it had been drafted so as to affect only discharged schizophrenics and not those suffering from other mental illnesses. The Government response, delivered by Lord Henley, a Lord in Waiting appointed in February 1989, concentrated on this point, suggesting that it would be discriminatory to deal with schizophrenia in isolation not only from other mental illnesses but also from mental handicap and physical illnesses.[28] The bill received an unopposed second reading.

Lord Mottistone decided to take the bill a stage further. Debate in committee on Wednesday 10 May for one hour twenty-four minutes revealed further the anxiety felt by many peers, notably Lord Ennals on behalf of the Opposition, at the exclusion of other medical conditions. Given the scope of the bill as introduced, it was procedurally impossible to broaden it.[29] The debate was evidently seen as a means of influencing future legislation, and Lord Henley confirmed that 'the care and thought that has gone into my noble friend's Bill will undoubtedly be helpful in providing a model'.[30]

Debate in committee also brought up a point over the libertarian implications of the proposed unqualified duty to provide information on a former patient's whereabouts, which was

[26] Lord Henley, HL Debs., 10 May 1989, col. 724.
[27] HL Debs., 12 Apr. 1989, col. 328; interview with Lord Mottistone.
[28] HL Debs., 12 Apr. 1989, cols. 358, 362; HL Debs., 10 May 1989, col. 722.
[29] Ibid., col. 726. [30] Ibid., col. 724.

amended on Lord Mottistone's initiative in a twelve-minute report stage on 20 June 1989.[31]

The bill was given a third reading on 26 June 1989 in four minutes. Lord Henley brought proceedings to and end with the remark that 'Ministers have followed these proceedings with keen interest and I hope will shortly be responding to the concerns expressed in an effective and practical way'.[32]

The bill was taken up in the Commons by Mr David Atkinson, but it made no progress.

The passage of the bill gave an opportunity for a particular issue—the after-care of schizophrenics—to be brought before the House four times in as many months, taking up four and a quarter hours of debate. It obliged the Government to give repeated consideration to these matters and to answer points raised at a time when the Government was known to be about to produce its response to the Griffiths Report on Community Care.[33] Lord Mottistone and the interest groups involved judged that the extended discussion of these matters had indeed influenced the Government in its response to the Griffiths Report, which was made in July,[34] and included a statement on the questions of notification and assessment raised in the bill.[35]

Unborn Children (Protection) Bill: a dress rehearsal

The Unborn Children (Protection) Bill was introduced on 1 February 1989 by the Duke of Norfolk, a Conservative hereditary peer, the premier Duke, and a leading figure among Britain's Roman Catholic community. The bill sought to prohibit the creation or retention of a human embryo for any purpose other than enabling a child to be borne by a specified woman. It was very closely modelled on the terms of the private member's bill introduced into the Commons in session 1984–5 by Mr J. Enoch Powell.

[31] HL Debs., 20 June 1989, cols. 208–12.

[32] HL Debs., 26 June 1989, col. 533.

[33] 'Community Care: Agenda for Action', a report to the Secretary of State for Social Services by Sir Roy Griffiths (HMSO, 1988).

[34] Statement to the House of Commons by the Secretary of State for Health, HC Debs., 12 July 1989, cols. 971–5. The statement was repeated in the House of Lords (HL Debs., 12 July. 1989, cols. 287–92).

[35] Interview with Lord Mottistone.

The bill was debated on second reading for three hours and fifty minutes on Wednesday 8 March 1989. Twenty-four peers took part in the debate, in addition to the sponsor and the minister. A majority favoured the bill. Those opposed to the bill in many cases expressed opposition not only to its purpose, but also to the timing of its introduction. The Warnock Report on Human Fertilization and Embryology had been the subject of a full debate in the House of Lords just over a year earlier,[36] and the Government had undertaken to bring forward legislation on embryo research, with alternative clauses, during the current Parliament. Lord Houghton of Sowerby described the bill as 'a futile exercise', accused the Duke of Norfolk of 'damaging the repute of the House',[37] and moved an amendment to refuse the bill a second reading on the ground that it was premature. Several other peers echoed this criticism in their contributions: Lord Henderson of Brompton, for example, described it as otiose, premature, and pre-emptive[38] and Baroness Llewelyn-Davies of Hastoe found it difficult to understand why it had been brought in, in view of the Government's commitment.[39] Other opponents of the bill included Earl Jellicoe, Chairman of the Medical Research Council, and Baroness Warnock. For the Government, Lord Henley repeated the undertaking to introduce legislation during the Parliament, and announced the Government's neutrality on the general question of embryo research.[40] Lord Houghton's amendment was negatived without a vote, and the bill received a second reading. It was, however, withdrawn on 26 April 1989 before its committee stage; more than sixty amendments had been tabled by a number of peers, raising the possibility of an unduly extended committee stage.

The debate was to an extent overshadowed by some sense of procedural futility, in that the House was aware that it had debated the matter fifteen months earlier, and would be doing so again shortly. Argument on the merits of the bill was therefore rather one-sided. In the event, the Government introduced its Human Fertilisation and Embryology Bill into the Lords in session 1989–90. On 8 February 1990, the House of Lords voted

[36] HL Debs., 15 Jan. 1988, cols. 1450–508.
[37] HL Debs., 8 Mar. 1989, cols. 1542–3.
[38] Ibid., col. 1577. [39] Ibid., col. 1559. [40] Ibid., cols. 1585–6.

by 234 to 80 in favour of permitting embryo research: in other words, against the sense of the bill promoted by the Duke of Norfolk.

The proponents of the bill may have hoped to put added pressure on the Government to introduce its promised bill, and to demonstrate the strength of the 'pro-life' group in the House of Lords, as a dress rehearsal for the coming debate. One supporter of the bill, wrongly anticipating a vote, referred to 'sending a message to the Government and to the other place as to how the feeling of this House is shown by a Division'.[41] Lord Rawlinson of Ewell, winding up the debate, said:

> The opportunity has been given in this Bill presented by the noble Duke for this House to think about these matters and debate them and to make the Minister . . . repeat that he will bring forward a Bill on this matter. . . . I hope that the Government see, by the majority which is given to this Bill and the defeat of the amendment, the seriousness with which this House views these vital issues.[42]

Employment (Age Limits) Bill: 'the beginning of a campaign'[43]

The Employment (Age Limits) Bill introduced on 2 March 1989 by Baroness Phillips, a Labour life peer and former Government whip, sought to prohibit discrimination against older people by the use of upper age limits in job advertisements, appointments, training, promotion, and retirement. After a fifty-minute debate on Thursday 4 May 1989, in which four peers spoke in addition to the bill's sponsor and the minister, the bill received an unopposed second reading.[44] Those participating included Lord Seebohm, the President of Age Concern, and Lord McCarthy, the Opposition front-bench spokesman on employment. There was no further debate as it passed its remaining stages, and it was sent to the House of Commons on 18 October, shortly before the end of the session; it was not taken up. A similar bill had been introduced into the Commons under the ten-minute rule procedure on 22 February 1989 by Mr Barry Field.

The bill may be seen as an opening shot in a campaign against

41 The Earl of Halsbury, ibid., col. 1561.
42 Ibid., col. 1590.
43 HL Debs., 18 Oct. 1989, col. 980.
44 HL Debs., 4 May 1989, cols. 319–33.

discrimination on grounds of age. In a brief speech on third reading, Baroness Phillips told the House that 'this is only the beginning of a campaign . . . a campaign like this is not won overnight'.[45] The length of the Government response on second reading delivered by Lord Skelmersdale, in which 'a voluntary approach based on persuasion' was advocated,[46] suggested that the campaign was indeed viewed as having begun.

Trade Union Act 1984 (Amendment) Bill: the Campbell amendment

The Trade Union Act 1984 (Amendment) Bill arose out of the dispute in 1989 between the port employers and the Transport and General Workers' Union. A strike ballot held by the Union favoured a strike, but the time taken to complete court actions meant that the statutory period of four weeks within which a strike permitted by such a ballot has to begin for the trade union to qualify for such statutory immunity as is afforded had elapsed. The bill, introduced on 11 October 1989 by a Conservative back-bench peer and expert on employment law, Lord Campbell of Alloway, sought to give to the courts a discretion to extend the four-week period imposed by section 10(3) of the Trade Union Act 1984.

The bill received an unopposed second reading on Tuesday 31 October 1989, in a debate of one hour and fifteen minutes. All eight peers in addition to the sponsor and the minister who participated supported the bill, including Lord Carr of Hadley, a former Conservative Secretary of State for Employment, and Lord Brightman, a Lord of Appeal, who also conveyed the support of the Master of the Rolls for the principle of the bill.[47] Lord Strathclyde, Parliamentary Under-Secretary of State at the Department of Employment, expressed the Government's reservations and its doubts as to whether such a case was likely to recur.[48] The bill had no further debate. It was passed on 13 November 1989 and sent to the Commons, only three days before Parliament was prorogued.

[45] HL Debs., 18 Oct. 1989, cols. 980–1.
[46] HL Debs., 4 May 1989, col. 331.
[47] HL Debs., 31 Oct. 1989, col. 186.
[48] Ibid., cols. 198–201.

It was, of course, well understood that the bill would not be enacted in the 1988–9 session. The Government was, however, known to be planning to introduce an employment bill in the forthcoming session, and peers openly used the bill as a means of seeking the inclusion of its terms in the Government's bill. Lord Strathclyde observed: 'I have little doubt that noble Lords will hear more about these matters in the months ahead'[49] and Lord Campbell looked ahead to the House having to deal with the question again.[50] In the event, the matter was raised by the Opposition in standing committee on the Employment Bill in the Commons, with a proposed maximum extension of six weeks; the Government resisted the amendment, but agreed to 'keep the matter under review and listen to what is said'.[51] On 12 July 1990, during the committee stage of the bill in the House of Lords, Lord Strathclyde moved a Government amendment to provide for the possibility of time spent in court proceedings being discounted for the purposes of calculating the four-week period. He told the House: 'In particular, we recognized the clear strength of feeling that was apparent from the debates in this Chamber.'[52]

Baroness Turner of Camden suggested that it might become known as 'the Campbell amendment'.[53] The gradual passage into statute law of this small but far from insignificant provision offers a concrete example of one of the reasons for the introduction of private members' legislation in the Lords.

Licensing (Amendment) Bill: 'letting democracy prevail'[54]

The only Lords private member's bill to receive royal assent in the 1988–9 session was the Licensing (Amendment) Bill, presented on 4 April 1989 by Lord Brooks of Tremorfa, a Labour life peer and secretary of the all-party group for non-profit-making members' clubs. The bill sought to restore the parity between clubs and pubs in permitted opening hours on Sundays, which had been broken by the extension of pub opening hours on Sundays under the Licensing (Amendment) Act 1988. The Earl

[49] Ibid., col. 198. [50] Ibid., col. 202.
[51] Official Report, Standing Committee D, 29 Mar. 1990, col. 486.
[52] HL Debs., 12 July 1990, col. 460.
[53] Ibid., col. 462. [54] HL Debs., 9 May 1989, col. 620.

of Arran, a Government whip, announced in the course of the nineteen-minute second reading debate, held during a dinner break in proceedings on the Water Bill on Tuesday 9 May 1989, that the Government would adopt 'a neutral stance'.[55] Four peers briefly expressed support, and the bill received an unopposed second reading.

In a three-minute committee stage on 6 June, Lord Brooks successfully moved an amendment providing for the Act to come into force two months from the date of its enactment to provide time for the licensing authorities and the clubs to prepare for the change, and the bill received its third reading on 20 June 1989. It was taken up in the Commons by Mr David Clelland, Labour MP for Tyne Bridge and member of the Executive Committee of the all-party group, and passed all its stages after the moment of interruption—in other words, when only business which is wholly unopposed can be passed—on 7 July 1989. On 21 July 1989 it received royal assent.

While an apparently minor piece of legislation, the passage of the Licensing (Amendment) Act aptly demonstrates one facet of private members' legislation in the Lords. The subject, licensing law, is one on which five Lords private members' bills have been passed into law since 1975–6.[56] It is not a party matter, but one on which Governments of all shades are reluctant to take potentially controversial action. There would seem to be a particular role for Lords private members' bills in the tidying-up of small but significant legislative anomalies, which might arouse unexpected political passions if raised in the first instance in the House of Commons. Those enjoying a drink on a Sunday between 2 p.m. and 3 p.m. in a members' club—and there must be many thousands of such people—can bear witness to that.

Protection of Privacy (No. 2) Bill; Religious Prosecutions (Abolition) (No. 2) Bill

Two bills were introduced in the Lords during 1988–9 in identical form to bills introduced in the Commons. Neither bill was debated. Lord Stoddart of Swindon, a Labour life peer and

[55] HL Debs., 9 May 1989, col. 620.
[56] 1975–6, 1980–1, 1984–5, 1986–7, 1988–9.

former Labour MP, introduced his Protection of Privacy (No. 2) Bill on 16 February 1989. The identical bill had been introduced in the House of Commons by Mr John Browne, a Conservative member. The Commons bill received a second reading on 17 February 1989. Having completed its committee stage, it was due to be considered on 5 May 1989. On 21 April, the Minister of State at the Home Office, Timothy Renton MP, announced a general review of privacy law and related matters by David Calcutt QC. In response, Mr Browne withdrew his bill on 4 May, and Lord Stoddart did likewise on 11 May.

Lord Sefton of Garston, a Labour life peer, introduced the Religious Prosecutions (Abolition) (No. 2) Bill on 6 July 1989, in identical form to the bill introduced in the House of Commons by Mr Tony Benn MP on 12 April. Neither the Commons nor the Lords bill was debated.

Such bills may be introduced on the as yet unproven supposition that their passage in the Lords in advance of the anticipated arrival of the bill from the Commons will in some way facilitate the formal passage through its various stages of the Commons bill: for example, because certain issues will have been identified and discussed in advance, even though the newly arrived bill would have to go through the same stages.

Concluding Observations

Government responses

The character of responses made by the Government spokesmen in debates on private members' bills to some extent depended upon whether a debate was replied to in the Lords by a minister from the appropriate department, as opposed to a whip, without specific ministerial responsibility. The Government responses to the three 'major' bills initiated in the Lords were delivered not by departmental ministers but by Lords in Waiting acting as spokesmen for the departments concerned,[57] which may have contributed to the sense that they were by and large prepared statements rather than reactions to debate. Lord Hesketh's

[57] Lord Henley was appointed Parliamentary Under-Secretary of State at the Department of Social Security in July 1989.

speech on second reading of the Junior Hospital Doctors (Regulation of Hours) Bill provided an opportunity for an update of the Government's position, and included a report on the most recent meeting with the British Medical Association, and on the results of interim reports from regional health authorities on progress in reductions in onerous rota commitments.[58] Lord Henley presented the Government's case during proceedings on both the Unborn Children (Protection) Bill and the Schizophrenia After-Care Bill. Given the Government's neutrality on the issues presented by the former, detailed argument could not have been expected; but several points raised by individual peers were picked up, and a clear restatement of the Government's legislative intentions was given. Lord Henley's speeches during proceedings on the latter bill also showed attention to points raised in debate, bringing forth the complaint from the bill's sponsor, Lord Mottistone, that the minister had 'responded to everybody's speech except mine'.[59] By contrast, it may be significant that the debate on the Trade Union Act 1984 (Amendment) Bill was answered by Lord Strathclyde, Parliamentary Under-Secretary of State at the Department of Employment; it was the same minister who a year later moved the amendment giving effect to the purpose behind the bill. Peers are inevitably interested in the quality and content of speeches by ministers in response to private legislative initiatives, since the Government at least as much as the House of Lords is the audience at which these initiatives are aimed.

In the debates on most of those bills emanating from the Commons, the response was given by a minister from the department concerned. This is particularly important to the fortunes of bills at committee stage when an amendment which is unwelcome to the Government could jeopardize the prospects of a bill becoming law. In the case of the bill which failed to complete all of its stages, the Licensing Amendment (Scotland) Bill, the Government's position was outlined by the Lord Advocate, Lord Fraser of Carmyllie, who set out the arguments for continuing with the bill unamended and relying on later legislative opportunities for consideration of amendments being offered to the bill.

[58] HL Debs., 25 Jan. 1989, col. 811.
[59] HL Debs., 12 Apr. 1989, cols. 362–3.

Pressure groups[60]

All three major bills introduced in the Lords owed something to the work of outside bodies: the Medical Practitioners Union and the British Medical Association Hospital Junior Staff Committee, 'pro-life' groups, and the National Schizophrenia Fellowship respectively. Lord Rea's Junior Hospital Doctors (Regulation of Hours) Bill was indeed a constituent part of a wider strategy designed to put the issue of junior doctors' hours in the headlines and to win public support for it.[61] Both he and the bodies involved felt that the bill had helped to raise public awareness of the situation and had stirred up the Government in its efforts to improve it. The National Schizophrenia Fellowship also considered that 'their' bill had been useful in influencing the Government's thinking. A bill obliges ministers and civil servants to address a specific proposal in some detail, and if necessary on more than one occasion. It is questionable whether a general debate on mental health provision or doctors' hours would have had similar results. The Licensing (Amendment) Bill, subsequently enacted, also owed its origins to interests outside the House, apparently conveyed through a large all-party group.

There was relatively little evidence of pressure-group activity in the Lords with regard to bills emanating from the Commons. This may be due in part to the fact that in each of the debates there was an awareness that extended proceedings or amendments could put at risk a bill's chance of reaching the statute book. Only in the case of the Licensing Amendment (Scotland) Bill were there substantial references to the views of interested bodies—in that case the Scottish Consumer Council and the Retail Consortium. Much was also made of a campaign being run by the *Daily Record* for stricter controls on the sale of alcoholic drink.

Why a bill?

There are several factors which may persuade a peer to introduce a private member's bill as a means of bringing a matter before the House of Lords, rather than pursuing other avenues. In the

[60] See Philip Norton, 'Public Legislation', in *Parliament and Pressure Politics*, ed. Michael Rush for the Study of Parliament Group (Clarendon Press, Oxford, 1990), esp. 200–4.

[61] Interview with Lord Rea.

first place, the successive stages in the passage of a bill mean that the subject-matter of the bill can be brought before the House on several occasions, permitting of sustained debate on matters of detail. Secondly, the Government are obliged to respond in detail to a specific set of published legislative proposals, rather than to propositions advanced with little or no notice in the course of debate. Thirdly, the possibility of a vote on a substantive motion, such as second reading or a significant amendment, can concentrate the minds of ministers and peers. Finally, the procedure for the introduction of a bill is relatively simple, and time will normally be found for a debate; by contrast, a peer may have to ballot for the right to introduce a short debate,[62] although it is usually possible to find time for an unstarred question. On the negative side, debates beginning at the supper hour and continuing until 10.30 or 11 p.m., as was the case with the three major debates in 1988–9, may not be popular, and participation may fall as a result.

Participation

The level of expertise and direct personal experience of those who spoke in all the debates was high. Surprisingly, given that all three major private members' bills introduced into the Lords dealt with health policy matters, only seven of the forty-two participants spoke in more than one second reading debate, including Lord Ennals, who spoke for the Opposition in all three debates, Lord Henley, who spoke for the Government in two, and Lord Winstanley, who spoke for the Social and Liberal Democrats in two.[63] The majority of those who spoke on the Junior Hospital Doctors (Regulation of Hours) Bill were distinguished members of the medical profession, and the debate included a maiden speech from Lord Butterfield, former Regius Professor of Physic at the University of Cambridge. Lords private members' bills provide an opportunity for the expertise and experience of members of the House of Lords to be displayed on legislative matters outside the Government's legislative programme.

[62] See Ch. 8.

[63] The other four were Lord Rea, Lord Pitt of Hampstead (both doctors), the Earl of Longford, and Lord Henderson of Brompton.

7

Private Legislation

Elizabeth Flood

Introduction

Erskine May defines private legislation as 'legislation of a special kind for conferring particular powers or benefits on any person or body of persons . . . in excess of or in conflict with the general law'.[1] The right to promote a bill seeking powers not permitted under the general law is based on the citizen's right to petition Parliament. Despite the fact that many areas previously covered by private legislation are now dealt with under other procedures, private bills still cover a wide range of subjects. These include especially the authorization of certain types of development (railways, tramways, canals; in some circumstances docks, harbours, and bridges) and the granting of special powers to local authorities, for example to regulate markets or to make special regulations for highways. Personal bills are a particular category of private bills, for example to enable marriage between people who, under the general law, are considered to be too closely related to marry.

Private bills are promoted by groups outside Parliament. They are not introduced by the Government, which customarily has remained neutral in respect of such bills. Those adversely affected by private bills may petition against them. After second reading, a private bill opposed by petitioners is referred to a select committee which may hear evidence for and against the bill and whose proceedings may well appear to have more in common with the law courts than with Parliament. Those bills against which no petitions are lodged are referred in the Lords to an unopposed bill committee which normally consists of the Chairman of Committees sitting alone, assisted by his counsel. Unlike public bills, any private bill which has failed to complete all its

[1] Erskine May, *Parliamentary Practice*, 21st edn. (Butterworths, London, 1989), 789.

stages by the end of a parliamentary session may be suspended, and in the new session consideration of it is resumed at the stage it had reached before suspension. This is known as 'carrying over' the bill.

Throughout most of this century private bill procedure had been an increasingly tranquil and apparently insignificant backwater of parliamentary life. But from the mid-1980s a series of highly controversial measures aroused growing interest both inside and outside Parliament and focused attention on private bill procedure to such an extent that in January 1987 a Joint Committee was established to consider private legislation. In October 1988 this Committee published its report, which was debated in both Houses during the 1988–9 session.[2] It is discussed further below.

Meanwhile, that session saw the introduction or carry over of several extremely controversial private bills and these aroused such determined opposition in the House of Commons that the entire private bill system showed increasing signs of strain, so much so that it became more and more difficult for any private bill to make progress in the Commons. This had a direct effect on the Lords because a large number of bills which had begun in the Commons stalled there and did not reach the upper House during the session. Other bills which had been considered and passed by the Lords did not re-emerge from the Commons. Only twelve bills completed all their stages in both Houses during the session. The fierce opposition which met some bills in the Commons underlined anxieties about the procedure felt in the Lords. This background should be borne in mind when considering the Lords' experience of private legislation during this session.

All told, sixty private bills were before one or other House during the 1988–9 session. Of these forty-one were new bills while nineteen were carried over from the previous session. The number of 'new' bills was comparatively high, confirming a trend evident in recent years. The 'new' bills were very varied in purpose. A high proportion of them (eighteen of the forty-one) were to empower their promoters to construct major works of various sorts—railways, tunnels, barrages, harbour develop-

[2] Report of the Joint Committee on Private Bill Procedure, HL Paper 97 (1987–8).

ments, and so on. Three others were intended to pave the way for works. Nine more were local authority bills seeking varied powers, but only one (the London Local Authorities (No. 2) Bill [HL]) was a genuinely wide-ranging miscellaneous provisions bill. The remaining bills covered most of the other normal subjects of private legislation: two company bills; a cemetery bill; two bills to reorganize colleges and medical schools of London University; three seeking various powers for harbour and other navigation authorities—enabling them to operate a lighthouse, for example; and two bills to empower bodies set up by residents of private estates to do such things as levy monies to maintain the private roads on the estate, or to control development on the estate. An unusual bill was one concerning the regulation of fares on London Regional Transport trains and buses. No personal bills were deposited in this session.

The nineteen bills carried over from the previous session consisted of ten works bills, two bills to pave the way for works, two local authority bills, two bills to confer new powers on harbour authorities, two bills to allow British Rail and London Regional Transport to impose on-the-spot penalty fares for fare-dodgers, and one bill concerned with a private housing estate.

Of the sixty bills before Parliament this session fifteen were never considered by the Lords because they were rejected in the Commons, the first House, or they were abandoned by their promoters, or they spent the entire session stuck in the Commons. A further seven bills had completed all their stages in the Lords by the end of the 1987–8 session, and were not therefore considered further by the House in 1988–9, but were simply noticed in the Journals of the House of Lords as having been passed and sent to the Commons. Four of these were sent back to the Lords for consideration of Commons amendments, but proceedings at this stage were purely formal.

Table 7.1 lists the remaining thirty-eight bills on which there were significant proceedings in the House of Lords in this session. These comprised nineteen works bills, two bills paving the way for works, six local authority bills, two company bills, three harbour bills, two university college or medical school bills, two private estate bills, one bill to impose penalty fares on fare-dodgers, and one cemetery bill.

It is interesting to compare the treatment of bills by the two

Table 7.1. *Private bills considered by the House of Lords, session 1988–9*

	First reading	Second reading	Committed	Committee to which bill initially referred	Reported from Select Committee	Reported from Unopposed Bill Committee	Third reading	Royal assent
A. *Bills carried over from session 1987–8*								
Birmingham City Council	29 Nov. pro forma	29 Nov. pro forma	—	—	—	29 Nov. pro forma	8 Dec.	20 Dec.
British Railways (No. 2)	29 Nov. pro forma	29 Nov. pro forma	29 Nov. pro forma	Select	8 Feb.	14 Mar.	22 Mar.	27 Apr.
British Railways (Penalty Fares) [HL]	29 Nov. pro forma	29 Nov. pro forma	29 Nov. pro forma	Unopposed	—	7 Dec.	20 Dec.	16 Nov.
City of London (Spitalfields Market)	25 Jan.	3 Apr. Debate	3 Apr.	Select	26 June	17 July	27 July Debate	—
Greater Manchester (Light Rapid Transit System) (No. 3) [HL]	29 Nov. pro forma	29 Nov. pro forma	29 Nov. pro forma	Unopposed	—	23 May	17 Oct.	—
London Docklands Railway (Beckton)	29 Nov. pro forma	29 Nov. pro forma	29 Nov. pro forma	Select	25 May	27 June	6 July	21 July
London Regional Transport	29 Nov. pro forma	29 Nov. pro forma	29 Nov. pro forma	Unopposed	—	15 Dec.	23 Jan.	7 Feb.
London Regional Transport (No. 2)	11 July	24 July	24 July	Unopposed	—	26 July	27 July	27 July
St George's Hill, Weybridge, Estate	29 Nov. pro forma	29 Nov. pro forma	29 Nov. pro forma	Select Discharged	—	10 July	17 July	—

Southern Water Authority	29 Nov. pro forma	29 Nov. pro forma	—	—	—	29 Nov. pro forma	8 Dec.	20 Dec.
B. *Bills introduced in session 1988–9*								
Associated British Ports (Hull)	16 June	28 June	28 June	Unopposed	—	11 July	19 July	27 July
Birmingham City Council (Miscellaneous Provisions) [HL]	18 Jan.	20 Feb.	20 Feb.	Select	16 Mar.	9 Oct.	24 Oct.	suspended 15 Nov.
Buckinghamshire County Council [HL]	18 Jan.	9 Feb.	9 Feb.	Unopposed	—	20 Mar.	11 Apr.	—
Cardiff Bay Barrage [HL]	18 Jan.	23 Feb. Debate	23 Feb.	Select	13 June	27 June	12 July Debate	suspended 15 Nov.
Greater Manchester (Light Rapid Transit System) [HL]	18 Jan.	21 Feb.	21 Feb.	Select Discharged	—	8 Nov.	suspended 8 Nov.	
Great Yarmouth Port and Haven [HL]	18 Jan.	16 Feb.	16 Feb.	Select	29 June	31 Oct.	suspended 2 Nov.	
Happisburgh Lighthouse [HL]	18 Jan.	8 Feb.	9 Mar.	Unopposed	—	1 Nov.	suspended 2 Nov.	
Hayle Harbour [HL]	18 Jan.	15 Feb.	20 Mar.	Unopposed	—	16 May	8 June	27 July
Heathrow Express Railway [HL]	18 Jan.	28 Feb., Debate	9 Mar.	Select	suspended 7 Nov.			
Hythe Marina Village (Southampton) Wavescreen	2 May	25 May	25 May	Select Discharged	—	22 June	28 June	—
International Westminster Bank	17 May	8 June	8 June	Unopposed	—	22 June	6 July	16 Nov.
Isle of Wight	16 June	29 June	29 June	Unopposed	—	17 July	24 July	—
Kingston upon Hull City Council [HL]	18 Jan.	20 Feb.	20 Feb.	Unopposed	—	15 Mar.	11 Apr.	3 July

Table 7.1. *(Contd.)*

	First reading	Second reading	Committed	Committee to which bill initially referred	Reported from Select Committee	Reported from Unopposed Bill Committee	Third reading	Royal assent
London Local Authorities (No. 2) [HL]	18 Jan.	15 Feb. Debate	15 Feb.	Select	16 Oct.	8 Nov.	suspended 8 Nov.	
Medway Tunnel [HL]	18 Jan.	2 Mar.	2 Mar.	Select	(*locus* disallowed)	17 July	26 July	—
Midland Metro	23 May	12 June	12 June	Select Discharged	—	25 July	17 Oct.	16 Nov.
New Southgate Cemetery and Crematorium Limited	22 June	5 July	5 July	Unopposed	—	13 July	20 July	—
Nottingham Park Estate [HL]	18 Jan.	8 Feb.	6 Apr.	Select Discharged	—	10 July	26 July	—
Penzance Albert Pier Extension	3 May	25 May	25 May	Select Discharged	—	1 Nov.	suspended 2 Nov.	
Queen Mary and Westfield College [HL]	18 Jan.	8 Feb.	8 Feb.	Unopposed	—	24 May	12 June	27 July
River Tees Barrage and Crossing [HL]	18 Jan.	17 May Debate	17 May	Select	26 Oct	suspended 2 Nov.		
Southampton Rapid Transit [HL]	18 Jan.	13 Apr. Debate	13 Apr.	Select	suspended 7 Nov.			
South Yorkshire Light Rail Transit [HL]	18 Jan.	15 Feb.	15 Feb.	Select Discharged	—	23 May	7 June	—

Tees (Newport) Bridge [HL]	18 Jan.	14 Feb.	14 Feb.	Unopposed	—	13 Mar.	22 Mar.	3 July
Tyne and Wear Passenger Transport	16 June	28 June	28 June	Unopposed	—	19 July	26 July	16 Nov.
United Medical and Dental Schools [HL]	18 Jan.	14 Feb.	6 Apr.	Unopposed	—	22 June	29 June	—
Vale of Glamorgan (Barry Harbour) [HL]	18 Jan.	14 Feb.	14 Feb.	Unopposed	—	17 May	6 June	—
Wesleyan Assurance Society	3 May	25 May	25 May	Unopposed	—	16 June	29 June	6 July

Houses to see whether one House passed private bills more expeditiously than the other. Taking the twelve bills which completed all stages in both Houses during the session we find that on average a bill in the Lords took about ten and a half weeks from first reading to third reading (the minimum time being four weeks and the maximum twenty-one weeks), whereas a bill in the Commons took nearly fifteen weeks (minimum six weeks, maximum twenty-one weeks), a rather small variation on what is a comparatively small sample. According to witnesses to the Joint Committee on Private Bill Procedure, Lords committees do have a reputation for being more meticulous and painstaking in examining promoters' claims than Commons committees.[3]

Stages of Bills

Allocation of bills to the two Houses

Those wishing to promote private bills have first to submit a petition requesting Parliament to consider their bills. Consultations between the Chairman of Committees in the House of Lords and the Chairman of Ways and Means in the Commons determine the division between the Houses. In general, the authorities of the two Houses try to divide the workload as evenly as possible. Of the forty-one bills deposited in the 1988–9 session, two were withdrawn before the division was made, nineteen were to originate in the Commons, and twenty in the Lords. The most obviously controversial bill introduced in that session, the King's Cross Railways Bill (to build the London terminus for the proposed new railway link to the Channel Tunnel), was allocated to the House of Commons, but other works bills likely to meet with strong opposition, such as the Heathrow Express Railway Bill and the two barrage bills, were to originate in the Lords. The local authority bill most akin to a 'jumbo' bill (the term often used to describe wide-ranging general powers bills), the London Local Authorities (No. 2) Bill, was sent first to their Lordships. The other eight local authority bills,

[3] Ibid., Paras. 37 and 117.

which all had limited purposes, were split evenly between the Houses.

It is impossible to judge the success of any attempt to divide the workload equitably between the Houses in this session because of the fact that, for reasons largely unconnected with the new bills, private legislation proceedings almost ground to a halt in the Commons. Usually, however, bottlenecks are avoided.

First, second, and third reading

The first reading of private bills is purely formal and is of no interest. Of the thirty bills which were given a second reading by the House of Lords in the 1988–9 session,[4] six were debated. Given that debates on second reading are fairly rare, this is a rather high proportion, but it is explained by the nature of these bills. Four were major works bills and one, the City of London (Spitalfields Market) Bill, although not itself a works bill, was intended to empower the Corporation of the City of London to move Spitalfields Market in order to clear the way for a large and controversial redevelopment of the site. The London Local Authorities (No. 2) Bill [HL] was a bill to empower local authorities to do things as diverse as licensing helicopter operations, regulating massage parlours and acupuncturists, and licensing private cemeteries. All six of the bills were prima-facie candidates for second reading debates.

Major issues of principle arose on only two of the six bills, the Cardiff Bay Barrage Bill [HL] and the London Local Authorities (No. 2) Bill [HL]. Several of the miscellaneous proposals in the London Bill met with criticism, not least from the Government.[5] The minister told the House that three Government departments had objected to the proposals to license helicopter movements and to control private cemeteries. Other peers considered that these matters were more suitable for public legislation than private legislation—a criticism frequently levelled at local authority bills. This did not prevent the House from giving the bill a second reading, however, because it was considered that a committee should sift through the bill. (In fact, the bill was

[4] Eight other bills were considered only at later stages.
[5] HL Debs., 15 Feb. 1989, cols. 265–6.

heavily amended by the committees to which it was referred and several of the clauses to which peers had objected in this debate were struck out.)

The debate on the Cardiff Bay Barrage Bill focused on the basic issue of the economic revitalization of the bay versus the environmental impact on people and local wildlife.[6] Peers expressed concern about the proposed destruction of a designated Site of Special Scientific Interest, which would be flooded if the barrier were built. As for the effects of the proposed barrage on people, peers debated the possibility that a large area of the docklands would be flooded periodically, and whether the lake created by the barrier would become stagnant and unhealthy. In all this they were aware of the danger that general legislation to protect the environment can be undermined in a piecemeal way by private legislation, but there was no attempt to defeat the bill outright on these grounds. It seems to have been accepted that these were matters for a committee to examine, since expert evidence was clearly needed.

This debate throws light on an interesting development in private bill procedure: an apparent shift in the attitude of governments to private bills. Unless they consider the proposals to be against the public interest, it is customary for ministers to express complete neutrality towards bills, but in recent years there have been indications that the Government is actively supporting some private bills. This became very evident on the Cardiff Bill, with the minister stating that the Government was very interested in its fate because of the importance it attached to the economic benefits of redeveloping the area.[7] At the end of the debate the bill was referred to a committee together with an Instruction that the committee pay particular attention to the question of water quality. The promoters did not oppose the Instruction.

The debates on the other four bills did not uncover issues of such wide concern but were limited to matters of more local interest. The Heathrow Express Railway Bill [HL] was controversial, not because anyone opposed the principle of building

[6] HL Debs., 23 Feb. 1989, cols. 788–815.

[7] This early indication of the Government's attitude to this bill was reinforced when the Government decided in 1991–2 to introduce it as a hybrid bill following its failure in the Commons in the 1990–1 session.

a railway link from London to Heathrow Airport but because there was fervent disagreement over the route.[8] No one in the debate queried the propriety of the private bill procedure to determine such planning matters. The debate on the City of London (Spitalfields Market) Bill centred not so much on the subject of the bill, the proposal to move the market, as on its consequences, the redevelopment of the market site.[9] In this case there was no question of promoters using a private bill to avoid normal planning procedure as an application for the proposed redevelopment was being made to the usual planning authorities. The main points at issue in the debate on the Southampton Rapid Transit Bill [HL] were whether the proposed aerial light-rail system would alleviate any of Southampton's transport problems and whether private enterprise really would be willing to finance the scheme.[10] As for the River Tees Barrage and Crossing Bill [HL] several peers were concerned that insufficient information was available about the impact of the barrage on the river regime upstream and on water quality, and that this lack of information would disadvantage the petitioners against the bill in the committee proceedings.[11]

No divisions took place at second reading on any of these six bills. The Lords usually respect the doctrine that, unless there are major objections of principle, the House should not reject a private bill at second reading but leave it to the committee to hear detailed evidence, and if necessary reject the bill.

At third reading it is rare for debates to take place given the earlier opportunities for scrutiny or rejection of a bill. But it is worth noting that, out of a total of thirty bills given a third reading by the House in this session, two—the Cardiff Bill and Spitalfields Market Bill—were debated on third reading.[12] In both cases peers wished to register disappointment with the select committees' conclusions, though many peers paid tribute to the care and thoroughness with which the committees had examined the evidence. The issues raised in debate were generally the same

[8] HL Debs., 28 Feb. 1989, cols. 1006–26.

[9] HL Debs., 3 Apr. 1989, cols. 959–76.

[10] HL Debs., 13 Apr. 1989, cols. 450–64.

[11] HL Debs., 17 May 1989, cols. 1247–60.

[12] HL Debs., 12 July 1989, cols. 331–42; HL Debs., 27 July 1989, cols. 1561–9.

as those discussed on second reading. In the end, neither bill was pressed to a division as their opponents considered it too late to seek to defeat them. The chief opponent of the Spitalfields Bill acknowledged at third reading that no new evidence had been produced, and on the Cardiff Bill the main critic stated that it was now for the House of Commons to decide the merits of the case.

Petitions

The committee procedures on private bills vary depending on whether petitions against the bill have been deposited. In the House of Lords those against which no petition has been deposited are referred immediately to an unopposed bill committee. Bills which have been petitioned against in the Lords are referred first to a select committee and then to an unopposed bill committee for consideration of the provisions of the bill to which petitioners have not objected.

Of the thirty-six bills considered by the House of Lords in this session that could potentially have been the subject of petitions,[13] eighteen were actually petitioned against, of which eleven were Lords bills, attracting a total of ninety-one petitions, and seven were Commons bills, attracting a total of thirty-one petitions. In the Commons twenty-two out of forty bills were the subject of petitions, a rate of petitioning higher than in recent years, partly because of the increase in the number of works bills. Although twenty-one bills could potentially have been petitioned against in both Houses, only five were. A total of twenty-eight petitions were deposited against these bills in the Lords and eighty-four in the Commons, there being a tendency for petitioners to concentrate on the first House to consider a bill.

A total of 122 petitions were deposited in the Lords, an average of about seven petitions per opposed bill. This average is distorted by a comparatively small number of bills which attracted most opposition; six bills, five of them works bills, together attracted over two-thirds of the petitions deposited in the Lords.

[13] Two other bills were carried over from the previous session and began again at third reading.

Over half of all the petitions in the Lords were withdrawn at some stage, and seven of the eighteen bills petitioned against became unopposed as a result. Petitions appear to have been withdrawn for a variety of reasons. Promoters are sometimes more willing to negotiate away objections when their bills are close to being enacted. The opponents who withdrew their petitions were composed disproportionately of limited companies and other large bodies. Forty-seven of the sixty-six petitions withdrawn had been deposited by companies, trade federations, statutory undertakers, and port authorities, while only nine of the forty-three petitions deposited by local groups or individuals were withdrawn. There are several possible reasons for this disparity. Large bodies often have specific objections to proposals which can be dealt with by amendments to the bill or legal agreements (undertakings) or the payment of compensation. Local groups and individuals—especially those opposing works—often object to the whole scheme and its effects and promoters find it difficult to persuade away such deep-rooted objections. At the same time, large bodies tend to be rather better organized than small groups or individuals and are more likely to be represented by lawyers or other experienced negotiators, which again makes it easier for promoters to negotiate with them.

Committee stage

Eleven bills were considered by Lords select committees in 1988–9, a slightly higher number than in recent years. One committee, on the Medway Tunnel Bill [HL], met only to disallow the locus of a single petitioner. The select committee stages of two bills, the Heathrow Express Railway Bill [HL] and the Southampton Rapid Transit Bill [HL], had not been completed by the end of the session; both bills were suspended in mid-committee. Only eight bills were reported from select committees, four of which were amended. Seven of the bills considered by select committees were also considered and amended by an unopposed bill committee. The select committees on two bills imposed written agreements on the parties without amending the bills concerned. Twenty-six bills in the Lords were referred only to an unopposed bill committee; twenty-three of them were amended.

Of the ten select committees which dealt substantively with bills in this session seven sat for more than four days. In general terms two related factors cause proceedings to be elongated: first, the number of petitioners; and second, the degree of complexity of the issues which have to be considered. The bill provoking the largest number of sittings, seventeen in all, was the Cardiff Bay Barrage Bill [HL] which attracted fifteen petitions and required detailed expert evidence on technical questions concerning flooding, the effects on the water-table, and river and tidal regimes. The committee on the Heathrow bill met for fourteen days; it had to consider complex arguments about the correct route for the railway and hear eight petitioners. The Spitalfields Bill also took fourteen days.

The number of committees and the length of time their deliberations took seem to have placed some strain on the House's ability to man committees. The Chairman of Committees customarily attempts to maintain a party balance, but it seemed that as the session continued and committee meetings began to overlap, it was increasingly difficult for him to do this. Altogether seventy-one appointments to committees were made in this session; twenty-seven peers were nominated to serve on only one committee, twelve to two committees, four to three committees, and two sat on four committees. In all, forty-five different peers were appointed to committees. The burden on individual peers varied widely. Eight peers nominated to committees never sat on them because they or their committees were discharged. Of the remaining thirty-seven, three served only on a committee which met once, but at the other end of the scale five peers spent more than twenty days sitting on private bill select committees, and another twenty-one peers spent ten or more days on these duties. Although the Chairman of Committees had told the Joint Committee on Private Bill Procedure in January 1988 that there were no major difficulties in manning committees in the Lords, in May 1989, when he spoke in the debate on the Joint Committee's report, he was expressing concern about the House's ability to continue to cope.[14]

Questions have been raised concerning the relative suitability

[14] Joint Committee's Report, 185 and Q. 470; HL Debs., 17 May 1989, col. 1185.

of parliamentarians for much of this work as compared with professional inspectors. Twenty-two of the thirty-seven peers who served on such committees this session had clearly relevant past experience, some through office as ministers or in local authorities or other public bodies, others as professional lawyers. Given that a comparatively small number of peers serve on such committees, those who do take part in this work tend to become relatively well experienced.

Decisions by select committees

It is instructive to look in slightly more detail at some of the matters decided by select committees. First we consider two contrasting works bills, the London Docklands Railway (Beckton) Bill and the British Railways (No. 2) Bill.

The British Railways (No. 2) Bill was one of the annual British Rail general powers bills which may cover anything from stopping up level crossings to minor works to alterations to the pension arrangements for British Rail staff. It attracted only two petitions in the Lords, one of which, from the British Waterways Board, was withdrawn on the day on which the committee first met, leaving a farmer as the sole petitioner to be heard. British Rail wished to acquire by compulsory purchase part of this farmer's property in order to strengthen an adjoining railway embankment. The petitioner did not dispute the fact that the embankment needed strengthening; hence much of the evidence was concerned with the detailed engineering question of what type of device should be used and how much land would be required. At the end of the first day of evidence, the chairman of the committee expressed the hope that the parties could reach an agreement between themselves, but when the committee resumed on the following day the parties reported that they had been unable to agree. By the end of the proceedings that morning, however, counsel put forward modified terms which both sides were able to accept, and the committee approved these with obvious relief. No amendment was made to the bill, but the agreement was incorporated into a written undertaking. However exasperating it may have been for the committee members to spend so much time and effort on a disagreement about comparatively small sums of money and areas of land, the committee's arbitration clearly helped considerably in solving a dispute which had reached deadlock. The final agreement between the parties even encompassed an earlier dispute which was about to be referred to the courts!

The other bill examined here is the London Docklands Railway (Beckton) Bill, the purpose of which was to enable the construction of an eastern extension of an existing light railway. Before the bill reached the Lords the committee in the House of Commons had required the promoters to alter the route. Ten petitions against it were deposited in the Lords, although by the time the committee met the opposition had shrunk to six petitions and three further petitions were withdrawn during the course of the committee stage. Despite this erosion of the opposition, the committee had to meet on ten days. Three major issues were put before the committee: noise from the trains, the design of the stations, and the provision of car parking at the eastern end of the line. None of the petitioners opposed the bill in principle and none sought amendments to the bill; instead they wanted written undertakings from the promoters. The bill was reported without amendment, with the committee deciding that undertakings should be given to petitioners only in respect of the question of noise. These involved London Regional Transport in a commitment to provide more double glazing for homes near the line than they had intended.

There were several other important decisions by select committees. A clause in the Cardiff Bay Barrage Bill [HL] had provided that the promoters would pay for surveys and remedial measures to properties within a certain area in the event of damage from a rise in the groundwater; the committee significantly extended the boundaries of this area and thus the promoters' liability. Another noteworthy feature of this committee was that it took evidence from the Welsh Water Authority, which was not a petitioner. This was necessary because of the House's instruction to the committee to pay particular attention to the water quality in the proposed lake. The committee on the Heathrow Express Railway Bill [HL] rejected the route put forward by the promoters of the bill, preferring an alternative, underground route. The promoters reluctantly accepted this and the committee adjourned while the promoters prepared a variation from the route originally designated in the bill.

Other Types of Private Legislation

Two confirming bills were presented under the Private Legislation Procedure (Scotland) Act 1936. The whole system of Scottish private legislation is intended to ensure that most of the debate and negotiation on proposed legislation takes place before the introduction of a bill. It is therefore not surprising that the two bills considered in 1988–9 passed largely unremarked.[15] Both were dealt with under expedited procedure. It is comparatively rare even for such a bill to be debated in either House.

Proceedings took place in the House on nine Special Procedure Orders.[16] Five of these were laid first during the 1988–9 session, while four were brought forward from previous sessions. Of the total of nine Orders, five were harbour revision orders, one was a harbour empowerment order, two were compulsory purchase orders, and the remaining one was a Field Garden Allotment Appropriation Order. None of the five laid in this session was petitioned against and no member of either House sought a debate on these Orders, so all five came into force in the minimum time (that is, after the lapse of the twenty-one-day period for petitioning and the subsequent twenty-one-day period during which either House may annul the order).

Three of the four Orders laid in earlier sessions met with opposition. The City of Westminster (Christchurch Gardens, SW1) Compulsory Purchase Order 1985 had been petitioned against and referred to a joint committee, but no proceedings on the Order took place during the 1988–9 session. Progress was, however, made with the London Docklands (East Docklands) Compulsory Purchase Order 1985, the petition of the Thames Water Authority against this Order being withdrawn in February 1989; the Order thereby became unopposed. The Harwich Dock Company Harbour Empowerment Order 1988 had a complicated history before the start of the session, having been laid, petitioned against, and withdrawn because it required some redrafting, and then relaid, so that the petitioning period extended into the 1988–9 session. The Order was referred to a joint

[15] The City of Glasgow District Council Order Confirmation Bill and the Scrabster Harbour Order Confirmation Bill.

[16] Special Procedure Orders provide a way of re-examining decisions taken by ministers and statutory authorities under certain legislation.

committee in December and the committee (containing three peers, one of whom was chairman, and three MPs) met in July 1989. It decided that the Order should be amended to provide that the dock extension should not take place until authorization had been given for the construction of a proposed bypass. This was in line with a petitioner's request and probably also with the promoter's intentions.

The Joint Committee on Private Bill Procedure

The debate in the House of Lords on the Joint Committee's report was held in May 1989.[17] The House supported the idea that promoters should not be able to obtain planning permission for their works by means of bills if other procedures were available to them. On balance peers who spoke were in favour of the establishment of alternative procedures for railways, tramways, and harbour works. Most of the detailed procedural recommendations were mentioned only briefly in debate. Overall, peers seemed to think that the increased burden of private bill work had shown some flaws in the procedure and that the Joint Committee's suggestions for changes were sensible. The House of Commons took a similar view of the Committee's report. Subsequently a number of changes have been made to the Standing Orders of both Houses to implement some of the recommendations. In November 1991 the Government introduced the Transport and Works Bill, creating a system of ministerial orders for authorizing certain transport schemes and works without the need for legislation.

Conclusion

The 1988–9 session was atypical for private bills. There were more controversial works bills than usual and the progress of bills was greatly delayed because of action in the Commons. But a few general conclusions about the House of Lords and private bill

[17] HL Debs., 17 May 1989, cols. 1180–1212; for debate in the House of Commons on this Report see HC Debs., 20 Apr. 1989, cols. 474–548.

procedure may be drawn. The most obvious is that, when party feelings are running high over a private bill, private legislation is more likely to receive calm consideration on its merits in the upper House than in the lower. The controversy over two ports bills disrupted other private business in the Commons: it is unlikely that any dispute would similarly spill over in the Lords. On the other hand, the doctrine that private bills stand outside the party political struggle may be less easy to maintain in the Lords in future; the Government's interest in the Cardiff Bay Barrage Bill [HL] may presage a change.

In regard to private legislation the traditional role of the Lords has not been simply that of a revising chamber. Both Houses attempt to scrutinize private bills carefully for their expediency and desirability. The Lords in this session did fulfil its function of scrupulous examination of complex local authority bills, but the two Houses displayed equal readiness to amend private bills and the Commons seemed in general more prepared to reject bills. An important difference between the Houses lies in the role of Counsel to the Chairman of Committees in the House of Lords. He ensures that all private bills are carefully examined for unnecessary, inappropriate, oppressive, or badly drafted provisions. Comments are supplied to promoters, in the form of 'Lord Chairman's observations', with a view to making any necessary amendments, normally in unopposed bill committees.

As far as committee proceedings are concerned, it is noteworthy that the Joint Committee heard criticisms about Commons committees but none specifically about Lords committees. Of course, committees in the Commons suffer from the fact that often their members have a heavier workload than peers, but the broad and relevant experience of many members of select committees in the Lords, as shown in this session, may also have contributed to the respect for Lords committees. Finally, there are signs that the authorities in the Lords considered that the expected increase in the number of works bills threatened the smooth working of private bill procedure in the Lords as in the Commons. Perhaps the 1988–9 session will be seen in retrospect as a turning-point both for the House of Lords and for private legislation: the session when it became clear that private legislation was beginning to impose too many burdens on members of both Houses and therefore was due for radical change.

8

Debates and Questions

R. L. Borthwick

There are broadly two views of debate in the House of Lords. The first tends to be disparaging: to see it as 'rhetoric from yesterday's men', an opportunity for bores to pontificate. The alternative view holds that one of the chief claims to usefulness that the House of Lords can advance is its capacity to debate issues of the day in the light of the experience and expertise of its members. Compared to the Commons, the Lords has greater flexibility in its timetable, less pressure of business (at least for part of the year), a wider range of expertise and experience, and last, but probably not least, a less partisan atmosphere in which, potentially, speakers may have more impact on their audience.

Certainly the pressure of time is less in the Lords. For most of the year the House does not find it necessary to sit on Fridays and, even though it sits longer than was the case thirty years ago, it still manages usually to end its day at a more civilized hour than does the Commons.

Within these confines there are a number of opportunities for peers to initiate debate. Wednesdays for much of the session and occasionally other days are devoted to debates on motions. In addition to debates on formal motions which, as Table 8.1 shows, occupied 17.1 per cent of the time of the House in 1988–9, there are other opportunities for discussion in the House.

Chief among these is the unstarred question. Taken as the last business on any day, they may appear analogous to the daily adjournment debate in the Commons but, as Shell points out, 'Unlike Commons adjournment debates, no time limit exists for debate on unstarred questions, which may range from half an hour or less to three hours or even more.'[1]

Starred questions (or questions for oral answer) also exist in the Lords. But whereas in the Commons these are limited by

[1] Donald Shell, *The House of Lords*, 2nd edn. (Harvester Wheatsheaf, London, 1992), 120.

Table 8.1. *Non-legislative debate and questions, 1988–9*

	Total no.	Total time (hrs. m.)	Time as a percentage of total time in session
Address in reply (Queen's Speech debate)	1	18:33	1.7
Motions to 'take note':			
Government	5	28:32	2.6
Others	2	7:57	0.7
EC Committee report	12	29:56	2.8
Science and Technology Committee reports	2[a]	2:57	0.3
Motions for papers:			
Balloted motions	12	26:14	2.4
Others	25	89:30	8.3
Unstarred questions	35	48:01	4.5
Private notice question	1	0:31	
Ministerial statements	31[b]	18:37	1.7
Starred (oral) questions	572	65:03	6.0

[a] Includes one report which was debated jointly with a report from the European Communities Committee; the time taken by this debate appears in the European Communities Committee entry. A motion on the Science and Technology Committee report was moved formally at the end of the debate.
[b] Includes two Private Notice Questions from the Commons repeated in the Lords as statements.

time, in the Lords they are limited by number: a maximum of four may be asked on any one day (including Fridays if the House is sitting, in contrast to House of Commons practice). Private notice questions also occur, though much more rarely than in the Commons. A further opportunity for quasi-debate is provided by ministerial statements, though these, as we shall see, are both less numerous than they used to be and less frequent than in the Commons. What is noticeably absent in the Lords is the range of post-question-time devices which are now so popular in the Commons: requests for emergency (Standing Order 20) debates, applications to introduce ten-minute-rule bills, and exploitation of (frequently bogus) points of order.

Central to the way the Lords operates is the fact that it controls its own procedures. The Lord Chancellor is not the equivalent of a Speaker when it comes to controlling debate. Suggestions that the House might create such a 'Speaker' have not met with approval.[2] The Lords relies on the collective will of its members, something which is not infrequently exercised.

A further feature that distinguishes debate in the Lords from its Commons counterpart is that the House acknowledges the existence of a list of speakers for debates (the list helpfully indicates also any maiden speech that is to be delivered). This makes life relatively predictable: there is no equivalent of the Commons scramble to catch the Speaker's eye and no sense of frustration at à speech undelivered. However, the very predictability of the order of speaking rules out the spontaneous intervention. As Shell points out: 'the word "debate" is in some ways a misnomer. Typically a motion (or unstarred question) gives rise to a series of speeches, each carefully prepared and often read almost verbatim. Succeeding speeches may deal with wholly diverse aspects of a subject.'[3]

The list is nearly always followed. For example, for a debate on Prisons and Alternatives to Custody on 30 November 1988 the list of those who spoke is nearly identical with the list published in advance: one speaker listed did not in the event speak. On the following day, for a debate on a European Communities Committee report, the list of those down to speak is exactly a list of those who did speak. The device operates also for unstarred questions: on each of the days mentioned the list for an unstarred question is precisely a list of those who spoke. Just occasionally there is minor embarrassment when a peer misreads the list and tries to speak at the same time as someone else. Occasionally a peer may drop out, or sometimes the order of the list may be varied by agreement. Peers whose names are not on the list may by custom intervene immediately before the winding-up speeches.

Debates on Motions

Non-legislative debate in the House of Lords takes place in a variety of forms. Most substantial are those debates that are held

[2] See the Report by the Group on the Working of the House, HL Paper 9, 1987–8, para. 15.
[3] Shell, *House of Lords*, 191.

on motions. These are principally of two types: motions to take note and motions for papers (that is, motions asking for papers on a subject to be laid before the House—such motions are never moved by ministers and are always withdrawn). A third type of motion is also possible, the so-called motion for a resolution. However, there were no debates of this sort in the 1988–9 session. That absence helps to explain why not a single division occurred during non-legislative debates in 1988–9. Chronologically, of course, the first debate each session is the debate on the address in reply to the Queen's Speech. This occupied three days of debate in 1988–9 but here too, in marked contrast to the equivalent debate in the Commons, there were no divisions (though in some sessions there may be divisions on amendments to the address).

During 1988–9 there were twenty debates held on take-note motions and thirty-seven on motions for papers. Of the twenty take-note debates, twelve were on reports of the House's European Communities Committee, one on a report from its Science and Technology Committee, one on a report from the Joint Committee on Private Bill Procedure, and one on a report from the Select Committee on Murder and Life Imprisonment. The remaining five motions were all moved by ministers and included some of the major debates of the session, notably the debate on the Government's proposals for reform of legal services (which is discussed more fully below), but also two debates relating to broadcasting ('Broadcasting and Terrorism' and 'Broadcasting in the 1990s'), a debate on the report of the inquiry into the King's Cross Underground fire, and finally the annual debate on the Defence White Paper.

However, in classifying debates in the House, the form of the motion may not be the most helpful tool. More useful may be the way debates are organized. Some non-legislative debates take place in time (almost always Wednesdays) allocated to the parties and cross-benchers; some arise from ballots which are held for the right to introduce topics on one Wednesday each month between the start of the session and the spring bank holiday recess, while others are held on days other than Wednesdays and represent agreement through the usual channels about the topics of debate. Debates on select committee reports and debates introduced by ministers are usually taken in this way.

A further complication is that debate may or may not be time-limited in some way. Balloted debates are always limited to 2½ hours, enabling two topics to be dealt with on each Wednesday set aside for such debates. These debates are known as 'short debates' and are thereby differentiated from debates which may also last 2½ hours in time allocated to the parties on other Wednesdays. On some party Wednesdays the time limit may be five hours (in which case only one subject is covered); while on others there may be no time-limit at all. The choice of format lies with the party introducing the debate, subject to the House's agreement to the necessary business motion.

The consequence of having a time-limit is that certain rules apply about the length of speeches. Short debates are governed by Standing Order No. 35, which may by motion of the House be applied to other debates with a time-limit.[4] In such cases, as the Companion to the Standing Orders puts it:

> Within the overall limit the amount of time allotted to particular speakers is agreed in advance and announced to the House. It is the practice to allow 15 minutes for the opening speaker and 20 minutes for the minister replying to the debate in the case of a 2½-hour limit, and 20 and 25 minutes respectively in the case of a 5-hour limit, and to divide the remaining time equally among the other Lords on the speakers' list.[5]

So, for example, before the debates on 14 December 1988 the Government Deputy Chief Whip announced that for the first debate there would be a time-limit of ten minutes per speaker (apart from the opening and closing speakers). However, such limitations are not always necessary: for the second debate on 14 December the Deputy Chief Whip had this to say: 'the number of speakers is such that it is not necessary to propose any formal time-limit but I am confident that noble Lords will keep the length of their speeches within the limits that are compatible with the spirit of these short debates'.[6]

As Table 8.2 indicates, nineteen Wednesdays from the start of the session to late June were devoted to debates initiated by the parties (and cross-benchers). They were divided up so that Conservative back-benchers had five, Labour eight, the Social

[4] On 1 July 1991 SO No. 35 was amended to apply to time-limited as well as short debates.

[5] *Companion to the Standing Orders and Guide to the Procedure of the House of Lords*, 1989 edn., 86.

[6] HL Debs., 14 Dec. 1988, cols. 941–2.

Table 8.2. *Motions debated in time allocated to parties, 1988–9*

Date	Peer	Party	Subject of motion	Time hrs. m.	No. of speakers
30 Nov.	Allen of Abbeydale, L.	X-B	Prisons and alternatives to custody	4:56	22
7 Dec.	Ewart-Biggs, B.	Lab.	Consumer debt	2:31	14
7 Dec.	Carter, L.	Lab.	Mentally ill and handicapped	2:28	14
21 Dec.	Blake, L.	Con.	Historic buildings and treasures	4:40	18
25 Jan.	Jenkins of Hillhead, L.	Dem.	Conduct of foreign relations	4:45	20
1 Feb.	Cledwyn of Penrhos, L.	Lab.	Pollution and the environment	4:57	29
8 Feb.	Boyd-Carpenter, L.	Con.	Sunday trading	5:03	27
22 Feb.	Hunter of Newington, L.	X-B	'Working for Patients'	6:16	29
1 Mar.	Gallacher, L.	Lab.	Food production policy	2:42	11
15 Mar.	Reay, L.	Con.	Crimes of violence	4:49	18
22 Mar.	McIntosh of Haringey, L.	Lab.	Non-elected body appointments	2:29	11
22 Mar.	Turner of Camden, B.	Lab.	Social policies	2:26	15
12 Apr.	Blackstone, B.	Lab.	Higher education	4:56	30
19 Apr.	Home of the Hirsel, L.	Con.	The Western Alliance	4:35	21
26 Apr.	McGregor of Durris, L.	Dem.	'The Press and the People'	2:31	12
26 Apr.	Ezra, L.	Dem.	The manufacturing base	2:28	10
3 May	Cledwyn of Penrhos, L.	Lab.	The challenge of 1992	4:43	24
17 May	Bancroft, L.	X-B	Private bill procedure[a]	2:11	11
17 May	McCluskey, L.	X-B	Legal profession in Scotland	2:26	10
24 May	Underhill, L.	Lab.	Traffic and transport in the UK	4:17	17
7 June	Chandos, V.	SDP	European Community: increased integration	2:24	13
7 June	Ross of Newport, L.	Dem.	Homelessness	2:31	16
14 June	Kimball, L.	Con.	Brewing industry	3:20	18
21 June	Ewart-Biggs, B.	Lab.	Hong Kong	2:28	19
21 June	Turner of Camden, B.	Lab.	Working women	2:20	10

[a] All debates were on motions for papers except that on private bill procedure, which was on a motion to take note.

and Liberal Democrats two and a half, the Social Democratic Party a half, and the cross-benchers three. Particularly for the smaller parties, the number of Wednesdays allocated is important as an indication of their status. In that respect the Social Democratic Party has suffered a reduction in its status, as it has in other ways; for example it is no longer automatically called to question Government statements.[7]

In 1988–9 the Conservatives used each of their Wednesdays to debate a single topic and without any recourse to a five-hour time-limit. The topics for their debates are chosen by the Association of Conservative Peers and the chairman of that body at the time (though his view is not necessarily overriding) disapproved of time limits. Labour used three of its days to hold two debates, while the Social and Liberal Democrats split one of their Wednesdays and shared another with the Social Democratic Party. One of the Wednesdays allocated to cross-benchers was also used for a 'double header'.

Table 8.2 also indicates that the topics covered in these debates were extremely diverse. Some covered major areas of domestic and foreign policy. A debate on the Government's proposals for the National Health Service, initiated by a cross-bencher, Lord Hunter of Newington, produced the longest of these debates, though having the same number of speakers as the debate introduced by Lord Cledwyn of Penrhos on environmental pollution. Measured in that way, the most popular debate in this group was that on higher education introduced by Baroness Blackstone, which attracted thirty speakers.

On six other Wednesdays from December to May, the topics for debate were chosen by ballot from among the motions on the Order Paper. As noted above, each of these Wednesdays is divided into two 'short debates'. In 1988–9 those successful in the ballot were three Conservative back-benchers, four Labour peers, two Social and Liberal Democrats, and three cross-benchers. Table 8.3 sets out the details of these debates. The topics covered ranged from southern Africa to Scottish devolution (the most popular in this category judged by number of

[7] See the exchange in HL Debs., 19 Dec. 1988, col. 1141, when Lord Walston on behalf of the SDP claimed the right to speak after the Liberal Democrats. This claim was not accepted and a back-bench Conservative, Lord Boyd-Carpenter, was given precedence.

Table 8.3. *Balloted short (2½-hour) debates, 1988–9*

Date	Peer	Party	Subject of motion	Time (hrs. m.)	No. of speakers
14 Dec.	Hatch of Lusby, L.	Lab.	Southern Africa	2:30	13
14 Dec.	Buckmaster, V.	X-B	Human rights	2:20	9
18 Jan.	Perth, E.	X-B	Scottish devolution	2:27	19
18 Jan.	Irvine of Lairg, L.	Lab.	Interpretation of Acts	2:13	13
15 Feb.	Somers, L.	X-B	Use of the railways	2:16	17
15 Feb.	Hanworth, V.	SDP	Trained engineers and technicians	2:26	10
8 Mar.	Stewart of Fulham, L.	Lab.	Teacher shortages	2:29	14
8 Mar.	Campbell of Croy, L.	Con.	Toxic waste disposal	1:33	6
5 Apr.	Brougham and Vaux, L.	Con.	Road users and the law	2:22	12
5 Apr.	Rochester, L.	Dem.	Training	1:47	7
10 May	Kinnoull, E.	Con.	Compulsory purchase compensation	1:22	6
10 May	Longford, E.	Lab.	Polytechnics	2:29	16

Note: All debates were on motions for papers.

participants). Some debates last much less than the allotted 2½ hours: for example, a debate on toxic waste disposal lasted just over 1½ hours and attracted just six speakers, and a debate on compulsory purchase compensation was over in less than 1½ hours and also had only six speakers.

The House of Lords is able to devote a good deal of time to discussing reports by its committees, particularly those on the European Communities and on Science and Technology (the work of which is described in Chapters 9 and 10 respectively). During 1988–9 no fewer than twelve debates were held on reports by the European Communities Committee and one on a report from the Science and Technology Committee; one of the European Communities Committee debates was combined with coverage of a Science and Technology Committee report, with the motion relating to the latter being taken formally. Such debates rarely last more than three hours and may occupy less than one hour. Table 8.4 gives details of these debates in 1988–9, and indicates that on two occasions the topics were dispatched in less than an hour. These debates are normally introduced, on motions to take note, by the peer who has chaired the sub-committee which produced the report. There were two exceptions to this in 1988–9: the reports on alternative energy sources and on package travel being introduced by other members of the subcommittees responsible.

Included in this group was a debate on the report of an *ad hoc* select committee, on Murder and Life Imprisonment. That committee is discussed in Chapter 10.

The final category of debates arising from motions is a more heterogeneous group. As Table 8.5 indicates, most are debates initiated by the Government, but included also is a debate initiated by a cross-bencher on the parole system. It is convenient to include under this heading also the debate on the address in reply to the Queen's Speech which occupied three days at the start of the session (technically part of a fourth day was also taken up with it but on that opening day the proceedings were largely of a formal kind). Each of the three main days was devoted to a separate topic, foreign and defence policy on the first, followed by home and social affairs and then economic and environmental affairs on the final day. Together these three days amounted to some thirteen hours of debate on the Government's proposals.

Table 8.4. *Debates on select committee reports, 1988–9*

Date	Peer	Party	Subject of motion	Time (hrs. m.)	No. of speakers
1 Dec.	Renwick, L.	Con.	Alternative energy sources (ECC)	3:00	12
15 Dec.	Broxbourne, L.	Con.	Package Travel (ECC)	2:40	9
23 Jan.	Kearton, L.	X-B	European Financial Area (ECC)	2:29	11
7 Feb.	Allen of Abbeydale, L.	X-B	Visual display units (ECC)	0:54	5
13 Mar.	Oliver of Aylmerton, L.	X-B	Public procurement directives (ECC)	0:55	4
13 Apr.	Robson of Kiddington, B.	Dem.	Fraud against the Community (ECC)	3:20	15
14 Apr.	Cranbrook, E.	Con.	Radioactive waste management (ECC)[a]	3:50	16
	Nelson of Stafford, L.	Con.	R. & D. in nuclear power (S. & T.)[a]	0:03	1
21 Apr.	Butterworth, L.	Con.	Agricultural and food research (S. & T.)	2:54	12
24 May	Oliver of Aylmerton, L.	X-B	Merger control (ECC)	2:12	10
27 July	Allen of Abbeydale, L.	X-B	Pensions benefits (ECC)	2:05	9
31 Oct.	Middleton, L.	Con.	Nitrate in water (ECC)	3:09	14
6 Nov.	Nathan, L.	X-B	Murder and Life Imprisonment	5:46	20
14 Nov.	Cranbrook, E.	Con.	Habitat and species protection (ECC)	2:00	11
15 Nov.	Kearton, L.	X-B	European Community and Japan (ECC)	3:22	13

[a] Debated jointly: proceedings on second report purely formal.
ECC: European Communities Committee Report; S. & T. Science and Technology Committee Report. All debates took place on motions to take note.

Table 8.5. *Other motions debated, 1988–9*

Date	Peer	Party	Subject of motion	Time (hrs. m.)	No. of speakers
22 Nov.	Colnbrook, L.	Con.	Queen's Speech: formal	1:01	6
23 Nov.	Glenarthur, L.	Con.[a]	Queen's Speech: foreign and defence policy	5:24	22
24 Nov.	Mackay of Clashfern, L.	Con.[a]	Queen's Speech: home and social affairs	5:04	20
29 Nov.	Caithness, E.	Con.[a]	Queen's Speech: economic and environmental affairs	7:55	31
8 Dec.	Ferrers, E.	Con.[b]	Broadcasting and terrorism[a]	3:08	16
12 Dec.	Brabazon of Tara, L.	Con.[b]	King's Cross Underground fire	2:51	12
13 Dec.	Ferrers, E.	Con.[b]	Broadcasting in the 1990s	5:59	25
7 Apr.	Mackay of Clashfern, L.	Con.[b]	Reform of legal profession	12:45	55
12 May	Allen of Abbeydale, L.	X-B	Parole system (motion for papers)	2:29	9
13 July	Trefgarne, L.	Con.[b]	Defence Estimates	3:49	16

[a] Government minister opening resumed debate.
[b] Government minister moving motion to take note.

However, this may not be enough. At the end of the session there was discussion of the arrangements for the equivalent debate in the 1989–90 session and it was suggested that the Government had refused requests for four days of debate even though at that stage the House was sitting on neither Friday nor Monday. The Leader of the House in responding defended the House's record of diligence and pointed out that the proposed arrangements had been agreed through the usual channels. However, he agreed to call a meeting to discuss the matter and to make a statement to the House. When he did so, it was to say that there would be four days for debate on the Address in 1989.[8]

As noted earlier, other debates were initiated by the Government, for example in December 1988 within a week there were two major debates relating to broadcasting. In the first the Government defended their plans to limit the access of terrorist organizations to the airwaves, while in the second there was a six-hour debate on the plan for 'Broadcasting in the 1990s'. It is customary for the House to spend one day each session debating the Government's Statement on the Defence Estimates and this it did in July 1989.

Undoubtedly the major non-legislative debate held in the House during the session took place on 7 April on the Government's proposals for reform of the legal profession. Not only was this a Friday but unusually the House began at 9.30 a.m. and, after a few items of preliminary business, settled down to a debate that lasted without a break until 10.41 p.m. At 12¼ hours this debate was easily the longest non-legislative debate of the session (apart from the three-day debate on the Address). Despite the length of the debate there was no time-limit on speeches. In all, fifty-four members of the House took part in the debate, with the Lord Chancellor, Lord Mackay of Clashfern, who both opened and wound up the debate, having to face some fierce criticism of his proposals from peers with a legal background.

The debate was formally to take note of three Green Papers but the bulk of attention was focused on one of these, The Work and Organization of the Legal Profession. By any standards it was one of the most remarkable debates the House has held for many years. As one participant commented later: 'It was an

[8] HL Debs., 13 Nov. 1989, cols. 1085–8, and 15 Nov. 1989, cols. 1318–19.

extraordinary scene . . . Never before have the Lord Chief Justice and the Master of the Rolls, flanked by Lords of Appeal, confronted a Lord Chancellor as though they were an opposition confronting a government. In this sense alone it was a unique debate.'[9] One participant described it as a 'marvellous debate'; another observed afterwards, 'The House was full; the subject was a major one; the atmosphere was tense.'[10]

Certainly the cast list was impressive. Apart from the Lord Chancellor, the Lord Chief Justice, and the Master of the Rolls, participants included three former Lord Chancellors, seven other current or former law lords, a former Law Officer, the chairman of a Royal Commission on Legal Services, and at least nineteen others with legal qualifications (the great majority of them as barristers). Even among the twenty speakers who lacked formal legal qualifications there was relevant expertise, for example two had experience as lay members of Bar Council committees. There was inevitably a sense of the debate being weighted down with lawyers; indeed it was said that both the Bar Council and the Law Society were so concerned about this in advance that they had encouraged non-lawyers to participate.[11]

Whatever the truth of that, certainly parts of the debate took on the appearance of the Bar versus the Lord Chancellor. The flavour of the Lord Chief Justice's remarks may be gauged from this sample (which by the standards of the House of Lords was a stinging rebuke): 'It would therefore perhaps have been courteous, or even helpful, if those responsible for drafting the paper on the organization of the legal profession had seen fit to consult the judges upon the draft, at least, before proposing in "white" rather than "green" terms to disembowel the system.'[12] The accusation of discourtesy was subsequently withdrawn. The Lord Chief Justice, however, was concerned with more than procedural courtesy. He claimed to detect a threat to freedom in the proposals before the House. In remarks more notable for their hyperbole than their syntax he suggested, 'Oppression does not stand on the doorstep with a toothbrush moustache and

[9] W. Rees-Mogg, 'The Lords is a devastating place for any failure of argument', *Independent*, 11 Apr. 1989.

[10] Ibid.

[11] See *The Times*, 7 Apr. 1989, 'Bar acts to cool Lords debate on law'.

[12] HL Debs., 7 Apr. 1989, col. 1329.

a swastika armband. It creeps up step by step; and all of a sudden the unfortunate citizen realizes that it has gone.'[13] Lord Hutchinson of Lullington was, if anything, more outspoken in his attack: 'The paper contains a mass of claptrap and many platitudes. It is woefully uninformed. At times it is misleading. It suppresses known facts and it is overwhelmingly authoritarian.'[14] (Lord Hutchinson is also credited in *Hansard* with a rather un-Lordslike comment on the remarks of another peer: 'Rubbish'.) A former Attorney-General spoke of the threat to 'the structure of the administration of justice'.[15]

Other peers, however, accused the legal profession of over-reacting. Lord Allen of Abbeydale argued that the Bar had done itself little good by its reaction to the proposals. The complaints about lack of consultation, he suggested, 'seemed to bear out the impression that lawyers were living in a world of their own if they could not understand that Green Papers are the beginning and not the end of consultation.'[16] Lord Henderson of Brompton, a former Clerk of the Parliaments, took a similar line: 'It is sad that otherwise sane, sensible, intelligent and wholly admirable people should so demean themselves in public by the extravagance of their utterance. I believe that they have lowered their estimation in the eyes of the public and have severely damaged the standing of the Bench and the Bar, I hope not permanently.'[17]

Overall, however, the reaction of those who spoke was critical of the Government's proposals. Apart from Lord Mackay, who spoke twice, fifty-three peers contributed to the debate. Of these the great majority had little good to say about the proposals. Even dismissing the hyperbole of some of the attacks there were legitimate areas of concern: for example about whether the proposals if implemented would represent a better or cheaper system; in particular there was concern at the possible loss of independence for the Bar, about the possible extension of the power of the state, and about the possible dangers to the consumer in the area of conveyancing.

Of course, the Lords debate was only one element in the response to the Government's proposals. During the debate the Lord Chancellor mentioned that his department had already received over 850 responses to the documents. One thing which

[13] Ibid., col. 1331. [14] Ibid., col. 1342. [15] Ibid., col. 1350.
[16] Ibid., col. 1358. [17] Ibid., col. 1379.

the debate may have helped to achieve was a slight extension of the deadline for responses.

In July 1989 the Government published its White Paper on these subjects. In this there were a number of concessions to critics but not the wholesale concessions that many had demanded. The central elements in the Government's plans remained, namely the opening up of conveyancing and the extension of rights of audience in higher courts, though around both there were greater safeguards than had been proposed in the Green Paper. It would be difficult to say that the changes resulted from the Lords debate, though undoubtedly that gave much publicity to many of the issues, as well as perhaps damaging the credibility of some of the critics. There was some feeling that the Bar had overplayed its hand. One observer noted the contrast between the turn-out for the debate on the reform of the profession and that a month later when the House debated the Carlisle Report on the parole system. On the latter occasion there were no law lords present and very few Conservative lawyers. Certainly none spoke in that debate.[18] Given the time which the Lords spent on its debate on 7 April, it was a little hard of *The Economist* when commenting on the White Paper to suggest that Parliament had played no role in debating these matters. It may have been true that 'The House of Commons never debated the green papers. . . . Translating them from radical thoughts to half-drafted legislation (for so they are now) involved ministers, civil servants, the press, PR companies, pressure groups and the professions.'[19] The House of Lords deserved at least some credit in all that. It had debated the proposals at some length.

The debate on the reform of the legal profession attracted a great deal of press and other media attention. Many other debates in the Lords during the year also attracted attention from

[18] 12 May 1989. Indeed no Conservatives, apart from Lord Carlisle himself and Earl Ferrers winding up for the Government, spoke in the debate. It should perhaps be added that the House had debated a similar topic in the previous November. On that occasion two law lords spoke. Apart, however, from the minister who wound up the debate, of the 22 speakers in the debate only three were Conservatives: Lords Carlisle and Elton (both former Home Office ministers) and Baroness Macleod of Borve, a former member of the Parole Board. That debate, like the later one, was introduced by Lord Allen of Abbeydale, a cross-bencher.

[19] *The Economist*, 22 July 1989, 30.

the press, albeit on a more modest scale. Notable examples include the debates on broadcasting and on the press and several of the debates on select committee reports.

Debates on legal matters enable the Lords to parade a great deal of expert knowledge. A more limited (and less heated) debate held earlier in the session on the question of how far the courts should take into account parliamentary debates in their interpretation of the resulting statutes illustrates this very well. Of the thirteen speakers in the debate all were legally qualified and all but one were entitled to put the letters QC after their name. Among those who spoke were the Lord Chancellor, a former Lord Chancellor, the Master of the Rolls, four other law lords, two former Recorders, and a former Home Office minister who had chaired a committee on the preparation of legislation. It would be hard to rival such a range of expertise in thirteen individuals. The subject-matter was not, of course, likely to give the debate great publicity.

However, it is not just the law which enables the House to parade expertise. For example, when the House debated higher education in April, of the twenty-nine peers who spoke, no fewer than eighteen had first-hand experience of the subject. Among them were nine current or former vice-chancellors or heads of colleges, including one peer who had been the vice-chancellor of two universities and was currently master of a Cambridge college. Another former vice-chancellor who spoke had also chaired the University Grants Committee. In addition there were three speakers with experience as chancellors or pro-chancellors of universities and six past or current university teachers. To this should be added the voice of a former Education Secretary (Lord Joseph). One significant absentee from the debate was Lord Chilver, the chairman of the Universities Funding Council (UFC). Lord Beloff drew attention to his role and his absence:

> I very much regret that the noble Lord, Lord Chilver, is not here to present his case for believing that he can carry out his duties on the UFC on the odd day. I still more deplore the fact that, the Government having appointed a Member of your Lordships' House to this important position, he has not seen fit to participate in any of the discussions that we have had on higher education.[20]

[20] HL Debs., 12 Apr. 1989, col. 284.

Those with experience of polytechnics were not very visible in the April debate. However, the polytechnics were the subject of a separate debate a month later. Of the sixteen speakers on this occasion, only five had participated in the earlier debate. On this occasion no vice-chancellor and only one head of an Oxbridge college participated. This suggests that polytechnics are less well represented in the Lords than are the universities. In this debate the polytechnic voice was put by a polytechnic chancellor (who was also a former Education Secretary), the chairman of the governors of another polytechnic, two former members of the Council for National Academic Awards (one of whom was a former polytechnic lecturer), and a member of the Polytechnics and Colleges Funding Council.

The law and higher education demonstrate something of the expertise available in the House. An example drawn from the field of foreign affairs may serve to show something of the depth of experience to be found there. In April 1989 the House had a debate on 'The Western Alliance' introduced by Lord Home of the Hirsel, a former Prime Minister and Foreign Secretary. Participants included two other former Foreign Secretaries, three other former Foreign Office ministers, and a former Permanent Under-Secretary at the Foreign and Commonwealth Office. Impressive though the credentials of many of the speakers were, it is hard to resist the impression that it was very much a gathering of 'former' men.

Unstarred Questions

Unstarred questions provide, in effect, another means of debate. As the Report by the Group on the Working of the House noted: 'Unstarred questions have proved to be a popular feature of Lords procedure, in large part because they are the only way in which back-bench members can initiate debates without party backing or luck in the ballot for Short Debates.'[21]

As noted above, they are always taken as the final item of business on those days when they occur. There are no formal

[21] HL Paper 9, 1987–8, para. 58.

limits on the number of such debates; presumably the peers' sense of self-restraint is sufficient to prevent an explosion in their number. Certainly that seems to work: on average about one such question was asked each week during the 1988–9 session (thirty-five unstarred questions and the House sat for parts of thirty-six weeks). The actual timing of a debate is a matter of discussion between the potential questioner and the Government Chief Whip's office to find 'a suitable day when business can be expected to finish at a reasonable hour'.[22] Of the thirty-five such questions in 1988–9 only four were asked after 9 p.m. Subject to that negotiation the device, in theory, allows matters to be raised at relatively short notice; in practice there is sometimes some delay.

The subjects raised vary from the very particular, for example, the protection of the World Heritage Site at Avebury (13 February) or the redeployment of two teachers at a school in East Sussex (21 July), to topics that might equally well have been taken on a formal motion, for example, the policy regarding the privatization of British Rail (21 December) or training and employment prospects (27 February).

The thirty-five debates were introduced by thirty different peers (the total in each case would have been one more had Lord St John of Fawsley not been unable to ask his planned question because of illness (16 March)). Four peers used the procedure more than once during the session: Earl Russell asked three questions, and Lords McCarthy and Harris of Greenwich and Baroness Cox two each.

One of Earl Russell's questions provoked particular controversy. On 15 February he used the procedure to ask a question about the inquiries into the collapse of a banking firm chaired by his cousin. It was felt in some quarters that this use was an abuse of his position since the matter was of private rather than public concern. It was reported that Labour peers planned to boycott the debate in protest. In the event the debate was brief, lasting only forty-four minutes and attracting only one speaker (Earl Russell's party colleague Lord Grimond) other than Earl Russell himself and the minister replying for the Government. Only one other unstarred question during the session attracted so few

[22] Shell, *House of Lords*, 1st edn. (Philip Allan, London, 1988), 159.

speakers. The average length of all such debates was 1 hour 22 minutes and the average number of speakers 6.8.

Other debates raise wider issues and attract more speakers. The three most popular debates during the session were on peers' voting rights (8 December), the Windlesham inquiry into the television programme, 'Death on the Rock', about the shooting of IRA suspects in Gibraltar (1 March), and the affairs of the Victoria and Albert Museum (22 March).

In the debate on peers' voting rights Lord Stoddart of Swindon invited the Government to consider relating the right to vote to attendance at the House. He pointed out that his question had been prompted by disquiet over the large number of backwoodsmen who had been persuaded to attend and help the Government avoid defeat on its poll tax proposals (and that his question had been put on the Order Paper in May!). Fifteen peers spoke in the debate, several of them expressing reservations about Lord Stoddart's proposal. The Government Chief Whip in closing the debate unequivocally rejected it. The Government based its case on the argument that the right to vote cannot be taken away. Other speakers had pointed out that primary legislation would be required to achieve the aim, a resolution of the House being insufficient for the purpose.

The question on the inquiry into the 'Death on the Rock' programme was asked by Lord Bonham-Carter. Here was a topic that had attracted considerable public attention. The debate, in which sixteen peers spoke, lasted over three hours (the longest on an unstarred question during the session). It is possible that the debate suffered from not having occurred earlier; the lack of media attention for the debate was attributed to the story having ceased to be newsworthy. Among those who spoke in the debate were Lord Windlesham himself, Baroness Warnock, a member of the Independent Broadcasting Authority, and a former Chief of the Defence Staff, Lord Carver. Great differences of opinion emerged during the debate, not only about the merits of the Windlesham report but about the decisions to make the programme and to allow it to be broadcast and about the propriety of the Government's request that it be not transmitted, as well as the events leading up to the actual shooting. Inevitably these different concerns became somewhat intertwined in the debate.

Events of a rather different character were before the House three weeks later when Lord Annan 'rose to ask Her Majesty's Government what information they have received from the trustees of the Victoria and Albert Museum about the recent reorganization of responsibilities in the museum and about the treatment of the curatorial staff who have been made redundant.'[23] There had been much discussion in the 'quality' press in the weeks prior to this debate about the policy and style of the Victoria and Albert Museum's new director. By its nature this topic is one rather remote from the great bulk of the population but equally it was one that the House was well qualified to debate. As one member of the House pointed out, 'The presence in the House of many of the chief actors, the elastic rules of debate, the fact that nothing is out of order unless their Lordships think it so, the high intellectual quality of the speeches, made it a unique inquiry into a controversial and important issue.'[24] Although formally addressed to the Government, the question was in effect answered by Lord Armstrong of Ilminster, the chairman of the trustees of the museum. The debate was described by Lord Rees-Mogg as 'dramatic' and 'one of the best debates I have ever heard'. He noted also that, of the fourteen speakers who took part, eleven had experience of museums and their administration. Clearly in this area the Lords maintained their reputation for debating on the basis of expertise. Again this was a debate that did not attract much press attention. Part of the explanation for this is probably that the debate did not begin until 8 p.m. and did not end until almost 11 p.m. In that respect debates on unstarred questions as the last item on the day's business are not well placed to receive press coverage, especially given the deadlines operated by modern newspapers.

Statements and Private Notice Questions

In the matter of ministerial statements the Lords has inevitably to play second fiddle to the Commons. The presence of so few senior ministers in the Lords means that almost all ministerial

23 HL Debs., 22 Mar. 1989, col. 765.

24 W. Rees-Mogg, 'Fifteen minutes that decided the careers of a lifetime', *Independent*, 28 Mar. 1989.

statements originate in the lower House. The Lords is thereby placed in the position of having to accept a large number of repeats of Commons statements or of ignoring the topics.

The Report by the Group on the Working of the House in 1987 recommended 'that most Commons' Statements should not be delivered orally, but printed in *Hansard*'.[25] The Lords Procedure Committee considered this recommendation and others relating to statements during the 1987–8 session and its recommendations in turn were accepted by the House in February 1988.[26] The Procedure Committee drew attention to the division of opinion which existed among peers regarding statements. Those who favoured existing arrangements argued that discussion of statements 'adds vitality to proceedings of the House, [and] allows topical issues to be raised without delay'. Moreover a reduction in the number of statements made would restrict the rights of the Opposition. Those who favoured change argued that 'repeated Statements interrupt the main business, cause unforeseen delays in the daily timetable, fail to receive media interest and that the proceedings on Statements are often long and unruly and degenerate into minor debates, without adequate preparation'.[27] The Procedure Committee were unwilling to go as far as the Group on the Working of the House had recommended, preferring to suggest that 'Commons' ministerial Statements should continue to be repeated when, in the opinion of the Leader of the House, after consultation through the usual channels, they are on a matter of national importance.'[28] The Committee recommended also that there be a time-limit of twenty minutes for discussion of repeated statements. These proposals were accepted by the House in February 1988. Exactly a year later the time-limit was extended to statements originating in the Lords.[29]

It had for some time been possible for Commons statements that were not repeated in the Lords to be printed in the Lords *Hansard*. The House agreed in 1988 to a Procedure Committee recommendation that this practice continue but in addition that it be possible for the Lords *Hansard* merely to contain an italic reference to the Commons statement. This has become the

[25] HL Paper 9, 1987–8, recommendation w.
[26] HL Debs., 22 Feb. 1988, cols. 937–40.
[27] HL Paper 46, 1987–8, 3. [28] Ibid.
[29] HL Debs., 22 Feb. 1989, cols. 656–8.

normal practice. During the 1988–9 session there were no Commons statements that were merely reprinted in the Lords *Hansard*; on the other hand, attention was drawn to thirty-seven Commons statements by italic references in the Lords *Hansard*.

Partly as a result of these changes only thirty-one ministerial statements were made in the Lords during 1988–9 (whereas in 1984–5, a session of almost identical length, 104 had been made). Of these thirty-one, twenty-six were repeats of Commons statements (included in this are two Commons private notice questions repeated as statements in the Lords).

Of the five statements that actually originated in the Lords, four were made by Lord Young of Graffham as Secretary of State for Trade and Industry and one by Lord Mackay of Clashfern as Lord Chancellor. Inevitably therefore the great bulk of Lords statements are made by junior ministers or whips. Not surprisingly press attention tends to be much greater for statements originating in the Lords. Those made by Lord Young were given a good deal of coverage, especially that outlining the Government's reaction to the report by the Mergers and Monopolies Commission on the brewing industry (10 July). Lord Mackay's statement (19 July), on the Government's White Paper proposals for the reform of the legal profession, also attracted considerable attention.

The Procedure Committee's hope that a twenty-minute time-limit would be observed for discussion of statements was not wholly met during 1988–9. The average time spent on statements was thirty-six minutes; even if one excludes the time taken in reading the statement itself, the average is still twenty-eight minutes. Excluding the time taken by the statement itself, only nine of the thirty-one statements were dealt with in twenty minutes or less. This suggests that peers find more political value in discussion of statements than the Procedure Committee acknowledged, and, of course, statements have the considerable advantage of providing an opportunity for comment on very topical issues. It is interesting to note also that while the Lords were spending 18½ hours on statements, in the same session the Commons were spending over sixty hours on this category of business (or over eighty hours if business statements are included).[30]

[30] House of Commons Sessional Information Digest, 1988–9.

In some respects private notice questions are very similar to statements. They are, however, now very rare in the House of Lords. During the 1988–9 session only one was asked. This was by Lord Williams of Elvel, the Opposition spokesman on trade and industry, to Lord Young of Graffham about the Government's failure to publish the report of the DTI inspectors into the Harrods takeover. This was a topic on which the Government and Lord Young were under considerable attack. On 3 April 1989, the House questioned Lord Young for half an hour on the matter. Lord Young began with what was described as a 'defiant' statement including the memorable line: 'I shall not publish and I shall not be damned.' He was then subject to some stiff questioning on the issues and rebuked sternly by Lord Williams of Elvel for using 'this House for personal attacks on people who are not members of the House'.[31] There was little support for Lord Young except on the issue of the behaviour of Lonrho and the *Observer* in publishing a copy of the report in question. At least on this occasion the Lords could not complain about neglect by the media; the questioning of Lord Young in the House was front-page news the following day.

Private notice questions in the Lords are fewer in number than they used to be. This is largely because until 1983 it was the practice of the House to repeat some Commons private notice questions by means of an arranged private notice question in the Lords. In November 1983 the House agreed to take such repeats as statements; as we have seen, two were so taken in 1988–9. In 1985 the House agreed to reduce the number of such statements. In 1987 the Report by the Group on the Working of the House recommended that the procedure be dispensed with altogether; this was rejected by the Procedure Committee on the grounds that it might lead to an increase in the number of Lords PNQs.[32]

Starred (Oral) Questions

According to the Report by the Group on the Working of the House, question time is regarded with mixed views by peers. For

[31] HL Debs., 3 Apr. 1989, cols. 897–906.
[32] HL Paper 46, 1987–8, 4.

some it was said to be 'a lively and popular part of the day's proceedings', while others thought that it was the occasion for 'abuse of the rules, in particular in the wording and content of Questions (including repetition and vagueness), verbose supplementaries and ministerial replies, reading of supplementaries and the stating of points of view'.[33] The Report went on to suggest that a majority of peers believed that the point of question time should remain the obtaining of information. In that respect perhaps question time in the Lords retains a purer ambition than its Commons counterpart.

Few would dispute that question time in the Lords lacks the reputation of its Commons equivalent. The reasons for this are obvious: notably the absence of major political figures and the lack of Government responsibility to the Lords. Moreover there can be no equivalent of questions to the Prime Minister in the Lords. The House has never sought to cover the volume of questions that traditionally has been associated with question time in the Commons (though even there numbers answered are many fewer than used to be the case). Nor has the House needed to develop things like a rota of departments to answer questions on particular days. On the other hand the House has in some respects more relaxed rules about whether questions are in order than does the House of Commons. It has been suggested, for example, that a question on whether the Government would advise the Queen to withdraw the knighthood conferred on President Ceauşescu would not have been allowed in the Commons.[34]

Since 1959 the maximum number of questions answered orally in the Lords has been four each day. Any individual peer is limited to having two questions answered on any day. Until recently peers were allowed to have three questions on the Order Paper at any one time. In February 1988 that limit was reduced to two. Part of the reason for the change, which had been recommended by the Group on the Working of the House, was the feeling that such was the pressure on the available four slots each day that topicality in questions was made more difficult by

[33] HL Paper 9, 1987–8, para. 43.

[34] HL Debs., 10 Apr. 1989, cols. 1–4. The comparison with the Commons was made by Christopher Jones on television in 'The Week in the Lords', 16 Apr. 1989.

the need to table questions well ahead of time. However, further steps, such as increasing the number of daily slots to six, or adopting the Commons practice of allowing written answers to be given to questions not answered orally, were not recommended.

Certainly the four slots are usually taken. The average over the 1988–9 session (ignoring the first and last days of the session) was 3.8 questions each sitting day. This is on a par with other sessions in the 1980s but is a far cry from the 1950s when the average tended to be between one and two each sitting day.[35] Table 8.6 indicates that during 1988–9 150 peers asked a total of 572 questions. In the same session something like 2,400 questions were answered orally in the Commons out of almost 24,000 tabled there for oral answer.[36]

The Lords total of 572 hides considerable variation in the use of starred questions by peers. Table 8.7 gives an indication of the distribution of questions among those who asked them (but of course says nothing about peers who asked no questions at all). The most obvious point to emerge from the figures is that, of those who do use starred questions, the overwhelming majority make very little use of them. Out of 150 peers asking questions during the session, 127 asked five or fewer. Indeed over one-third (fifty-nine) of questioners asked only a single question for oral answer.

At the other end of the spectrum are those who were conspicuous users of the procedure. Twelve peers asked ten or more questions each during the session. These twelve, although comprising only 8 per cent of the questioners, accounted for 41 per cent (236) of the questions asked. Of the twelve, five were Conservative, five Labour, and one each Social and Liberal Democrat and Social Democrat.

On the Conservative side the most active questioner was Lord Campbell of Croy, with thirty-three asked during the year. He was followed by Lord Boyd-Carpenter (twenty-seven oral questions), and then came Baroness Strange, Lord Gainford, and Lord Orr-Ewing. On the Labour side the field was led by Lord Molloy with thirty-one, closely followed by Lord Hatch of Lusby with twenty-nine. Then came Lord Dean of Beswick (twenty),

[35] HL Paper 9, 1987–8, Table XI.
[36] House of Commons Sessional Information Digest, 1988–9.

Table 8.6. *Starred (oral) questions, 1988–9*

	No. of questioners	No. of questions	Average per questioner
Conservative	62	229	3.7
Labour	39	200	5.1
Social and Liberal Democrat	17	56	3.2
Social Democrat	7	33	4.7
Cross-bench[a]	25	54	2.2
TOTAL	150	572	3.8

[a] Includes 1 question from a bishop.

Table 8.7. *Distribution of starred questions, 1988–9*

	No. asking					
	1–5	6–10	11–15	16–20	21+[a]	Total
Conservative	52	6	2	0	2	62
Labour	31	3	1	2	2	39
Social and Liberal Democrat	15	1	0	1		17
Social Democrat	5	1	1			7
Cross-bench	24[a]	1				25
TOTAL	127	12	4	3	4	150

[a] Includes 1 question from a bishop.

Lord Dormand of Easington (nineteen), and Lord Carter (twelve). For the Social and Liberal Democrats Lord Ezra (seventeen) was way out ahead, while the most active Social Democratic Party questioner was Baroness Burton of Coventry (thirteen). Some, but by no means all, of the active questioners were former members of the Commons. Lord Hatch of Lusby, for example, had never sat there.

On the whole, as Shell notes,[37] those peers who ask the most starred questions tend to spread themselves over a wide range of

[37] Shell, *House of Lords*, 2nd edn., 203.

topics. Lord Campbell of Croy's questions, for example, covered a considerable variety of themes. It is possible to detect some concentration on environmental issues and matters relating to driving, but that still leaves a vast range of other topics including the University of Glasgow Veterinary School, gazumping, the community charge, and the use of 'National' in the United Kingdom. Of Lord Boyd-Carpenter's twenty-seven questions, six related to air traffic and four to taxation. In the case of Baroness Strange it is possible to detect very little subject overlap in any of her questions apart from three with a naval focus. Lord Gainford asked four of his questions on defence matters but otherwise spread himself very widely, as did Lord Orr-Ewing, who, apart from three on aspects of Soviet defences, ranged from Cabinet records to the delivery of holiday postcards. Some of these peers may have been among a group of back-bench Conservatives tabling questions provided by Conservative Central Office and intended to be helpful to the Government.[38]

Among the most active Labour questioners there is rather more subject concentration. Eleven of Lord Molloy's questions were on aspects of the National Health Service and six on the Middle East. Lord Hatch of Lusby asked nine of his questions on aspects of nuclear power as well six on Namibia and a further four on other overseas matters. Lord Dean of Beswick was an Opposition front-bench spokesman on matters relating to the Department of the Environment and this is reflected in nearly half his questions being on matters related to housing. Lord Dormand of Easington, appropriately for a former MP for a mining constituency, asked six of his questions on matters relating to coal, while Lord Carter's front-bench responsibilities for agriculture were reflected in four of his twelve questions being in that area. Of the other substantial questioners, Lord Ezra asked three questions on energy efficiency and seven on various aspects of national finance. Baroness Burton was perhaps the most specialized questioner, with five questions on consumer matters and all of her other thirteen questions on matters relating to air transport.

The House is capable of taking big issues as well as small ones at question time. For example, on successive questions on

[38] Ibid., 205.

28 February it moved from discussing the release of a named individual from prison to the question of East–West relations. Sometimes the House can be parochial, as with its concern about the design of its own Christmas card on 25 January—one of the rare occasions when a question was answered by someone other than a Government minister. That question was answered by Lord Aberdare, the Chairman of Committees, and the topic was evidently sufficiently interesting for nine other peers to participate, in addition to Lord Aberdare and the original questioner.

Members of the Lords worry from time to time about the time taken by starred questions. Until 1991 the official view of the House was that question time should last no longer than twenty minutes.[39] In practice this limit seems to have been something of a lost cause: during the 1988–9 session only about one-sixth of the question times were completed within the target period. From time to time the Leader of the House intervened during questions to suggest that enough time had been spent on a particular question and to remind the House of its declared aim of a twenty-minute question time.[40]

There is clearly a tension between that desire to confine oral questions to a twenty-minute period and the aim of exploring a limited number of questions at some length, thereby enabling government to be scrutinized in some depth. Although question time in the Lords is a more genteel affair than its Commons counterpart, in some respects ministers have a more difficult task in the Lords. They lack the respites provided by the rota system in the Commons and may well find themselves answering on topics far removed from their nominal departmental responsibilities. So, for example, on 18 July the Minister of State for Defence Procurement found himself answering a question on coniferous afforestation in Wales. Such situations are inevitable in a system where questions are directed at the Government as a whole rather than at particular departments and where there are a limited number of ministers available to reply. Sometimes the situation produces grumbles, as when Baroness Seear complained,

[39] In 1991 the House agreed to a new formula whereby questions could last for up to half an hour but with the new limit more strictly applied. See 1st Report from the Procedure Committee, 1990–1 (HL Paper 17), paras. 13–14.

[40] See e.g. HL Debs., 24 July 1989, col. 1124, and 1 Nov. 1989, col. 242.

'with two Questions on the Order Paper dealing with foreign affairs and defence it is a pity that no one from either the Ministry of Defence or the Foreign Office is here to answer the Questions, on which the House can reasonably expect an informed Answer'.[41]

Although, in general, question time in the Lords is much less frenetic than in the Commons, trouble can break out. On a question on Palestine in July 1989, for example, the Opposition felt that they were being unduly restricted by the amount of time spent on the previous question (asked by a Conservative peer). As other peers were calling 'Next question' a disgruntled Baroness Phillips protested: 'If the Government like to take nearly twenty minutes on the first Question, what right do they have to cut down on the time available for other Questions?'[42] In fact she exaggerated somewhat but on that afternoon questions occupied nearly forty minutes.

Sometimes the disputes are between a minister and one of his own back-benchers. A tense exchange occurred between Lord Young of Graffham and Lord Cockfield during a question about fraud in the European Community. In the course of supplementaries Lord Cockfield asked about a 1986 decision in this area which Lord Young confessed himself unable to answer; after other peers had spoken, Viscount Whitelaw intervened to suggest that a question of such a specialized nature should be put down as a separate question. Lord Cockfield continued to press Lord Young who delivered the polite but stinging reply: 'My Lords, it is obviously some time since my noble friend stood in my position answering questions on these matters in your Lordships' House and he has perhaps forgotten the formalities of this matter.'[43]

In that example the supplementary asked was arguably unfair. In other cases ministers from time to time find themselves somewhat out of their depth or inadvertently giving misleading answers for which they have to apologize subsequently, as with Lord Skelmersdale on 20 December and Lord Trefgarne on 15 May. Part of the explanation for this is no doubt the relative political

[41] HL Debs., 22 May 1989, col. 5.
[42] HL Debs., 24 July 1989, col. 1125.
[43] HL Debs., 14 Feb. 1989, col. 68. Lord Cockfield returned to the point at question time two weeks later and was still pressing his argument in a debate on a European Communities Committee report in early Apr.

inexperience of the ministerial team in the Lords during 1988–9. None of them except Lord Fraser of Carmyllie, Lord Advocate from January 1989, had ever sat in the Commons.

Question time is flexible enough to provide for what are virtually mini-debates on topics that arouse the House's interest. So, for example it was possible to spend nearly twenty minutes on a question on salmonella in eggs and poultry in December 1988, at a time when the topic was creating a great furore in the media. Later in the month a question on unemployment produced an exchange lasting fifteen minutes in which eighteen supplementaries were asked. Evidently the notion that the purpose of a question is to ask for information does not wholly state the case. On the other hand the House is strict with questioners who seem in danger of failing to observe the interrogatory form.

It is rare for a starred question not to give rise to several supplementaries. Only one in the whole of the 1988–9 session was not followed by at least one supplementary,[44] and only six were followed by a single supplementary. The average number of supplementaries per question over the session was 7.1.

As might be inferred from that average figure, many questions attract numerous supplementaries. The House's Procedure Committee has tried to stop the practice of the original questioner asking the final supplementary. However much the Procedure Committee may deplore the custom, many peers seem to like it. The conflict occasionally shows as in comments like that by Lord Kennet, 'My Lords, I believe it is the custom that the questioner may round up'[45] and when Lord Denham pointed out to Lord Hatch of Lusby that 'he has no absolute right to ask the last question'.[46]

Sometimes the subject of a starred question is seen as too large and the suggestion made that it might have been more suitable as an unstarred question;[47] at other times it is suggested that the detail in the answer is such that the question ought to have been put down for written answer.[48] To questions for written answer we now turn.

44 HL Debs., 30 Jan. 1989, a question on historic vehicles.
45 HL Debs., 7 Feb. 1989, col. 1435.
46 HL Debs., 15 Feb. 1989, cols. 178–9.
47 See e.g. HL Debs., 5 Apr. 1989, col. 1096.
48 See e.g. HL Debs., 6 Nov. 1989, col. 429.

Questions for Written Answer

In the 1961–2 session seventy-two questions were tabled for written answer in the Lords; it was not until the 1969–70 session that the total reached three figures.[49] By these standards the 1988–9 total of 1,221[50] looks like an explosion. By comparison with the Commons, however, it appears the epitome of restraint. In 1988–9 in the Commons, 39,540 questions were tabled for written answer and, including those put down for oral answer but not receiving one, no less than 46,404 questions received written answers there.[51]

The House of Lords then has avoided the mushrooming of questions for written answer which has occurred in the Commons. In theory there would be nothing to stop peers asking a great many more questions for written answer than they do (though, of course, the absence of constituency pressures, the lesser attention paid by interest groups, and the absence of research assistants help to limit the number actually asked in the Lords).

The Report by the Group on the Working of the House took the view that the position regarding questions for written answer was generally satisfactory, though they noted that some peers favoured a ration of such questions, perhaps to two per day, with a maximum of six on the Order Paper at any one time. They did not recommend such a restriction, however. What is certainly clear, as Table 8.8 indicates, is that in 1988–9 the number of peers asking questions for written answer is not all that much greater than the number asking questions for oral answer. The additional number are almost entirely Conservative peers; the number in the other parties and among cross-benchers is almost identical for the two types.

As with questions for oral answer there are great disparities in the number of questions asked, with a handful of peers each asking a lot and the great bulk of questioners each asking very

[49] HL Paper 9, 1987–8, Table X.

[50] There is a slight difficulty in determining how many questions for written answer were asked during the session. The official figure given in the Sessional Statistics is 1,202. My reading of replies in *Hansard* suggests that the figure should be 1,221. The scope for confusion arises from the habit of ministers of sometimes answering more than one question with a single answer.

[51] House of Commons Sessional Information Digest, 1988–9.

Table 8.8. *Questions for written answer, 1988–9*

	No. of questioners	No. of questions	Average per questioner
Conservative	100	481	4.8
Labour	41	294	7.2
Social and Liberal Democrat	18	92	5.1
Social Democrat	7	199	28.4
Cross-bench[a]	25	155	6.2
TOTAL	191	1,221	6.3

[a] Includes 1 question from a bishop.

Table 8.9. *Distribution of questions for written answer, 1988–9*

	No. asking					
	1–5	6–10	11–15	16–20	21+	Total
Conservative	73	17	5	1	4	100
Labour	24	6	5	3	3	41
Social and Liberal Democrat	14	0	1	3		18
Social Democrat	5	0	1	0	1	7
Cross-bench	20[a]	2	1	1	1	25
TOTAL	136	25	13	8	9	191

[a] Includes 1 question from a bishop.

few. As Table 8.9 indicates, 137 peers who asked questions for written answer asked five or fewer. In other words 71 per cent of the peers using this device fall into the low-use category. Those 71 per cent accounted for 21 per cent of the questions asked whereas the nine peers who asked the most questions constituted less than 5 per cent of the questioners but were responsible for 38 per cent of the questions. Equally striking is the fact that just seventeen of the questioners were responsible for almost half the questions asked (49.6 per cent). In other words seventeen peers asked virtually as many questions as the remaining 174 who were involved.

Top of the league table of questioners by a vast margin as Table 8.10 shows was Lord Kennet who asked the quite prodigious number of 173 (14 per cent of the total number asked in the session), more than 100 ahead of his nearest rival. What Table 8.10 indicates also is that the peers most active in asking questions for written answer were not especially active among those asking questions for oral answer. Four of the top eleven did not ask a single starred question. Conversely, the peers most active in asking starred questions were, with one exception, rather inactive in the other category: Lord Campbell of Croy asked two questions for written answer, Lord Molloy thirteen, Lord Hatch of Lusby one, and Lord Boyd-Carpenter five.

It is possible to detect particular themes among the questions asked by the most active questioners. Lord Kennet, for example, asked about one-third (fifty-six) of his questions on defence-related topics. At that time he was the Social Democratic Party spokesman on defence and foreign affairs. Other areas where his attention was concentrated included the environment (twenty questions at least), water (twelve questions), the Victoria and Albert Museum (eight questions), and the Channel Tunnel (five questions).

Of Lord Hylton's seventy questions, the largest number were about prisoners and the court system (nineteen questions), with at least another seven on refugees and five on human rights. Labour peers who revealed a considerable degree of specialization in their questions included Lord Mason of Barnsley with eighteen questions relating to salmon-fishing, Lord Graham of Edmonton with twenty-three out of his thirty-two on prisons, Lord Northfield with ten on deer and related matters, and Lord Jenkins of Putney with fifteen on matters relating to nuclear fuel. Among Conservative peers the most specialized of the active questioners was the MEP Lord O'Hagan, all of whose twenty-seven questions had a European Community angle to them, though that was not always obvious at first sight since they dealt with such things as lead paint in historic houses and the liability of village halls for VAT. Lord Brougham and Vaux spread himself over a vast range of topics, with no more than five or six questions in any one definable area. Lords Chelwood and Kimberley were less catholic in their interests but even they covered nine or ten topics each.

Table 8.10. *Peers asking twenty or more questions for written answer 1988–9*

Peer	Party	No. of questions
Kennet, L.	SDP	173 (5)
Hylton, L.	X-B	70 (9)
Brougham and Vaux, L.	Con.	57 (2)
Mason of Barnsley, L.	Lab.	33 (–)
Graham of Edmonton, L.	Lab.	32 (2)
Jenkins of Putney, L.	Lab.	27 (3)
O'Hagan, L.	Con.	27 (–)
Chelwood, L.	Con.	21 (2)
Kimberley, E.	Con.	21 (–)
Denning, L.	X-B	20 (–)
Northfield, L.	Lab.	20 (1)

Note: Figures in brackets are the number of starred (oral) questions asked in 1988–9.

Lord Denning is one of only two cross-benchers on the list of the most active questioners in Table 8.10. He did not ask a question until the middle of June but thereafter followed with a steady stream, nearly all of which were related to the disposal of church school property. Clearly Lord Denning had a particular worry, as he had in a quite different area with two questions relating to a single driving prosecution. His position as a member of the House of Lords enabled him to pursue these worries in a way that is denied to an ordinary member of the public.

Of course it is not only the most active questioners who can pursue particular issues or obsessions. Lord Fanshawe of Richmond asked nine questions for written answer during the session. Of these, six were concerned with the problem of litter on the A4 between Hammersmith and Chiswick. Lord Fanshawe was obviously dissatisfied with progress in this matter as his regular questions from April to October 1989 indicate. By the final questions in October it did seem that he was at last achieving some results.

Questions for written answer then cover a variety of topics from the local to the national to the international. A number of the questions asked are obviously prompted by the Government themselves, as for example those which ask for reports of meetings of European Community ministers. On other occasions no doubt the Government help to stimulate questions when they have information they wish to impart or achievements they wish to boast about.

Conclusion

At the outset of this chapter a contrast was drawn between two views of the value of the House's efforts in the area of non-legislative debate. It is probably not possible to demonstrate that either is wholly correct. As we have seen, the House succeeds in airing a range of topics that would otherwise receive less attention, and on many subjects it speaks with considerable authority. However, it is as well to remember the warning given by Shell: 'The mere fact that peers taking part in a debate have an impressive list of qualifications is not in itself evidence for the political importance of those debates . . . Lucid, original and sparkling speeches may have no more influence than boring and repetitive ones.'[52]

The target of debates varies according to subject-matter. For some debates it may be the Government, as it was with Lord Boyd-Carpenter's debate on Sunday trading. Likewise the Government was clearly the target of the speeches in the debate on reform of the legal profession. More often debates or questions are aimed at officials, as with Lord Harris of Greenwich's debate on crime on London Underground. In other cases it may be intended to influence the public or interest groups.

How far such efforts succeed is very difficult to say. With legislative debate there are more tangible yardsticks: amendments are made or defeated. However, non-legislative debate is much more diffuse: what is said in the Lords will usually be only part of a larger discussion. Peers themselves are inclined to rank non-legislative debate behind work on legislation and some of the committee work of the House.

In general it is probably the case that the more precise the topic the greater the potential for influence. Low-key discussions

[52] Shell, *House of Lords*, 2nd edn., 209.

of practical subjects, for example interpreting Acts of Parliament, are likely to have more notice taken of them than are big debates on broad subjects, for example the Western Alliance. On the latter it is unlikely that much new will be said or that civil servants will be forced to focus on new issues. Where the topic is more limited and where peers are speaking with direct knowledge then at the very least officials are obliged to address matters they might otherwise not. Of course, peers often show no greater knowledge than ordinary citizens, but they have the very considerable advantage over the latter that they can obtain answers from the government of the day to the things that worry them. So Lord Denning can nag away about the disposal of church school property, Lord Fanshawe of Richmond can keep pressing about litter on the A4, and Lord Mason of Barnsley can keep raising issues connected with salmon-fishing. Concentrating on a single parliamentary session may not reveal the extent to which peers pursue topics over a longer period. Assuming such tenacity does not result in the peer in question simply becoming regarded as an eccentric or a bore, then the potential exists for civil servants to be kept under pressure.

On the other hand influence may be limited by the fact that while Governments have to respond to peers, the ministers who are members of the House may not carry much weight in government circles. Equally, media attention may be less if major political figures are not present in the Lords. In 1988–9 press attention seemed greater on matters affecting Lords Mackay of Clashfern and Young of Graffham. Aside from seeking to influence ministers and officials, debate may sometimes have other targets, as with the debate on the Victoria and Albert Museum. There is, of course, an immediate target for debate, namely other peers. In that respect the audience for debate is probably better in the Lords than it is in the Commons, both in size and openness to persuasion.

Outside the House public opinion, both special and general, is a target, and specialized publications may well give coverage to proceedings in the House. For example, the debates on higher education were reported in the *Times Higher Education Supplement* but with only a small number of speeches mentioned. Moreover, it is difficult to say how much influence debates have with the wider public. For example Lord Wyatt of Weeford may use a variety of devices in the House to keep the issue of Hong Kong in the public gaze, but is that more effective than an article on the subject by him in *The Times*?

It is certainly the case that much of the debate in the House is quickly forgotten even by those involved. Peers frequently have difficulty recalling significant debates during the session. Those inclined to dismiss the value of the Lords' efforts may agree with Gilmour (admittedly writing over twenty years ago) that in the Lords 'the individual actors are good, there is no play'.[53] However, it may be important that some things are debated in the Lords; partly because otherwise they may not be debated in Parliament at all.

What this chapter has tried to show is that the House of Lords covers a wide range of subjects in the course of a session by way of non-legislative debate and questions. In pursuing these activities peers display considerable breadth of knowledge and experience, as well as occasionally prejudice, ignorance, and irrelevance. Assessing the impact of these activities is, as the preceding paragraphs may have demonstrated only too well, not an easy matter.

Moreover, there is no way of knowing whether the session looked at was typical. In formal terms such as length it was, but in one respect it may come to be regarded as different. It was the last session in which the House of Lords was the only House having its proceedings televised. Before the Commons joined in, there is no doubt that more publicity was given to activities in the Lords, particularly via such programmes as 'The Week in the Lords'. In that respect debates in the Lords may never again achieve quite the coverage they received during the sessions up to and including 1988–9.

[53] I. Gilmour, *The Body Politic* (Hutchinson, London, 1969), 304.

9

The European Communities Committee

*Donald Shell**

The Select Committee on the European Communities has become a major element in the work of the House of Lords. Every session since its establishment in 1974 between eighty and one hundred peers have been involved in the work of this Committee, producing some twenty to thirty reports annually. While the House of Commons has invested heavily since 1979 in departmental select committees, the House of Lords has directed much of its available capacity into the European Communities Committee and its several subject-based subcommittees. The Committee has gained a high reputation outside the House, based largely it would seem on the thoroughness and the competence of its reports. Almost wherever the role of the House is spoken of, the work of this Committee is emphasized. The survey cited above, in Chapter 3, suggested that peers themselves saw the work of this Committee as second only in importance to the work of revising legislation. Before examining what the Committee did during the 1988–9 session it is desirable briefly to set the context for its work.

Parliament and the European Community

The basic principle upon which select committees on European Community legislation in both Houses were established in 1974 was that draft legislation could be scrutinized before it went to the legislative body of the European Community, the Council, and that such scrutiny, together with the opinions expressed by Parliament, would constrain the actions of British ministers when exercising their legislative role within the Council.[1] The select

* For help and advice on many matters in relation to this chapter I am very grateful to Dr Philippa Tudor, a clerk in the House of Lords.

[1] On the European Community see S. George, *Politics and Policy-Making in*

committee set up by the House of Lords was given the following terms of reference:

> to consider Community proposals, whether in draft or otherwise, to obtain all necessary information about them, and to make reports on those which, in the opinion of the Committee, raise important questions of policy or principle, and on other questions to which the Committee consider that the special attention of the House should be drawn.[2]

In three significant respects these terms of reference and the way they were subsequently interpreted were different from those given to the parallel Commons select committee. First, the Lords Committee made substantive reports on policy questions, quickly developing the practice of taking a wide range of evidence very like the Commons departmental select committees, while the Commons committee made more narrowly focused reports aimed at identifying proposals which raised questions of legal or political importance, and which the Committee therefore felt should receive further consideration not by the Committee but by the House. Second, the terms of reference for the Lords Committee included a general permissive clause whereas the Commons Committee had no such clause. The Lords Committee has used this power to examine wide-ranging questions concerning the development of the Community, especially through *ad hoc* subcommittees. It has thus at times been specifically proactive rather than simply reactive in its approach.[3] Finally, while the Commons Committee was limited to sixteen members, and could only establish subcommittees from within this membership, no fixed limit was prescribed for the Lords Committee, which also had the power to co-opt on to subcommittees any peer not

the European Community (2nd edn., Clarendon Press, Oxford, 1991); also N. Nugent, *The Government and Politics of the European Community* (Macmillan, London, 1989).

[2] First Report from the Select Committee on Procedure 1973–4, HL 58.

[3] The Commons Committee has itself from time to time sought an extension of its terms of reference. A slight change took place in 1976, and then a further change in 1990. On this see 2nd Special Report from the House of Commons Select Committee on European Legislation 1985–6, HC 400, where the Committee specifically referred to the wider terms of reference of the Lords Committee in seeking for itself the power to report on wider issues affecting the Community; no change was made. See also 1st Special Report 1988–9, HC 533, where the Committee made a similar recommendation, later supported by the Commons Procedure Committee in its Report on the *Scrutiny of European Legislation*, HC 622, 1988–9, paras. 19–22.

already appointed to the main Committee. This provided a flexible means by which the large part-time membership of the House could be deployed.

Structure and Method of Work of the Committee

The European Communities Committee has generally consisted of some two dozen peers, presided over by the Principal Deputy Chairman of Committees, a salaried post created in 1974 to allow for the extra work anticipated as a result of the establishment of this Committee.[4] The Principal Deputy Chairman works almost exclusively on Community business. But the real work of inquiry and the drawing up of reports is carried out by subcommittees. The subcommittee structure has varied slightly over the years; in 1988–9 it was as follows:

A: Finance, Trade and Industry, External Relations
B: Energy, Transport, Technology
C: Social and Consumer Affairs
D: Agriculture and Food
E: Law and Institutions
F: Environment

Ad hoc subcommittees have been used with some regularity (eleven all told, to 1991) to investigate topics which do not lie easily within the purview of any single subcommittee. During the 1988–9 session an *ad hoc* committee reported on Fraud against the Community (see below).

For every Community document deposited in Parliament by the Government[5] an explanatory memorandum is provided by

[4] For a general view of the work of the European Communities Committee see T. St. J. N. Bates, 'Select Committees in the House of Lords', *The New Select Committees*, ed. G. Drewry (2nd edn., Clarendon Press, Oxford, 1989).

[5] The terms of reference of the Commons Committee define the range of documents that are deposited with both Committees. All proposals from the Commission to the Council for legislation are deposited, unless they are certified as confidential; confidential documents include those submitted to Inter-governmental Conferences and to the European Council (composed of heads of Government). Other documents for submission to the Council are deposited, as are any other documents published by one Community institution with a view to submission to another and other documents relating to Community matters which the Government might choose to deposit. The decision as to precisely which documents lie within these terms of reference rests with the Government. On the

the relevant government department; this indicates the anticipated implications the proposal has, and says something about its likely treatment, the expected timing of decisions and so on. With advice from the legal adviser to the Committee, and with the help of the explanatory memorandum, the Lords Committee chairman makes a weekly sift of all documents deposited (see Table 9.1). This is done on the chairman's responsibility but is confirmed at the next meeting of the main Committee. Those sifted to List A consist of documents which are not considered to require further scrutiny. Proposals referred to subcommittees make up List B, and from these the subcommittees themselves decide which to make the subject of inquiry. Those documents which subcommittees decide not to investigate are then listed as List C, while a final List D shows those upon which reports have been made by subcommittees. Every fortnight while the House is sitting a progress report is published indicating the state of the sift. Reports are submitted to the main Committee for approval before publication, but when published the subcommittee responsible for the report and its membership are always identified. Reports may be either recommended for debate in the House or simply made for information.

It is for the subcommittees to decide whether or not to report on a document. Given that each subcommittee can only undertake a limited number of inquiries in a session, the decision where to direct their energies may not be easy. Sometimes short inquiries taking a limited amount of written evidence only are undertaken. This allows a subcommittee to put in a report relatively quickly, perhaps breaking off its main current inquiry for a couple of weeks or so in order to do this. The subcommittee may decide not to conduct any inquiry, and not to make any report, but to indicate a view about a proposal by sending a letter to the Government minister concerned, a procedure used particularly where the subcommittee has already inquired into an earlier draft of the proposal or into a related area. Letters are also used to follow up inquiries, and to seek information about

face of it this seems curious in that the Executive has the responsibility to decide which documents Parliament's Standing Orders require to be submitted. In practice there seems to have been little difficulty over this.

Table 9.1. *European Communities Committee Documents: sift statistics, 1988–9*

	Total no.	No. as % of total
Documents deposited	901	100
Documents sifted A	618	69
Documents sifted B	283	31

Note: A Sift: not requiring further scrutiny; B Sift: referred to subcommittee for consideration.

Government and Community decisions after a report has been made. The practice of reporting such correspondence to the House in published form began in 1988.

Table 9.2 lists all reports made during the 1988–9 session. Of the ten recommended for debate eight were debated fairly soon after publication, one (9th) not until almost a year after publication, and one (2nd) was never made the subject of a motion for debate in the House. All substantive reports received replies from the Government, usually published as letters to the subcommittee chairman. It has become more difficult to find time for debates because of the pressure of legislative business. Elsewhere in this volume, Table 1.2 shows that in the 1988–9 session less than 3 per cent of the time on the floor of the House was spent on debating reports from the European Communities Committee.

In the 1988–9 session subcommittees generally met weekly while the House was sitting, though in the past fortnightly meetings had been more normal. About one-third of the meetings were for deliberation, or to consider draft reports, while the remainder involved the hearing of evidence, which was invariably undertaken in public. Some meetings combined both activities. Subcommittees have the opportunity to travel in the course of their inquiries both within the United Kingdom and overseas, though the amount of travel undertaken is very limited compared with Commons select committees.

Each subcommittee had a clerk attached to it, though clerks working for subcommittees were required to carry out other

Table 9.2. *European Communities Committee Reports, 1988–9*

	No. of pages			Information or debate
	Report	Appendices	Evidence	
1st	Inter-Regional Air Services (B)			
	17	4	129	information
2nd	Air Pollution from Municipal Waste Incineration Plants (F)			
	14	8	55	debate
3rd	Review of the Beef and Veal Regime (D)			
	19	6	100	information
4th	Anti-Fouling Paints (F)			
	2	2	10	information
5th	Fraud against the Community (*ad hoc*)			
	35	7	113	debate 13 Apr. 1989
6th	Merger Control (E)			
	22	13	114	debate 24 May 1989
7th	Farm Price Proposals 1989/90 (D)			
	4	2	50	information
8th	Efficiency of Electricity Use (B)			
	12	12	146	information
9th	1992: Health Controls and the Internal Market (D)			
	28	2	122	debate 5 Apr. 1990
10th	Equal Treatment for Men and Women in Pensions and Other Benefits (C)			
	20	21	140	debate 27 July 1989
11th	Withholding Tax (A)			
	6	2	31	information
12th	Correspondence with Ministers			
	—	—	(51)	
13th	Relations between the Community and Japan (A)			
	23	2	260	debate 15 Nov. 1989
14th	Marketing and Use of Pentachlorophenol (F)			
	5	3	11	information
15th	Habitat and Species Protection (F)			
	16	21	275	debate 14 Nov. 1989
16th	Nitrate in Water (D)			
	43	2	288	debate 31 Oct. 1989
17th	Burden of Proof in Sex Discrimination Cases (E)			
	12	11	33	information
18th	Blood Alcohol Levels for Drivers (B)			
	5	3	9	information

19th	Motor Insurance (B)				
	3	2	5	information	
20th	Aircraft Noise (B)				
	7	5	14	information	
21st	Transport Infrastructure (B)				
	29	9	288	debate 11 Dec. 1989	
22nd	1992: Border Control of People (E)				
	27	31	194	debate 5 Apr. 1990	
TOTAL	349	168	2,438		

Subcommittee responsible for report indicated by letter in brackets after report title.

duties in the House as well. In 1988–9 outside specialist advisers were invariably appointed for all major inquiries, and quite often for short inquiries too. Advisers were more often than not drawn from universities (see Tables 9.4 to 9.10 below). Recruiting advisers of the right quality at short notice has not always been easy. In autumn 1988 a post of Specialist Assistant was created, initially for two years, to serve the Committee. The post was filled by an agricultural specialist, who worked mainly for Subcommittee D.

Subcommittee E, unlike the other subcommittees, had quite specific terms of reference, namely:

to consider and report on (*a*) any Community proposal which would lead to significant changes in UK law, or have far-reaching implications for areas of UK law other than those to which it is immediately directed, (*b*) the merits of such proposals as are referred to it by the select committee, (*c*) whether any important developments have taken place in Community law, and (*d*) any matters which they consider should be drawn to the attention of the Committee concerning the vires of any proposal.

The chairman of this subcommittee has always been a Lord of Appeal in Ordinary, and it is also assisted by the Legal Adviser to the Committee and a Legal Assistant, the former being a relatively senior appointment. This subcommittee has in particular examined the treaty base, legal implications, and vires of proposals, including some which have also been examined by other subcommittees in regard to their policy implications.

Membership and Attendance

During the session under review eighty-one different peers at some stage served on the European Communities Committee, with the main Committee comprising twenty-four peers, and each subcommittee containing two to four members of the main Committee, and between five and ten co-opted peers. The Standing Orders of the House specifically provide that any peer has the right to attend meetings of select committees and to take part in evidence-taking sessions. The European Communities Committee has gone further than this by issuing a general invitation to any peer to attend its private deliberative meetings as well. However, during the 1988–9 session only five peers who were not named as members of the Committee or a subcommittee did actually attend any meetings of any of the subcommittees.

Members retire from the Committee after five sessions' service. The Committee appoints the chairmen of subcommittees, who are then exempt from the retirement rule for three sessions after being appointed as chairman.[6] It is worth noting that a high proportion of the active members of the House have served on the European Communities Committee or a subcommittee at some stage or other; of the peers who attended the House during the 1988–9 session, well over a quarter (218 out of 816) had served on the Committee or a subcommittee. As a result the House is imbued with an awareness of the practicalities of European Community membership.

The total membership of the Committee and its subcommittees in 1988–9 was somewhat less than it had been in the late 1970s and early 1980s, when around 100 peers were involved. There were probably various reasons for the decline, including the competing demands of other select committees, notably since 1979 the Select Committee on Science and Technology, as well as a fairly steady stream of *ad hoc* select committees. Nor has the supply of new recruits to the House been as abundant in the 1980s as it was in the 1970s, while the demands of work on the floor of the House have considerably increased. It has to be remembered too that the House is composed of unpaid

[6] On these rules see *Standing Orders*, No. 63 (1989 edn.) and *Companion to the Standing Orders* (1989 edn.), 166–7 and 174.

Table 9.3. *Attendance at European Communities Committee and subcommittees, 1988–9*

	No. of members	No. of meetings	Infrequent attenders	Percentage attendance
Main committee	24	16	9	55.4
Subcommittee A	12	25	3	59.5
Subcommittee B	18	23[a]	4	60.0
Subcommittee C	10	18	3	54.3
Subcommittee D	12	26	1	64.4
Subcommittee E	15	23	7	50.6
Subcommittee F	13	16	3	59.9
Ad hoc Subcommittee (Fraud)[b]	12	5	4	71.7

[a] Excludes one meeting of which no record of attendance is available; subcommittee actually met 24 times.
[b] This *ad hoc* subcommittee only held five meetings during the 1988–9 session, completing the work it had commenced in the previous session.
Notes: Members: all who served at any time during the session, but excluding non-members who attended meetings.
Meetings: all meetings, excluding visits away from Westminster.
Infrequent attenders: number of peers who attended half the meetings or less.
Percentage attendance: number of peers recorded as present at meetings expressed as a percentage of the total of members multiplied by meetings, allowing for peers who were members for only part of the session.

volunteers. This fact no doubt helps to account for the generally rather low rates of attendance at committee meetings revealed in Table 9.3—attendance levels are considerably lower than attendance at Commons departmental select committees. Nor do the aggregate figures reveal partial attendance at committee meetings, though not infrequently the verbatim record of evidence taken at a meeting includes apologies from members for missing part of the meeting, or even rebukes to latecomers.[7]

The elderly character of the House was not only reflected but accentuated within the European Communities Committee. Taking the main Committee and all the subcommittees, less

[7] See 14th Report 1988–9, HL Paper 71, Q. 60, where the chairman abruptly cuts off a fellow committee member's question, saying, 'We did deal with this quite well before you came in.'

than a quarter of the members were under the age of sixty (eighteen out of eighty-one; see Tables 9.4 to 9.10). The availability of younger members of the House to be active members of select committees is limited in many cases by their need to earn their living elsewhere. Those who are free to give time to parliamentary work tend to be sucked into front-bench positions, though several opposition party front-benchers did take part in committee work; of Labour's thirteen members of the Committee, six held front-bench posts. Overall the Committee was roughly representative of the parties in the House, with twenty-nine Conservatives, thirteen Labour, nine Social and Liberal Democrats, and four Social Democrats. But it also contained twenty-six cross-bench peers, a disproportionately high figure.

The Chairman of the main committee was Baroness Serota, who had first been appointed to that post in 1986. A Labour baroness, she had become a peer in 1967 after an active career in local politics in London. A veteran of many commissions and committees of inquiry, she had also held office in the Wilson Government from 1968 to 1970. Near the end of the 1988–9 session she attained the age of seventy, but some thirty other peers who served on the Committee or subcommittees during the session were senior to her in age! As well as attending all sixteen recorded meetings of the main Committee, which of course she chaired, she also managed to attend over half of all the subcommittee meetings which took place, a total of nearly 100 meetings overall in the session. It is to the analysis of the subcommittees, and in particular the reports they produced, that we now turn.

Subcommittee A: Finance, Trade and Industry, External Relations

The main inquiry conducted by this subcommittee was into relations between the Community and Japan. The European Community Commission had published a paper which concluded that the 'relationship was moving in the right direction . . . but not fast enough to reduce tensions significantly'. But according to

Table 9.4. *Membership of Subcommittee A*

Peer	Date of birth	Peerage	Party	Experience/posts held
Chairman				
Kearton, L.	1911	LP	X-B	Chairman Industrial Reorganization Corporation 1966–8 and British National Oil Corporation 1975–9
Members				
Greenhill of Harrow, L.	1913	LP	X-B	Head Diplomatic Service 1969–73
Murray of Epping Forest, L.	1922	LP	Lab.	General Secretary TUC 1973–84
Peston, L.[a]	1931	LP	Lab.	Academic economist
Co-opted Members				
Benson, L.	1909	LP	X-B	Accountant
Butterworth, L.	1918	LP	Con.	Vice-Chancellor Warwick University 1963–85
Camoys, L.	1940	H	Con.	Banker
Geddes, L.	1937	H	Con.	Businessman
Kissin, L.[b]	1912	LP	X-B	Businessman
MacLehose of Beoch, L.	1917	LP	X-B	Diplomat; Governor of Hong Kong 1971–82
Meston, L.	1950	H	Dem.	Barrister
Roll of Ipsden, L.	1907	LP	X-B	Banker; Permanent Secretary DEA 1964–6
Advisers				
Sir Michael Wilford, formerly Ambassador to Japan (Relations between the Community and Japan)				
Andrew Dilnot Esq., Institute of Fiscal studies (Taxation of Savings)				
Professor David Begg, Birkbeck College, London (Delors Report on Monetary Union)				

[a] Not a member of the subcommittee throughout the session.
[b] Although listed as a member recorded a nil attendance.
Advisers: Those appointed advisers during the 1988–9 session are listed, together with the inquiry upon which they advised. Some of the resulting reports were not published until the following session.

Baroness Elles, a member of the European Parliament, that important document had not been the subject of any debate or further study, apart from that by this committee.[8] As well as being advised by Sir Michael Wilford, a former British ambassador to Japan, members of the subcommittee visited Japan, and also went to northern England to look at examples of Japanese-managed industrial plants. In its report the subcommittee emphasized that Japan's purpose was to 'dominate in ever more sectors of business, finance and technology'; the Community would have to make greater efforts if it were to compete successfully with this economic superpower.[9]

When the report was debated in the House the Labour frontbench spokesman, Lord Bruce of Donington, spoke of it 'as a good example of the excellent and thorough work carried out by select committees in your Lordships' House'; most speeches were in quite sombre terms, emphasizing the growing imbalance between the Community and Japan. But the Government spokesman, Viscount Ullswater, exuded an air of relative complacency, which Lord Kearton rebuked in his closing response to the debate, suggesting that the Government 'look into a mirror of their own devising and are absolutely dazzled by their reflection'.[10]

While conducting this inquiry, Subcommittee A broke off for a time to make a brief examination of a proposal for a Community withholding tax, that is a tax on investment income at source. This had been put forward in a draft directive in February, apparently following concern expressed by the French Government about the liberalization of capital movements. Decisions were to be reached by ministers at a Council meeting in late June. Curiously the subcommittee did not commence its inquiry until May, by which time the proposal was effectively dead owing to opposition publicly expressed from both Germany and Britain. (Germany had introduced a withholding tax, and then withdrawn it after suffering a flight of capital.) At the very commencement of the first evidence-taking session, the Treasury witness being examined said that in the Government's view such a tax would

[8] HL Debs., 15 Nov. 1989, col. 1362.

[9] 13th Report 1988–9, HL Paper 65, *Relations between the Community and Japan*, para. 97.

[10] HL Debs., 15 Nov. 1989, cols. 1321–84.

be 'unnecessary, ineffective and damaging'.[11] Presumably the evidence the subcommittee took from the main banks, Stock Exchange, and other bodies further strengthened the argument against such a tax. But one wonders why the subcommittee bothered to interrupt its main inquiry to add weight to the already overwhelming opposition to this proposal.

One other published response from this subcommittee during the 1988–9 session was a letter concerning Community financial regulations applicable to banks. No detailed scrutiny was given to this, but the subcommittee decided it wished to raise three points on a draft regulation, which it did through an exchange of correspondence between the chairman of the main Committee, Baroness Serota, and the Paymaster-General.[12] Before the end of the session the subcommittee was well into its next major inquiry (completed the following year) on the subject of the Delors Committee Report.

Subcommittee B: Energy, Transport, and Technology

This was the largest of the subcommittees, with numbers rising to eighteen for an inquiry into Transport Infrastructure.

The subcommittee undertook two major inquiries during the session. The first of these was into a Commission proposal for improving electricity use. The efficient use of energy and associated questions of conservation had been matters of long-standing concern to this committee. In the previous session it had examined Alternative Energy Sources, and its report on this subject was debated in the House in December 1988.[13]

Two basic themes which ran through both the inquiry and the subcommittee report were the extent to which governments should concern themselves with efficiency, and the extent to which the Community as a whole as opposed to member states

[11] 11th Report 1988–9, HL Paper 55, *Withholding Tax*; see Q. 2.

[12] 12th Report 1988–9, HL Paper 56, *Correspondence with Ministers*, 22–3.

[13] 16th Report 1987–8, HL Paper 88, *Alternative Energy Sources*; HL Debs., 1 Dec. 1988, cols. 411–54. Following this debate an exchange of letters took place between Baroness Hooper, Under-Secretary at the Department of Energy, and Lord Shepherd, chairman of the Subcommittee; see 12th Report 1988–9, HL Paper 56, 37–9.

should stipulate policy in this area. On the first issue it was notable that Government witnesses believed the demand for efficiency was 'market-led' while almost all other witnesses took a different view. Thus for example argument took place over whether the testing and labelling of domestic appliances to show their relative efficiency should be left simply to manufacturers or whether some Government- or Community-imposed framework should be stipulated. The ineffectiveness of incentives for consumers to undertake additional investment to save energy was illustrated by one witness, a domestic appliance manufacturer, when he was sharply critical of the inefficient lighting in the House of Lords itself![14] The subcommittee in its report recommended that external funding should be made available to poor households to provide capital for efficiency improvements; it deplored the cuts in the Energy Efficiency Office, but drew back from requiring—preferring simply to encourage—companies to provide energy audits in their annual reports.

In the background throughout this inquiry was the Government's Electricity Bill then going through Parliament with debate focusing on incentives to energy efficiency in a privatized industry. During the bill's committee stage Lord Shepherd, the chairman of the subcommittee, with support from several other members, and amid much citation of evidence presented to the subcommittee, moved an amendment the purpose of which was to ensure that the electricity supply industry had a statutory obligation to be efficient. The Government resisted this, but were defeated by 126 votes to 114.[15] The House of Commons Select Committee on Energy then issued a special report which supported the Lords amendment, and the Labour front-bench spokesman back in the Commons referred to the Lords Committee as the source of the amendment, saying 'it was supported by the House of Lords Select Committee on Energy, which moved it . . .' (*sic*).[16] But it was rejected by the Government to be replaced by their own amendment. However, ministers did

[14] 8th Report 1988–9, HL Paper 37, *Efficiency of Electricity Use*; see QQ. 341–4.

[15] HL Debs., 16 May 1989, cols. 1044–58.

[16] 5th Report 1988–9, Select Committee on Energy, *Electricity Bill: Lords Amendments on Efficient Use of Electricity*, HC 478; HC Debs., 20 July 1989, cols. 553, 558.

Table 9.5. *Membership of Subcommittee B*

Peer	Date of birth	Peerage	Party	Experience/posts held
Chairman				
Shepherd, L.	1918	H	Lab.	Government minister 1964–70, Leader of the House 1974–6
Members				
Greenhill of Harrow, L.[a]	1913	LP	X-B	Head Diplomatic Service 1969–73
Kearton, L.	1911	LP	X-B	Chairman Industrial Reorganization Corporation 1966–8 and British National Oil Corporation 1975–9
Lucas of Chilworth, L.	1926	H	Con.	Motor industry, Government minister 1983–7
Renwick, L.	1935	H	Con.	Stockbroker
Rodney, L.	1920	H	Con.	Printing industry
Co-opted Members				
Chilston, V.	1946	H	Con.	Film producer
Ezra, L.	1919	LP	Dem.	Chairman National Coal Board 1971–82
Gorell, L.	1927	H	X-B	Shell International
Gregson, L.	1924	LP	Lab.	Engineer
Hanworth, V.	1916	H	Dem.	Engineer
Hood, V.	1914	H	Con.	Company director
Ironside, L.	1924	H	Con.	Business, Electronics
Lauderdale, E.	1911	H	Con.	MP 1951–9; industrial consultant
Llewelyn-Davies of Hastoe, B.	1915	LP	Lab.	Government minister 1974–9; Chairman European Communities Committee 1982–6
Lloyd of Kilgerran, L.	1907	LP	Dem.	Barrister, Patent bar
Portland, D.	1897	H	Con.	Career diplomat
Stedman, B.[a]	1916	LP	SDP	Government minister 1975–9

Table 9.5. *(contd.)*

Advisers
Professor M. A. Laughton, Queen Mary College, London (Efficiency in Electricity Use)
Professor T. E. H. Williams, Southampton University (Transport Infrastructure)
Andrew Hofton Esq., Cranfield Institute of Technology (Air Traffic Control and Aircraft Noise)

[a] Not a member of the subcommittee throughout the session.

claim subsequently that the 'strengthened provisions for energy efficiency [in the Act] were introduced in response to representations, including those made by the Committee'.[17]

In the same report, when discussing the role of the Community, the subcommittee was critical of the Commission for the narrow scope of its proposals. When the Director-General of the appropriate section of the Commission was examined, subcommittee members indicated by the tone of their questioning their dissatisfaction with the vagueness of the proposals put forward and their view that firm proposals were necessary rather than exhortation. In his second question the chairman asked: 'Is it because the Commission has such limited resources that you are required to take this line, or is it political?'[18] Though the subcommittee wanted the Commission to sharpen up its programme, their report was directed as much to domestic concerns as it was to Community policy decisions. The committee was clearly very keen to encourage efficiency in electricity use, but saw this as more the responsibility of national institutions than of Community institutions. The Government's response to the report was seen as weak by the subcommittee, which reiterated the main points of its own criticism.[19]

[17] 8th Report 1989–90, HL Paper 28, *Correspondence with Ministers*, 69. See also debate on Commons amendments in the Lords, HL Debs., 25 July 1989, cols. 1339–49..

[18] Ibid., Q. 197.

[19] 8th Report 1989–90, HL Paper 28, *Correspondence with Ministers*, 67–70.

The second major inquiry conducted during the session was into Transport Infrastructure. This covered five different Commission communications, but was mainly directed at a draft action programme for the five-year period 1988–92, running up to completion of the internal market. While Government witnesses argued against both Community funding for transport infrastructures and against Community institutions deciding priorities in this area, many witnesses drew attention to the way United Kingdom expenditure on transport had been falling in relative terms, with the CBI asserting that trade and the movement of goods had 'already outstripped the supply of transport facilities'.[20]

Evidence from the Commission spoke of the fact that the Court of Auditors had noted that in Britain (and Germany) funds granted from Community sources for transport projects had been deducted from national funds allocated to the area concerned. The subcommittee took this issue of 'additionality' up with the Minister of State at the Department of Transport, Mr Michael Portillo, who defended such action on the grounds that 'Community funds are merely funds which are provided by Member States into a pot and redistributed'.[21] This point was taken up again when the report was debated by the House, an occasion for a series of speeches mainly directed at the unsatisfactory nature of the transport situation in Britain. The deputy Chief Whip, Viscount Davidson, answered for the Government with a rather unconvincing speech. Lord Shepherd, the subcommittee chairman, subsequently wrote to the Secretary of State for Transport pressing the Government further both on the question of additionality and on funding for transport links with peripheral areas.[22]

Four other short reports were made during the session from this subcommittee. A proposed draft directive to standardize the blood alcohol level allowable for drivers throughout the Community at a maximum considerably lower than the British standard (0.50 mg/ml rather than 0.80 mg/ml) was heavily

[20] 21st Report 1988–9, HL Paper 84, *Transport Infrastructure*, para. 20.
[21] Ibid., QQ. 727–30.
[22] 8th Report 1988–9, HL Paper 28, *Correspondence with Ministers*, 71–2.

criticized. Written evidence only was taken on this occasion, but the subcommittee unequivocally concluded that enforcement of the 'lower limit would be difficult, costly and almost certainly unproductive'.[23] Ministers expressed their agreement, and Britain was by no means alone in expressing hostility to the proposal, which was later shelved by the Council of Ministers.[24]

A directive on motor insurance was criticized by the subcommittee because it was so loosely drafted.[25] Again written evidence only was taken on this. Subsequently no alterations to the text of the directive were agreed, but the Government in its reply to the subcommittee claimed that other member states supported an interpretation of the directive which was more favourable to the subcommittee's view.[26]

Finally, a draft directive on aircraft noise was also criticized by the subcommittee, partly because it was discriminatory, in exempting aircraft below a certain size (which the subcommittee claimed effectively meant one particular aircraft), and also because the subcommittee believed that the European Civil Aviation Conference (ECAC), which had a wider membership than the Community, was the better body through which recommendations on this subject should be made; certainly it wanted to see an effort made to harmonize the ECAC and the Community proposal.[27]

At the commencement of the session the subcommittee had reported on Inter-Regional Air Services, a subject on which it had taken evidence during the previous session. This was a narrowly focused inquiry into the extent to which greater choice for consumers and alleviation of congestion might result from a proposed directive on the authorization of services. The subcommittee welcomed the proposal 'as a small step towards the liberalisation of air transport within the Community', but there was a general tone of weariness, even cynicism, to the report. Among the witnesses was Lord Bethell, a member of the Lords

[23] 18th Report 1988–9, HL Paper 81, *Blood Alcohol Levels for Drivers*, para. 18.

[24] 8th Report 1988–9, HL Paper 28, *Correspondence with Ministers*, 71; also 18th Report 1988–9, HL Paper 81, App. 3.

[25] 19th Report 1988–9, HL Paper 82, *Motor Insurance*.

[26] See 8th Report 1988–9, HL Paper 28, *Correspondence with Ministers*, 71.

[27] 20th Report 1988–9, HL Paper 83, *Aircraft Noise*.

and also of the European Parliament, and a long-time crusader for change in this area.[28]

Subcommittee C: Social and Consumer Affairs

This was the smallest of the subcommittees, with only nine members until Lord Rochester joined it almost at the end of the session. It published only one report during the session (though it published no fewer than five reports the following session). From December 1988 until March 1989 it took evidence on a draft directive on 'completing the implementation of the principle of equal treatment for men and women in statutory and occupational social security schemes'. In its report on this highly complex subject the subcommittee welcomed the proposal, but called for certain aspects of it to be clarified, in particular the meaning of the term indirect discrimination.[29] On the vexed subject of pension ages the subcommittee favoured a 'decade of retirement' enabling anyone to commence their pension at any age between sixty and seventy. The subcommittee appeared to direct itself as much to British domestic policy as to Community policy; during debate in the House on this report Lord Allen of Abbeydale said: 'There are a number of issues here in which action ought to be taken by the Government quite apart from what happens to the Directive. They are matters of great interest and importance.' Lord Allen was rather less than flattering to the Government spokesman who replied to the debate; drawing on his own experience as a civil servant he suggested that the minister's speech had 'sounded distinctly like some of the pieces I used to write when I was a civil servant and when I had not the slightest idea what to do and could only write something which I hoped would put off the decision to some distant date in the future'. No Conservative peer—other than the minister—took part in the debate, which may have been because of its subject-matter, or possibly because it took place on the last day before the summer recess, keeping the House conveniently occupied until legislation was ready for royal assent.[30] In October Lord Allen asked a question

[28] 1st Report 1988–9, HL Paper 10, *Inter-Regional Air Services*.

[29] 10th Report 1988–9, HL Paper 51, *Equal Treatment for Men and Women in Pensions and Other Benefits*.

[30] HL Debs., 27 July 1989, cols. 1571–1608.

Table 9.6. *Membership of Subcommittee C*

Peer	Date of birth	Peerage	Party	Experience/posts held
Chairman				
Allen of Abbeydale, L.	1912	LP	X-B	Permanent Secretary Home Office 1966–72
Members				
Attlee, E.[a]	1927	H	SDP	British Rail 1970–6
Hunter of Newington, L.	1915	LP	X-B	Medical academic; Vice Chancellor Birmingham University 1968–81
Rochester, L.[b]	1916	H	Dem.	ICI 1964–72
Co-opted Members				
Bonham-Carter, L.	1922	LP	Dem.	MP 1958–9; former Chairman Race Relations Board and Community Relations Commission
Bucking-hamshire, E.	1944	H	Con.	Finance and banking
Cox, B.	1937	LP	Con.	Nurse, sociologist, academic
Hayter, L.	1911	H	X-B	Business; Security industry
Lockwood, B.	1924	LP	Lab.	Labour Party agent 1952–75; Chairman Equal Opportunities Commission 1975–83
Turner of Camden, B.	1927	LP	Lab.	Trade unionist
Adviser				
Sir Alec Atkinson, former Permanent Secretary, Department of Health and Social Security (Equal Pensions Treatment)				

[a] Although listed as a member recorded a nil attendance.
[b] Not a member of the subcommittee throughout the session.

about progress being made on this subject, and in the ensuing exchanges a number of references were made to the report from his subcommittee.[31]

Subcommittee D: Agriculture and Food

As might have been expected, this subcommittee had a membership rich in agricultural experience but less obviously qualified in regard to other aspects of the food industry. The only non-agriculturalist member was Baroness Gardner of Parkes, a dentist, but she recorded no attendances at any of the meetings of the subcommittee during the session. Lord Middleton took over the chairmanship at the start of the session. One member, Viscount Ullswater, left the committee upon his appointment to the Government late in the session.

At the commencement of the session this subcommittee was already part way through an inquiry into draft regulations concerning the beef and veal regime, a subject examined back in 1983, when the generation of surpluses had been criticized by the subcommittee. In the years since it found 'little improvement has been made'.[32] For a start the subcommittee was very critical of the fact that, though the old regime was due to expire on 31 December 1988, no proposals for its replacement were published until 25 October 1988. But it was also critical of the proposals themselves, as was the Minister for Agriculture, Mr MacGregor, who subsequently told the subcommittee that when the Council agreed a package of beef reforms the United Kingdom and several other member states voted against. Further correspondence between the minister and the committee revealed that a high measure of agreement existed between them. Both were eager to reinforce the arguments of the other.[33]

The subcommittee took written evidence on the Farm Price Proposals for 1989–90, following which the chairman wrote to the minister in advance of the publication of the report so as to make clear the subcommittee's views before the relevant

[31] HL Debs., 11 Oct. 1989, col. 298.

[32] 3rd Report 1988–9, HL Paper 22, *Review of the Beef and Veal Regime*, para. 1.

[33] 12th Report 1988–9, HL Paper 56, *Correspondence with Ministers*, 44–8.

Table 9.7. *Membership of Subcommittee D*

Peer	Date of birth	Peerage	Party	Experience/posts held
Chairman				
Middleton, L.	1921	H	Con.	Land agent; President, Country Landowners Association, 1981–3
Members				
Carter, L.	1932	LP	Lab.	Agriculturalist, farmer, Opposition whip and agriculture spokesman
Ullswater, V.[a]	1942	H	Con.	
Co-opted Members				
Brookeborough, L.	1952	H	Con.	Farmer
Elliot of Harwood, B.	1903	LP	Con.	Farmer
Gardner of Parkes, B.[b]	1927	LP	Con.	Dentist
Mackie of Benshie, L.	1919	LP	Dem.	MP 1964–6; fruit-grower
Northbourne, L.	1926	H	X-B	Farmer
Radnor, E.	1927	H	Con.	Landowner
Raglan, L.	1927	H	SDP	Farmer
Somerset, D.	1952	H	X-B	Farmer and landowner
Stodart of Leaston, L.	1916	LP	Con.	MP 1959–74; minister in MAFF 1970–4
Advisers				
Dr John Strak, Manchester University (Review of the Beef and Veal Regime)				
Dr Tony Andrews, Royal Veterinary College (Plant Health and Veterinary Checks)				
Dr Robert Maude, Institute of Horticultural Research (Plant Health and Veterinary Checks)				
Simon Harris Esq., professional economist (Farm Price Proposals)				
Professor J. K. Syers, Newcastle University (Nitrate in Water)				
Professor Bevan Mosley, Institute of Food Research (Irradiation of Foodstuffs)				

[a] Not a member of the subcommittee throughout the session.
[b] Although listed as a member recorded a nil attendance.

Agriculture Council. On this subject, too, points of dispute between the subcommittee and the minister were much less prominent than areas of agreement.[34]

Health checks on plants and animals transported across frontiers within the Community was a subject given salience because of the commitment to a single market in 1992. The Commission's concern was to dismantle all barriers to trade, but its whole approach was vigorously criticized by the subcommittee and most of its witnesses. Relaxed border controls, placing the onus for providing adequate health checks on the exporting country rather than the importing country, quarantine (where necessary) being provided at the point of destination rather than at the border, were all Commission proposals hardly likely to commend themselves to the British agricultural community. However, the Commission witnesses did provide a robust defence of their position against some hostile questioning from subcommittee members. Unusually the Government reply to this report was published as a separate command paper; this indicated the wide area of agreement between the subcommittee and the Government, which was further illustrated when the report was eventually debated in the House in April 1990.[35]

The longest inquiry undertaken by the subcommittee during this session dealt with a wide-ranging draft directive on nitrate in water, concerned not only with drinking-water but with fresh, coastal, and marine waters suffering from eutrophication. The subcommittee criticized the directive on three main grounds: first, it involved the adoption of a lower permissible nitrate level than members felt to be justified on the basis of scientific evidence; second, it was based almost entirely on a preventative approach, while the subcommittee argued that a curative approach was justified in some circumstances; third, the subcommittee was very critical of the Commission for its failure to consult more widely in advance of drafting its proposals. At its eighth and final oral evidence-taking session, members challenged Commission witnesses to examine the evidence more carefully (even asking if

[34] 7th Report 1988–9, HL Paper 34, *Farm Price Proposals 1989–90*; see also 12th Report 1988–9, HL Paper 56, *Correspondence with Ministers*, 50–4.

[35] 9th Report 1988–9, HL Paper 47, *1992: Health Controls and the Internal Market*; Government Response, Cm. 815; HL Debs., 5 Apr. 1990, cols. 1548–85.

they would read the committee report), while the witnesses were reduced to pleading lack of resources to do their job properly.[36]

When the report was debated in the House in October, the Commission came in for further severe criticism and the subcommittee for high praise. Lord Nugent of Guildford suggested that the Commission should accept an obligation to publish the scientific evidence on which its proposals were based; Lord Raglan claimed that the Commission had not done its research, while Lord Crickhowell, chairman of the National Rivers Authority, said he had never read a select committee report that impressed him more, and suggested it was 'almost certainly the most complete compendium of information, practical experience and scientific knowledge on the subject of nitrates in water that exists anywhere'.[37] While the subcommittee was conducting this inquiry the Water Bill was passing through Parliament, prompting questions about standards of water cleanliness in the context of the privatization of the water industry. The subject was frequently raised on the floor of the House with the evidence the subcommittee had gathered being cited.[38]

Subcommittee E: Law and Institutions

Lord Oliver of Aylmerton, who had entered the House as Lord of Appeal in Ordinary in 1986, chaired this subcommittee, which, as would be expected, contained a preponderance of legal expertise.

This subcommittee's distinctive terms of reference were reflected in its output, which differed from that of the other subcommittees in more frequently taking the form of letters addressed to ministers rather than substantive reports. In particular in 1988–9 the committee was concerned about the use of Article 100A (which dealt with the removal of barriers to the internal market) as a treaty base for a number of directives which, it felt, should more correctly have been drawn from some

[36] 16th report 1988–9, HL Paper 73, *Nitrate in Water*; see esp. QQ. 716 and 756.

[37] HL Debs., 31 Oct. 1989, cols. 141–84; for quotations see cols. 146 and 169.

[38] See e.g. HL Debs., 6 July 1989, cols. 1278–1303; also for questions HL Debs., 22 Feb. 1989, col. 654; 23 Mar. 1989, col. 827; 11 Apr. 1989, col. 240.

Table 9.8. *Membership of Subcommittee E*

Peer	Date of birth	Peerage	Party	Experience/posts held
Chairman				
Oliver of Aylmerton, L.	1921	A	X-B	Lord of Appeal in Ordinary
Members				
Allen of Abbeydale, L.[a]	1912	LP	X-B	Permanent Secretary Home Office 1966–72
Broxbourne, L.[a]	1910	LP	Con.	MP 1945–83; barrister
Mackenzie-Stewart, L.[a,b]	1924	LP	X-B	President European Court of Justice 1984–8
Robson of Kiddington, B.	1919	LP	Dem.	Past president Liberal Party
Co-opted Members				
Birk, B.	1919	LP	Lab.	JP; journalist; local government and Labour Party activist
Bledisloe, V.	1934	H	X-B	Barrister
Carnegy of Lour, B.	1925	LP	Con.	Farmer 1956–89
Colville of Culross, V.	1933	H	Con.	Barrister; Government minister 1972–4
Dilhorne, V.	1932	H	Con.	Barrister
Grantchester, L.	1921	H	X-B	Barrister, Recorder
Hacking, L.[a]	1938	H	X-B	Solicitor
Lloyd of Hampstead, L.	1915	LP	X-B	Barrister; Professor of Jurisprudence 1956–82
McGregor of Durris, L.	1921	LP	Dem.	Professor of Social Institutions
Wilberforce, L.	1907	A	X-B	Lord of Appeal in Ordinary 1964–82

Advisers

Stephen Richards, Barrister (Merger Control)

Professor W. R. Cornish, London School of Economics (Biotechnological Inventions)

[a] Not a member of the subcommittee throughout the session.
[b] Although listed as a member recorded a nil attendance.

other treaty base. The tone of Lord Oliver of Aylmerton's replies to ministers was slightly pained as he thanked them for their explanations, but insisted that the subcommittee retained its doubts about their validity.[39] Sometimes the legal implications of a proposal were examined by this subcommittee at the same time as another was looking at policy implications. For example Subcommittee E decided that the Commission was wrong in the treaty article upon which it sought to base its proposed directive on harmonization of blood alcohol levels for drivers; subsequently Subcommittee B also criticized this proposal (see above).[40]

Subcommittee E also published three reports during the year. The first of these concerned draft regulations on the 'control of concentrations between undertakings' or Merger Control;[41] this acknowledged the need for some transfer to the Community of the power to block mergers, but also urged caution. Lord Peston from the Opposition front bench described the report as 'immensely useful'.[42] Later in the year the Commission brought out a revised proposal, whereupon Baroness Serota wrote to the minister concerned that the subcommittee, having considered the revised draft, 'noted with satisfaction that on a number of points where they criticized the terms of earlier drafts, negotiations have altered it in line with their recommendations'.[43]

The subcommittee also inquired into a proposed directive on the burden of proof in sex discrimination cases, a subject of considerable complexity on which Britain found itself in a minority of one in the Council.[44] The final report concerned abolition of controls on persons at intra-community borders, and a draft directive on the acquisition and possession of weapons. The subcommittee held seven evidence-taking sessions, producing a lengthy report, which while acknowledging the ideal of a 'Europe without Frontiers' nevertheless argued that for assorted reasons, including terrorist threats, drug smuggling, and the need

[39] 12th Report 1988–9, HL Paper 56, *Correspondence with Ministers*, 26–8; see also 8th Report 1989–90, HL Paper 28, *Correspondence with Ministers*, 41–6.
[40] 8th Report 1989–90, HL Paper 28, *Correspondence with Ministers*, 70.
[41] 6th Report 1988–9, HL Paper 31, *Merger Control*.
[42] HL Debs., 24 May 1989, cols. 461–92.
[43] 8th Report 1989–90, HL Paper 28, *Correspondence with Ministers*, 66–7.
[44] 17th Report 1988–9, HL Paper 76, *Burden of Proof in Sex Discrimination Cases*.

to prevent illegal immigration from outside the Community, border controls ought to remain. The report was debated concurrently with a report from Subcommittee D on health controls in April 1990.[45]

Subcommittee F: Environment

The fifth Earl of Cranbrook chaired this subcommittee, as he had done from 1980 to 1984. Lord Cranbrook had become a prominent naturalist, having obtained a Ph.D. in anatomy from Birmingham University, before becoming a university lecturer, chairman of the Rain Forest Club, editor of the journal of the British Ornithologists' Union, and other assorted posts.

At the commencement of the session the subcommittee had already begun an inquiry into air pollution from incineration plants. It reported that a proposed directive if implemented would require the closure of many existing municipal plants in Britain, which it argued would be undesirable. It also argued that 'a national waste policy cannot be *laissez-faire*', and that local authorities would have to spend more than the one per cent of their budgets (the amount they currently spent) on waste-management.[46] Though recommended for debate, no debate took place on this report.

The subcommittee produced a short report on the subject of Anti-Fouling Paint in February 1989.[47] Unusually no Government department gave evidence, and the subcommittee expressed its concern that scant attention had been paid to the environmental effects of this programme by the Government. However, after the report had been published a Department of the Environment minister submitted a reply somewhat longer and more detailed than the original subcommittee report. This drew from the chairman of the Committee, Baroness Serota, the rejoinder that 'if the Department had submitted such a detailed document in time for the Committee to have had the benefit of it

[45] 22nd Report 1988–9, HL Paper 90, *1992: Border Control of People*; HL Debs., 5 Apr. 1990, cols. 1548–85.

[46] 2nd Report 1989–90, HL Paper 17, *Air Pollution from Municipal Waste Incineration Plants*.

[47] 4th Report 1988–9, HL Paper 23, *Anti-Fouling Paints*.

Table 9.9. *Membership of Subcommittee F*

Peer	Date of birth	Peerage	Party	Experience/posts held
Chairman				
Cranbrook, E.	1933	H	Con.	University lecturer in Zoology
Members				
Bridges, L.	1927	H	X-B	Career diplomat
Nicol, B.	1923	LP	Lab.	Local government
Shannon, E.	1924	H	X-B	Businessman
Young, B.	1923	LP	Con.	Government minister 1979–87
Co-opted Members				
Blyth, L.	1931	H	X-B	
Moran, L.	1924	H	X-B	Career diplomat
Norrie, L.	1936	H	Con.	Army 1956–70
Rugby, L.	1913	H	X-B	Farmer
Thomas of Gwydir, L.	1920	LP	Con.	MP 1951–66, 1970–87; Government minister 1959–64, 1970–4
Walston, L.	1912	LP	SDP	Farmer; Government minister 1964–7
Warnock, B.	1924	LP	X-B	Mistress, Girton College, Cambridge; philosopher
White, B.	1909	LP	Lab.	MP 1950–70; Government minister 1964–70
Advisers				
Dr A. J. Mitchell-Jones, Nature Conservancy Council (Use of Pentachlorophenol)				
Robin Grove-White Esq., Imperial College, London (Habitat and Species Protection)				
W. Short Esq., consultant on energy and resources (Air Pollution from Municipal Waste Incineration Plants)				
Stephen Tromans Esq. (Access to Information on the Environment)				
David Baldock Esq., Institute of Environmental Policy (Tropical Forests)				

in preparing their report, the Committee might not have expressed the concern it did'.[48]

The subcommittee's next report was on a draft directive which would have limited the use of Pentachlorophenol (PCP), a dangerous chemical used in wood treatment. The Department of the Environment was seeking a derogation for three years 'for treatment by professional users in cases of dry rot'. The subcommittee refused to support this, arguing that it would be unworkable (attempting to restrict use to 'professionals'), that it would diminish the incentive to seek other treatments, and that the Government in seeking it had failed to evaluate scientific evidence on the toxic effects of PCP on bats. This latter point was almost certainly picked up because Lord Cranbrook, the chairman of the subcommittee, was a particular expert on bats.[49] In advance of the report being made Baroness Serota wrote to the minister responsible expressing the concern of the Committee.[50]

The most extensive inquiry undertaken by this subcommittee was into a proposed directive on the protection of natural and semi-natural habitats and of wild fauna and flora, the basic purpose of which was to establish by the year 2000 a comprehensive network of protected areas to ensure the survival of threatened species. The subcommittee decided not to look at detailed questions but to examine the extent to which existing obligations were being honoured within the Community, and to consider what role the Community ought to play in this area. It was common ground between the subcommittee and the Government that the existing system of nature protection within Britain was one of the best. But while the Government tended to rest its case at that point, and dispute whether the subject was a fit one for Community action at all, the subcommittee took the view that Britain was well placed to give a lead to the Community, and it criticized the Government for its lack of willingness if not enthusiasm to do this. Though the draft proposal was 'unwieldy and over-ambitious', nevertheless the objective of environmental quality could be 'attained better at Community level than at

[48] 8th Report 1989–90, HL Paper 28, *Correspondence with Ministers*, 49–65.

[49] 14th Report 1988–9, HL Paper 71, *Marketing and Use of Pentachlorophenol*.

[50] 12th Report 1988–9, HL Paper 56, *Correspondence with Ministers*, 12.

the level of the individual member states'.[51] Among the thirty-three different bodies listed as witnesses, conservation interests predominated.

The themes of this report were taken up when it was debated in the House. Several peers criticized the Government witnesses for their negative and passive attitude. When the draft directive had first been published, the Earl of Caithness, speaking on behalf of the Government, had suggested that the Brussels bureaucrat be added to the official pest list! When Lord Reay responded to the debate for the Government, he sought to repair the damage done by such intemperate remarks and to mollify the subcommittee. He spoke glowingly of its work, saying that 'no other member state had the benefit of such an extended study by experts taking evidence from all sides of the argument', and that the greater flexibility being shown by the Commission was in no small measure attributable to the Committee's report, which, he claimed, had been widely circulated in Europe.[52]

Ad hoc Subcommittee: Fraud against the Community

This subcommittee was set up midway through the 1987–8 session. Its report was published a year later in March 1989, and debated in the House the following month. The subcommittee drew on the other subcommittees for its members and was chaired by Baroness Robson of Kiddington. The decision to establish it was triggered by an annual report from the Community Court of Auditors and a Commission report on 'Tougher Measures to fight against Fraud'. Press reports, suggesting that fraud was depriving the Community of between £2 billion and £6 billion per year, were feeding a public sentiment of hostility to the Community, and were no doubt also very much in the Committee's mind. Their report and accompanying evidence made disquieting reading. The conclusion was blunt: 'the responsibilities of the Community's institutions for managing funds have not been complied with satisfactorily . . . the administrative controls on

[51] 15th Report 1988–9, HL Paper 72, *Habitat and Species Protection*; for quotations see paras. 78 and 85.

[52] HL Debs., 14 Nov. 1989, cols. 1248–79; see cols. 1273–5 for remarks made by Lord Reay.

income and expenditure are inadequate . . . the deterrents against fraud are insufficient . . . the potential for fraud is enormous'.[53] The subcommittee were particularly concerned that in some important respects the structures of the Community actually encouraged member states to connive in fraud perpetrated by bodies within their territorial boundaries, and that so long as detection and prosecution remained a matter for national Governments rather than Community institutions such incentives to fraud would remain. While recommending that the responsibilities of the Court of Auditors should be increased, the report emphasized that the real difficulty lay in the lack of political will on the part of the Council of Ministers to overcome the problem.

When the report was debated in the House this view received powerful endorsement in a devastating and bitter twelve-minute speech from Lord Cockfield, formerly a European Community Commissioner. Why, he asked, had proposals put forward by him on behalf of the Commission in 1986 and 1987 to deal with fraud been vetoed by the United Kingdom in conjunction with other ministers? In replying for the Government Lord Belstead described his speech as 'enormously interesting' but went on to explain that on grounds of practicality and principle the Government remained opposed to allowing members of the Commission to lead investigations on fraud in member states.[54] This illustrated the dilemma. If the Community was to be given the means to fight fraud effectively, then it was hard to see how this could be done in a way which did not encroach on the authorities of member states concerned with the detection and prosecution of crime. The subcommittee had not resolved this dilemma. Giving the Court of Auditors more power to investigate and the statutory duty to express opinions, might shame national governments into doing more. But within the culture of the Community these could hardly be seen as effective remedies. The leading accountant, Lord Benson, a member of the subcommittee, suggested in his speech in the debate on the report that the 'financial misfeasance' which resulted in some 10 to 20 per cent of the revenues of the Community being lost through fraud should bring 'a blush of shame to all'. But he went on to say that 'in the

[53] 5th Report 1988–9, HL Paper 27, *Fraud against the Community*, para. 2.
[54] HL Debs., 13 Apr. 1989, cols. 387–432.

last three months a good deal more attention has been given to this subject partly as a result of this report'.[55] Maybe focusing greater attention on the problem was as much as the subcommittee could be expected to do, and in itself a far from worthless task. Certainly in the months after the publication of the report a steady stream of questions kept the subject before the House.[56] The chairman of the Committee did subsequently claim that this report had been both timely and influential particularly on the British Government.[57]

Summary and Conclusion

What criteria should be employed in assessing the work of select committees? Answers to such a question would normally speak of the importance of Parliament scrutinizing the work of government and holding government to account for what it does. A select committee in the Lords affords the opportunity for scrutiny, but not for accountability other than in a very weak sense of the term. Furthermore, in the case of the European Communities Committee the scrutiny is not so much of Government action or inaction, but of Community policy, and this does involve at least a difference of emphasis in regard to the work of this Committee.

Of course, the first task of the Committee is to report to the House. But as we have noted the House spends only a tiny fraction of its time debating Committee reports, not infrequently on the eve of the recess or at other relatively obscure times, and sometimes long after they have been published. This might suggest that the House does not value the work of its select committee very highly. But that would be too facile a conclusion. In the Commons very few select committee reports are debated; the work of the Public Accounts Committee is highly valued, but only one day a year is given to debate its reports.

Perhaps anyone puzzled at the lack of enthusiasm for debates

[55] Ibid., col. 399. See also the evidence from Baroness Serota to the Commons Procedure Committee, HC 622–II, 1988–9, QQ. 414–16.

[56] See HL Debs., 14 Feb. 1989, col. 64; 23 June 1989, cols. 418–20; 13 July 1989, col. 424; 20 July 1989, cols. 912–14.

[57] See the evidence from Baroness Serota to the Commons Procedure Committee, HC 622–II, 1988–9, Q. 418.

on reports should read some of the debates that do take place. They seldom add to what has already been so well stated in the report itself. If not dominated by speeches from peers who drew up the report, such speeches typically are a large component to the debate.[58] During debate a gloss may be added here and there, or the opportunity given for an especially experienced peer to place his views on record (as for example Lord Cockfield on fraud against the Community). Perhaps a fragment of publicity may be gained through the debate. But what more has been achieved? A Government spokesman replies to the debate, but unless a minister with direct responsibility for the policy area concerned happens to be a member of the House, such a reply will simply involve the reading out of a brief prepared by civil servants, with the ritual promises to write to peers whose concerns go beyond the bounds of the spokesman's brief. Holding a debate is not necessary in order to obtain a reply from the Government. Indeed a written reply to a Committee report from the senior minister responsible may well be preferable to a speech in the House, and, as the reports of correspondence made to the House indicate, such replies regularly lead to an exchange of letters in which the Government's and the Committee's position can be further clarified.

Sometimes Committee inquiries impinge directly on legislation and this can result in Committee members moving amendments to bills (as was the case with the Electricity Bill and the Water Bill). Committee reports may also be cited in questions in the House, or in responses to Government statements. In all these ways the Committee may be said to furnish peers with materials useful to them in their activities on the floor of the House. But the extent to which this results in any genuine accountability of government is very doubtful.

As public documents Committee reports may be taken up elsewhere, either in the media, in the Commons, or by interest groups of one sort or another. There is no doubt that anyone seriously concerned about nitrate in water or about the transport infrastructure of the United Kingdom would be well advised to

[58] In debates on the 9 reports made in 1988–9 that were subsequently debated in the House, 36 of the 84 speeches were made by members of the subcommittees responsible for the reports.

study the Committee reports cited above. In this way reports work by osmosis, transferring information and ideas around the body politic (and who is to say when a report reaches the vital parts of the body that other sources have not reached?). This may be a haphazard process, but that fact should not be used as a reason for ignoring it. Beyond that it could be argued that the work of this select committee has over the years ensured that, at least from somewhere within the British political system, a serious and well-informed response to the practicalities of Community policy-making has been forthcoming.

A leading article in *The Times* in July 1989 discussed the relationship between the United Kingdom and the European Community. The article was headed 'Strangers no More', and emphasized that both Westminster and the European Parliament must scrutinize and monitor Community policy-making more carefully. 'Westminster's machinery has been overwhelmed by the quantity and detail of European regulations. . . . The approach to monitoring Community regulations taken by most Westminster MPs must rapidly change. The work of the select committee on European legislation and the debates in the House [of Commons] are adequate only for considering general principles. Large areas of detailed and specialist monitoring—the true province of MEPs and of the specialist select committees of the House—are left uncovered.' And so the article went on about the importance of 'putting domestic monitoring on a proper footing'. But nowhere was a mention made of the House of Lords and the work of its European Communities Committee![59]

One response would be to say that such a failure even to mention the work of the Lords reveals far more about the current condition of that once great newspaper than it does about the House of Lords. Be that as it may, the fact is that the work of the European Communities Committee of the House is—if not invisible—certainly lacking in any clear public profile. But it would be wrong to look only at the domestic consumption of these reports. They are distributed widely in Europe. The

[59] See *The Times*, 24 July 1989. See also the wry comments on this article made by Lord Allen of Abbeydale when introducing a debate on a committee report three days later: HL Debs., 27 July 1989, col. 1578.

Committee has built up a range of formal and informal contacts, and seeks to make the most of these.[60] It is concerned to inject ideas into the European policy-making processes at all stages, including the earliest. To this end some of its inquiries are deliberately forward-looking, examining issues that have not yet reached the formal agendas of ministers but look set to surface there soon. Other inquiries may be intended to warn the Commission of difficulties ahead unless it changes course. The Committee works on the assumption that good well-researched reports, pushing forward ideas at timely moments, showing both their relevance and their practicality, can be influential.

Sometimes there is a definite sense that ministers have appreciated some report made by the Committee. When tangling with colleagues in the Council, or looking for help in some battle with the Commission, Government ministers are no doubt glad of all the support they are offered. And in this regard it is not so much how the Committee is viewed in London that matters, but its standing elsewhere in Europe that counts. The Committee has cultivated its contacts throughout Europe with great care, not only in Brussels, but in other European capitals. If the Committee is better known on mainland Europe than it is within Britain, then this should not be seen as detracting from the value of its work. On the contrary the very fact that the Committee has a higher profile and is more highly regarded elsewhere in the Community than here should be regarded as its strength. As far as the domestic political scene is concerned, the work of the Committee is accomplished largely by stealth.

[60] See the matter-of-fact way in which Baroness Serota described the Committee's approach to a somewhat bemused Commons Procedure Committee on 19 July 1989: 4th Report from the Select Committee on Procedure 1988–9, *The Scrutiny of European Legislation*, HC 622–II, QQ. 411, 414–16.

10

Select Committees

*Cliff Grantham**

Introduction

The House of Lords has the power to appoint select committees to 'examine any matter which, in the opinion of the House, requires investigation'.[1] In the period from 1945 to 1970, it was a power employed essentially for the purposes of internal organization and for fulfilling the judicial functions of the House. By 1970, the House had several 'domestic' committees, for such matters as administration and privilege; four committees for the purposes of exercising its judicial function; a special orders committee; and it participated in a joint committee on Consolidation Bills. What it did not have was any committee for scrutinizing particular sectors of public policy or the merits of bills. One such committee (a joint committee on censorship of the theatre) had been appointed in the 1966–7 session, but that was exceptional.

The position changed in the 1970s. The Government White Paper on House of Lords Reform in 1968 (Cmnd. 3299) had envisaged a greater use of select committees. A growth in the active membership of the House, particularly through the influx of life peers, provided a greater pool of personnel—and some impetus—for such committees. Since 1970, the use of committees for the scrutiny of public policy has become a regular feature of the upper House. Fourteen have been appointed on an *ad hoc* basis: nine to consider the merits of proposed public bills (ranging

* My thanks go to the 12 members of the Science and Technology Committee who responded so fully to my questionnaire. Lord Shackleton provided some useful additional material. I am grateful to him. I am also grateful to Baroness Ewart-Biggs—a member of the Murder and Life Imprisonment Committee—for her insights. My thanks also go to Philip Norton of the University of Hull and to Rhodri Walters, Clerk to the Select Committee on Science and Technology, for their valuable assistance.

[1] Erskine May, *Parliamentary Practice*, 21st edn. (Butterworths, London, 1989), 574.

from the Anti-Discrimination (No. 2) Bill in 1972–3 to the Infant Life (Preservation) Bill in 1986–7) and five to consider issues of public policy (ranging from sport and leisure, appointed in 1971 and reporting in 1973, to murder and life imprisonment, appointed in 1988 and reporting in 1989).[2]

The 1988–9 session provides a good, and fairly typical, illustration of both the extensive work of the sessional Science and Technology Committee and of the value of an *ad hoc* committee—that on Murder and Life Imprisonment.

The Select Committee on Science and Technology

The Lords Select Committee on Science and Technology was first appointed in December 1979 following the demise of the Science and Technology Committee in the House of Commons.[3] Its terms of reference were as broad as they were concise: 'to consider science and technology'. A fuller explication of its terms of reference, provided by *Erskine May*, serves to emphasize the wide nature of its remit: 'Subjects are chosen which concern areas where Parliament can help and stimulate the advancement and application of science and technology in the United Kingdom, aspects of science and technology in which the Government or statutory bodies are involved, or issues of science and technology over which there is public concern.'[4] It is not surprising, given this, that topics chosen for inquiry tend to cross departmental boundaries and, by their nature, are seldom highly contentious in party political terms.

[2] Select committees have been appointed to consider the following public bills: Anti-Discrimination (No. 2) (1972–3); Lotteries (1974–5); Licensing (Scotland) (1975–6); Hare Coursing (1976); Foreign Boycotts (1978); Laboratory Animals Protection (1979–80); Parochial Charities (Neighbourhood Trusts) and Small Charities (1983–4); Infant Life (Preservation) (1986–7).

Select committees have been appointed on the following issues of public policy: Sport and Leisure (1971–3); Commodity Prices (1975–7); Bill of Rights (1977–8); Unemployment (1979–82); Overseas Trade (1984–5); Murder and Life Imprisonment (1988–9). The Select Committee on a Bill of Rights was appointed in the context of the introduction of a private member's bill, but the bill itself was not committed to the Committee.

[3] The Commons committee was disbanded when departmentally related select committees were established.

[4] Erskine May, *Parl. Practice*, 584.

Within the first decade of its existence, the Committee had established itself as an influential and authoritative committee of the House, the quality of whose investigations, according to one of its members, gave it 'an almost worldwide reputation'. It was a reputation that was firmly augmented during the 1988–9 session.

Membership and structure

The Committee divides into two subcommittees for the purpose of conducting inquiries, the powers and procedures of each being akin to those of the full Committee. Inquiries, which last for approximately one full year, are undertaken simultaneously by Subcommittees I and II and are normally synchronized with one another so that members can alternate between them depending on the subject-matter. A third subcommittee (Subcommittee III) is appointed for general purposes: it meets once a year and its main function is to recommend topics for inquiry. Each subcommittee has the power to appoint its own chairman.

Six reports were published under the aegis of the Committee during the 1988–9 session. The first two—those on agricultural and food research and on research and development (R. & D.) in nuclear power—were the result of work undertaken principally during the previous session. The Committee's third and fourth reports—on civil R. & D. and on hazardous waste—were shorter, essentially follow-up reports, the work having been undertaken by the full committee. The Committee published the Government's response to its report on nuclear power R. & D. as its fifth report. Of the two major inquiries undertaken during the session—on the Greenhouse effect (by Subcommittee II) and on scientific and technical aid to developing countries (Subcommittee I)—only one, the former, was published in 1988–9—the sixth report of the Committee. The work of Subcommittee I came to fruition in the first report of the following session, published in January 1990.

The fifteen members of the select committee are notable for three things: their degree of expertise, their continuity in membership, and their commitment. A significant proportion of the members of the full committee had backgrounds in science and technology: five were scientists and six engineers. Six were Fellows of the Royal Society.

This expertise—shared between the nine life and six hereditary peers—is reinforced through the capacity of the committee to co-opt other peers. During the 1988–9 session, ten peers were co-opted, three of whom, Lords Gregson, Nelson of Stafford, and Sherfield, were involved in four of the Committee's five inquiries. A survey of members of the Committee undertaken by the author in 1990 (see Annexe), found that at least two-thirds of members regarded their co-opted colleagues as 'very valuable' or 'valuable'; only one respondent of twelve classified them as 'unnecessary'.

Table 10.1 lists all peers who served on the Committee or a subcommittee in 1988–9. Details of members' involvement in inquiries are given in Table 10.2.

As with the European Communities Committee, peers may serve on the Committee for five sessions, after which they must retire. The Committee appointed for the session in November 1988 resembled closely that of the previous session, twelve of the fifteen members having served on it in the 1987–8 session. A significant degree of continuity has thus been sustained. The power to co-opt provides an additional dimension. One co-opted member, Lord Gregson, chaired the inquiry into hazardous waste; he had chaired the previous 1981 inquiry into the same subject. Lord Sherfield had been a co-opted member since 1980.

This combination of expertise and continuity would appear to contribute to the commitment shown by members. Though peers are, in effect, unpaid volunteers, two of the respondents in our survey devoted more than six hours a week when the House is sitting to committee work, a further nine (three-quarters of the respondents) devoted between three and six hours each week. Most found the work 'very rewarding': none of the respondents in our survey found it 'not very rewarding'.

Membership is also notable because of absence of partisanship. Members are drawn from all parts of the House, no one party enjoying a majority (five cross-benchers, four Conservative, four Labour, one Social and Liberal Democrat, and one SDP). Party allegiance is essentially irrelevant on subcommittees and in the co-option of members. The subcommittees are, according to one observer, 'essentially expert-driven rather than party-driven'. The 'typical' committee member, then, is someone with an academic

Table 10.1. *Members of the Select Committee on Science and Technology, 1988–9*

Peer	Date of birth	Peerage	Party	Experience/posts held
Chairman				
Shackleton, L.	1911	LP	Lab.	MP 1946–55; Leader of the House of Lords 1968–70; President Royal Geographical Society 1971–4; Deputy Chairman RTZ 1975–82; Chairman East European Trade Council 1978–86
Members appointed by the House				
Adrian, L.	1927	H	X-B	Professor of Cell Physiology, Cambridge University
Butterworth, L.	1918	LP	Con.	Former Vice-Chancellor, University of Warwick; member Foundation for Science and Technology
Caldecote, V.	1917	H	Con.	Engineer; Director English Electric Co. 1953–69; President Fellowship of Engineering 1981–6
Carver, L.	1915	LP	X-B	Chief of Defence Staff 1973–6
Clitheroe, L.	1929	H	Con.	Former member Chemical Industries Association; former Chairman RTZ Borax Limited
Erroll of Hale, L.	1914	C	Con.	MP 1945–64; Engineer; President Electrical Research Association 1971–3; Vice-President London Chamber of Commerce 1966–9
Flowers, L.	1924	LP	X-B	Physicist; Chairman Science Research Council 1967–73; Member Atomic Energy Authority 1971–81

Ilchester, E.	1920	H	X-B	Engineer; President Society of Engineers 1974–5; President Institute of Nuclear Physics 1982–4
Kearton, L.	1911	LP	X-B	Member Atomic Energy Authority 1955–81; Chairman Electricity Supply Research Council 1960–77; Chairman British National Oil Corporation 1975–9
Kirkwood, L.	1931	H	Dem.	Engineer
Lockwood, B.	1924	LP	Lab.	Chairman Equal Opportunities Commission 1975–83
Perry of Walton, L.	1921	LP	SDP	Professor of Pharmacology, University of Edinburgh, 1958–68; Vice-Chancellor Open University 1969–81
Taylor of Blackburn, L.	1929	LP	Lab.	Director of companies
White, B.	1909	LP	Lab.	MP 1950–70; Member Royal Commission on Environmental Pollution 1974–81; Chairman University of Wales Institute of Science and Technology
Co-opted members				
Gregson, L.	1924	LP	Lab.	Engineer; Director British Steel; President Defence Manufacturers' Association
Nelson of Stafford, L.	1917	H	Con.	Engineer; Chairman General Electric Company 1968–83
Sherfield, L.	1904	C	X-B	Diplomat; joint Permanent Secretary HM Treasury 1956–60; Chairman UK Atomic Energy Authority 1960–4
Subcommittee members				
Chilver, L.	1926	LP	Con.	Professor of Civil Engineering University College London 1961–9; Vice-Chancellor Cranfield Institute of Technology 1970–89

Table 10.1. *(contd.)*

Peer	Date of birth	Peerage	Party	Experience/posts held
Chorley, L.	1930	H	X-B	President Royal Geographical Society 1987–90; member Natural Environment Research Council since 1988
Dainton, L.	1914	LP	X-B	Professor of Chemistry Oxford University 1970–3; Chairman National Radiological Protection Board 1978–85
Elliott of Morpeth, L.	1920	LP	Con.	MP 1957–83; Director Port of Tyne Authority
Lewis of Newnham, L.	1928	LP	X-B	Professor of Chemistry Cambridge University since 1970; Chairman Royal Commission on Environmental Pollution since 1986
Swann, L.	1920	LP	X-B	Professor of Zoology, University of Edinburgh, 1952–65; Chairman BBC 1973–80
Torrington, V.	1943	H	Con.	Chairman Moray Firth Exploration PLC; Chief Executive Exploration and Production Services (Holdings) Ltd.

or practical knowledge of one of the sciences; in party terms, there is no typical member.

Mode of inquiry

As with other committees, the Science and Technology Committee invites evidence (via letters, memoranda, press releases, etc.) from interested groups and individuals. Written evidence is considered and the Committee invites approximately 10 per cent of those submitting evidence to give oral evidence. As a matter of course, oral evidence will be taken from the relevant Government departments.

Of the five reports published by the Committee in 1988–9, three had involved extensive evidence-taking inquiries. The inquiry into Agricultural and Food Research, for example, attracted 117 submissions, from bodies as diverse as the Countryside Commission for Scotland, the British Embassy in Tokyo, ICI, the Medical Research Council, Plymouth Polytechnic, the Water Research Centre, and the Home-Grown Cereals Authority. Nineteen witnesses, including the Minister of Agriculture, appeared before the Committee.

Though the Committee and each subcommittee enjoyed substantial expertise derived from the experience and qualifications of the members, the Committee none the less made use of its power to appoint specialist advisers. For its inquiry into Agricultural and Food Research, Subcommittee I had the services of Professor John Harley FRS, Emeritus Professor of Forest Science at Oxford University, and Dr Anthony James FRS, former head of Biosciences at Unilever Research Colworth Laboratory. Subcommittee II, considering research and development in nuclear power, similarly had the services of two advisers: Sir John Hill FRS, former Chairman of the UK Atomic Energy Authority, and Professor Roger Williams, Professor of Government and Science Policy at Manchester University. The same Subcommittee, when it turned its attention to the Greenhouse Effect, drew on the services of a former director of the Meteorological Office (Andrew Gilchrist), the Professor of Oceanography at Southampton University (Professor Harry Charnock), and the Professor of Environmental Physics at Nottingham University (Professor Michael Unsworth). Though

Table 10.2. *Science and Technology Committee Reports, 1988–9: participation of members*

	Agriculture and Food Subcttee. I 1.	R. & D. in Nuclear Power Subcttee. II 2.	Civil R. & D. Full Cttee. 3.	Hazardous Waste Full Cttee. 4.	Greenhouse Effect Subcttee. II 6.
Members appointed by the House					
Adrian, L.	√		√	√	
Butterworth, L.	√ (ch)		√	√	
Caldecote, V.		√	√	√	
Carver, L.		√	√	√	√ (ch)
Clitheroe, L.			√	√	√
Erroll of Hale, L.		√	√	√	√
Flowers, L.		√	√	√	√
Ilchester, E.		√	√	√	
Kearton, L.		√	√	√	√
Kirkwood, L.	√		√	√	√
Lockwood, B.	√		√	√	√
Perry of Walton, L.	√		√	√	
Shackleton, L.	√		√	√	
Taylor of Blackburn, L.		√	√	√	
White, B.	√		√	√	
TOTAL 15					

Co-opted members					
Chilver, L.	√				
Elliott of Morpeth, L.	√				
Swann, L.	√				
Dainton, L.		√			√
Gregson, L.		√	√	√ (ch)	√
Nelson of Stafford, L.		√ (ch)	√	√	√
Sherfield, L.		√	√ (ch)	√	√
Torrington, V.		√			
Chorley, L.					√
Lewis of Newnham, L.					√

the practice of appointing advisers is common to committees in the House of Commons, the distinction between lay members and specialist advisers that exists in the Commons is less clearly drawn in the Lords, given the expertise of the peers themselves. Indeed, for its follow-up inquiries into civil R. & D. and hazardous waste, the committee relied on its own resources.

The specific expertise of the advisers has none the less been valued by the Committee. In our survey of Committee members, all twelve respondents judged specialist advisers to be 'very valuable' (the response of seven of the twelve) or 'valuable'.

The committee also made use of its power to 'adjourn from place to place'. Subcommittee I visited four of the institutes of the Agricultural and Food Research Council as well as the Agriculture Ministry's Central Veterinary Laboratory at Weybridge, the 1988 Royal International Agricultural Show, and Unilever Research Colworth Laboratory. Subcommittee II went further afield. For its inquiry into R. & D. in nuclear power, it visited British Nuclear Fuels at Capenhurst and Sellafield; the UK Atomic Energy Authority at Windscale, Dounreay, and Culham; the joint European Torus (JET) at Culham; the EC Commission in Brussels; and Paris, where it held discussions with officials of the French Government, electricity industry, and atomic energy commission. For its inquiry into the Greenhouse Effect, it visited Washington DC—concurrently with members of the Commons Energy Committee—to hold discussions with a wide range of bodies, including the Department of Energy, the National Aeronautics and Space Administration (NASA), the World Bank, the President's Science Adviser, and, perhaps most valued of all, some leading individual scientists.

Reports and responses

The Committee itself has decided whether its reports should be classified as 'for debate'. In practice, time is found for debate following negotiation through 'the usual channels'. As Table 1.2 shows, debates on reports occupied less than one per cent of the time of the House.[5] Members of the Committee were generally satisfied with the amount of time devoted to Committee reports

[5] See also the Report by the Group on the Working of the House, HL Paper 9, 1987–8, para. 7.

on the floor of the House, though two would have preferred a more central slot for debates. Even when debated at what for the House constitutes a relatively late hour, reports can attract significant attention from peers. For example, the Sixth Report from the Committee on the Greenhouse Effect—debated on a Tuesday at seven o'clock—attracted contributions from six members of the Committee and, more importantly, twelve other peers, including the Archbishop of York, as well as the Opposition and Government spokesmen.[6]

The primary audience for each report, of course, is the House itself, and the topic of the inquiry will invariably determine the secondary audience. Most recommendations emanating from the Committee are directed at the Government. Others are directed at different public bodies, such as local authorities, and—an important 'attentive public'—the research councils. The Government normally makes a written response to each report, and the Committee will follow up the Government's response in whatever manner seems appropriate. Sometimes this has taken the form of a short report approximately twelve to twenty-four months after the Government's response. It may also take the form of a substantive return to the issue, involving a new report, some years after its initial inquiry. In the 1988–9 session, the two follow-up reports from the Committee both fell in the former category. Its short report on civil R. & D. was a follow-up to its major report (published in three substantial volumes) on the subject two sessions previously.[7] Its report on hazardous waste followed two earlier reports from the Committee (in 1981 on hazardous waste disposal and in 1985 on the scientific and technical services of local authorities, in which it argued for the creation of single-service waste disposal authorities for hazardous waste control).[8] In its inquiry on Agricultural and Food Research, the Committee issued an interim report in October 1988 (on the reorganization of the research councils concerned with the biological sciences, arguing that the AFRC and NERC should be merged into a Natural Resources Research Council) before issuing its full report two months later.[9]

[6] HL Debs., 30 Jan. 1990, cols. 224–84.
[7] HL Paper 24, 1988–9; HL 20, 1986–7.
[8] HL Paper 40, 1988–9; HL 273, 1980–1; HL 11, 1985–6.
[9] HL Paper 104, 1987–8; HL Paper 13, 1988–9.

Impact

The Committee's reports, as we have noted already, have different audiences. The Committee is able to ensure that its findings and recommendations receive attention on the floor of the House and it is clear from their contributions to debates that interested members of the House subject reports to close textual analysis:

I turned with particular interest to paragraphs 10.32 and 10.39 of the report which consider the international dimension of emissions control. That part of the report deals with the matter of forests. I have also followed up the extremely interesting references in the evidence on which these paragraphs are based.[10]

My second and central point is to be found in paragraph 13.44 and concerns nuclear energy. I have spoken about that subject many times and noble Lords know my views.[11]

It is also not uncommon for this analysis to derive from a degree of knowledge or experience of the topic under debate. In the debate on the Greenhouse Effect, contributions came from a former chairman of the National Coal Board (Lord Ezra), the chairman of the Advisory Committee on Pollution at Sea (Lord Campbell of Croy), a former chairman of the Parliamentary Liaison Group for Alternative Energy Strategies and former member of the European Communities Subcommittee on Energy, Transport, Research and Technology (Lord Tanlaw), and a former chairman of the Meteorological Committee (Earl of Halsbury). Combined with contributions from Committee members, reports from the Committee thus create the basis for informed debate on scientific issues.

Indeed, it is within the House itself that Committee reports are seen as having the greatest impact. Of the twelve members of the Committee consulted, eleven judged the impact of Committee reports in the House to be 'significant'; one judged them to have 'some impact'; none considered that they had 'little or no impact'. Perhaps not surprisingly, no other body (the House of Commons, the European Parliament, the European Commission) was accorded such a positive rating.

But what of the impact on Government? The quality of the work undertaken by the Committee is generally acknowledged by

[10] Archbishop of York, HL Debs., 30 Jan. 1990, cols. 231–2.
[11] Lord Hatch of Lusby, ibid., col. 236.

ministers.[12] And the reports were difficult for ministers to ignore: in part because the reports themselves—unlike those in the Commons—regularly came to the floor of the House for debate. Government spokesmen thus had to appear at the dispatch-box to offer a view.

Members of the Committee themselves considered that their reports had an impact on Government thinking. Of the members consulted, seven felt the reports had 'significant' impact on Government thinking, four felt they had 'some impact', and only one felt they had 'little impact'. This generally positive assessment appears to derive not so much from the extent to which the Government accepted and implemented recommendations immediately, but rather from the extent to which recommendations enter the thinking of Government over a longer period, achieving implementation several years later. 'My most clear impression', records one senior member of the Committee, 'is that the recommendations of the Committee on Science and Technology are usually resisted initially by Government but liable to appear as Government proposals three to five years later! Influencing Government is a slow business!'

Assessment of the immediate impact of reports is less positive. According to one Committee member, 'there is a tendency for Government to "welcome" reports, give assurances that most of the recommendations are in line with their policy and are already in operation, and then to oppose the few recommendations which would involve significant change. This sometimes reduces the value of a report which had unanimous, usually cross-party, support by experienced people.' The Government response to the Committee's Second Report of the session—on research and development in nuclear power—illustrated this admirably. In thirty-seven often short paragraphs, the phrase 'the Government agrees' appears nine times, 'the Government welcomes' appears twice, and 'the Government endorses' three times. Apart from welcoming and endorsing the Committee's recommendations (especially those placing present and future responsibilities on the industry and operators), the Government adopted an essentially non-committal position on various recommendations necessitating

[12] See e.g. paras. 78–81 of the Report from the Select Committee on the Committee Work of the House (HL Paper 35–I, 1991–2).

Government action; furthermore, on the specific question of keeping open the Pressurized Fuel Reactor at Dounreay beyond 1994—one of the principal recommendations in the report—the Government rejected the Committee's finding out of hand. Thus, in the final paragraph: 'The Government will bear in mind the comments of the Committee in considering the future role of the [UK Atomic Energy] Authority. This consideration will include the question of the statutory constraints on the authority (paragraph 3.76). A statement on the future of the UKAEA will be made in due course.'[13] The Committee had expressed the view that the UKAEA 'must be restructured', a process necessitating substantial support from Government.

However, Government resistance to recommendations was not quite as pervasive as these observations may imply. The Committee's report on civil R. & D. in 1986–7, for example, produced some immediate changes—including the creation of the Advisory Committee on Science and Technology (ACOST); it may also have been the genesis of a number of other—less immediate—changes, including the Government's decision in 1989 to force companies to declare the amount of R. & D. spending in their accounts.

Government resistance, moreover, may not always be definitive. Members of the Committee supported by other members of the House may be able to force a change of view. Though a committee *qua* committee cannot table amendments to a bill, individual members of the committee may table amendments designed to fulfil committee recommendations and the genesis of such amendments is usually apparent to other members of the House. There are various examples of this technique proving successful. To take one from the session under review: arising out of the Committee's nuclear research report, an amendment was tabled to the Electricity Bill to safeguard R. & D., an amendment that the Government deemed prudent to accept (see Chapter 4).

Furthermore, Committee influence on Government cannot be measured solely in terms of the number of recommendations accepted, either immediately or in the long term. The Committee is in a position to exercise an important role of agenda setting or

[13] HL Paper 41, 1988–9.

raising the profile—and understanding—of an issue once it is on the agenda of political debate. Most of its reports in the 1988–9 session did this. The work of the Committee on civil R. & D., especially in the earlier 1986–7 session, raised the profile significantly of the problem of civil R. & D. in the UK, attracting major publicity and an immediate response from the Government, the then Prime Minister herself declaring her intention to take a lead in a field in which she had some professional experience. The Committee's reports in the 1988–9 session continued to attract media coverage, for example its Fourth Report, on hazardous waste disposal, was well written up in *The Times* and the *Financial Times*.

In terms of other potential 'attentive publics', the impact of the Committee's work is less obvious. Members of the Committee themselves considered that their reports had 'some impact' on the House of Commons. (Nine of the twelve respondents to our questionnaire gave that response; two judged the reports to have 'significant' impact, only one that it had 'little or no impact'.) One interesting feature of Committee activity in the 1988–9 session was the extent to which it overlapped with the work of the Commons Energy Committee. As already noted, Subcommittee II visited the USA concurrently with the Commons Energy Committee. In its report on hazardous waste disposal, the Committee also noted a report from the Commons Environment Committee on toxic waste. Such overlapping activity appears to encourage a greater awareness on the part of each House of what the other House is doing, and committees are able to draw on the work of related committees in the other place.

Members of the Committee also judged that their work had 'some impact' in the European Commission, but somewhat less in the European Parliament. That the work of the Committee should attract some attention in the institutions of the European Community is not surprising, given that much of the subject matter of their inquiries (such as the Greenhouse Effect) recognizes no state boundaries, and, as we have seen, Subcommittee II spent some time in Brussels in discussion with members of the EC Commission during their inquiry into nuclear R. & D. Equally, it is not surprising that the institutions of the Community are more likely to have a greater and more consistent interest in the work of the Lords EC Committee.

Beyond political institutions, the Committee also had some impact on a range of public, and several private, bodies operating in the science sector. Most notable among these were the research councils and the Advisory Board for the Research Councils (ABRC) as well as, not surprisingly, ACOST. Individual members of the Committee also identified the Royal Society, the Fellowship of Engineering, and the Confederation of British Industry (CBI) as being among other bodies on which the Committee had had some influence.

Overall, this evidence—though largely imprecise and impressionistic—would suggest that the Science and Technology Committee played an important role in contributing to debate on scientific issues in Britain, helping keep Government—and public scientific establishments—on their toes, and having some influence, through issuing substantial, well-informed and largely partisan-free reports, on Government thinking and, variously, public policy.[14]

The Select Committee on Murder and Life Imprisonment

As Michael Wheeler-Booth has noted, the genesis of *ad hoc* committees varies.[15] Some are established on the initiative of Government. Others have their origins in debates in the House. The Select Committee on Murder and Life Imprisonment has its genesis in debate on the Criminal Justice Bill in 1987. During deliberations on the bill, it was clear that there was general dissatisfaction with the existing state of the law on the offence of murder and a desire for change. By the time of third reading, it was too late to make any radical change to the bill. Speaking during the debate, Lord Windlesham suggested that a select committee should look into the whole matter. 'So, with Lord Mackay's [the Lord Chancellor's] blessing, the select committee was born.'[16]

[14] See also 'The Parliamentary Monitoring of Science and Technology in Britain' by P. D. G. Hayter (Clerk to the Science and Technology Committee 1980–90), *Government and Opposition*, 26(2), 149–66.

[15] M. A. J. Wheeler-Booth, 'The House of Lords', in J. A. G. Griffith and Michael Ryle, *Parliament: Functions, Practice and Procedures* (Butterworths, London, 1989), 494.

[16] Sheila Gunn, 'How Long is Life?', *The House Magazine*, 23 Oct. 1989, 10.

The Committee was appointed on 21 July 1988 to consider the scope of the crime of murder, the question of whether imprisonment for life should remain mandatory rather than a maximum penalty for murder, and the working of the arrangements for reaching decisions on the release of those serving life sentences for murder. Eleven peers were appointed to the Committee, comprising a mix of lawyers, people with experience of the penal system and system of parole (including two former Home Office ministers), and—as the Committee's final report put it—others who had 'wide experience of public life' (see Table 10.3). Among the former category—that is, those with applicable experience—three were barristers and three solicitors; between them, they had wide experience of the legal system in both England and Scotland. Lord Nathan, one of the solicitors, was appointed as chairman. He brought a certain amount of international experience to the Committee as an associate member of the Bar Association of the City of New York and of the New York County Lawyers Association. The cross-benchers on the Committee formed the largest single grouping, the others being drawn from each of the main political parties: Conservative (3), Labour (2), Social and Liberal Democrats (1), and SDP (1).

The Committee employed its power to appoint specialist advisers. Two were appointed: an academic QC (Professor J. C. Smith of Nottingham University) and an academic criminologist (Professor Keith Bottomley of Hull University). In the course of its inquiry, it also made considerable use of its power to adjourn from place to place, visiting four prisons in England (Parkhurst, Kingston, Leyhill Open Prison, and Durham) and the Special Unit at HMP Barlinnie, Glasgow, part of a three-day visit to Scotland: on each occasion, Committee members met a number of prisoners as well as staff. Some members of the Committee also made visits to the panels of the Parole Board of England and Wales.

More conventional evidence-taking sessions were held in London and, in total, the Committee received evidence—in oral and/or written form—from more than eighty organizations and individuals. These included the Lord Chief Justice, the National Council for Civil Liberties, the Home Office, the Association of Chief Police Officers, the Howard League for Penal Reform, the Voluntary Euthanasia Society, and prisoners serving life

Table 10.3. *Members of the Select Committee on Murder and Life Imprisonment*

Peer	Date of birth	Peerage	Party	Experience/posts held
Ackner, L.	1920	A	X-B	Lord of Appeal in Ordinary
Campbell of Alloway, L.	1917	LP	Con.	QC; Recorder of the Crown Court 1976–89
Darcy (de Knayth), B.	1938	H	X-B	No legal background; member of IBA Advisory Council
Ewart-Biggs, B.	1929	LP	Lab.	No legal background; Opposition front-bench spokesman
Harris of Greenwich, L.	1930	LP	Dem.	Home Office Minister 1974–9; Chairman Parole Board 1979–82
Morton of Shuna, L.	1930	LP	X-B	QC (Scotland); Opposition spokesman on Scottish Legal Affairs 1985–8; Senator of the College of Justice in Scotland since 1988
Nathan, L. (Chairman)	1922	H	X-B	Solicitor
Platt of Writtle, B.	1923	LP	Con.	No legal background; Chairman Equal Opportunities Commission 1983–8
Prys-Davies, L.	1923	LP	Lab.	Solicitor
Wilson of Langside, L.	1916	LP	SDP	QC (Scotland); Lord Advocate 1967–70
Windlesham, L.	1932	H	Con.	Home Office Minister 1970–2; Leader of the House of Lords 1973–4; Chairman Parole Board 1982–8

sentences in a number of prisons. (Indeed, one of the most articulate submissions came from a young 'lifer' who had written a book about his experiences.) The Committee also received some assistance from the Secretariat of the Council of Europe, which co-ordinated a questionnaire on practice in member states.

The Committee met thirty-two times—including twice at the end of the previous session—before publishing its report in October 1989.[17] This ran to three volumes and included nearly 800 pages of evidence and appendices. Its recommendations went somewhat beyond the Committee's formal terms of reference to study the law and its application: 'the Committee are convinced that such a study cannot be undertaken in isolation from the human and social factors surrounding the crime of murder'.[18] The Committee thus invited such organizations as the Parents of Murdered Children Group and Victim Support to submit evidence and in its report put forward a number of recommendations relating to the supply of information to the families of murder victims.

On the central question of the inquiry—the imposition of a mandatory life sentence for certain categories of murder—the Committee, with one exception (Baroness Platt of Writtle), were unanimous: 'The Committee agree with the majority of their witnesses that the mandatory life sentence should be abolished.'[19] The Committee argued instead for a discretionary sentence, with judges specifying in open court the period of years to be served. This period—referred to by the Committee as 'the penal sanction'—should not, it argued, be subject to revision by ministers. In order to counter perceived criticism that the Committee had 'gone soft', the Committee was careful to emphasize that in the case of extremely grave and heinous crimes, abolition of the mandatory sentence could actually lead to a longer period being served. 'The Committee expect that their proposals will lead to very lengthy penal sanctions being set in the most grave cases. In some cases, this may result in imprisonment for the rest of the prisoner's life.'[20]

The release of the report excited considerable interest, not least in the national press; *The Times* leaked the findings some

[17] HL Paper 78, 1988–9. [18] Ibid., para. 11.
[19] Ibid., para. 118. [20] Ibid., para. 178.

weeks in advance with a front-page article headed 'Peers demand tougher terms for murderers'.[21]

The report was debated in the House on 6 November 1989, just weeks after its publication. Twenty peers (including eight members of the Committee) spoke during the 5¾-hour debate, described by one of the later speakers as 'one of the most interesting debates we have had in the area of criminal justice policy for some years'.[22] Though not all agreed with the Committee's key recommendations, peers were unanimous in their appreciation and admiration of the work undertaken by the Committee, variously referring to it as 'a meritorious accomplishment which may well be copied by future select committees of your Lordships' House';[23] 'an excellent report, easy to read, mostly simple to follow and attractively pragmatic in its recommendations';[24] 'interesting reading from which I am sure I shall derive much profit';[25] 'comprehensive and informative . . . a painstaking exercise which makes fascinating reading'.[26]

The Home Office Minister, Earl Ferrers, was no less effusive. Speaking during the debate, he referred to the report as 'clear and comprehensive'. 'No one can accuse it of being stuffy. Behind every recommendation there is careful consideration of what are difficult and delicate.'[27] On the central recommendation, however—the abolition of the mandatory life sentence—he was cautious, suggesting that it was not one that would endear itself to the public. 'I fancy that there would be many eyebrows which would move smartly in an upward direction if it were realized that the act of murder may attract neither the death penalty nor life imprisonment but merely a predetermined number of years in prison.'[28]

The Government's official position was soon confirmed. The White Paper, 'Crime, Justice and Protecting the Public', published in February 1990, announced its decision that the mandatory life sentence should remain 'to mark the heinous nature of this

[21] *The Times*, 22 Sept. 1989.
[22] Lord Harris of Greenwich, HL Debs., 6 Nov. 1989, col. 513.
[23] Lord Mishcon, ibid., col. 458.
[24] Lord Hutchinson of Lullington, ibid., col. 463.
[25] Lord Goff of Chieveley, ibid., col. 467.
[26] Lord Macaulay of Bragar, ibid., col. 501.
[27] Ibid., col. 452. [28] Ibid., col. 456.

crime'. It was a decision that caused genuine and considerable disappointment among members of the Committee, who felt they had put forward a comprehensive and convincing case in favour of abolition.

The one area in which the Committee could claim some success related to the supply of information to families of murder victims. The Committee's recommendations that the families of victims should be kept informed of release decisions and resettlement plans of offenders as well as being given a channel through which to express their anxieties, were endorsed by the Home Office and later incorporated in the so-called 'Victims Charter', published in February 1990, which set out for the first time how victims of crimes should be treated.

The members of the Murder and Life Imprisonment Committee —and other peers who supported their recommendations— had an early opportunity to return to the issue and to press for a change in the law. In April 1991, during the passage of the Criminal Justice Bill, peers inflicted a heavy defeat on the Government, an amendment tabled by Lord Nathan and others to do away with the mandatory life sentence for murder being carried by 177 votes to 79.[29] Supporters of the amendment included Lord Windlesham and two former Lord Chancellors, Lord Hailsham of Saint Marylebone and Lord Havers; Lord Lane, the Lord Chief Justice, spoke in favour of the amendment.

The issue of mandatory life imprisonment came to dominate the passage of the bill; at one point, the Government appeared almost isolated, many of its supporters—not only in the upper House, but also among the leader writers in the quality press— lining up in favour of abolition. Throughout lengthy deliberations on the issue in both Houses, the earlier work of the select committee was variously invoked. In speaking against the amendment, Lord Waddington, the Leader of the House, began by paying tribute to the members of the Committee and addressed many of his subsequent remarks to points raised in the report.

The Lords amendment was later reversed in the Commons, but only after the Home Secretary himself had gone to the House to argue in favour of the present arrangements, and not before their Lordships had wrung a number of significant concessions from

[29] HL Debs., 18 Apr. 1991, cols. 1559–86.

the Government, including the creation of a new life-sentence review procedure for discretionary life-sentence cases and an end to the Home Secretary's power to delay a prisoner's release by six months.[30]

It is questionable that without the earlier select committee inquiry and report, the issue would have come to dominate the passage of the Criminal Justice Bill in the way that it did, causing ministers at one point to fear that the whole Bill may be threatened and, as a result, to go a good deal further than they had intended in agreeing to other Lords amendments.

Conclusion

Select committees of the House of Lords are notable for their quality rather than their quantity. The disparity is not coincidental. The upper House boasts peers who are specialists in a number of areas, but those peers are of necessity limited in number. Furthermore, peers being unpaid volunteers, there is a limit to the time they can devote to the activities of the House. Consequently, the expertise that is available to serve on committees is sufficient to furnish the members of the Science and Technology Committee and the EC Committee, plus at any time one *ad hoc* committee, but probably not sufficient to sustain committees, especially sessional committees, in other sectors of government responsibility. Moreover, any major extension in the Lords committee structure—for example, by the increased use of *ad hoc* select committees—is unlikely to ever find favour with the Government of the day, on whose support any extension would depend.

The existing committees are also limited in terms of resources. They can call upon the services of a clerk, specialist advisers, and some secretarial support, but that—not dissimilar to the position in the Commons—is the extent of it. Of the twelve members of the Science and Technology Committee who responded to the questionnaire, half felt the existing resources were adequate to meet the Committee's existing needs while the other half felt they were not adequate, wanting instead more clerks, more

[30] HC Debs., 25 June 1991, cols. 866–913.

secretarial back-up, the capacity to commission research, and better resources for visits away from Westminster.

The capacity of the House to sustain a system of specialist committees is thus limited by available members and resources. However, our evidence suggests that those committees it does have are noteworthy for their authority. They draw upon a degree of expertise not possible in the Commons, where expertise in the science field is notably lacking and no longer covered on any central or continuous basis by a select committee. (Science constitutes a rather marginal part of the remit of the Education, Science and Arts Committee, and science-related topics get dealt with by other committees as they deem appropriate.) Recognizing this, the Commons Procedure Committee raised in a report in 1990 the possibility of a joint committee to look at science and technology.[31]

The body of expertise that exists in the Lords, consolidated by the willingness of committees to utilize their powers to appoint subcommittees and co-opt members, provides the basis for much of the authority accorded reports emanating from the Lords committees. The Archbishop of York's description of the Science and Technology Committee's report on the Greenhouse Effect as 'sober, factual, well balanced and properly agnostic where it is not possible to be certain'[32] offers a good illustration of how the reports are seen. Their potential impact on Government is enhanced by the non-partisan nature of their deliberations and conclusions and also by the fact that they are able to delve into important areas for which the House of Commons has neither the time, the political inclination, nor an appropriate committee structure to venture. Lords committees thus have the potential to influence political debate, and, at times, set it. The Science and Technology Committee provides an example of a well-informed committee able to undertake substantial inquiries, some

[31] 'The proposal has the advantage of maximising the present standing of science and technology in the deliberations of the House of Lords and of enabling the Commons to participate in the examination of those matters. It would also provide a useful source of information and recommendations for consideration on the floor of the House, without creating any extra work for Ministers who already serve their Lordships' Committee.' (2nd Report from the Select Committee on Procedure, 1989–90, *The Working of the Select Committee System* (HC 19), para. 284.)

[32] HL Debs., 30 Jan. 1990, col. 231.

coterminously, on a continuous basis; the Committee on Murder and Life Imprisonment was a good example of an *ad hoc* committee able to focus informed attention on a specific issue. Both contributed significantly during the 1988–9 session to understanding in their respective fields, in a way that almost certainly could not be emulated by the House of Commons nor probably by many other legislative bodies. The authority of the House of Commons derives from election, the authority of the House of Lords—and especially its committees—from its expertise.

ANNEXE

A survey of the fifteen members of the Science and Technology Committee was conducted in the early part of 1990 in the form of a questionnaire. Twelve members responded. The text of the questionnaire is printed below. Where respondents were asked to tick boxes in questions 3 to 12, the number ticking each box is indicated.

QUESTIONNAIRE

1. Are you a: (please tick) Life Peer [ ] Hereditary Peer [ ]
2. Are you: (please tick)
   Conservative [ ] Labour [ ] SLD [ ]
   SDP [ ] Independent/Cross-bench [ ]
3. On average, how much time would you estimate you devote to the work of the Committee each week when the House is in session?
   Up to 3 hours [1]
   3–6 hours [9]
   6–9 hours [1]
   9–12 hours [ ]
   More than 12 hours [1]
4. How rewarding do you find serving on the Committee? (Please tick)
   Very rewarding [9] Quite rewarding [3] Not very rewarding [ ]
   Other [ ] (please specify) ____________
5. What impact do you think the Committee's reports have on Government thinking? (Please tick)
   Significant impact [7] Some impact [4] Little impact [1]
6. How do you view the contribution to the work of the Committee of specialist advisers? (Please tick)

Very valuable [7] Valuable [5] Some use [ ] Unnecessary [ ]

7. Do you believe that more time ought to be devoted on the floor of the House to debating reports from the Committee? (Please tick)
   No [8] Yes [4] If yes, how much: ______________________
8. Do you think that the present resources of the Committee are adequate for it to fulfil its present responsibilities? (Please tick)
   Yes [6] No [6]
   If no, what extra resources do you believe to be necessary:

9. How do you view the contribution to the work of the Committee of co-opted members? (Please tick)
   Very valuable [5] Valuable [5] Some use [1] Unnecessary [1]
10. Would you like to see the committee structure in the House of Lords extended to encompass scrutiny of other policy sectors?
   No [7] Yes [3]
   If yes, what sectors would you like to see covered?
11. What impact do you believe that reports from the Committee have on the thinking and actions of the following bodies? (Please tick)

	Significant impact	Some impact	Little or no impact
House of Lords	[11]	[1]	[ ]
House of Commons	[2]	[9]	[1]
European Commission	[2]	[6]	[3]
European Parliament	[2]	[2]	[5]

   Are there any other bodies—national or international—on which you believe Committee reports have significant influence? (Please specify)

12. Can and should more be done to link the Committee and its reports to those bodies identified above? (Please tick)
   No [5] Yes [3] If yes, what (please specify):

13. Are there any general observations you would like to make on the role and impact of the Science and Technology Committee, especially in the 1988/89 session?

14. Name (optional):
   Thank you very much for your co-operation.

11

Services and Facilities

Michael Rush and David Jones

Introduction

The House of Lords shares the Palace of Westminster with the House of Commons, but for the most part the two Houses operate quite separately within the building. This is most importantly the case procedurally, as is evident from other chapters, but it is also true of the provision of services and facilities. There are a few services common to both Houses, such as the telephone system, the post office, and many aspects of security, but in the provision of procedural advice, library and information services, accommodation, and refreshment facilities, there are separate arrangements. Similarly, there are also separate arrangements for the preparation of each House's Official Report (*Hansard*) and other publications.

The House of Lords also differs from the Commons in three other respects. First, the membership of the Commons has a specific limit, the number of constituencies varying only in consequence of boundary redistributions. In the 1987 Parliament, the number of MPs was 650, but the membership of the Lords needs to be seen in terms of attendance rather than absolute numbers, as Chapter 2 makes clear. Second, unlike MPs, peers have no constituency responsibilities and to that extent they could be said to require fewer services and facilities than members of the Commons. Third, peers (other than those who are Ministers or office-holders) are not given any remuneration for their services, however assiduous they may be in attendance or active in the work of the House, so that whereas MPs receive salaries and expenses, peers may receive only expenses.

The services and facilities available to members of both Houses have grown significantly since the 1960s, but the expansion for

MPs has been vastly greater.[1] In comparison the expansion of services and facilities for peers has been significant but modest. The pressure on space in the Palace of Westminster has been such that there have been periodic demands that accommodation currently used by the House of Lords be made available to the Commons. While almost all accommodation and services and facilities for peers are within the Palace of Westminster, services and facilities for members of the Commons extend beyond the Palace of Westminster to various buildings near by.

A small part of the Lord Chancellor's Department, which is a Government department, is located in the Lords' part of the Palace of Westminster. The Lord Chancellor personally epitomizes the constitutional fusion of powers by being a member of the legislature as Speaker of the House of Lords, a member of the Cabinet, and head of the Judiciary, while his Permanent Secretary, the Clerk of the Crown in Chancery, is both a civil servant and an officer of the House of Lords and of the House of Commons.[2] The Clerk's deputy is also both a civil servant and an officer of both Houses.

Government Ministers in the House of Lords, the Leader of the Opposition and Opposition Chief Whip in the Lords, and the Chairman of Committees and the Principal Deputy Chairman, are all paid salaries, as shown in Table 11.1, and receive a secretarial allowance. All peers have at their disposal the

[1] In effect the job of an MP has been treated as a full-time occupation since the First Report of the Top Salaries Review Body (TSRB) on MPs' salaries and allowances in 1971, when for the first time a clear distinction was drawn between salaries and expenses. For further details on MPs' pay, allowances, services, and facilities, see Michael Rush and Malcolm Shaw (eds.), *The House of Commons: Services and Facilities* (Allen & Unwin, London, 1970); Michael Rush (ed.), *The House of Commons: Services and Facilities 1972–1982* (Policy Studies Institute, London, 1983); and comparative surveys by Michael Rush in vol. 2 of TSRB *Report No. 20* (Cmnd. 8881–II, May 1983) and vol. 2 of TSRB *Report No. 24* (Cm. 131–II, Apr. 1987).

[2] The Clerk of the Crown in Chancery heads the Crown Office, which prepares and sends writs to peers and instructs returning officers in constituencies to hold elections and return the names of those elected to the Crown Office, where they are recorded. The Crown Office also receives all ballot papers and other documents relating to elections and retains them for a year, except for those relating to Scottish constituencies, which are kept by the sheriff clerk of the county in which the constituency is situated. The Clerk of the Crown in Chancery also reads out the titles of bills in the House of Lords when they receive the royal assent, and the Great Seal is affixed to state documents in the Crown Office.

Table 11.1. *Salaries of Ministers and other office-holders in the House of Lords in 1989*

Post	Salary Annual (£)
Lord Chancellor	91,500
Cabinet ministers	41,997
Lord Advocate	42,067
Ministers of State	37,047
Captain of the Honourable Corps of Gentlemen-at-Arms (Government Chief Whip)	37,047
Parliamentary Secretaries	30,647
Captain of the Queen's Bodyguard of the Yeoman of the Guard (Government Deputy Chief Whip)	30,647
Lords in Waiting (Government whips)	27,377
Leader of the Opposition	30,647
Opposition Chief Whip	27,377
Chairman of Committees	37,047
Principal Deputy Chairman of Committees	33,537

Notes: The above rates were introduced with effect from 18 Apr. 1989 in the case of the Lord Chancellor and from 1 Jan. 1989 in the case of all others. The figures exclude a London supplement of £1,222 payable to Ministers and other office holders without an official residence. 14 per cent of the Lord Chancellor's salary (£12,810) relates to his duties as Speaker of the House of Lords and is paid from the House of Lords Vote (HL 260, 1985–6). Back-bench MPs in 1989 received a basic salary of £24,107.

Sources: Ministerial and other Salaries Order 1988 (SI 1988 No. 2253), Lord Chancellor's Salary Order 1989 (SI 1989 No. 681), *Civil Service Year Book 1989* (HMSO, London, 1989), *Whitaker's Almanack 1990* (Whitaker, London, 1989).

procedural advice of the clerks in the House, information services through the Library of the House of Lords, access to parliamentary papers and various other official documents, computer services, postal and telephone services, and refreshment and a number of other facilities. In addition, as already noted, peers who are not salaried office-holders may claim the reimbursement of various expenses incurred in carrying out their parliamentary duties.[3]

allowance, was introduced with effect from 6 Apr. 1990 by s. 5 of the Ministerial

The Control of Services and Facilities

The Palace of Westminster is a royal palace and until 1965 control of it was vested in the Lord Great Chamberlain, an hereditary royal official, but in 1965 control of those parts of the Palace used by the Commons and the Lords was transferred to each of the two Houses. The Lord Great Chamberlain remains in charge of the Queen's Robing Room and the Royal Gallery, both used on state occasions, notably the annual state opening of Parliament. He also has joint control with the Speakers of the two Houses over Westminster Hall and the Crypt Chapel. In the Commons ultimate responsibility now lies with the House of Commons Commission, chaired by the Speaker, and it is the Commission, rather than the Government, which approves the annual estimates for the Commons before their presentation to Parliament, and which has overall responsibility for services and facilities. The Speaker is advised on matters relating to services and facilities by a Board of Management, consisting of heads of departments, and by the House of Commons (Services) Committee.

The House of Lords, however, has different and basically simpler arrangements. Control of services and facilities is ultimately the responsibility of the Select Committee on the House of Lords' Offices, which until 1991 operated through seven specialized subcommittees.[4] The main committee, which in 1989 had fifty-eight members, is chaired by the Chairman of Committees (the principal Deputy Speaker of the Lords). In 1988–9 the membership of the Offices Committee included the Lord Great Chamberlain, the Leader of the House (Government leader in the Lords), the Government Chief Whip, the Opposition Leader and Chief Whip, the chief whips of the Liberal Democrats and the SDP, and the convenor of the cross-bench peers. The principal official of the House of Lords, the Clerk of the Parliaments, attends the Committee and may attend any of its subcommittees. The seven subcommittees in 1988–9 were Administration, Finance, Staff of the House (all chaired by the Chairman of Committees), Computers, Library, Refreshment

[4] The subcommittee structure was altered from that described at the beginning of the 1991–2 session.

Department, and Works of Art (chaired by other members of the Committee). Several of the subcommittees have co-opted members, who are not members of the main Committee.

The Cost of the House of Lords

Assessing the cost of the House of Lords is complicated by two factors: first, some costs cover both Houses of Parliament or relate to the whole of the Palace of Westminster; and second, financial years operate from April to March, whereas the parliamentary year is normally from November to October. However, since there were 145 sitting days in the House of Lords in the financial year 1988–9 and 153 sitting days in the 1988–9 session, figures for the financial year 1988–9 provide a reasonably accurate assessment of the cost of operating the House during the session with which this book is primarily concerned. The principal costs which do not fall on the House of Lords Vote are the upkeep of the Palace of Westminster, the cost of parliamentary printing, and office and general accommodation services. Details of costs under the House of Lords Vote in 1988–9 are shown in Table 11.2.

The expenditure shown in Table 11.2 does not include the cost of stationery and printing for the House of Lords, nor the Lords' share of the rates on Government property, neither of which is reported in detail in the Appropriation Accounts. However, the estimates for these items for 1988–9 were £3.97 million and £0.35 million respectively, a further £4.32 million. In addition, no account is taken of the upkeep of the Palace of Westminster, which is the responsibility of the Property Services Agency, and the estimate for this was £25.3 million for 1988–9. Assuming a proportional division between the two Houses the same as that for rates (for which the estimate in respect of the Commons was £0.9 million in 1988–9), a further £7.1 million needs to be added. This, together with the £12.9 million shown in Table 11.2 and the £4.32 million mentioned above, gives a total cost of the House of Lords in 1988–9 of £24.4 million. Compared with this the cost of the House of Commons for 1988–9 was £105.3 million, more than four times that of the Lords. Moreover, about a quarter of

Table 11.2. *The House of Lords vote for the financial year, 1988–9*

Item of expenditure	Cost (£'000)
Expenses of peers	4,009[a]
House of Lords' Offices	4,108
House of Lords Staff Pension Scheme	577
Police (50% share of Palace of Westminster costs)	4,011
Refreshment Department	505
Computer services	129
Subtotal	13,339
Less various receipts[b]	392
TOTAL	12,947

[a] Includes an estimated £65,000 to cover the London supplement and secretarial allowance for parliamentary work payable to ministers and other paid office-holders.
[b] e.g. fees from judicial proceedings and private bills, and profits of the Refreshment Department.

Source: *Appropriation Accounts 1988–89*, HC 15–XII, 1989–90.

Commons expenditure is accounted for by the various allowances to members, compared with a sixth of Lords expenditure.

The Staff of the House of Lords

The two principal permanent members of the staff of the House of Lords are the Clerk of the Parliaments, whose counterpart in the Commons is the Clerk of the House, and the Gentleman Usher of the Black Rod, whose nearest equivalent in the House of Commons is the Serjeant-at-Arms. Black Rod's deputy is the Yeoman Usher of the Black Rod.

The departmental structure of the Parliament Office, which is headed by the Clerk of the Parliaments, is shown in Table 11.3. It consisted of twelve offices with a complement of 198 staff (including Library staff) at the beginning of 1989. The Clerk of the Parliaments is appointed by the Crown on the advice of the Prime Minister and is the Accounting Officer for the House of Lords Vote. The Clerk advises generally on points of order and

Table 11.3. *The twelve offices of the Parliament Office, 1988–9*

Senior officer responsible to the Clerk of the Parliaments	Office(s)
Clerk Assistant	Journal and Information Office Printed Paper Office Establishment Office Accountant's Office
Reading Clerk	Public Bill Office Record Office Office of the Official Report (*Hansard*) [Library]
Fourth Clerk at the Table	Judicial Office
Principal Clerk	Committee Office Refreshment Department (from April 1989)
Principal Clerk	Private Bill Office Overseas Office

procedure and is custodian of the records of both Houses of Parliament kept in the House of Lords Record Office, but this task is deputed to a Clerk of the Records appointed by the Clerk of the Parliaments. The latter is also responsible for the accuracy of the texts of all Acts of Parliament and Measures. The Clerk's deputy is the Clerk Assistant, who is responsible for the Minutes of Proceedings of the House and, in 1988–9, was in charge of the Journal and Information Office and the Printed Paper Office. The Clerk Assistant and two other senior clerks, the Reading Clerk (who in 1988–9 was also Principal Clerk of Public Bills) and the Fourth Clerk at the Table (Judicial), are appointed by the Lord Chancellor subject to the approval of the House. The Fourth Clerk at the Table (Judicial) is head of the Judicial Office which, as its name implies, is concerned with the appellate work of the House. Three other offices in the Parliament Office, the Committee Office, the Private Bill Office, and the Overseas Office, were in 1988–9 headed by two other Principal Clerks. The House of Lords Library was not in 1988–9 part of the Parliament Office, the Librarian at that time being appointed on the recommendation of the Offices Committee,[5] but the Deputy Librarian and all other Library staff were appointed and employed by the Clerk of the Parliaments, who delegated to the Reading Clerk the oversight of the Library.

The Clerk of the Parliaments also appoints the Editor of Debates, who is responsible for the House of Lords Official Report (*Hansard*). The Shorthand Writer to the House, who is responsible for recording evidence presented to select committees, is appointed jointly by the Clerk of the Parliaments and the Clerk of the House of Commons. The Shorthand Writer, however, is not on the staff of the House of Lords or the House of Commons, but is head of an independent firm of shorthand writers which also serves the law courts.

The Refreshment Department, the services of which are described in the next section, was formerly a separate organization but since 1980 has formed part of the Clerk of the Parliaments' Department. At the beginning of the 1988–9 session the Superintendent was responsible directly to the Clerk of the Parliaments (as well as to the Refreshment Department Subcommittee of the Offices Committee) but from April 1989 the Clerk of the Parliaments delegated the oversight of the Department to the Principal Clerk of Committees. In terms of staff numbers the Refreshment Department is the largest office in the Parliament Office, with a complement of 61 at the beginning of 1989.

The clerks of the House of Lords are recruited on its behalf by the Civil Service Commission[6] in open competition and are paid salaries linked to those of civil service grades. All staff of the House of Lords are, nevertheless, employees of the House and not civil servants. Senior positions, including that of the Clerk of the Parliaments, are usually filled by internal promotion.

Black Rod is responsible for accommodation, cleaning services, messenger services, the public galleries, and security. Security, like telephone and postal services, are common to both Houses, but Black Rod has jurisdiction over passes for peers' staff.

[5] In 1991 the Offices Committee agreed that in future the Librarian should be appointed by the Clerk of the Parliaments (2nd Report, 1990–1, HL Paper 36).

[6] In 1991 the part of the Civil Service Commission responsible for this recruitment became an agency under the name Recruitment and Assessment Services.

Black Rod is appointed by the Crown on the advice of the Lord Chamberlain; Black Rod himself appoints his deputy the Yeoman Usher. Both posts are normally held by former senior officers of the armed forces. Their duties are carried out under the auspices of the Administration Subcommittee of the Offices Committee. At the beginning of 1989 Black Rod's Department had a complement of 87 staff.

Accommodation and Other Services

All Government ministers who are members of the House of Lords are provided with office accommodation in the Lords' area of the Palace of Westminster. In 1988–9 there were a maximum of twenty-three such ministers, including whips. The Leader of the House, the Deputy Leader, the Government Chief Whip, and a few others have single rooms, but the majority share offices. The Opposition Leader and Deputy Leader, the Opposition Chief Whip, the Chairman of Committees and Principal Deputy Chairman of Committees, the Leader of the Social and Liberal Democrats, and the convenor of the cross-bench peers, are also provided with rooms, as are each of the Lords of Appeal in Ordinary. In 1988–9 approximately 150 other peers had desks in shared offices. All peers with a room are provided with basic office furniture. Limited parking facilities are available to peers.

Peers with offices have telephones, but telephones are also available in various locations for the use of other peers, and all calls on parliamentary business within the United Kingdom are free.

Postal services are provided by the branch post office located in the Central Lobby, but members of the House are responsible for the cost of postage and other postal services, which may be reclaimed under the expenses allowance. Supplies of House of Lords stationery are made directly available to peers and in the Library and the Prince's Chamber (which adjoins the chamber of the House).

The Refreshment Department operates the three dining-rooms and three bars in the House of Lords, which provide meals and other refreshments during sittings (including days when only the Appellate Committee is sitting), but not during recesses. There have been periodic proposals that the two Houses should operate joint refreshment facilities, but these have never been accepted.[7] Peers and staff may also use certain of the Commons' refreshment facilities, and peers who are former MPs may use most of the Commons' facilities.

Information Services

Procedural advice

Information and advice on procedure is available from the clerks in the House of Lords and any peer may obtain their assistance in tabling questions, amendments to bills, motions, and amendments to motions, or in introducing a private member's bill. The Committee Office services all select committees and individual clerks are responsible for the administration of, and giving procedural advice to, each committee.

The House regulates its business through its *Standing Orders relating to public business*,[8] though these are less extensive than the Commons' Standing Orders. The House of Lords also publishes, however, a lengthy and detailed *Companion to the Standing Orders and Guide to the Proceedings of the House of Lords*, which is now in it sixteenth edition,[9] having originated in 1862. The House also provides, for peers, a *Brief guide to the procedure and practice of the House of Lords*.

Assistance to select committees

The specialized select committees of the House of Lords regularly use the services of outside specialist advisers for particular inquiries. In 1988–9 the European Communities Committee employed seventeen specialist advisers, the Science and Technology Committee five, and the Select Committee on Murder and Life Imprisonment two.

In autumn 1988 temporary specialist assistants were appointed

[7] See e.g. House of Commons (Services) Committee, *Fifteenth Report*, HC 652, 1966–7, p. x.
[8] The latest edn. (July 1989) is HL Paper 77, 1988–9.
[9] HMSO, London, 1989.

on an experimental basis to the Science and Technology Committee and the European Communities Committee. Their tasks included writing specialist papers, analysing evidence, keeping the committees informed of recent developments, and developing a supporting role in their area of expertise. The purpose of these posts was to bring specialist knowledge into the Committee Office. The experiment was for two years in the first instance, though it was subsequently extended and one of the specialist advisers continued for a further two years, the other for a further year.

Documentation

The formal records of the activities of the House of Lords are contained in its *Minutes of Proceedings*, published daily after each sitting, and the Journals of the House of Lords, published sessionally. Annexed to the *Minutes* are details of future business which has been tabled. The Official Report (*Hansard*) is the verbatim record of speeches made in the House during its proceedings, but also includes some formal entries of proceedings (such as messages brought from the Commons relating to bills), the text of replies to questions for written answer, and division lists. *Hansard* is published in daily and weekly parts, and in corrected bound volumes. Select committee minutes of evidence and reports, public bills and amendments, and various other documents, are published as House of Lords Bills and Papers.

The House also produces, for internal use, *Lords Spiritual and Temporal: General Information*, commonly known as the *Grey Book*. A new edition is produced after each recess and includes a list of all peers (indicating whether they have taken the oath of allegiance, are on leave of absence from the House, have not received a writ of summons, have not taken their seats, or have not made a maiden speech), a list of ministers in the Lords, official Opposition and other party spokesmen, membership of select committees, and brief details of the Parliament Office.

All peers who attend the House are provided with copies of the *Standing Orders* and the *Companion*, and may receive *Hansard* and the *Minutes* regularly. In addition they may, on request, have free copies of other official publications which they require in order to discharge their parliamentary duties. These include

House of Lords Papers, House of Commons Papers (which include many reports made to Parliament by statutory bodies and office-holders), and Command Papers (which include Government white papers, green papers, and departmental reports), and European Community publications, details of all of which are circulated weekly. Peers may also receive copies of non-parliamentary papers published by HMSO or Government departments. These are all obtainable from the Printed Paper Office.

The Journal and Information Office is responsible for producing the *Grey Book*. It also produces a number of Factsheets and Information Sheets. The Office has also prepared educational material and deals with public enquiries.

The House of Lords Library and computer services

The House of Lords Library occupies a suite of five large rooms on the terrace side of the Palace of Westminster and in 1989 had a staff of eighteen. Its principal function is to provide information services for peers, including the loan of material from its own collection and from other sources, including the House of Commons Library. Although the libraries of the two Houses are separate, they are linked through a liaison committee, which includes a representative from the House of Lords Record Office, and efforts are made to avoid unnecessary duplication of holdings.

The Lords Library holds some 45,000 titles in approximately 100,000 volumes. The stock is heavily biased towards law, partly because of the House's work as a revising chamber and partly because of its judicial role. The Library, in fact, supplies the law lords with the authorities for their judicial work and has a fine collection of English and Scottish law. There is also a good collection on British history. The limited book holdings on contemporary affairs are 'weeded' at irregular intervals and contemporary matters are covered primarily by the Library's subscription to about 600 newspapers and periodicals, of which some fifty are kept permanently.

Three members of the Library staff, two Library Clerks and a Legal Library Executive, are engaged in research for peers, and during the 1988–9 session they produced 737 research briefs in response to requests from peers. These are related to debates in or legislation before the House, since peers do not, of course, have the constituency responsibilities of MPs. Quick reference requests are dealt with at an Information Desk.

Other information can be extracted from various computerized databases. The Library's catalogue is on computerized microfiche, can be searched on-line, and is updated monthly. Regular use is made of the Parliamentary On-Line Information System (POLIS) operated by the Commons Library, of PROFILE for on-line searching of newspapers, LEXIS for the searching of statutes and law reports, and JUSTIS for European Communities material. The Library also subscribes to BBC Data, a commercial service for the provision of press cuttings. The Journal and Information Office maintains a database of peers' political interests, but it is available only to peers and officers of the House of Lords. The responsibility for computer services throughout the House lay, in 1988–9, with the Computer Subcommittee of the Offices Committee, and the Computer Officer, who supervises the computer services of both Houses.[10]

The Library is undoubtedly one of the most important of the services and facilities provided for peers. Not only is it a major source of information, but for the many peers without offices it is a workplace when they attend the House. It is invariably full each afternoon when the House is sitting, and is one of the major meeting places for peers, and there is close co-operation between peers and the Library staff.

Expenses

Peers are currently entitled to travel expenses and to an expenses allowance when the House or one of its committees is sitting. Travel expenses were introduced in 1946, when peers were able to claim reimbursement of first-class rail travel between the nearest station to their homes and London. This was, however, subject to an assiduity rule requiring attendance at a minimum of one-third of the sittings. In 1947 the rule was abolished for

[10] In Nov. 1990 the House of Lords appointed its own Computer Executive, since when the Computer Officer has acted mainly in an advisory capacity.

peers living in Scotland and in 1972 abolished altogether. A car allowance was introduced in 1961 as an alternative to first-class rail travel. Initially, however, it was limited to the cost of rail travel, but eventually linked to the car mileage allowance of civil servants.

The daily attendance allowance, which was renamed in 1981 'the reimbursement of expenses allowance', was introduced in 1957, but the expenses that could be claimed under it were not fully clarified until 1977, when the TSRB observed that the expenses were the subject of 'a great deal of confusion'.[11] In its report the TSRB recommended that the allowance should cover four types of expenses: overnight subsistence, day subsistence and incidental travel, secretarial costs, and postage and additional expenses, such as the 'purchase of books and periodicals or the payment of a professional subscription relevant to a specialist interest directly related to parliamentary duties'.[12] In 1979 the TSRB recommended that the third and fourth categories should be amalgamated to create a secretarial and research allowance because peers had experienced difficulty in distinguishing between the two. The expenses allowance was linked to civil service rates in 1984.[13]

The rates in force during the 1988–9 session are shown in Table 11.4.[14] The figures given are *maxima*, and expenses must be claimed, normally monthly, within three months of being incurred. A survey of peers eligible to attend the House conducted on behalf of the TSRB in 1975 found that 82 per cent of non-office holders made claims against the travel and expenses allowance.[15] A subsequent survey in 1986 dealt only with the secretarial and research allowance and recorded a take-up figure of 62 per cent of a sample of peers who had attended the House during the previous session.[16] Statistics giving details of take-up

[11] TSRB, *Report No. 9*, Cmnd. 6749 (Mar. 1977), para. 20.

[12] Ibid., paras. 22 and 33.

[13] A new formula governing certain aspects of the allowance was introduced in 1991: see HL Debs., 25 July 1991, cols. 884–7.

[14] For the rates in earlier years, and further details of the history of the allowance, see Donald Shell, *The House of Lords*, 2nd edn. (Harvester Wheatsheaf, London, 1992), App. A.

[15] TSRB, *Report No. 9*, App. A, Table 12.

[16] TSRB, *Report No. 24*, vol. 2, Cm. 131–II, Apr. 1987, App. D, Section 3, Table 3.1, note b.

Table 11.4. *Expenses allowance rates (maxima), 1988–9*

Year from 1 Aug.	Day subsistence	Secretarial and research	Overnight subsistence	Total
1988	£23	£23	£60	£106
1989	£24	£25	£64	£113

are not published, but by reference to the published Estimates and Appropriation Accounts and using attendance figures it has been estimated that in 1988–9 the total amount claimed was about 66 per cent of the theoretical maximum. The 1975 survey data show that take-up, as would be expected, is more common amongst regular attenders and peers living outside London. It is also higher among life than hereditary peers.[17]

Satisfaction with both the travel and the expenses allowance has tended to increase as they have become more flexible and generous. The 1975 survey found as many as 54 per cent of non-office-holders *dissatisfied* with allowances, with the highest levels of dissatisfaction amongst peers living outside London and attending frequently.[18] A further survey in 1982 found that the proportion dissatisfied had fallen to 41.0 per cent, but was as high as 64.9 per cent amongst those who attended 125 or more days per year.[19]

Conclusion

The House of Lords is almost certainly the only chamber in a major national legislature whose members are not remunerated for their services. Nor, for that matter, are they regarded as full-time legislators, except, of course, for Government ministers and other office-holders. Curiously and illogically, in 1977 the Labour Government refused to accept the recommendation of the TSRB that the expenses allowance be increased to £24.50, on the

[17] TSRB, *Report No. 9*, App. A, Table 12.
[18] Ibid., Table 13.
[19] TSRB, *Report No. 20*, vol. 2, Cmnd. 8881–II, May 1983, S. 4, Table 5. 51.3% were satisfied and 7.7% did not reply.

grounds that it would breach its pay policy, even though it allowed MPs' allowances to rise in accordance with TSRB recommendations.[20]

The question of remuneration has been considered on a number of occasions, including the Lawrence Committee on the Remuneration of Ministers and Members of Parliament in 1964 and the TSRB in 1977, 1983, and 1986. The Lawrence Committee took the view that the introduction of remuneration for peers, whether in the form of a salary or an annual fee, should not precede reform of the upper chamber and that to do so 'might well amount to a recommendation on the reform of the House of Lords itself'.[21] In its 1977 Report the TSRB agreed with this view, also pointing out that there were problems with the taxation of allowances if remuneration were introduced.[22] The TSRB returned to the question in 1983, but, whilst agreeing that 'the case for remuneration . . . [has] . . . some force, particularly in relation to those peers who devote a great deal of time and effort to the work of the House', again felt that it 'would constitute a significant change . . . which it would be wrong for us to initiate'.[23] In 1986 the TSRB considered only allowances and was unwilling to recommend the payment of higher allowances to more active back-bench peers, although it did suggest that a proposal for a special secretarial allowance for such peers was 'a matter which the Leader of the House might wish to invite the House to consider further'.[24]

Apart from suggestions for the remuneration of more active peers, there have, in the various surveys, been proposals for the reimbursement of lost earnings, an entertainment allowance, better secretarial and research facilities and the provision of office equipment (such as word processors), and more office accommodation. These are fairly modest claims, all the more so when they and the existing expenses allowance are compared with the provision of services and facilities for MPs. As already

[20] See Michael Rush, 'Members' Salaries, Allowances, Pensions and Related Facilities' in Rush (ed.), *House of Commons: Services and Facilities*, 116–18.

[21] *Report of the Committee on the Remuneration of Ministers and Members of Parliament (The Lawrence Committee)*, Cmnd. 2516, Nov. 1964, para. 158.

[22] TSRB, *Report No. 9*, paras. 10–13.

[23] TSRB, *Report No. 20*, para. 179.

[24] TSRB, *Report No. 24*, paras. 69–71.

noted, the House of Commons costs four times more than the House of Lords, a difference which is not accounted for simply by the payment of salaries to and the provision of a pension scheme for MPs. Services and facilities for back-bench MPs are considerably more extensive, not only in terms of accommodation (much as MPs may complain), but also in many other respects, notably in the level of the MPs' secretarial and research allowance. However, a reformed and probably elected second chamber, which undoubtedly would have to consist of acknowledged full-time members who would demand services and facilities comparable to those of MPs, would cost considerably more. This additional cost would arise only in part from the provision of salaries, a pension scheme, and improved services and facilities, and the greater staffing they would involve; a major capital investment would also be required in providing accommodation. It is therefore arguable that, given the work done by the House of Lords and the considerable efforts this involves for its more active members, the services of the upper House are bought at a bargain price.

12

Conclusion

Donald Shell

The purpose of this book has been to examine and evaluate the work of the House of Lords. To that end contributors have looked closely at every aspect of the work of the House in the 1988–9 session (except its judicial activities). In order to provide adequate explanation and context for the analysis of that particular session, contributors have found it desirable to say a little about how the House in general goes about that aspect of its activities which they have analysed, why it follows the procedures it does, and so on. Contributors have also offered their own conclusions about what they have found, and compared these with the findings of others, and to some extent the views and opinions offered elsewhere.

The purpose of this final chapter is to try to provide an overall assessment of the role of the House. Before summarizing and reviewing what we have found in relation to the 1988–9 session, it may be helpful to consider for a moment two different perspectives from which an evaluation can be made. One perspective simply looks at the House as a discrete institution, a distinct part of a given political system, and evaluates its activities without reference to the effectiveness or otherwise of other parts of that system. From this point of view the functions of the House can be examined, assessing, for example, how adequately it revises bills brought from the Commons, how useful it is for the introduction of some bills before they go to the Commons, how effective its select committee work is in scrutinizing policy, and so on. Reform of the House can also be considered, but very much from the point of view of how the House could better fulfil the functions it at present attempts to carry out. Thus one may consider, for example, procedural changes designed to improve the scrutiny of legislation, or how best to ensure that the House mobilizes a membership adequate for its select committee work, or other similar matters.

A different perspective, however, is to consider the work of the House within the wider context of the parliamentary and constitutional system, a system which many would argue is itself in need of fundamental reform. If devolution to regional assemblies took place, if electoral reform were introduced, if a codified Constitution were enacted, how then might a second chamber be constituted and what functions might it have? Discussion about such reform developed very much during the late 1980s, so much so that it has become rather difficult not to adopt this latter perspective at least to some extent when discussing the role of the Lords in the early 1990s. Perhaps this point can be seen rather more clearly if we glance back over the earlier post-war period for a moment.

In the 1950s and the 1960s the basic shape of the British Constitution was widely viewed as highly satisfactory. Increasingly in the 1960s the need for institutional reform was discussed, but this was seen very much as a question of updating and modernizing specific institutions. Local government, the civil service, and the House of Commons were all approached in this piecemeal way. The abortive attempt to reform the Lords in 1968–9 was very much in this tradition. It was a perspective shared by both major parties. In the 1970s a more sweeping critique of the entire political system developed. As economic difficulties intensified and talk of British decline became more widespread, the search for the roots of this decline led to a focus on the role of the political parties. Attention switched from modernizing institutions (increasingly seen as exhausting, expensive, and ineffective—a mere palliative) to the complacency and stagnation induced by consensus politics, or the evils attendant on adversarial politics, depending on one's point of view. Either way the operation of the political system became subject to more sweeping critique. In the 1980s both the need to modernize the institutional bits and pieces of British government (so readily perceived in the 1960s), and the attack on the political system (characteristic of the 1970s), were gradually eclipsed by more sweeping calls for constitutional reform. The House of Lords was not singled out as particularly or especially in need of change; rather its reform or replacement was discussed in the context of a fundamental review, perhaps culminating in the formal enactment of a written Constitution.[1]

This concluding chapter first and foremost takes up the more limited perspective of how the House operated in the 1988–9 session as an institution within the constraints exerted by the present constitutional and political systems, and how it might be changed to enhance its value within the existing structure and practice of parliamentary government in Britain. But the point needs to be emphasized that this should not be seen as the only legitimate perspective. Indeed it may be (and this is the crucial point) that the House by performing relatively well its present role is in effect assisting the continuation of a system that otherwise would more obviously stand in need of fundamental reform. The House may plug gaps that ought not to exist and would not if changes elsewhere took place.

The 1988–9 Session

The fact that the session studied was during a period of Conservative government should be noted as a preliminary point to our summary. Clearly in all sorts of ways statistics concerned with the work of the House have been different under Labour Governments—most obviously the much larger number of Government defeats in the division lobby. The success rate for amendments moved from the Opposition benches has been much higher when those benches have been occupied by Conservative peers. But though the statistics, and indeed the style of the House, have been very different under Conservative Governments from Labour Governments, there is probably a greater danger in being misled about the role of the House through exaggerating the differences than there is through ignoring them. We would not wish to ignore them. But two points need to be emphasized. First, the way the House operates has been different

[1] See e.g. *Charter 88*; *1688–1988: Time for a New Constitution*, eds. R. Holme and M. Elliott (Macmillan, London, 1988); *New Constitution for the United Kingdom*, Institute for Public Policy Research, 1991; *Constitutional Reform in the UK: An Incremental Agenda*, F. Vibert, Institute of Economic Affairs. See also the discussion contained in R. Brazier, *Constitutional Reform* (Clarendon Press, Oxford, 1991).

from Parliament to Parliament, irrespective of any change in the party in office. After the Conservative Government greatly increased its majority in 1983 there was a noticeably enhanced determination on the part of the House to play the role of responsible opposition to the Government precisely because of the weakness of the Labour Opposition in the Commons. Similar sentiments were expressed after the 1987 election, though there was also then a greater resolve on the part of the Thatcher Government, by that time obviously irritated by the House, to curb the enthusiasm of peers for fulfilling the role of 'Her Majesty's Alternative Opposition'.[2] In the same sort of way the Labour Government of the 1970s with its precarious existence in the Commons found distinct differences from the House it had experienced in the 1960s. What we have done is to study the House as it was in the middle of the 1987–92 Parliament, and we acknowledge that there will be changes in any subsequent Parliament, whichever party is in office. But the second point is that on past evidence those changes are unlikely to alter the role of the House in any very significant way. In most major respects that role is similar as between Governments of different parties. Of course, there have been many more Government defeats when Labour has been in office, but the vast majority of these (certainly in the 1974–9 period) were reversed by the Commons, whose decisions were accepted without more ado by the Lords. Only in a small number of cases did the Lords dig their heels in and offer any serious resistance. A former Chief Whip in the Lords with very long experience of the House has argued that the actual extent of revision of bills that takes place through the House has been very similar under Governments of both Parties, and a majority of active peers have expressed similar views.[3]

If by general consent the most important work of the House is the revision of Government legislation, then Chapters 3 and 4 above deserve particularly close attention. Apologists for the House frequently give prominence to statistics indicating the

[2] See HL Debs., 22 June 1983, esp. comments by Lord Cledwyn of Penrhos at col. 13; his view was partially contradicted by Lord Hailsham of Saint Marylebone at col. 129; see also comments by Viscount Whitelaw, HL Debs., 25 June 1987, col. 21; also 'The Other Opposition', Radio 4 Analysis, 5 Nov. 1987.

[3] Lord Denham in interview. For survey evidence see N. Baldwin, 'The House of Lords', Ph.D. thesis, University of Exeter, 1985, esp. App. 10.

very large number of amendments made to Government bills. Certainly the crude total of amendments made (and accepted by the Commons), at 2,339, sounds impressive. If the usefulness of the House—or even the productivity of peers—were to be gauged by such statistics then the House could take pride in its record, up from 700 or so amendments per year in the 1970s to over 1,200 in the early 1980s to over 2,000 in the period 1985–90. But reading the above chapters at least prompts the question: are such figures as much—or perhaps more—a symptom of sickness in the legislative system as a whole, rather than an indication of the health and vigour of the upper House? Has the House become first and foremost a convenience for government rather than a forum for the testing and proving of government policy in the eyes of the nation?

The argument for the former view finds some support in the degree to which the Government appears to dominate the legislative work of the House. On the case-study bills not simply a majority but an overwhelming majority—more than nineteen out of every twenty amendments that were agreed—were moved by Government spokesmen. A further suggestive piece of evidence is the fact that over 99 per cent of all amendments moved by the Government were successful, while amendments moved from all other quarters of the House achieved a success rate of only just over 6 per cent. While it is reasonable to argue that some amendments moved by Government spokesmen were responses to points raised on the back benches and elsewhere, Chapter 4 also shows that the process worked the other way round, with non-Government peers bringing forward amendments drafted by the Government. What is very clear is that the vast majority of amendments made to bills were the result of second (third, fourth, and fifth?) thoughts by the Government itself as its legislation was squeezed through the so-called legislative sausage machine. This on the face of it implies a very high degree of control by the Government over the legislative process.

What though of the relative significance of amendments made? Miers and Brock conclude in Chapter 4 that 'the extent to which the House has a significant impact depends on the standpoint of the observer'. Their discussion illustrates this point. For example, the 341 amendments made to the Water Bill included several adjustments important to particular groups. It is surely appropriate to expend much effort to try and get the detail of such legislation right, to try and balance economic and environmental interests to maximum mutual benefit, to remove any unnecessary obfuscation, and so on. There is a good case for arguing that the details of such legislation should be discussed both in a highly political forum (as an elected chamber inevitably is), and in a rather less politicized and perhaps more expert body (as a second chamber can be). But if the House is to be more than a body which conveniently tidies up bills, or makes improvements in drafting and allows adjustments agreed by Government, then one must look for examples where the Government has given ground on points of some significance.

This scarcely happened on the Water Bill, upon which few if any major changes appear to have been made by the House. This was not for want of trying—at least by some peers. 'Much was expected of the Lords' debates on the Water Bill,' write Miers and Brock, but from their detailed account it would seem that little was delivered. To extend the prohibition on charging for water for fire-fighting to include water for fire-fighting training, or to alter the rules under which water companies obtain access to private land to lay pipes, may be worth-while improvements to the bill as originally drafted. To someone, somewhere, sometime, such changes may indeed be significant. But in the context of a bill privatizing the water industry they were the merest incidentals. Pressure in the House may have led to some revision of the code to be followed by the private water companies before disconnection of customers took place, and if so that was surely a more significant change. But when Lord Nugent of Guildford, a peer who was not only a lifelong Conservative, but someone recognized as one of the country's leading experts on the water industry,[4] moved an amendment to substitute statutory water companies for private companies he was firmly rebuffed. This was not (he claimed) a wrecking amendment, because it left alone the privatization of the industry while restraining the capacity of the privatized water companies to make unlimited profits. But the Government regarded the amendment as a

[4] Lord Nugent of Guildford had been an MP from 1950 to 1966; a minister 1951–9; chairman of the Select Committee on the Nationalised Industries 1961–4; President of the Association of River Authorities 1965–74; and Chairman of the National Water Council 1973–8.

violation of its bill, and it was rejected. Clearly had it been passed ministers would have sought (and obtained) its reversal in the Commons, and the Lords would have dutifully submitted.

Reading the above chapters it seems fair to say that in the 1988–9 session the Government did not give way to the House of Lords on any matter which ministers regarded as of major significance, at least on the case-study bills. Looking at the non-case-study bills it is difficult to find any evidence that would require this conclusion to be modified. An amendment to the Electricity Bill imposing a statutory duty on the electricity companies to be energy-efficient was passed by 126 votes to 114, and though acknowledged to be technically defective the principle of the amendment was supported by the Commons Energy Select Committee in a special report, as well as by an Early Day Motion signed by forty Conservative back-bench MPs. But the Government was prepared to make only a limited concession.[5] On the Social Security Bill, even though nineteen Conservative MPs defied a three-line whip to support a Lords' amendment on the uprating of child benefit, the Government overturned this amendment. On the same Bill, Lords' amendments to broaden the scope of the disability allowance were rejected in the Commons, causing one former Conservative cabinet minister to express himself 'appalled at this act of social cruelty', while the Liberal Democrat, Earl Russell, said that he 'could not recall any amendment carried on division in this place which had been fully accepted in the Commons'.[6] This latter view was contradicted by the Leader of the House and others with long years of experience in the Lords, but it is significant that Lord Russell was speaking of his own experience in the House which he had entered in 1987.

Sometimes proceedings in the Lords afforded an opportunity for Opposition parties to inflict embarrassment upon the Government. An example was the 'ambush' defeat the Government suffered on the Companies Bill over donations to political parties. True, such setbacks can usually be quickly reversed by a

[5] See HL Debs., 16 May 1989, cols. 1044–58; HC Debs., 20 July 1989, cols. 553–87; HL Debs., 25 July 1989, cols. 1337–49; 5th Report from the Select Committee on Energy, *Electricity Bill: Lords Amendment on Efficient Use of Electricity*, HC 478, 1988–9.

[6] On the Social Security Bill see HC Debs., 19 July 1989, cols. 435–83; HL Debs., 20 July 1989, cols. 917–29.

party 'in control' of the Commons. Nevertheless what happened in the Lords may have had some marginal effect in raising slightly the threshold of public awareness of the fact that ministers were unprepared to allow shareholders to decide whether companies should make donations to political parties, while requiring trade unions to seek approval from their members before making such donations.

Most of the legislative work of the House involves making what may fairly be described as minor, technical, and drafting amendments to bills. This work is concentrated on a small number of bills primarily because bills vary so much in length and complexity, as Table 3.3 shows. It is not surprising that the Lords, like the Commons, devotes a much higher proportion of its time to long complex bills than to short simple ones. The technical improvement of legislation is not only important but all the more necessary for those bills subjected to the guillotine in the Commons. However, the frequently made claim that the House of Lords gives special attention to matters guillotined in the Commons needs to be treated with some scepticism. Table 3.3 shows that as a proportion of the time spent by the Commons, the time spent by the Lords on bills guillotined in the lower House was only very slightly higher than the time spent on non-guillotined bills. The reader of *Hansard* is more likely to be struck by the extent to which argument and debate in the two Houses tends to focus on the same points. The fact that the most vitriolic exchange in the Lords in the 1988–9 session took place as peers argued over the rights and wrongs of the Government use of the guillotine in the Commons on the Official Secrets Bill illustrates this point. It seemed less the substance of the bill, more the fact that it had been guillotined, which really upset peers!

It is worth taking particular note of the treatment by the House of those Government bills introduced there. For seventy years lip-service has been paid to the Bryce Commission view that one of the major functions of the House has been to initiate bills which may have an easier passage through the Commons if they have been fully discussed and put into 'a well-considered shape before being submitted' to the lower House.[7] But in 1988–9, of

[7] Report of the Conference on Reform of the Second Chamber (Chairman Viscount Bryce), Cd. 9038 (1918).

the two major Government bills introduced into the Lords, one was 'largely rewritten in the Commons' and the other was returned from the Commons to the Lords 'almost double the length that it left the Lords' (the Companies Bill and the Children Bill respectively). It is worth noting that another bill introduced into the Lords, the Football Spectators Bill, was, in regard to its main provision, legislatively stillborn. Neither Lords nor Commons could deflect the Prime Minister's obdurate determination to see this bill through, despite the many predictions of the unworkability of its central provision for a football membership scheme. But after the Hillsborough disaster and the Taylor Report thereon, and some six months after the bill reached the statute book, the Government announced that, though the Act would not be repealed, the membership scheme for which it made provision would be indefinitely postponed.[8]

As Table 3.3 shows, the House of Lords spent a long time on these bills but the House of Commons spent a very similar amount of time dealing with them. Whether the House of Lords actually saved the House of Commons time is a moot point. Nevertheless debate in the Lords clearly served various purposes. On the Children Bill complex issues were unravelled, no doubt helping (as the Lord Chancellor put it) to 'inform progress in the Commons'. But for the bill to return from the Commons with over 400 new amendments, and this in the final week of the session, suggests that if it had been properly thought out from the start the potential for the House to save the Commons time would have been greater. What happened could hardly be said to represent effective management of the legislative process! Baroness Seear's protest that the House was being treated with contempt was understandable.

Overall it does seem fair to say that the usefulness of the House has been primarily, if not overwhelmingly, to the Government rather than to the Commons, to interest groups, or to the public. The House is a place where errors and omissions can be corrected, where at least some details can be put right even if others are ignored. From this point of view it is better to have the House than to be without it. If political ambition and ministerial

[8] See Statement from the Home Secretary, HC Debs., 29 Jan. 1990, cols. 19–36. When the Statement was repeated in the House of Lords it prompted some sharp comments from peers, see HL Debs., 29 Jan. 1990, cols. 19–31.

vanity result in a 'legislate as you go' mentality then it is useful to have a second chamber like the House of Lords, reasonably diligent and generally dull, with a whiff of expertise but no real boldness, with conscience but not too much credibility, with a little public profile but no actual power. The House can act as a kind of legislative long-stop. If it did not exist more care would have to be taken with the earlier stages of bills, or indeed more stages would be necessary in the Commons. The real question though is whether the whole legislative process could not be reformed and improved in such a way as to reduce the demands made on the second chamber (and on the first for that matter). This point finds some reinforcement when the position in regard to delegated legislation is considered.

Alongside the considerable expansion in the quantity of primary legislation that has taken place there has been immense growth in the volume of delegated legislation. Figures cited by Borthwick (p. 137) show how the number of pages of statutory instruments enacted each year has increased, giving rise to another expanded parliamentary task. And apart from instruments dealing exclusively with finance all are potentially subject to debate in the Lords as well as in the Commons. Statutory Instruments (SIs) are also subject to the scrutiny of the joint select committee which draws its membership equally from both Houses. The work of this committee is described above in Chapter 5 as 'obscure, unglamorous, and drab'. The scrutiny it undertakes is largely technical in nature, probing the vires of instruments, assessing 'unexpected or unusual use of powers' and so on. While it may be thought praiseworthy that at least four MPs can be found who are prepared to attend its meetings more or less every sitting week, in principle this does seem to be the kind of task which members of a second chamber might disproportionately bear. That it should have been disproportionately borne by MPs seems surprising. Yet, as Chapter 5 shows, peer members of the joint select committee were on balance slightly less assiduous attenders than the MP members.

As regards debate on SIs, it is worth underlining the fact that the Commons spends over three times as long as the Lords on this task. Furthermore, the lower House usually debates instruments in advance of the upper House. Essentially the Lords seems to be doing 'more of the same' as the Commons. The procedural constraints—the inability to amend SIs, the single stage or once only debate, the conventions disallowing rejection of SIs in the Lords—these all might be said to inhibit the role of the House. That it does continue to spend 3 per cent of its time debating SIs is worth noting, and as Borthwick shows that does result in some instruments receiving brief explanation in the Lords when no such opportunity for explanation has been found in the Commons. Furthermore the House of Lords does retain a special niche for hybrid instruments, which can result in select committee inquiries, one of which took place in 1988–9 and did result in an Urban Development SI being altered by an amending Instrument. The very fact that the House of Lords retains a distinctive procedure here deserves emphasis, and a question worth posing is, should other distinctive procedures be adopted in this area? This is a point to which we return in the next section of this chapter.

In terms of the quantity of legislation placed on the statute book private members' bills appear relatively insignificant. As Tables 6.3 and 6.4 show, the nine private members' bills enacted in the 1988–9 session together added only forty-three pages of legislation, while the thirty-three Acts introduced by the Government ran to over 2,300 pages. However, the relative importance of private members' legislation cannot be entirely assessed in so simple a way. Chapter 6 brings this point out well. While only a single private member's bill introduced into the Lords was enacted (and that a mere single page of legislation), eight other bills introduced by peers were discussed in the House and, as the discussion in Chapter 6 shows, these undoubtedly did bear fruit in various ways. It would be silly to attempt to justify the existence of a second chamber because of its work on private members' bills. But a second chamber being in existence, one should note its modest usefulness in respect of such legislation. This usefulness extends to private members' bills brought from the Commons. The severe constraints which operate in the lower House (which have intensified in recent years) underscore one aspect of the value of the Lords. Some bills, if they pass the Commons at all, only do so entirely undebated because of time-table constraints; such bills will always receive a brief debate in the Lords, so *Hansard* will contain an explanation of what the bill is about (as for example with the Dangerous Dogs Bill). But more generally the House affords opportunities for issues to be taken up, causes to be advocated, and campaigns launched. It also enables cockshies to be made at translating ideas into legislation, some at least of which bear fruit in subsequent bills introduced by Governments or back-benchers.

Private legislation remains something of a curiosity. Yet it is obvious from Chapter 7 that considerable importance attaches to private bills. Whether this should be so or not is another matter. Perhaps new forms of planning inquiries are needed to facilitate the expression of public opinion while not leaving the burden of recommendation or decision on the lonely shoulders of an inspector or secretary of state. But 'lay involvement' in the shape of select committees of either House has both its supporters and its value. Here the Lords is able to play a role of something akin to equality with the lower House. From Chapter 7 it is clear that uncertainties surround the future of the whole private bill procedure. Apart from responding to the recommendations of the joint select committee, creeping party politicization in the Commons appears to have rendered private bill procedures in the lower House of increasingly limited value. Meanwhile it is clear that in this admittedly rather marginal area, the Lords really does save the time of the Commons. And so long as the private bill procedure exists the need for a contribution from a second House is likely to remain, if not be enhanced.

The role of the House in non-legislative debate is something of an enigma. Again given the existence of a second chamber it would be very odd if no opportunities were afforded in that chamber for members to initiate and take part in such debates, or ask questions of the Government. Equally though, it would be hard to justify the House of Lords on the basis of such activity. The value of this work is hard to assess. Much of it appears to have a haphazard, perhaps idiosyncratic, even quirky character. Given that the most senior judges sit in the Lords it is not surprising that the House should make something of a spectacle of debating the Government's proposals for fundamental reform of the legal profession (see pp. 221–4). But it would be hard to establish a justification for this debate in terms of its measurable impact in bringing adjustments to Government policy. And it is clear that all who took part could (and no doubt many did) add their responses to the 800-plus responses received by the Government to its Green Paper. It could certainly be argued that a House of Commons select committee established to conduct hearings on the proposals would have been not only a more effective mechanism for ensuring that these were taken note of, but also a procedure more in keeping with a democratic political system.

The upper House does provide a public platform for peers to express views. But its members tend to be the sort of people who could find other platforms without difficulty. A more pertinent question perhaps is, would they choose to do so? Lord Windlesham might have been ready enough to answer critics of his report on the 'Death on the Rock' TV programme in the columns of a serious newspaper, but it is unlikely that a former chief of defence staff would have offered his views on the subject, unless prompted to do so through a debate in the House of which he happened to be a member (p. 228). The House of Lords has provided a form of accountability for some of those in public positions. Lord Armstrong of Ilminster was able to answer directly critics of his role as chairman of the trustees of the Victoria and Albert Museum through a Lords debate (p. 229). For a peer holding some public office to decline to answer his critics in the Lords is itself something to be noted, as was the case with Lord Chilver, chairman of the Universities Funding Council, whose absence from a debate on higher education occasioned adverse comment in the House (p. 225).

The House may also provide a forum which brings together individuals whose views on a subject are important because the Government is unwilling to introduce legislation or even to formulate policy until a measure of consensus has been publicly expressed. For example since 1986 the Government has refused to legislate on Sunday trading until a greater measure of agreement between interests involved has been secured. A debate in the House of Lords, such as that initiated by Lord Boyd-Carpenter (see p. 244) with leading retailers, churchmen, and trade unionists taking part, is a public way of signalling how near or distant such agreement might be. The fact that the Government is answerable in the Lords ensures that a public statement of the Government's position on a matter has to be made. The House sometimes provides an opportunity for an issue to be raised in a timely way when for one reason or another this cannot or will not happen in the House of Commons.

The House of Lords has no direct part in the struggle for the hearts and minds of the electorate. It has no role in that contest of wills which can sometimes in the Commons threaten to break a Government. But in a civilized democracy, where fact and reason, where experience and expertise, also count in forming opinion and in shaping policy, a role for a second chamber in debating and defining views on some of the issues of the day may be thought to be justified.

The select committee work of the House is reviewed in Chapters 9 and 10. In summarizing this it is worth emphasizing three points. First, the House has undertaken work that complements rather than in any sense rivals that of the Commons. It was because the Commons disbanded its committee on science and technology that the Lords set up a committee in this area. And as far as the European Communities Committee is concerned, the House has consciously struck out in a direction different from that taken by the Commons. Second, the House has been able to provide at least some very distinguished and experienced members to serve on select committees. This has been most markedly the case in relation to the Science and Technology Committee, but it is also evident elsewhere, for example with the *ad hoc* Committee on Murder and Life Imprisonment discussed in Chapter 10. Third, the House *in toto* has sustained a high level of committee work bearing in mind that it is a House not composed of full-time professional politicians but of unpaid volunteers. It is apparent from the analysis given in Chapter 5 of the joint select committee on statutory instruments and the analysis in Chapter 9 of the attendance of peers at the European Communities Committee that some members of these select committees have found it difficult to attend meetings regularly. It has also been evident in recent years that the House has considered establishing further select committees, but drawn back from doing so because of the lack of staff, and perhaps uncertainty about the capacity of the House to sustain any higher level of committee work than it does at present. Prompted in part by these considerations the House itself in 1991 established a select committee to examine its own select committee work.[9]

It seems reasonable to suggest that the reports from the select committees of the House help towards an effective public

[9] This committee reported in Feb. 1992 (HL Paper 35, 1991–2).

monitoring of Government activity in certain selected areas. The scientific press has taken a consistent interest in the reports of the Science and Technology Committee. Perhaps the House should derive encouragement from the fact that the Secretary of State for Education and Science was stung into making a sharp attack upon this committee in December 1991.[10] Reports from the European Communities Committee, while rarely achieving much by way of publicity, do bring together important collections of views and facts on selected policy issues. They also afford government the opportunity to define its view on these issues. Perhaps of greatest interest is the fact that such reports have been quite widely circulated within the European Community, thus indicating the way towards a different kind of parliamentary role from that which has before been experienced.

To summarize: this review of the activity of the Lords in the 1988–9 session suggests that the House fulfils a useful if modest role. It is convenient to a number of groups. To the Government some bills can be tidied up in the Lords; others can be introduced there relieving the Commons of some of the initial work involved in scrutinizing them. To outside groups the House is a useful forum for attempting to get the details of legislation adjusted. Its value is almost certainly enhanced precisely because it is not merely a party-dominated chamber. To the Opposition the House is a place where a little useful spadework can be done, turning Government policies over, probing here and there for weak spots which may then be further exposed and perhaps exploited elsewhere. For all the above groups the select committee work of the House can also be helpful. It is not difficult to talk up the role of the House. Apologists for the House can fasten on to evidence suggesting that it has a role of some significance, if in general a rather shadowy one. But equally it is not difficult to talk down the role of the House, to dismiss its revising work as of very minor consequence, to argue that if it were otherwise Governments would simply not tolerate the House, to see its non-legislative debate as little more than a 'hard core of wind',[11] and to argue that in general whatever it does do it lacks

[10] Ibid.

[11] The title of a book by a former employee of the House, S. Braham (Val Publishing, London, 1986).

the legitimacy to do, and that such tasks should really be done by other bodies, or rendered unnecessary by reforms elsewhere.

The House from 1989 to 1992

Before addressing the subject of reform, a further brief glance at the period since 1988–9 is appropriate. It seems fair to say that in the following two sessions nothing happened which would require any significant alteration to the picture presented by our study of the 1988–9 session. We have argued that since 1987 there had been evidence of a hardening attitude by ministers towards the House, a change which would appear to have been sustained throughout the 1987–92 Parliament. For example, despite considerable unease on Conservative benches in the Commons, amendments made by the House of Lords to the National Health Service and Community Care Bill, the Education (Student Loans) Bill, and the Social Security Bill in the 1989–90 session were all reversed with only very limited concessions being made. When in the same session the Lords voted for a dog-registration scheme the Government insisted on rejecting this despite widespread support for the idea on the Conservative benches in the Commons.[12]

In the 1990–1 session peers voted to amend the Criminal Justice Bill so as to abolish the mandatory life sentence for murder. As Chapter 10 indicates, this was a subject upon which the House had established a select committee, and peers were simply voting in line with the recommendation of their select committee report (see p. 302). The Government however insisted on overturning the view expressed by the House.[13] Press reports suggested that peers were feeling more and more demoralized at the apparent contempt with which their House was being treated.[14] If the House was unable to change the minds of ministers even on such an issue as this about which peers had thought

[12] See Donald Shell, *The House of Lords*, 2nd edn. (Harvester Wheatsheaf, London, 1992), 173–5.

[13] HL Debs. 18 Apr. 1991, cols. 1559–86; HC Debs., 25 June 1991, cols. 866–913; HL Debs., 3 July 1991, cols. 991–6, 1006–66.

[14] See e.g. 'Peers' self-confidence is fading', S. Gunn, *The Times*, 23 Apr. 1991.

so deeply, was it worth retaining the House at all in all its panoply as the second chamber of Parliament?[15]

Most notable was the outright defeat at second reading in the Lords, by a massive 207 votes to 74, of the War Crimes Bill. This was a Government measure which had received no imprimatur in a manifesto, and was in no genuine sense a party matter at all. It raised in acute form various legal and ethical questions. The view of the House of Lords on the subject of altering the law so as to prosecute alleged Nazi war criminals had been made abundantly clear well before the legislation was introduced. Peers felt strongly that no such change in the law should be made.[16] But the Government pushed ahead with a bill, and following its rejection by the Lords decided to use Parliament Act procedures to have the measure enacted. In the 1990–1 session peers again rejected the bill at second reading (by 131 votes to 109), thereby depriving themselves of the opportunity to put forward amendments which conceivably might have diminished the unacceptability of the bill. Lord Jenkins of Hillhead, whose study on the passage of the original Parliament Act was well known,[17] declared that the use of the Parliament Act to secure the passage of the bill was a 'constitutional monstrosity' and he continued 'if anyone had tried to advocate the need for that Act in 1911 or 1949, in terms of a measure such as this Bill, he would not have begun to be taken seriously in either House of Parliament'.[18] Though in no sense precipitating an immediate constitutional crisis this episode did indicate the constitutional impasse the House of Lords had come

[15] One peer who was very doubtful was Lord Stoddart of Swindon who in a speech in 1989 protested: 'What on earth is the use of good-hearted people, with a conscience about and a feeling for their country, coming along here day by day to thrash out the bills that come before us and to give their considered opinion to the Government and to the country if they are to be overruled at a stroke with no reasons properly given. . . . We have become nothing more than a curiosity, and an expensive curiosity at that. . . . By accepting . . . diktats from the House of Commons the House of Lords is getting rid of itself . . . the House is a waste of some £12 to £15 million a year and if the electorate realised . . . they would demand that it be closed and be used merely as a tourist attraction for foreign visitors' (HL Debs., 20 July 1989, col. 924).

[16] For debate on the Chalmers–Hetherington Report (Cm. 744) see HL Debs., 4 Dec. 1989, cols. 604–79; for second reading debates see HL Debs., 4 June 1990, cols. 1080–1208, and 30 Apr. 1991, cols. 619–743.

[17] R. Jenkins, *Mr Balfour's Poodle* (Heinemann, London, 1954).

[18] See HL Debs., 30 Apr. 1991, col. 633.

to occupy. Between Labour hostility and the Conservative indifference, what future was there for the House?

The Question of Reform

Before examining what the major Parties were actually suggesting by way of reform in the early 1990s, it seems best to reflect on the question of reform from the perspective developed in this study on the work of the House. We can consider first proposals for changes which lie within the competence of the House itself to initiate and at least in part to execute, before looking at proposals for fundamental change in the House in terms of its composition and functions.

As indicated above (p. 13) the House itself examined its own procedures in 1987 and concluded that it did not wish to introduce changes of any significance. Marginal adjustments relating to the rules and conduct of the House will no doubt continue to be made. It is of no consequence whatsoever to the outside world whether a bishop votes with his robes on or off—to take one recent example of a question addressed by the Procedure Committee of the House![19]

But there are certainly more significant changes which the House itself could implement. The evidence cited earlier concerning the increased time spent by the House on Government bills, and the very considerable pressures the House is under, which undoubtedly sometimes result in the work of revision being carried out with unseemly haste, prompt reconsideration of procedures for dealing with legislation. Experiments involving the committee stage of a bill being taken off the floor of the House have taken place, but only intermittently. Such committees, analogous to standing committees in the Commons, have been known in the Lords as Public Bill Committees. But in a politically unrepresentative House largely composed of part-timers the basis for the selection of the members of these committees can prove difficult. Partly for this reason, peers who have not been members of such committees have hitherto been entitled to attend, speak, and even move amendments. At the

[19] HL Paper 76, 1990–1.

report stage back on the floor of the House a good deal of repetition of what has been said in committee can take place. Continued reluctance to impose restraints on members of the House, or to provide for the selection of amendments for debate at later legislative stages, can only limit the extent to which such committees can save time on the floor of the House. For such committees to have this effect, their introduction must be accompanied by other changes either procedural or behavioural (or a combination of both). As the House gradually becomes more of a professional legislative chamber, with a higher proportion of peers effectively working there fulltime, and a growing acceptance of constraints on procedural freedom, then conditions may become more favourable for the use of such committees. But it is unlikely that their use would diminish the total number of peer-hours (including time on committees) needed to do the work of the House; indeed the opposite effect is more probable. And this question of the capacity of the House to sustain a higher workload is one to which we must return.

From what has been said earlier in this chapter, and from the analysis provided in Chapters 3 and 4 above, it is clear that saving the time of the House is closely related to improving the quality of legislative scrutiny. The latter certainly suffers at present because of the haste with which much legislative work has to be undertaken. Some proposed reforms have been directed more specifically at improving the quality of legislative scrutiny. In 1976 the Select Committee on Practice and Procedure recommended the establishment of a range of committees covering different policy areas with each being responsible for legislative scrutiny in their particular area.[20] It was recommended that in the case of Commons bills such committees would act as select committees taking evidence on a bill while it was before the lower House. Such committees would also monitor a bill's progress in the Commons, thus being in a position to report factual details such as the time spent on various stages in the Commons, the undertakings given by ministers there, and other matters. After a bill had received its second reading in the Lords the same committee would then form the nucleus of a public bill committee

[20] 1st Report from the Select Committee on Practice and Procedure, HL 141, 1976–7.

for further consideration of the bill. For bills introduced into the Lords the committee could perform both the scrutiny and evidence-taking function and the normal debating and amending function in an extended committee stage, thus being very similar to the special standing committees that operated so intermittently in the House of Commons in the early 1980s.[21]

When the motion to establish a select committee to examine the committee work of the House was moved in April 1991, one peer, Lord Northfield, intervened to request that the new select committee be invited to consider the proposals made by the 1976 select committee of which he had himself been a member. He had also written an article urging strongly the case for the development of a system of select committees to deal with legislation in the House.[22] Whether as a result of this intervention or not, it was apparent at the end of 1991 that the select committee was conducting a wide-ranging inquiry.

Recommendations for select committee type scrutiny of legislation impinge directly on the relationship between the Government and Parliament. Ministers therefore take a keen interest in such matters, and it has to be said ministers have consistently and quite strenuously resisted changes of this kind. That has been evident in the Commons, and when the report of the 1976–7 select committee was debated in the Lords it found very few friends on the front benches.[23] Much was made by the report's critics of the difficulties that would result from a timetabling point of view if such changes were introduced. Doubt was also expressed about whether the House had the capacity to sustain such a development of its committee work.

But that is to take refuge behind present constraints when the focus of discussion really needs to move on from how to improve the present legislative system by various minor adjustments, to the question of how to reshape that system to improve the quality of the end-product. The proper objective of reform must be to make a substantial improvement in the whole legislative system. But from the bunkers in Whitehall such reform would not be

[21] See 2nd Report from the Select Committee on Procedure, HC 49, 1984–5.

[22] HL Debs., 18 Apr. 1991, cols. 1561–3; See also Lord Northfield 'Reforming Procedure in the House of Lords', in *Policy and Politics*, eds. D. Butler and A. H. Halsey (Macmillan, London, 1978).

[23] HL Debs., 5 July 1977, cols. 166–265.

seen this way. Nor is it likely that the Commons would show any enthusiasm for reforms of the upper House which would enhance its credibility with interest groups generally in regard to making changes to legislation, and add to the self-confidence and clout which the House might display. Governments have a vested interest in keeping the capacity of both Houses to review their legislation as weak as it usually is now, at least in normal times of one-party majority rule. To the Government, making the system more efficient means little more than enabling it to deliver their bills more speedily. Furthermore, to implement comprehensive reforms would almost certainly require a fundamental reform of the composition of the House, which of course depends on the House of Commons and the Government. None the less the House could itself establish experimental select committees in one or two policy areas to embark on the kind of role outlined above.

This theme of how the House of Lords might initiate reform of the legislative process is further illustrated when we examine secondary or delegated legislation. The way in which the variety and complexity of creatures in the 'delegated legislation zoo' (p. 137) have multiplied without being systematized or shaped by any obvious principles indicates a need to reflect on the question: what forms should legislation take, and how ought these to be related to each other?—surely a pertinent question for Parliament to consider.

On the one hand it may be argued that a 'sovereign' Parliament can do what it likes. If it chooses to confer power on ministers by statute to introduce fundamental change by means of SIs (even the power to amend Acts of Parliament, as with the so-called 'Henry VIII clauses') then so be it. That is within its powers. Likewise the line between what is contained in an Act of Parliament, say one reforming the law on children, and what is decided in SIs laid subsequent to the Act, cannot be a hard and fast one. Whether an Act aimed at regulating the behaviour of football spectators, or introducing student loans, should be primarily declaratory or whether it should contain much of the detail about how the objectives concerned are to be realized, these it might be argued are matters which a sovereign Parliament should freely decide. Likewise whether provision should be made for the affirmative procedure (requiring parliamentary debates and votes) or the negative procedure (simply allowing the possibility of parliamentary debates and votes), indeed whether an instrument should be laid before Parliament at all (and whether it should have any legal force, that is, be recognized as law by the courts, or be simply advisory), all these it may be said are matters for Parliament to decide on an *ad hoc* basis, bill by bill.

But adherence to this one principle—of letting Parliament decide—all too readily means that no other principles are recognized. The question of how much detail is in primary legislation, how much goes into secondary legislation, and what form the secondary legislation takes, become matters merely of expediency and convenience. If a Government has not yet decided what it really wants to do, or how to do it, then a bill can be skeletal, to be filled in later with SIs. For reasons associated with the parliamentary timetable it may suit to keep a bill short, or conversely for political or personal reasons a minister may have ambitions to have a very long bill, the length and complexity of which becomes a source of pride.

The existing joint select committee on Statutory Instruments exists to probe the delegated legislation undergrowth, but its point of departure is always the parent Act. A more fundamental, systematic, and applied scrutiny of bills, and the kinds of powers they confer on ministers, would be appropriate. The House could itself set up a select committee to monitor public bills with a view to systematizing more the powers they contain to make delegated legislation. Reference is made by Borthwick to a debate in the Lords in which the possibility of establishing such a select committee was argued (p. 164). Government ministers may resist such changes and even resent them being proposed, but the outside observer can only suggest that the House takes this kind of initiative in order the better to fulfil its parliamentary role.

This review of possible reforms which lie within the power of the House itself to initiate (if not consummate) has focused very much on legislation. In regard to non-legislative debate and parliamentary questions the House has modified its procedures over the years in ways which provide structures for these activities at least as satisfactory as those which exist in the Commons. The introduction some twenty years ago of time-limited debates was initially made with considerable caution. But the spread of this practice suggests the innovation has been regarded as generally satisfactory.[24] A further area of innovation concerns select committee work, and here the House appears to have made good use of its available membership. While the scope of select committee work has remained limited because of the part-time character of the House, there are no obvious procedural changes that the House could itself make to enhance the effectiveness of its select committees, nor indeed of the time it spends on non-legislative debate and questions. The main weakness of the work of the House in these areas is precisely its inability to do more than publish its reports and its views, hoping that those with the power to make decisions take some notice.

This consideration of the functions of the House and the changes that might be made appears irresistibly to push the argument on towards a consideration of more fundamental reform. In part this is because it seems unlikely that the House as at present constituted could really do much more than it now does. Indeed, reading the chapters of this book one might well conclude that the House is already in some danger of finding itself unable to sustain the range and level of activities that it already undertakes. Committee attendance is poor; the Government front bench lacks the experience and in some cases the abilities considered essential for ministers in the Commons; bills are often revised in haste and with superficiality. But the case for fundamental reform can also be made out on the grounds that the House is simply misconceived for the modern world. It is a relic from a past age. Though its very antiquity may confer upon it an air of mystique and even a form of legitimacy, its aristocratic flavour and its lack of any democratic basis represent fundamental handicaps in the late twentieth century. The House lacks both the capacity and the standing to do the job that needs to be done by a second chamber in a large modern democratic state.

Fundamental Reform, Replacement, or Abolition

How then might the House be reformed? Numerous proposals have been advanced, and it is not our purpose here to provide

[24] See HL Paper 9, 1987–8, paras. 66–71.

any comprehensive review of these. But at the beginning of the 1990s we may at least note the position of the major parties.

The Conservatives had apparently ceased to have any policy on the subject of Lords reform, or indeed on virtually any constitutional question whatsoever.[25] What had become notable, however, within the party was the increased irritation felt by Conservatives towards the House in the 1980s, and the growing indifference to—and even contempt of—the House evident among Conservative ministers and some MPs. Certainly it is hard to imagine the modern Conservative Party defending the House of Lords or even the retention of a second chamber with any real conviction or vigour. Their thoughts and energies appear to be directed elsewhere—for better or for worse.

While inertia in respect of Lords reform has overtaken the Conservatives, Labour in opposition in the 1980s, as in the period 1970–4, has again recognized that the House can have some value in resisting some Government measures and attracting publicity to such opposition. The Party has modified its early 1980s policy of abolition followed by unicameralism to a policy of abolition followed by replacement—the creation of a new second chamber. This was outlined in the Party's policy review proposals in 1989.[26] These were part of a more sweeping scheme for constitutional reform, with the new chamber being an entirely elected body having certain specific powers to delay for a whole Parliament any legislation which breached a Charter of Fundamental Rights which the Party also proposed to promulgate. Apart from this power, the new House would not, however, be able to do other than ask the House of Commons to think again about any amendments to legislation it proposed. Furthermore it

[25] In the 1991 Swinton Lecture *Political Culture, Conservatism and Rolling Constitutional Change* (Conservative Political Centre, 1991) John Patten MP provides an elegant argument for doing nothing about the Constitution except 'tackling proven abuses', but in his analysis such abuses scarcely exist, and certainly the House of Lords seems—to him—free from perpetrating any abuse. Individual Conservatives entertain aspirations for change; e.g. Douglas Hogg MP in a televised conversation with his father, Lord Hailsham of Saint Marylebone, criticized the present House of Lords for its lack of authority and expressed a wish for a second chamber which would exercise more authority, but his father seemed, somewhat forlornly, to think that leaving everything alone was the best way to bring this about (Channel Four, 'A Week in Politics', 6 Dec. 1990).

[26] *Meet the Challenge: Make the Change*, Final Report of Labour's Policy Review for the 1990s (Labour Party).

would contain no ministers and legislation could not be introduced there. Clearly many details about these proposals remained to be filled in, but as they stood they were subject to heavy criticism not least from within the Labour Party itself. Who would stand for election to a body devoid of power in respect of almost all its legislative work? How seriously would the work of revising bills be undertaken if no one answered in the House for the Government? It was surely significant that when the House of Lords itself debated its own powers and composition in 1990, of the Labour peers who spoke in the debate not one provided a defence of their Party's proposals.[27] The desire on the part of Labour to remove the spectacle of an upper House still predominantly composed of peers by succession has not been matched by the ability to put forward a credible alternative.

The Liberal Democrats have advanced proposals for an entirely elected 100-member Senate which would represent the nations and regions of the United Kingdom. Such a chamber would revise legislation, with ministers from the Commons having the right to attend and contribute to its proceedings though not to vote. The power of the Senate to delay legislation would be increased, and its assent would be required to any amendments to the written Constitution, the introduction of which the Party has also proposed.[28]

What is most apparent from this cursory discussion of the various Parties' proposals is that no deep thought has actually been given to the subject of the second chamber. Nor is there anything like a consensus between the parties about what might be done. It seems unlikely in these circumstances that anything actually would be done to replace the existing House. While a Party with a secure Commons majority could bring forward legislation to abolish and replace the House of Lords, the enactment of such a bill would be fraught with much difficulty and would almost certainly make heavy demands upon the parliamentary timetable. Other legislation would surely be perceived as deserving a higher priority.

[27] HL Debs., 25 Apr. 1990, cols. 606–37.

[28] *We the People . . . Towards a Written Constitution*, Federal Green Paper No. 13 (Liberal Democrat Publications).

But a simple measure to remove hereditary peers from the House (without further interfering with the peerage) could be passed quite easily. The Life Peerages Act of 1958 affords an obvious precedent. This was a measure that had been talked about for decades but about which no inter-party consensus existed. The Labour Opposition actually opposed it, but the Conservative Government took it through. A Government of either party could introduce such a measure in the 1990s and it is unlikely that any serious difficulty would arise. Polls suggest public opinion would be ambivalent about such a change, certainly not hostile, possibly supportive.[29] Once hereditary peers had been removed it would be possible to consider how to supplement a House consisting entirely of nominated life peers with an elected element. Perhaps a basis for elections would be best devised in the context of other reforms, such as devolution to national and even regional assemblies, or some further reform of local government.

At various times proposals have been put forward for a second chamber constituted on corporate lines.[30] Such a chamber would include representatives of major groups in society who may be elected or appointed. Such ex-officio membership would follow the example of the bishops in the present House. No major party includes such proposals in its policy documents at the time of writing. There are several obvious difficulties, including decisions about which groups should be represented and in what numbers. Doubts about the availability of members so appointed to work regularly enough in the House to give its activities adequate coherence have also been expressed. But such objections need not preclude the idea of extending a little the ex-officio principle in a House composed of part appointed and part elected members.

[29] A poll taken for BBC Radio, the results of which were broadcast on 10 Jan. 1991 as part of a programme on Patronage presented by R. Oakley, included a question about reform of the Lords which found 9% supporting unicameralism, 18% an elected second chamber, 19% some other changes to the existing House, and 30% the status quo. When asked specifically about the retention of hereditary peers in the House another question found almost half supported their removal while only a quarter of respondents supported their retention.

[30] See e.g. R. Butt 'The Case for a Stronger Second Chamber', *People and Parliament*, ed. J. P. Mackintosh (Saxon House, 1978); *Reshaping Britain* (Political and Economic Planning, 1974).

It has been commonplace to say that no such institution as the House of Lords would (or indeed could) be created today, but that the House, being there already, cannot be easily or obviously improved upon, and actually does a tolerably useful job. But that argument (if argument it can be called) has declining force. It is foolish to pretend that a House of accidentally selected part-timers can function adequately as a second chamber in a country as large and as complex as the United Kingdom. To make this point is not to belittle the very considerable efforts made by many very able peers in the existing House. Experience and wisdom can be (and often have been) put to good use in the House through diligence and industry. But there is something mildly eccentric in expecting a 'House of Lords' to function as a modern parliamentary chamber. Of course, this very eccentricity gives the House of Lords what some would describe as its quintessentially English flavour. But if defending the 'tribe's customs and weathered monuments'[31] becomes a more dominant impulse than the attempt to arrest decline, to modernize British democracy, and to remain competitive in the modern world, then the price for retaining what is quintessentially English has surely become too high.

[31] A phrase taken from Tom Nairn talking of the House of Lords in 'The Politics of the New Venice', *New Society*, vol. 42, 17 Nov. 1977; quoted in M. J. Wiener, *English Culture and the Decline of the Industrial Spirit 1850–1980* (Penguin edn., 1985), 161.

APPENDICES

compiled by David Beamish

Appendix A: Sittings of the House of Lords, 1988–9

Table A lists each of the 153 sittings of the House of Lords during the 1988–9 session. Sittings purely for judicial business are excluded. There follow notes on certain columns in the table.

Lords present

The number of lords present each day is based on the lists of lords present and voting published in vol. 222 of the House of Lords Journals.

Lords voting

On days when divisions took place, this column shows the number of lords voting in one or more divisions.

Other columns

The columns to the right of the 'Lords voting' column contain an analysis of the number of lords attending by party, peerage type, and attendance record. Party affiliations are based on the Parties' own lists of lords taking their whip. The columns from 'Con' to 'Bp' inclusive, and from 'Bp' to 'H' inclusive, each constitute a complete breakdown, by Party and peerage type respectively, of lords attending on a particular day. The columns are as follows:

Con	Conservative
Lab	Labour
Dem	Social and Liberal Democrat
SDP	Social Democratic Party
X-B	Cross-bencher in receipt of the 'unlined whip'
Oth	Other (excluding bishops)
Bp	Bishop or Archbishop
A	Life peer created under the Appellate Jurisdiction Act 1876
L	Life peer created under the Life Peerages Act 1958
C	Hereditary peer of first creation
H	Hereditary peer by succession

The last three columns show the number of lords attending who, during the whole of the 1988–9 session, attended not more than ⅓, ⅒, and 1/20 of the sittings which they were eligible to attend.

Table A *Sittings of the House of Lords, 1988–9*

					Sitting began	Sitting ended	Hours sat	No. of divs	Lords present	Lords voting	Con	Lab	Dem	SDP	X-B	Oth	Bp	A	L	C	H	≤1/3	≤1/10	≤1/20
1	Tue	22	Nov.	1988	15:30	16:46	1:16		303		134	78	25	11	48	5	2	2	151	8	140	45	14	8
2	Wed	23	Nov.	1988	14:30	20:02	5:32		346		148	79	29	12	71	3	4	3	178	8	153	61	15	8
3	Thu	24	Nov.	1988	15:00	20:11	5:11		323		140	73	31	13	60	5	1	2	161	5	154	53	15	6
4	Tue	29	Nov.	1988	14:30	21:58	7:28		379		171	85	30	12	77	3	1	7	202	8	161	70	15	8
5	Wed	30	Nov.	1988	14:30	21:43	7:13		376		164	75	33	11	86	4	3	11	197	7	158	64	18	9
6	Thu	1	Dec.	1988	15:00	19:36	4:36		317		136	70	31	12	65	2	1	4	166	6	140	41	11	7
7	Tue	6	Dec.	1988	14:30	20:03	5:33		360		163	80	31	12	69	3	2	5	187	12	154	58	10	3
8	Wed	7	Dec.	1988	14:30	20:50	6:20		355		150	81	33	12	72	3	4	3	181	9	158	56	12	1
9	Thu	8	Dec.	1988	15:00	20:45	5:45		361		162	74	28	10	80	4	3	8	169	8	173	67	16	5
10	Mon	12	Dec.	1988	14:30	18:03	3:33		289		130	67	25	10	54	2	1	3	148	6	131	34	4	2
11	Tue	13	Dec.	1988	14:30	21:48	7:18		389		177	81	33	11	79	3	5	3	206	8	167	76	17	8
12	Wed	14	Dec.	1988	14:30	19:54	5:24		340		154	74	29	10	67	3	3	4	180	7	146	51	16	7
13	Thu	15	Dec.	1988	15:00	21:42	6:42		314		143	68	27	9	61	3	3	7	155	5	144	40	5	0
14	Mon	19	Dec.	1988	14:30	22:33	8:03		310		144	68	28	10	55	3	2	4	158	7	139	31	5	1
15	Tue	20	Dec.	1988	14:30	22:39	8:09		335		150	74	29	12	64	4	2	3	174	7	149	53	8	1
16	Wed	21	Dec.	1988	14:30	20:46	6:16		281		122	57	27	10	59	2	4	2	138	6	131	36	9	3
17	Thu	22	Dec.	1988	11:00	13:17	2:17		189		73	47	18	10	39	1	1	1	97	1	89	9	2	0
18	Mon	16	Jan.	1989	14:30	20:00	5:30		280		124	61	22	12	55	3	3	3	146	4	124	32	7	4
19	Tue	17	Jan.	1989	14:30	22:50	8:20	1	375	224	180	76	33	13	63	4	6	2	183	8	176	66	13	4
20	Wed	18	Jan.	1989	14:30	21:08	6:38		349		156	71	29	13	75	2	3	7	171	6	162	61	13	6
21	Thu	19	Jan.	1989	15:00	22:52	7:52	1	333	183	153	69	32	9	66	2	2	8	163	5	155	45	11	3
22	Mon	23	Jan.	1989	14:30	0:16	9:46		315		144	64	29	10	64	3	1	3	159	5	147	44	4	2
23	Tue	24	Jan.	1989	14:30	21:56	7:26		352		166	73	32	9	68	2	2	4	180	7	159	49	8	2
24	Wed	25	Jan.	1989	14:30	23:00	8:30		351		158	71	36	12	68	3	3	4	175	7	162	55	10	0
25	Thu	26	Jan.	1989	15:00	18:10	3:10		316		140	70	27	10	64	4	1	8	164	5	138	43	7	2
26	Mon	30	Jan.	1989	14:30	22:43	8:13	1	318	199	134	74	31	11	62	2	4	3	164	6	141	33	6	0
27	Tue	31	Jan.	1989	14:30	20:16	5:46		368		178	79	35	11	57	3	5	3	197	9	154	58	14	5
28	Wed	1	Feb.	1989	14:30	22:21	7:51		355		164	72	30	13	62	3	11	4	174	7	159	64	18	8
29	Thu	2	Feb.	1989	15:00	21:31	6:31		329		151	78	27	9	57	3	4	5	164	5	151	44	11	4
30	Mon	6	Feb.	1989	14:30	22:22	7:52	2	308	216	146	80	25	8	43	4	2	2	152	6	146	35	9	4

Table A *(contd.)*

					Sitting began	Sitting ended	Hours sat	No. of divs	Lords present	Lords voting	Con	Lab	Dem	SDP	X-B	Oth	Bp	A	L	C	H	≤1/3	≤1/10	≤1/20
31	Tue	7	Feb.	1989	14:30	22:06	7:36	2	367	281	175	86	36	9	57	3	1	7	191	6	162	61	14	6
32	Wed	8	Feb.	1989	14:30	21:30	7:00		337		148	77	24	9	70	4	5	4	175	7	146	55	12	6
33	Thu	9	Feb.	1989	15:00	20:45	5:45		313		144	72	26	8	59	3	1	11	157	3	141	43	11	0
34	Mon	13	Feb.	1989	14:30	18:11	3:41		270		127	64	24	9	43	2	1	2	134	4	129	26	5	4
35	Tue	14	Feb.	1989	14:30	21:36	7:06		350		171	80	26	10	58	3	2	3	176	5	164	51	10	2
36	Wed	15	Feb.	1989	14:30	22:03	7:33		327		149	70	36	9	56	4	3	4	169	5	146	46	10	5
37	Thu	16	Feb.	1989	15:00	21:47	6:47	1	315	114	141	70	31	9	60	3	1	9	151	6	148	45	13	4
38	Mon	20	Feb.	1989	14:30	22:15	7:45	2	346	272	164	74	33	10	60	3	2	3	167	5	169	55	11	4
39	Tue	21	Feb.	1989	14:30	22:58	8:28	1	371	184	178	80	32	9	68	3	1	7	184	7	172	58	11	2
40	Wed	22	Feb.	1989	14:30	21:33	7:03		333		148	73	26	11	70	4	1	3	168	7	154	44	11	4
41	Thu	23	Feb.	1989	15:00	21:38	6:38		323		144	76	23	11	64	3	2	3	159	6	153	43	9	5
42	Mon	27	Feb.	1989	14:30	20:03	5:33		285		122	72	25	11	51	2	2	3	144	4	132	25	5	3
43	Tue	28	Feb.	1989	14:30	20:45	6:15	2	349	276	167	81	26	13	56	5	1	4	174	6	164	50	9	2
44	Wed	1	Mar.	1989	14:30	20:57	6:27		317		142	70	25	9	67	3	1	3	161	5	147	44	10	8
45	Thu	2	Mar.	1989	15:00	22:15	7:15	1	346	189	157	71	30	12	71	3	2	15	163	5	161	68	15	3
46	Mon	6	Mar.	1989	14:30	20:57	6:27	3	328	224	167	71	25	7	52	2	4	3	164	5	152	51	9	1
47	Tue	7	Mar.	1989	14:30	22:54	8:24	2	380	305	181	84	33	11	65	4	2	3	191	5	179	68	15	3
48	Wed	8	Mar.	1989	14:30	22:42	8:12		349		158	74	24	7	78	4	4	4	179	4	158	64	22	13
49	Thu	9	Mar.	1989	15:00	21:39	6:39		323		145	75	25	8	65	4	1	4	169	4	145	44	10	4
50	Mon	13	Mar.	1989	14:30	19:29	4:59	2	310	215	149	69	23	7	58	3	1	4	160	4	141	43	7	3
51	Tue	14	Mar.	1989	14:30	0:22	9:52	2	353	267	170	76	33	10	58	3	3	4	183	4	159	53	9	6
52	Wed	15	Mar.	1989	14:30	21:15	6:45		329		147	73	28	7	66	5	3	4	170	4	148	45	1	1
53	Thu	16	Mar.	1989	15:00	21:57	6:57		328		142	68	30	12	71	3	2	11	161	5	149	53	11	2
54	Mon	20	Mar.	1989	14:30	21:13	6:43	1	330	188	157	73	27	10	58	4	1	2	170	7	150	48	7	3
55	Tue	21	Mar.	1989	14:30	21:28	6:58	1	370	255	179	83	30	8	64	4	2	2	191	7	168	59	10	2
56	Wed	22	Mar.	1989	14:30	22:59	8:29		304		134	69	25	8	63	4	1	0	159	3	141	39	11	5
57	Thu	23	Mar.	1989	11:00	15:08	4:08		205		88	55	15	6	39	2	0	0	105	4	96	16	1	1
58	Mon	3	Apr.	1989	14:30	22:05	7:35	3	343	279	171	73	38	7	51	2	1	2	176	7	157	51	12	3
59	Tue	4	Apr.	1989	14:30	20:16	5:46	1	372	268	186	78	37	8	57	4	2	3	192	7	168	63	15	4
60	Wed	5	Apr.	1989	14:30	20:34	6:04		274		132	68	20	5	45	2	2	1	143	8	120	24	5	2

61	Thu	6	Apr.	1989	15:00	21:27	6:27	1	309	169	142	72	24	9	56	4	2	3	159	5	140	41	4	0
62	Fri	7	Apr.	1989	9:30	22:41	13:11		235		100	51	18	4	60	2	0	12	117	3	103	41	14	9
63	Mon	10	Apr.	1989	14:30	22:56	8:26	4	325	269	161	71	27	8	53	3	2	1	164	5	153	41	7	1
64	Tue	11	Apr.	1989	14:30	22:10	7:40	1	363	182	191	73	24	9	60	5	1	1	180	7	174	62	10	3
65	Wed	12	Apr.	1989	14:30	23:36	9:06		356		152	72	32	10	79	4	7	2	180	7	160	68	10	4
66	Thu	13	Apr.	1989	15:00	21:54	6:54	1	338	70	152	70	33	12	67	3	1	8	166	8	155	59	10	0
67	Fri	14	Apr.	1989	11:00	15:18	4:18		160		66	39	16	4	32	2	1	1	72	4	82	18	5	1
68	Mon	17	Apr.	1989	14:30	23:35	9:05		322		149	70	28	12	59	3	1	2	156	7	156	47	7	4
69	Tue	18	Apr.	1989	14:30	19:46	5:16	1	375	267	191	73	28	7	69	4	3	2	187	5	178	66	8	3
70	Wed	19	Apr.	1989	14:30	21:17	6:47		327		150	67	30	9	62	5	4	2	165	8	148	48	6	1
71	Thu	20	Apr.	1989	15:00	21:49	6:49	4	321	233	153	67	27	7	60	4	3	6	159	8	145	49	10	1
72	Fri	21	Apr.	1989	11:00	15:19	4:19		177		75	46	17	6	28	2	3	0	84	5	85	13	2	1
73	Mon	24	Apr.	1989	14:30	21:13	6:43	1	309	194	151	72	22	8	51	3	2	2	157	4	144	41	4	2
74	Tue	25	Apr.	1989	14:30	22:40	8:10		333		152	78	25	11	62	4	1	3	171	7	151	45	10	2
75	Wed	26	Apr.	1989	14:30	20:49	6:19		321		138	72	31	7	65	4	4	1	163	8	145	51	18	7
76	Thu	27	Apr.	1989	15:00	17:17	2:17	1	276	172	133	62	20	10	45	4	2	0	142	6	126	40	6	2
77	Tue	2	May	1989	14:30	23:27	8:57	4	364	321	174	80	35	9	62	3	1	4	180	8	171	70	13	7
78	Wed	3	May	1989	14:30	21:18	6:48		311		136	70	27	9	63	3	3	2	157	5	144	44	11	3
79	Thu	4	May	1989	15:00	23:35	8:35	5	430	344	234	75	30	9	78	3	1	10	186	8	225	134	46	21
80	Mon	8	May	1989	14:30	0:21	9:51	2	295	234	142	71	30	6	42	2	2	1	146	5	141	35	4	2
81	Tue	9	May	1989	14:30	22:04	7:34	5	325	276	160	67	28	9	55	3	3	3	162	7	150	57	8	3
82	Wed	10	May	1989	14:30	20:21	5:51		287		129	64	26	10	51	2	5	1	145	6	130	39	11	3
83	Thu	11	May	1989	15:00	22:44	7:44	1	304	194	143	68	25	7	56	4	1	2	153	5	143	42	8	2
84	Fri	12	May	1989	11:00	14:25	3:25		140		51	38	18	5	25	2	1	0	66	4	69	5	2	0
85	Mon	15	May	1989	14:30	22:44	8:14	3	277	234	124	77	24	7	41	3	1	1	140	4	131	31	9	2
86	Tue	16	May	1989	14:30	23:30	9:00	1	351	240	165	79	31	11	57	3	5	1	178	7	160	53	12	0
87	Wed	17	May	1989	14:30	21:30	7:00		340		160	71	27	10	67	4	1	5	169	9	156	56	11	1
88	Thu	18	May	1989	15:00	23:27	8:27	2	337	186	160	72	27	11	63	3	1	11	161	4	160	55	14	4
89	Mon	22	May	1989	14:30	23:00	8:30	3	332	253	166	71	28	6	56	4	1	2	156	5	168	49	9	2
90	Tue	23	May	1989	14:30	4:44	14:14	2	336	214	163	70	29	8	61	2	3	1	159	5	168	59	10	2
91	Wed	24	May	1989	14:30	21:37	7:07		278		120	70	24	11	47	2	4	2	132	5	135	33	5	1
92	Thu	25	May	1989	11:00	16:30	5:30		249		103	62	21	12	48	1	2	2	117	3	125	29	5	2
93	Mon	5	June	1989	14:30	23:20	8:50	2	322	252	152	77	26	13	51	3	0	2	163	5	152	48	9	1
94	Tue	6	June	1989	14:30	23:26	8:56	5	351	288	171	77	29	10	60	3	1	3	178	9	160	58	8	0
95	Wed	7	June	1989	14:30	19:59	5:29		312		135	65	26	11	69	3	3	4	154	5	146	51	16	6
96	Thu	8	June	1989	15:00	23:18	8:18	3	330	201	157	70	26	12	60	3	2	5	158	8	157	56	15	7

Table A (contd.)

					Sitting began	Sitting ended	Hours sat	No. of divs	Lords present	Lords voting	Con	Lab	Dem	SDP	X-B	Oth	Bp	A	L	C	H	≤1/3	≤1/10	≤1/20
97	Fri	9	June	1989	11:00	14:56	3:56		160		60	48	14	6	29	2	1	1	74	2	82	13	4	2
98	Mon	12	June	1989	14:30	23:29	8:59	3	339	275	168	72	32	12	50	4	1	3	173	6	156	48	13	5
99	Tue	13	June	1989	14:30	0:08	9:38	1	355	215	175	76	30	10	59	4	1	4	181	6	163	58	10	3
100	Wed	14	June	1989	14:30	20:12	5:42	1	319	86	145	77	26	9	57	4	1	3	172	7	136	44	7	0
101	Thu	15	June	1989	15:00	22:47	7:47		319		162	68	25	7	53	3	1	2	157	8	151	41	7	2
102	Fri	16	June	1989	11:00	14:17	3:17	2	226	188	101	53	25	7	36	3	1	1	113	3	108	28	11	2
103	Mon	19	June	1989	14:30	22:12	7:42	1	322	233	162	69	32	9	46	3	1	0	152	7	162	44	10	3
104	Tue	20	June	1989	14:30	20:10	5:40	3	329	266	162	70	26	11	56	3	1	2	166	4	156	49	8	4
105	Wed	21	June	1989	14:30	19:46	5:16		246		104	55	25	10	47	4	1	5	122	3	115	35	6	3
106	Thu	22	June	1989	15:00	22:48	7:48	2	334	221	151	73	34	13	59	3	1	2	156	4	171	53	9	3
107	Fri	23	June	1989	11:00	15:05	4:05	1	176	110	82	45	13	9	24	2	1	0	87	3	85	7	1	0
108	Mon	26	June	1989	14:30	20:41	6:11		301		154	65	25	10	41	3	3	3	145	6	144	32	5	1
109	Tue	27	June	1989	14:30	0:17	9:47	7	386	337	196	80	34	12	56	3	5	0	186	8	187	66	16	5
110	Wed	28	June	1989	14:30	21:07	6:37	2	290	229	146	62	24	9	44	3	2	1	139	6	142	35	5	2
111	Thu	29	June	1989	15:00	23:46	8:46	2	325	224	153	72	30	9	56	3	2	3	159	8	153	36	3	1
112	Mon	3	July	1989	14:30	21:06	6:36	1	317	186	159	66	25	11	45	4	7	4	154	8	144	48	13	6
113	Tue	4	July	1989	14:30	20:30	6:00		320		145	72	32	9	58	2	2	3	161	7	147	39	4	0
114	Wed	5	July	1989	14:30	22:26	7:56	2	287	213	140	67	29	8	40	2	1	2	147	7	130	32	3	1
115	Thu	6	July	1989	15:00	22:10	7:10	2	365	299	181	81	34	10	53	3	3	2	190	7	163	67	15	5
116	Mon	10	July	1989	14:30	20:00	5:30	3	324	263	157	77	27	10	49	3	1	2	164	6	151	43	9	4
117	Tue	11	July	1989	14:30	1:05	10:35		332		164	69	28	11	54	4	2	1	164	7	158	42	11	3
118	Wed	12	July	1989	14:30	0:12	9:42	6	340	289	176	70	25	9	56	2	2	3	179	5	151	61	11	7
119	Thu	13	July	1989	15:00	20:54	5:54		296		128	66	28	11	59	3	1	1	148	3	143	35	2	2
120	Fri	14	July	1989	11:00	13:57	2:57		144		59	42	18	4	18	2	1	0	68	4	71	6	2	1
121	Mon	17	July	1989	14:30	22:32	8:02	4	331	281	159	72	30	11	54	4	1	1	180	7	142	43	6	2
122	Tue	18	July	1989	14:30	19:41	5:11	3	326	266	172	70	27	8	45	3	1	2	172	8	143	52	9	2
123	Wed	19	July	1989	14:30	1:16	10:46	3	360	252	161	80	29	11	75	3	1	4	184	7	164	55	7	0
124	Thu	20	July	1989	15:00	22:25	7:25	1	347	199	164	74	32	10	63	2	2	4	181	7	153	59	14	3
125	Fri	21	July	1989	11:00	16:26	5:26	2	172	60	71	46	16	7	29	2	1	0	90	5	76	8	4	1
126	Mon	24	July	1989	14:30	1:07	10:37	4	311	253	148	71	29	11	48	3	1	2	164	7	137	33	6	2

127	Tue	25	July	1989	14:30	22:18	7:48	1	368	258	185	76	34	11	58	3	1	3	191	9	164	59	13	6
128	Wed	26	July	1989	14:30	22:53	8:23	1	295	167	147	61	26	9	47	3	2	1	152	7	133	33	10	4
129	Thu	27	July	1989	11:00	21:12	10:12		252		104	60	27	9	49	2	1	4	125	6	116	21	6	1
130	Mon	9	Oct.	1989	14:30	23:38	9:08	5	311	273	150	68	30	8	50	3	2	0	155	5	149	45	6	0
131	Tue	10	Oct.	1989	14:30	23:58	9:28	3	330	256	153	74	33	9	56	4	1	2	162	6	159	54	7	1
132	Wed	11	Oct.	1989	14:30	4:39	14:09	2	327	173	150	71	29	9	59	3	6	2	161	6	152	55	11	3
133	Thu	12	Oct.	1989	15:00	21:30	6:30		297		128	74	29	8	54	3	1	1	150	6	139	37	3	0
134	Mon	16	Oct.	1989	14:30	23:50	9:20	5	286	250	138	70	26	8	42	1	1	2	143	5	135	27	3	1
135	Tue	17	Oct.	1989	14:30	22:56	8:26	4	340	268	160	80	29	10	56	4	1	2	174	6	157	53	10	3
136	Wed	18	Oct.	1989	14:30	21:55	7:25	1	312	195	143	74	29	8	54	3	1	1	152	8	150	46	9	6
137	Thu	19	Oct.	1989	15:00	22:42	7:42	1	310	134	138	73	28	9	58	3	1	3	150	6	150	43	7	2
138	Mon	23	Oct.	1989	14:30	22:29	7:59	3	299	237	142	71	22	10	51	2	1	2	151	6	139	30	6	2
139	Tue	24	Oct.	1989	14:30	22:01	7:31	4	327	274	151	76	30	9	55	2	4	2	167	8	146	44	7	2
140	Wed	25	Oct.	1989	14:30	0:51	10:21	4	354	282	160	80	36	9	61	4	4	2	172	9	167	59	16	7
141	Thu	26	Oct.	1989	15:00	18:58	3:58	1	303	168	134	69	28	10	57	4	1	3	161	5	133	36	8	1
142	Mon	30	Oct.	1989	14:30	23:24	8:54	4	320	259	149	71	26	9	61	3	1	2	167	7	143	39	8	3
143	Tue	31	Oct.	1989	14:30	21:31	7:01		327		154	69	28	10	62	3	1	3	164	5	154	47	6	2
144	Wed	1	Nov.	1989	14:30	20:14	5:44	3	370	266	178	76	30	11	69	3	3	3	186	6	172	63	15	4
145	Thu	2	Nov.	1989	15:00	19:59	4:59	3	323	240	154	66	28	10	60	2	3	2	169	6	143	37	4	1
146	Mon	6	Nov.	1989	14:30	21:33	7:03		302		141	67	23	10	53	3	5	8	150	7	132	42	7	5
147	Tue	7	Nov.	1989	14:30	22:53	8:23	5	428	366	236	80	33	12	62	3	2	1	208	10	207	105	35	19
148	Wed	8	Nov.	1989	14:30	23:15	8:45		316		150	68	22	11	57	2	6	2	160	9	139	46	13	4
149	Thu	9	Nov.	1989	15:00	21:55	6:55	1	332	27	149	70	32	10	65	4	2	3	165	8	154	49	10	3
150	Mon	13	Nov.	1989	14:30	18:33	4:03	1	290	166	143	63	19	8	52	4	1	3	148	5	133	38	4	1
151	Tue	14	Nov.	1989	14:30	19:35	5:05		358		164	71	33	9	75	3	3	3	179	8	165	61	9	4
152	Wed	15	Nov.	1989	14:30	19:38	5:08		319		140	69	30	10	65	4	1	2	165	7	144	39	4	0
153	Thu	16	Nov.	1989	9:30	10:05	0:35		123		46	38	14	6	17	1	1	0	75	1	46	5	0	0
TOTAL (153 days):							1,076:51	189	48,399		22,531	10,716	4,208	1,452	8,694	469	329	487	24,338	924	22,321	7,068	1,449	502

Appendix B: Divisions in the House of Lords, 1988–9

Table B lists each of the 189 divisions in the House of Lords during the 1988–9 session. All the divisions were on public bills. For the 186 divisions on Government bills, votes have been categorized as anti-Government or pro-Government. For the three divisions on private members' bills (shown in italics), votes have been categorized as 'Content' or 'Not-content'. Votes on each side have been broken down by Party and peerage type, using the same abbreviations as in Appendix A.

Stage

The following abbreviations are used:

CWH	Committee of the whole House
Re-CWH	Committee of the whole House on recommitment
Rpt	Report stage
3R	Third reading
HC amdt	House of Commons amendment to a House of Lords bill
HC Reason	House of Commons reason for disagreeing to a Lords amendment
Adjt	Motion to adjourn consideration of House of Commons reasons (Electricity Bill, division 138)

Tellers

Each side appoints two tellers for a division. The party affiliations of the tellers are shown using the same abbreviations as in Appendix A, but are shown either wholly in capitals to indicate front-benchers or wholly in lower case to indicate back-benchers or cross-benchers.

Table B *Divisions in the House of Lords, 1988–9*

No.	Date (1989)	Time	Bill	Stage	Anti-Govt. or *C*	Pro-Govt. or *NC*	Total votes	Daily attce	Breakdown of anti-Government votes/*Contents*												Breakdown of pro-Government votes/*Not-Contents*												
									Con	Lab	Dem	SDP	X-B	Oth	Bp	A	L	C	H	Tellers	Con	Lab	Dem	SDP	X-B	Oth	Bp	A	L	C	H	Tellers	
1	Tue 17 Jan	17:25	Children [HL]	CWH	110	114	224	375	3	60	24	8	15				81	2	27	2LAB	104				10				37	3	74	2CON	
2	Thu 19 Jan	16:15	Children [HL]	CWH	59	124	183	333		42	14		3				49	1	9	2LAB	103		1	5	14		1		43	2	78	2CON	
3	Mon 30 Jan	15:28	Companies [HL]	CWH	106	93	199	318	1	57	28	8	11		1		80	1	24	LAB, SLD	80				13				29	2	62	2CON	Govt defeat No. 1
4	Mon 6 Feb	16:35	Children [HL]	Rpt	83	112	195	308		54	16	6	7				62	1	20	2LAB	106				5	1			37	3	72	2CON	
5	Mon 6 Feb	17:23	Children [HL]	Rpt	82	99	181	308		51	15	3	12		1		58		23	2LAB	94				4	1			34	4	61	2CON	
6	Tue 7 Feb	15:59	Children [HL]	Rpt	109	128	237	367	4	65	27	5	6	1	1		84	1	23	2x-b	112				16			1	49	3	75	2CON	
7	Tue 7 Feb	17:03	Children [HL]	Rpt	112	128	240	367	2	67	26	5	12				84	2	26	x-b, lab	121				6	1		1	48	4	75	2CON	
8	Thu 16 Feb	18:19	Children [HL]	Rpt	47	67	114	315	2	23	10		12				32		15	2LAB	62				5				14	1	52	2CON	
9	Mon 20 Feb	16:33	Football Spectators [HL]	CWH	124	121	245	346	12	64	24	7	15	1	1	1	85		37	LAB, con	101			2	18			1	43	2	75	2CON	Govt defeat No. 2
10	Mon 20 Feb	19:13	Football Spectators [HL]	CWH	59	80	139	346	1	34	15	2	6	1			47		12	LAB, SLD	72				8				24	1	55	2CON	
11	Tue 21 Feb	18:18	Companies [HL]	CWH	90	94	184	371	12	47	15	3	12	1		1	59	1	29	LAB, con	90				4				29	2	63	2CON	
12	Tue 28 Feb	16:00	Prevention of Terrorism (Temp Prov)	CWH	54	191	245	349		53				1			48	1	5	2LAB	129	2	22	7	29	2		2	75	4	110	2CON	
13	Tue 28 Feb	18:51	Prevention of Terrorism (Temp Prov)	CWH	41	97	138	349		36	1		3	1			36		5	2LAB	78		11	2	6				33	2	62	2CON	
14	Thu 2 Mar	16:38	Companies [HL]	CWH	64	125	189	346		42	12	6	4				49	2	13	2LAB	107	1			17			2	41	2	80	2CON	
15	Mon 6 Mar	17:39	Companies [HL]	CWH	66	124	190	328		47	14	1	3	1			53	2	11	2LAB	114				10			1	48	2	73	2CON	
16	Mon 6 Mar	20:11	Elected Authorities (Northern Ireland)	Rpt	52	67	119	328	3	25	19		4	1			36	1	15	LAB, SLD	61				6				23	1	43	2CON	
17	Mon 6 Mar	20:30	Elected Authorities (Northern Ireland)	Rpt	36	49	85	328	2	22	8		3	1			26		10	2LAB	45				4				17		32	2CON	
18	Tue 7 Mar	15:48	Prevention of Terrorism (Temp Prov)	Rpt	108	149	257	380		59	27	8	11	3			80	2	26	2LAB	132				16	1			45	3	101	2CON	
19	Tue 7 Mar	18:57	Football Spectators [HL]	CWH	72	109	181	380	2	43	20	2	4	1			52	1	19	LAB, SLD	94				15				34	1	74	2CON	
20	Mon 13 Mar	15:43	Elected Authorities (Northern Ireland)	3R	82	114	196	310	4	49	12	3	13	1			60	1	21	LAB, SLD	107				6	1			39	1	74	2CON	
21	Mon 13 Mar	16:05	Elected Authorities (Northern Ireland)	3R	83	109	192	310	5	49	15	3	10	1			61	2	20	LAB, x-b	103				6				42		67	2CON	
22	Tue 14 Mar	16:20	Football Spectators [HL]	CWH	107	113	220	353	4	57	24	7	12	3		1	76	2	28	SLD, lab	99				14				40	1	72	2CON	
23	Tue 14 Mar	17:52	Football Spectators [HL]	CWH	80	121	201	353		47	23	3	5	2			60	2	18	2LAB	106				14	1			40		81	2CON	
24	Mon 20 Mar	16:16	Companies [HL]	Rpt	70	118	188	330	5	44	14		7				47		23	LAB, con	106	1		5	6				46	3	69	2CON	
25	Tue 21 Mar	18:25	Security Service	CWH	99	156	255	370		68	23	2	5	1			78	1	20	LAB, SLD	130				26			1	60	5	90	2CON	
26	Mon 3 Apr	17:33	Official Secrets	CWH	101	157	258	343	2	56	34	4	5				72	2	27	LAB, SLD	138				19				62	3	92	2CON	
27	Mon 3 Apr	18:35	Official Secrets	CWH	85	120	205	343	2	46	29	1	7				62	2	21	2LAB	114				6				48	3	69	2CON	
28	Mon 3 Apr	19:26	Official Secrets	CWH	64	95	159	343	1	35	23	1	4				47	1	16	LAB, SLD	86				9				34	3	58	2CON	
29	Tue 4 Apr	16:18	Official Secrets	CWH	97	171	268	372		60	33		4				74	2	21	LAB, SLD	142				28		1		69	5	96	2CON	
30	Thu 6 Apr	16:37	Companies [HL]	Rpt	64	105	169	309	1	38	17	3	5				45	1	18	2LAB	94				11				41		64	2CON	
31	Mon 10 Apr	16:07	Football Spectators [HL]	Rpt	91	123	214	325		50	23	6	11	1			62	1	28	LAB, SLD	107				15		1		47	3	72	2CON	
32	Mon 10 Apr	17:58	Football Spectators [HL]	Rpt	69	120	189	325		45	16	3	5				52		17	LAB, SLD	107				13				47	1	72	2CON	
33	Mon 10 Apr	18:39	Football Spectators [HL]	Rpt	57	90	147	325		36	15	2	4				43		14	LAB, SLD	80				10				37	2	51	2CON	
34	Mon 10 Apr	22:03	Football Spectators [HL]	Rpt	22	34	56	325	1	10	7		4				14		8	LAB, SLD	32				2				9	1	24	2CON	
35	Tue 11 Apr	17:48	Companies [HL]	Re-CWH	61	121	182	363	3	36	15	5	2				46	1	14	LAB, SLD	99				21	1			45	2	74	2CON	
36	Thu 13 Apr	19:45	Football Spectators [HL]	Rpt	25	45	70	338		15	8		2				18		7	2LAB	41				4				10		35	2CON	

Table B *(contd.)*

No.	Date (1989)	Time	Bill	Stage	Anti-Govt. or *C*	Pro-Govt. or *NC*	Total votes	Daily attce	Breakdown of anti-Government votes/*Contents* Con	Lab	Dem	SDP	X-B	Oth	Bp	A	L	C	H	Tellers	Breakdown of pro-Government votes/*Not-Contents* Con	Lab	Dem	SDP	X-B	Oth	Bp	A	L	C	H	Tellers	
37	Tue 18 Apr	17:13	Official Secrets	Rpt	99	168	267	375	3	52	28	6	10				71	2	26	LAB, SLD	145				22	1		2	60	1	105	2CON	
38	Thu 20 Apr	15:51	Security Service	Rpt	71	122	193	321		45	18	4	3	1			54	3	14	LAB, SLD	102				18	1	1		43	3	75	2CON	
39	Thu 20 Apr	17:20	Security Service	Rpt	51	107	158	321	1	33	10	3	4				37	2	12	LAB, SLD	99				7		1		38	3	65	2CON	
40	Thu 20 Apr	17:45	Companies [HL]	Rpt	43	100	143	321		29	9	2	3				28	2	13	LAB, sld	93				7				37	3	60	2CON	
41	Thu 20 Apr	21:40	Companies [HL]	Rpt	5	16	21	321		3	1		1				3		2	LAB, SLD	16								6		10	2CON	No quorum
42	Mon 24 Apr	16:02	Official Secrets	3R	73	121	194	309		44	16	7	5	1			56		17	LAB, SLD	102				19			1	42	2	76	2CON	
43	Thu 27 Apr	16:40	Companies [HL]	3R	70	102	172	276		43	13	6	8				53	2	15	LAB, x-b	93				9				37	3	62	2CON	
44	Tue 2 May	17:03	Water	CWH	127	161	288	364		66	32	9	19	1			88	2	37	LAB, SLD	143				17	1			61	4	96	2CON	
45	Tue 2 May	18:37	Water	CWH	85	134	219	364		49	24	5	6	1			62		23	LAB, SLD	119				15				48	2	84	2CON	
46	Tue 2 May	19:24	Water	CWH	56	111	167	364		36	15	3	2				43		13	LAB, SLD	96				13	1	1		36	2	72	2CON	
47	Tue 2 May	21:16	Water	CWH	34	72	106	364		12	13	2	6		1		20		13	2x-b	69				3				26	2	44	2CON	
48	Thu 4 May	17:43	Water	CWH	112	208	320	430	9	55	21	4	22	1			71	2	39	con, x-b	198				10				61	6	141	2CON	
49	Thu 4 May	18:35	Water	CWH	52	141	193	430		28	15	3	6				35	1	16	LAB, SLD	134				7				28	2	111	2CON	
50	Thu 4 May	18:58	Water	CWH	54	116	170	430		28	12	3	11				32	1	21	LAB, SLD	110				6				23	2	91	2CON	
51	Thu 4 May	19:07	Water	CWH	47	91	138	430	4	23	12	2	6				28	1	18	2con	88				3				16	1	74	2CON	
52	Thu 4 May	21:02	Water	CWH	23	70	93	430		12	6		5				13		10	LAB, sld	66				4				19	1	50	2CON	
53	Mon 8 May	16:12	Water	CWH	92	108	200	295		52	23	6	11				65		27	LAB, SLD	98				9		1		37	3	67	2CON	
54	Mon 8 May	17:42	Water	CWH	71	109	180	295		50	14	4	3				52	1	18	LAB, SLD	98				11				37	2	70	2CON	
55	Tue 9 May	15:29	Water	CWH	48	120	168	325		43	2		3				40	1	7	2LAB	102				17	1		1	42	4	73	2CON	
56	Tue 9 May	16:33	Water	CWH	76	119	195	325	1	46	20	6	3				57	2	17	LAB, SLD	109				9	1			44	4	71	2CON	
57	Tue 9 May	17:56	Water	CWH	69	108	177	325		37	18	5	9			1	47		21	2LAB	99				8	1			45	2	61	2CON	
58	Tue 9 May	18:57	Water	CWH	50	92	142	325		28	15	4	3				37		13	2LAB	80				11	1		1	31	2	58	2CON	
59	Tue 9 May	19:34	Water	CWH	44	59	103	325		22	13	2	7			1	30		13	LAB, SLD	52				6	1			17	2	40	2CON	
60	Thu 11 May	16:04	Electricity	CWH	84	110	194	304		50	18	6	9		1		62	2	19	LAB, SLD	97				11	2			37	2	71	2CON	
61	Mon 15 May	15:42	Water	CWH	64	97	161	277		44	9	4	6		1		48	1	14	LAB, SLD	86				10	1			29	1	67	2CON	
62	Mon 15 May	18:24	Water	CWH	52	85	137	277	1	37	7	4	3				39	1	12	LAB, sld	73				12				28		57	2CON	
63	Mon 15 May	21:06	Water	CWH	81	47	128	277		60	19	1	1				63	1	17	LAB, sld	41				6				16		31	2CON	Govt defeat No. 3
64	Tue 16 May	15:46	Electricity	CWH	126	114	240	351	5	69	24	7	21				90	3	33	LAB, SLD	108				5	1			44	3	67	2CON	Govt defeat No. 4
65	Thu 18 May	17:35	Water	CWH	73	102	175	337		43	13	2	15				50	2	21	LAB, SLD	98				4				32	2	68	2CON	
66	Thu 18 May	18:13	Water	CWH	51	86	137	337		35	9	1	6				39	1	11	LAB, sld	81				5				27	2	57	2CON	
67	Mon 22 May	15:30	Water	CWH	74	117	191	332		47	18	3	5	1			56	2	16	LAB, SLD	103				13	1			38	1	78	2CON	
68	Mon 22 May	17:20	Water	CWH	73	133	206	332		51	14	3	5				56	1	16	LAB, SLD	116				16	1			47	1	85	2CON	
69	Mon 22 May	17:40	Water	CWH	61	123	184	332	1	46	11	2	1				49	1	11	LAB, sld	107				16				42	1	80	2CON	
70	Tue 23 May	15:48	Water	CWH	84	121	205	336		51	19	5	8	1			64	1	19	LAB, SLD	108				13				38	1	82	2CON	
71	Tue 23 May	23:58	Water	CWH	15	45	60	336	1	4	5		5				5		10	sld, x-b	45								14		31	2CON	
72	Mon 5 Jun	15:31	Electricity	CWH	112	104	216	322		69	20	11	12				88	1	23	LAB, SLD	95				8	1			34	2	68	2CON	Govt defeat No. 5

73	Mon	5 Jun	18:57	Electricity	CWH	65	67	132	322	11	28	13	3	10			41		24	LAB, con	63			4			22	1	44	2CON	
74	Tue	6 Jun	15:40	Water	Rpt	80	132	212	351		55	17	3	5			62	2	16	2LAB	111			20	1		48	2	82	2CON	
75	Tue	6 Jun	17:49	Water	Rpt	75	133	208	351	2	48	15	5	5			58		17	LAB, sld	116			16	1		50	3	80	2CON	
76	Tue	6 Jun	18:37	Water	Rpt	69	111	180	351	4	43	13	4	5			53		16	LAB, SLD	106			5			39	2	70	2CON	
77	Tue	6 Jun	18:47	Water	Rpt	60	106	166	351	4	40	11	2	3			47		13	LAB, SLD	99			7			34	2	70	2CON	
78	Tue	6 Jun	21:27	Water	Rpt	33	55	88	351		20	9		4			23		10	lab, sld	51			4			16	1	38	2CON	
79	Thu	8 Jun	17:44	Water	Rpt	78	110	188	330		50	18	5	5			59	2	17	LAB, sld	100			10			33	4	73	2CON	
80	Thu	8 Jun	18:17	Water	Rpt	52	92	144	330		32	12	4	4			38	2	12	LAB, sld	86			6			25	2	65	2CON	
81	Thu	8 Jun	21:46	Water	Rpt	12	25	37	330	1	7	4					9		3	LAB, sld	24			1			8	1	16	2CON	
82	Mon	12 Jun	15:43	Water	Rpt	98	118	216	339		58	23	8	8	1		76		22	LAB, sld	107			10	1		45	3	70	2CON	
83	Mon	12 Jun	17:31	Water	Rpt	89	111	200	339	2	51	21	5	9	1		63	2	24	LAB, sld	106			4	1		44	2	65	2CON	
84	Mon	12 Jun	18:16	Water	Rpt	65	108	173	339		45	13	5	1	1		53		12	2LAB	98			9	1		41	1	66	2CON	
85	Tue	13 Jun	15:54	Water	Rpt	90	125	215	355		50	25	7	8			67	2	21	LAB, sld	116			7	2		46	4	75	2CON	
86	*Wed*	*14 Jun*	*18:56*	*Control of Pollution (Amendment)*	*CWH*	*41*	*45*	*86*	*319*	*3*	*25*	*9*	*1*	*3*			*28*		*13*	*2lab*	*44*			*1*			*13*	*1*	*31*	*2CON*	*private member's bill*
87	Fri	16 Jun	13:09	Football Spectators [HL]	3R	83	96	179	226	2	49	22	2	7	1		62	1	20	LAB, SLD	77		1	17	1		32	1	63	2CON	
88	Fri	16 Jun	13:54	Football Spectators [HL]	3R	53	65	118	226		24	19	3	6	1		33	1	19	LAB, SLD	57			7	1		18	1	46	2CON	
89	Mon	19 Jun	16:30	Electricity	CWH	107	126	233	322	3	57	29	5	13			72	1	34	LAB, x-b	123			1	1	1	46	4	75	2CON	
90	Tue	20 Jun	15:58	Dock Work	CWH	47	148	195	329		45			1	1		44		3	2LAB	107	18	2	19	1	1	56	2	89	2CON	
91	Tue	20 Jun	17:39	Dock Work	CWH	49	117	166	329		44		1	1	3		42	1	6	2LAB	87	13		17			43	1	73	2CON	
92	Tue	20 Jun	19:09	Dock Work	CWH	37	79	116	329		22	9	4	1	1		29		8	2LAB	70	1		8			24		55	2CON	
93	Thu	22 Jun	17:42	Social Security	CWH	115	94	209	334	5	54	29	7	18	1	1	76	2	36	con, x-b	86			8			27		67	2CON	Govt defeat No. 6
94	Thu	22 Jun	21:04	Social Security	CWH	21	49	70	334		14	5	1	1			16		5	LAB, lab	46			3			17	1	31	2CON	
95	Fri	23 Jun	12:42	Electricity	CWH	41	69	110	176		20	9	6	5	1		30		11	2LAB	62			7			22		47	2CON	
96	Tue	27 Jun	16:16	Water	3R	113	167	280	386		63	29	11	9		1	83	2	27	LAB, SLD	152			15			62	3	102	2CON	
97	Tue	27 Jun	17:13	Water	3R	115	121	236	386	8	56	24	7	18	1	1	77	2	35	2con	120			1			45	3	73	2CON	
98	Tue	27 Jun	17:31	Water	3R	96	136	232	386	1	55	25	7	7	1		72		24	LAB, SLD	127			9			49	3	84	2CON	
99	Tue	27 Jun	18:36	Water	3R	74	119	193	386	1	46	18	6	2	1		56		18	LAB, sld	110			8	1		44	2	73	2CON	
100	Tue	27 Jun	21:42	Water	3R	61	67	128	386		39	11	5	6			42	1	18	LAB, lab	64			2	1		22	1	44	2CON	
101	Tue	27 Jun	23:00	Water	3R	62	53	115	386	8	33	9	2	9	1		33	1	28	LAB, sld	52			1			18		35	2CON	Govt defeat No. 7
102	Tue	27 Jun	23:50	Water	3R	52	58	110	386	1	31	11	2	6	1		33		19	LAB, SLD	56			2			19		39	2CON	
103	Wed	28 Jun	16:14	Dock Work	Rpt	79	130	209	290		51	17	8	1	2		61	2	16	LAB, SLD	113	1		15	1		46	3	81	2CON	
104	Wed	28 Jun	18:12	Dock Work	Rpt	42	102	144	290		39	1	1		1		40		2	2LAB	84	8		10			37	2	63	2CON	
105	Thu	29 Jun	16:18	Social Security	CWH	95	115	210	325	1	55	23	7	9			67	2	26	LAB, sld	101			13	1		35	5	75	2CON	
106	Thu	29 Jun	20:52	Social Security	CWH	18	45	63	325	1	11	5		1			15		3	LAB, sld	41			4			11	1	33	2CON	
107	Mon	3 Jul	15:35	Dock Work	3R	69	117	186	317		47	13	6	1	1	1	55	2	11	2LAB	104			12	1		42	4	71	2CON	
108	Wed	5 Jul	16:23	Electricity	Rpt	117	91	208	287	14	55	24	5	19			75	2	40	LAB, con	87			4			38	3	50	2CON	Govt defeat No. 8
109	Wed	5 Jul	22:11	Electricity	Rpt	13	33	46	287	1	5	7					9		4	LAB, SLD	32			1			8		25	2CON	
110	Thu	6 Jul	16:28	Water	HC Reason	114	168	282	365		64	30	8	10	1	1	83	2	28	LAB, SLD	149			18		1	63	3	101	2CON	
111	Thu	6 Jul	17:36	Electricity	Rpt	81	110	191	365	1	52	15	2	9	2		57	2	22	LAB, sld	106			4			41	2	67	2CON	
112	Mon	10 Jul	16:35	Electricity	Rpt	100	126	226	324	3	59	23	8	7			75		25	LAB, sld	118			8			43	3	80	2CON	
113	Mon	10 Jul	18:17	Electricity	Rpt	72	99	171	324		42	18	8	4			51	1	20	2LAB	89			10			40	1	58	2CON	
114	Mon	10 Jul	18:59	Electricity	Rpt	54	82	136	324		38	11	3	2			41	1	12	2LAB	75			7			31	1	50	2CON	
115	Wed	12 Jul	16:31	Social Security	Rpt	124	114	238	340	14	55	19	7	28	1		79	2	43	LAB, x-b	112			2			53	2	59	2CON	Govt defeat No. 9
116	Wed	12 Jul	18:15	Social Security	Rpt	79	129	208	340.	1	45	15	3	15			57	1	21	LAB, sld	125			4			55	1	73	2CON	

Table B *(contd.)*

No.	Date (1989)	Time	Bill	Stage	Anti-Govt. or *C*	Pro-Govt. or *NC*	Total votes	Daily attce	Breakdown of anti-Government votes/*Contents*: Con	Lab	Dem	SDP	X-B	Oth	Bp	A	L	C	H	Tellers	Breakdown of pro-Government votes/*Not-Contents*: Con	Lab	Dem	SDP	X-B	Oth	Bp	A	L	C	H	Tellers	
117	Wed 12 Jul	19:13	Social Security	Rpt	67	95	162	340	2	34	13	3	15				46		21	LAB, x-b	93				2				33	1	61	2CON	
118	Wed 12 Jul	22:12	Social Security	Rpt	28	50	78	340	1	12	9		6				18		10	LAB, con	47				3				23		27	2CON	
119	Wed 12 Jul	23:17	Social Security	Rpt	26	36	62	340	3	9	6		8				16		10	con, x-b	36								14		22	2CON	
120	Wed 12 Jul	23:36	Social Security	Rpt	18	33	51	340		8	6		4				11		7	2SLD	33								11		22	2CON	
121	Mon 17 Jul	15:27	Social Security	3R	90	114	204	331		54	21	5	9	1			70	1	19	LAB, sld	104				8	2			43	1	70	2CON	
122	Mon 17 Jul	16:48	Social Security	3R	91	121	212	331		55	22	8	5	1			72	2	17	LAB, SLD	114				6	1			49	3	69	2CON	
123	Mon 17 Jul	18:58	Fair Employment (Northern Ireland)	Rpt	63	75	138	331		42	14	6	1				51	1	11	LAB, sld	69				6				27		48	2CON	
124	Mon 17 Jul	21:08	Fair Employment (Northern Ireland)	Rpt	28	48	76	331		21	5	2					23	1	4	LAB, SLD	44				4				15	1	32	2CON	
125	Tue 18 Jul	16:10	Electricity	3R	97	146	243	326	4	51	22	3	16	1			68	2	27	LAB, SLD	139				7				57	5	84	2CON	
126	Tue 18 Jul	16:47	Electricity	3R	78	146	224	326	1	49	20	3	4	1			61	2	15	2LAB	139				7				57	5	84	2CON	
127	Tue 18 Jul	17:31	Electricity	3R	75	130	205	326		49	18	5	3				59	1	15	2LAB	125				5				49	3	78	2CON	
128	Wed 19 Jul	17:27	Local Government and Housing	CWH	84	112	196	360		45	22	5	10	1	1		62	2	19	2LAB	105				7				41	2	69	2CON	
129	Wed 19 Jul	18:37	Local Government and Housing	CWH	64	90	154	360		38	20	5	1				47	2	15	2LAB	81				9				26	2	62	2CON	
130	Wed 19 Jul	21:09	Local Government and Housing	CWH	77	43	120	360		63	11	2	1				64	1	12	2LAB	39				4				15	1	27	2CON	Govt defeat No. 10
131	Thu 20 Jul	17:21	Local Government and Housing	CWH	78	121	199	347		53	16	4	5				56	2	20	2LAB	111				10				43	3	75	2CON	
132	*Fri 21 Jul*	*14:57*	*Licensing Amendment (Scotland)*	*CWH*	*38*	*20*	*58*	*172*	*21*	*1*	*5*	*1*	*10*				*12*	*1*	*25*	*2con*	*6*	*14*							*14*		*6*	*2lab*	*private member's bill*
133	*Fri 21 Jul*	*15:08*	*Licensing Amendment (Scotland)*	*CWH*	*35*	*22*	*57*	*172*	*21*	*1*	*5*	*1*	*7*				*13*		*22*	*con, x-b*	*6*	*15*			*1*				*15*		*7*	*2lab*	*private member's bill*
134	Mon 24 Jul	15:46	Local Government and Housing	CWH	55	152	207	311		50			5				47		8	2LAB	110		16	8	17		1		56	4	91	2CON	
135	Mon 24 Jul	19:12	Local Government and Housing	CWH	38	83	121	311		32	2	2	2				35		3	2LAB	72				11				30	1	52	2CON	
136	Mon 24 Jul	21:10	Local Government and Housing	CWH	32	53	85	311		16	9	3	4				23		9	2LAB	48				5				19	1	33	2CON	
137	Mon 24 Jul	21:40	Local Government and Housing	CWH	23	45	68	311		10	6	2	5				15		8	2LAB	44				1				19		26	2CON	
138	Tue 25 Jul	16:40	Electricity	Adjt	110	148	258	368		54	28	10	17	1			77	2	31	LAB, SLD	137				11				61	5	82	2CON	
139	Wed 26 Jul	17:44	Local Government and Housing	CWH	59	108	167	295		40	13	2	3	1			51		8	2LAB	96				12				39	2	67	2CON	
140	Mon 9 Oct	16:14	Local Government and Housing	CWH	92	128	220	311		53	25	6	7		1		67	2	22	2LAB	110				17	1			42	2	84	2CON	
141	Mon 9 Oct	16:44	Local Government and Housing	CWH	82	123	205	311		51	23	5	1	2			65	2	15	2LAB	106				17				41	1	81	2CON	
142	Mon 9 Oct	18:02	Local Government and Housing	CWH	77	106	183	311		46	19	4	8				57	2	18	LAB, SLD	99				7				36	2	68	2CON	
143	Mon 9 Oct	19:05	Local Government and Housing	CWH	47	94	141	311		30	13	3	1				40		7	2LAB	86				8				32	2	60	2CON	
144	Mon 9 Oct	21:22	Local Government and Housing	CWH	16	48	64	311		11	5						13		3	LAB, sld	44		2		2				11	1	36	2CON	
145	Tue 10 Oct	16:07	Local Government and Housing	CWH	93	122	215	330		54	26	6	6	1			73	2	18	2LAB	103				16	2	1	1	43	3	74	2CON	
146	Tue 10 Oct	16:27	Local Government and Housing	CWH	89	114	203	330		55	26	6	2				68	2	19	2LAB	102				10	2			42	3	69	2CON	
147	Tue 10 Oct	17:53	Local Government and Housing	CWH	69	113	182	330		45	16	5	2	1			50	2	17	2LAB	100				12	1		1	40	2	70	2CON	
148	Wed 11 Oct	18:16	Local Government and Housing	CWH	69	96	165	327		41	19	4	4	1			50	2	17	2LAB	87				9			1	33	1	61	2CON	
149	Wed 11 Oct	0:17	Local Government and Housing	CWH	17	29	46	327	3	8	5		1				10		7	2LAB	25				4				8		21	2CON	
150	Mon 16 Oct	15:40	Employment	CWH	75	113	188	286	1	52	15	4	3				59	2	14	LAB, SLD	100				13			1	36	3	73	2CON	
151	Mon 16 Oct	16:22	Employment	CWH	66	114	180	286		48	11	4	3				53	2	11	LAB, SLD	104				10			1	36	3	74	2CON	
152	Mon 16 Oct	17:47	Employment	CWH	71	100	171	286		49	17	4	1				53	2	16	2LAB	90				10				35	2	63	2CON	

153	Mon	16 Oct	18:30	Employment	CWH	64	87	151	286		44	15	5					47	1	16	2LAB	79			8				28	2	57	2CON	
154	Mon	16 Oct	21:35	Employment	CWH	12	43	55	286		11	1						10		2	LAB, sld	42			1				12		31	2CON	
155	Tue	17 Oct	15:51	Employment	CWH	83	115	198	340		57	20	5	1				71	2	10	2LAB	96			18	1			38	1	76	2CON	
156	Tue	17 Oct	16:44	Employment	CWH	81	109	190	340		57	17	5	2				67	2	12	2LAB	98			10	1			36	2	71	2CON	
157	Tue	17 Oct	17:36	Employment	CWH	80	111	191	340		57	17	6					67	1	12	2LAB	102			8	1			34	2	75	2CON	
158	Tue	17 Oct	19:44	Employment	CWH	42	67	109	340		28	11	1	2				31		11	LAB, sld	60			7				20		47	2CON	
159	Wed	18 Oct	16:19	Self-Governing Schools etc. (Scotland)	CWH	81	114	195	312		54	21	4		2			63	2	16	2LAB	100			14				35	4	75	2CON	
160	Thu	19 Oct	18:08	Local Government and Housing	Rpt	54	80	134	310		39	10	3	2				44	1	9	2LAB	71			9				22	2	56	2CON	
161	Mon	23 Oct	15:50	Local Government and Housing	Rpt	76	99	175	299		46	11	5	13		1		53	2	20	LAB, SLD	93			6				38	3	58	2CON	
162	Mon	23 Oct	17:22	Local Government and Housing	Rpt	74	99	173	299		48	12	5	8	1			55	2	17	2LAB	93			6				35	2	62	2CON	
163	Mon	23 Oct	18:52	Local Government and Housing	Rpt	49	76	125	299		35	10	4					37	1	11	2LAB	66			10				20	2	54	2CON	
164	Tue	24 Oct	15:30	Local Government and Housing	Rpt	90	111	201	327		55	21	8	6				75	2	13	2LAB	101			10				41	2	68	2CON	
165	Tue	24 Oct	16:40	Local Government and Housing	Rpt	90	127	217	327		55	23	6	4	1	1		71	2	16	2LAB	113			14				44	4	79	2CON	
166	Tue	24 Oct	17:07	Local Government and Housing	Rpt	90	111	201	327		56	23	7	2	1	1		74	2	13	2LAB	100			11				38	3	70	2CON	
167	Tue	24 Oct	20:40	Local Government and Housing	Rpt	25	51	76	327	1	12	8	1	3				18		7	LAB, con	47			4				17		34	2CON	
168	Wed	25 Oct	16:30	Local Government and Housing	Rpt	85	126	211	354	1	50	22	6	3	1	2		63	1	19	2LAB	112			14				39	2	85	2CON	
169	Wed	25 Oct	17:54	Local Government and Housing	Rpt	75	116	191	354		47	20	6	2				62	1	12	LAB, SLD	103			12	1			37	2	77	2CON	
170	Wed	25 Oct	21:43	Local Government and Housing	Rpt	111	38	149	354	10	56	27	4	11	1	2		66	2	41	con, x-b	37			1				11		27	2CON	Govt defeat No. 11
171	Wed	25 Oct	22:26	Local Government and Housing	Rpt	94	36	130	354	1	54	24	2	11	1	1		61	1	31	2LAB	35			1				9		27	2CON	Govt defeat No. 12
172	Thu	26 Oct	16:45	Self-Governing Schools etc. (Scotland)	Rpt	61	107	168	303		37	13	7	3	1			48	1	12	2LAB	94			13				34	2	71	2CON	
173	Mon	30 Oct	15:11	Employment	Rpt	71	98	169	320	1	43	11	6	10			1	56	2	12	LAB, SLD	86			12				27	3	68	2CON	
174	Mon	30 Oct	16:24	Employment	Rpt	51	118	169	320		49			2				46		5	2LAB	99			19				44	2	72	2CON	
175	Mon	30 Oct	17:31	Employment	Rpt	72	99	171	320		50	11	4	7				52	1	19	LAB, sld	91			8				32	1	66	2CON	
176	Mon	30 Oct	18:13	Employment	Rpt	67	90	157	320		50	9	5	3				51		16	LAB, SLD	78			12				34	1	55	2CON	
177	Wed	1 Nov	16:28	Local Government and Housing	3R	91	137	228	370		60	23	4	3	1			73	2	16	LAB, SLD	120			17				48	3	86	2CON	
178	Wed	1 Nov	17:05	Local Government and Housing	3R	86	124	210	370	1	53	20	5	6	1			65	2	19	2LAB	112			12				41	1	82	2CON	
179	Wed	1 Nov	17:33	Local Government and Housing	3R	85	105	190	370	4	53	17	4	6	1			62	1	22	lab, con	98			7				36	1	68	2CON	
180	Thu	2 Nov	16:12	Employment	3R	57	147	204	323	1	41			15			2	41		14	2LAB	107	21	3	14		2		62	4	79	2CON	
181	Thu	2 Nov	18:18	Football Spectators [HL]	HC amdts	35	84	119	323		23	6	3	3				27	1	7	LAB, sld	74			10				36		48	2CON	
182	Thu	2 Nov	19:20	Football Spectators [HL]	HC amdts	19	56	75	323		10	8		1				13		6	LAB, sld	53			3				21		35	2CON	
183	Tue	7 Nov	16:38	Companies [HL]	HC amdts	110	223	333	428		66	29	10	5				87	2	21	LAB, SLD	208			14	1			76	6	141	2CON	
184	Tue	7 Nov	18:26	Companies [HL]	HC amdts	62	136	198	428		43	13	4	2				47		15	2LAB	128			7	1			48	3	85	2CON	
185	Tue	7 Nov	19:22	Companies [HL]	HC amdts	39	86	125	428	1	24	8	1	4		1		30		8	LAB, lab	85			1				27	1	58	2CON	
186	Tue	7 Nov	20:44	Companies [HL]	HC amdts	21	70	91	428		12	6	1	2				14		7	2LAB	65			4	1			26	1	43	2CON	
187	Tue	7 Nov	22:24	Companies [HL]	HC amdts	7	39	46	428		5	1		1				5		2	2LAB	38			1				10		29	2CON	
188	Thu	9 Nov	21:46	Companies [HL]	HC amdts	8	19	27	332		3	4		1				4		4	LAB, sld	18			1				4		15	2CON	No quorum
189	Mon	13 Nov	15:19	Companies [HL]	HC amdts	62	104	166	290		39	12	5	5	1			48	2	12	2LAB	86			16	2		1	34	1	68	2CON	

Appendix C: Participation by Members of the House of Lords, 1988–9

Table C lists each of the 816 lords who attended the House of Lords during the 1988–9 session, plus Lord Melchett who did not attend but asked questions for written answer.
Titles are abbreviated as follows:

Abp	Archbishop
B.	Baroness
Bp	Bishop
C.	Countess (of)
D.	Duke of
E.	Earl (of)
L.	Lord
Ly.	Lady
M.	Marquess (of)
V.	Viscount (of)

For each lord the peerage type and Party affiliation are given using the same abbreviations as in Appendix A.

Lords who were not eligible to attend throughout the session are marked by a + (for those who became eligible during the session) or a – (for those who died or ceased to be eligible during the session) before their names.

Figures for percentage attendances and percentage votes are based on the number of sittings and divisions when the lord concerned was eligible to attend.

For an explanation of the measurement of the number of interventions by each lord, see Chapter 2.

Table C *Participation by members of the House of Lords, 1988–9*

	Peerage type	Year of birth	Party	Attces	% attces	Total votes	Anti-Govt. votes	Pro-Govt. votes	% votes on Govt. bills	Interventions
Abercorn, D.	H	1934	Con.	26	17.0	11		11	5.9	1
Aberdare, L.	H	1919	X-B	140	91.5					63
Aberdeen and Temair, M.	H	1920	X-B	4	2.6	1		1	0.5	2
Abinger, L.	H	1914	Con.	34	22.2	30		30	16.1	
Ackner, L.	A	1920	X-B	36	23.5					4
Addington, L.	H	1963	Dem.	152	99.3	132	124	5	69.4	29
Adrian, L.	H	1927	X-B	19	12.4	1	1		0.5	2
Ailesbury, M.	H	1926	X-B	118	77.1	39	5	31	19.4	5
Ailsa, M.	H	1925	Con.	11	7.2	3		3	1.6	
Airedale, L.	H	1915	Dem.	136	88.9	132	127	4	70.4	15
Airey of Abingdon, B.	L	1919	Con.	126	82.4	60	1	59	32.3	
Airlie, E.	H	1926	X-B	2	1.3					2
Alanbrooke, V.	H	1932	X-B	9	5.9					
Albemarle, E.	H	1965	X-B	1	0.7					
Aldenham, L.	H	1948	Con.	10	6.5	5		5	2.7	
Aldington, L.	C	1914	Con.	70	45.8	31	1	30	16.7	9
Alexander of Potterhill, L.	L	1905	X-B	6	3.9					
Alexander of Tunis, E.	H	1935	Con.	135	88.2	94		94	50.5	2

Table C *(contd.)*

	Peerage type	Year of birth	Party	Attces	% attces	Total votes	Anti-Govt. votes	Pro-Govt. votes	% votes on Govt. bills	Interventions
Alexander of Weedon, L.	L	1936	Con.	54	35.3	46		46	24.7	7
Allen of Abbeydale, L.	L	1912	X-B	106	69.3	21	18	3	11.3	32
Allenby of Megiddo, V.	H	1931	X-B	68	44.4	50	5	45	26.9	3
Allerton, L.	H	1903	Con.	67	43.8	79		79	42.5	1
Alport, L.	L	1912	Oth	93	60.8	52	17	35	28.0	9
Amherst, E.	H	1896	Dem.	144	94.1	83	79	3	44.1	
+Amherst of Hackney, L.	H	1940	X-B	1	1.0					
Ampthill, L.	H	1921	X-B	151	98.7	89	34	54	47.3	17
Annaly, L.	H	1927	Con.	38	24.8	43		43	23.1	
Annan, L.	L	1916	X-B	133	86.9	15	9	6	8.1	25
Annandale and Hartfell, E.	H	1941	Con.	2	1.3					
Ardwick, L.	L	1910	Lab.	148	96.7	111	111		59.7	16
Armstrong of Ilminster, L.	L	1927	X-B	3	2.0					2
Arran, E.	H	1938	Con.	137	89.5	183		183	98.4	117
Ashbourne, L.	H	1933	Con.	132	86.3	49		49	26.3	5
Ashcombe, L.	H	1924	Oth	1	0.7					
Astor, V.	H	1951	Con.	12	7.8	12		12	6.5	
Astor of Hever, L.	H	1946	Con.	10	6.5	5		5	2.7	

Atholl, D.	H	1931	Con.	11	7.2	10		10	5.4	1
Attlee, E.	H	1927	SDP	96	62.7	63	60	3	33.9	9
Auckland, L.	H	1926	Con.	150	98.0	76	7	68	40.3	25
Avebury, L.	H	1928	Dem.	5	3.3	4	4		2.2	18
Aylesford, E.	H	1918	Con.	2	1.3					
Aylestone, L.	L	1905	SDP	108	70.6	92	87	5	49.5	11
Baldwin of Bewdley, E.	H	1938	X-B	45	29.4	6	6		3.2	6
Balfour, E.	H	1925	Con.	61	39.9	82		82	44.1	20
Balfour of Burleigh, L.	H	1927	X-B	9	5.9	1		1	0.5	
Bancroft, L.	L	1922	X-B	26	17.0	1	1		0.5	1
Banks, L.	L	1918	Dem.	54	35.3	22	21	1	11.8	13
Barber, L.	L	1920	Con.	38	24.8	29		29	15.6	1
Barnard, L.	H	1923	X-B	1	0.7					
Barnett, L.	L	1923	Lab.	112	73.2	25	25		13.4	10
–Basnett, L.	L	1924	Lab.	10	43.5					
Bathurst, E.	H	1927	Con.	5	3.3	4		4	2.2	1
Bauer, L.	L	1915	Con.	60	39.2	40		39	21.0	2
Beaumont of Whitley, L.	L	1928	X-B	14	9.2	15	13	2	8.1	1
Beaverbrook, L.	H	1951	Con.	62	40.5	40		40	21.5	7
Belhaven and Stenton, L.	H	1927	Con.	152	99.3	66	1	65	35.5	2
Bellwin, L.	L	1923	Con.	82	53.6	19		19	10.2	7
Beloff, L.	L	1913	Con.	134	87.6	103		101	54.3	35
Belstead, L.	H	1932	Con.	150	98.0	180		179	96.2	97
Benson, L.	L	1909	X-B	55	35.9	8		8	4.3	14
Bernstein, L.	L	1899	Lab.	1	0.7					
Bessborough, E.	H	1913	Con.	152	99.3	100		98	52.7	6

Table C *(contd.)*

	Peerage type	Year of birth	Party	Attces	% attces	Total votes	Anti-Govt. votes	Pro-Govt. votes	% votes on Govt. bills	Interventions
Bethell, L.	H	1938	Con.	27	17.6	8		8	4.3	16
+Biddulph, L.	H	1959	Con.	4	3.4	4		4	2.2	
Birdwood, L.	H	1938	Con.	131	85.6	45		44	23.7	1
Birk, B.	L	1919	Lab.	110	71.9	92	92		49.5	32
Birkett, L.	H	1929	X-B	7	4.6					2
Blackstone, B.	L	1942	Lab.	105	68.6	63	63		33.9	18
Blake, L.	L	1916	Con.	47	30.7	34		34	18.3	3
Blakenham, V.	H	1938	X-B	1	0.7					1
Blanch, L.	L	1918	X-B	34	22.2	3		3	1.6	
Blatch, B.	L	1937	Con.	139	90.8	152	2	148	80.6	62
Blease, L.	L	1914	Lab.	106	69.3	81	81		43.5	39
Bledisloe, V.	H	1934	X-B	18	11.8	5	3	2	2.7	4
Blyth, L.	H	1931	X-B	150	98.0	113	29	83	60.2	7
Boardman, L.	L	1919	Con.	31	20.3	33		32	17.2	4
Bolton, L.	H	1929	Con.	32	20.9	16		16	8.6	
Bonham-Carter, L.	L	1922	Dem.	143	93.5	98	95	3	52.7	48
Borthwick, L.	H	1905	Con.	114	74.5	116	1	113	61.3	9
Boston, L.	H	1939	Con.	7	4.6	1	1		0.5	
Boston of Faversham, L.	L	1930	Lab.	143	93.5	70	70		37.6	
Bottomley, L.	L	1907	Lab.	146	95.4	92	91		48.9	14

Boyd-Carpenter, L.	L	1908	Con.	144	94.1	142		141	75.8	143
Brabazon of Tara, L.	H	1946	Con.	113	73.9	125		125	67.2	206
Bradford, Bp	B	1932	Bp	10	6.5	1	1		0.5	1
Bradford, E.	H	1947	Con.	1	0.7					
Brain, L.	H	1926	X-B	37	24.2	12	7	5	6.5	5
Bramall, L.	L	1923	X-B	38	24.8	4	1	3	2.2	7
Brandon of Oakbrook, L.	A	1920	X-B	13	8.5					
Braye, B.	H	1941	Con.	18	11.8	14		14	7.5	
Brentford, V.	H	1933	Con.	85	55.6	7		7	3.8	6
Bridge of Harwich, L.	A	1917	X-B	19	12.4					2
Bridgeman, V.	H	1930	Con.	12	7.8	10		10	5.4	3
Bridges, L.	H	1927	X-B	24	15.7					6
Briggs, L.	L	1921	X-B	1	0.7					
Brightman, L.	A	1911	X-B	87	56.9	18	4	14	9.7	14
Briginshaw, L.	L	1908	Lab.	125	81.7	43	43		23.1	
Brimelow, L.	L	1915	Lab.	2	1.3	2	2		1.1	
Broadbridge, L.	H	1938	X-B	139	90.8	75	63	10	39.2	5
Brocket, L.	H	1952	Con.	7	4.6	5		5	2.7	1
Brookeborough, V.	H	1952	Con.	58	37.9	36	4	32	19.4	7
Brookes, L.	L	1909	Coṅ.	28	18.3	27	1	26	14.5	
Brooks of Tremorfa, L.	L	1927	Lab.	117	76.5	70	70		37.6	7
Brougham and Vaux, L.	H	1938	Con.	138	90.2	146	2	142	77.4	77
Broxbourne, L.	L	1910	Con.	11	7.2	2		2	1.1	3
Bruce of Donington, L.	L	1912	Lab.	145	94.8	96	96		51.6	54
Bruce-Gardyne, L.	L	1930	Con.	66	43.1	36		36	19.4	20
Buccleuch and Queensberry, D.	H	- 1923	Con.	3	2.0	3		3	1.6	

Table C *(contd.)*

	Peerage type	Year of birth	Party	Attces	% attces	Total votes	Anti-Govt. votes	Pro-Govt. votes	% votes on Govt. bills	Interventions
Buchan, E.	H	1930	X-B	3	2.0					2
Buckinghamshire, E.	H	1944	Con.	18	11.8	3		3	1.6	1
Buckmaster, V.	H	1921	X-B	63	41.2	32	26	6	17.2	9
Burton, L.	H	1924	Con.	11	7.2	5		5	2.7	3
Burton of Coventry, B.	L	1904	SDP	99	64.7	22	19	3	11.8	27
Butterfield, L.	L	1920	X-B	55	35.9	12	4	8	6.5	8
Butterworth, L.	L	1918	Con.	129	84.3	122	1	119	64.5	6
Buxton of Alsa, L.	L	1918	Con.	15	9.8	5		5	2.7	3
+Byron, L.	H	1950	X-B	5	20.8	1		1	2.0	
Caccia, L.	L	1905	X-B	78	51.0	17		17	9.1	
+Cairns, E.	H	1939	X-B	1	1.6					
Caithness, E.	H	1948	Con.	98	64.1	160		159	85.5	184
Caldecote, V.	H	1917	Con.	63	41.2	27	4	23	14.5	25
Callaghan of Cardiff, L.	L	1912	Lab.	88	57.5	58	58		31.2	16
Camden, M.	H	1930	Con.	7	4.6	8		8	4.3	
Cameron of Lochbroom, L.	L	1931	Con.	9	5.9					1
Camoys, L.	H	1940	Con.	7	4.6	1		1	0.5	
Campbell of Alloway, L.	L	1917	Con.	146	95.4	93	3	90	50.0	80
Campbell of Croy, L.	L	1921	Con.	141	92.2	104		102	54.8	78

Campbell of Eskan, L.	L	1912	Lab.	55	35.9	30	30		16.1	
Canterbury, Abp	B	1921	Bp	4	2.6					2
Caradon, L.	L	1907	Lab.	6	3.9	2	2		1.1	
−Carlisle, Bp	B	1919	Bp	42	37.8					1
Carlisle, E.	H	1923	X-B	1	0.7					
Carlisle of Bucklow, L.	L	1929	Con.	26	17.0	3		3	1.6	4
Carmichael of Kelvingrove, L.	L	1921	Lab.	145	94.8	143	143		76.9	42
Carnarvon, E.	H	1924	X-B	27	17.6	7		7	3.8	1
Carnegy of Lour, B.	L	1925	Con.	123	80.4	128	3	122	67.2	44
Carnock, L.	H	1920	Con.	134	87.6	163		162	87.1	
Carr of Hadley, L.	L	1916	Con.	79	51.6	39	1	37	20.4	15
Carrington, L.	H	1919	Con.	12	7.8	4		4	2.2	1
Carter, L.	L	1932	Lab.	131	85.6	117	115		61.8	81
Carver, L.	L	1915	X-B	30	19.6	5		5	2.7	5
Cathcart, E.	H	1919	Con.	44	28.8	19		19	10.2	2
Cawley, L.	H	1913	Con.	18	11.8	15		15	8.1	
Cayzer, L.	L	1910	Con.	38	24.8	10		10	5.4	
Chalfont, L.	L	1919	X-B	23	15.0	1		1	0.5	4
Chandos, V.	H	1953	SDP	13	8.5	2	2		1.1	5
Charteris of Amisfield, L.	L	1913	X-B	20	13.1	1		1	0.5	2
Chelmer, L.	L	1914	Con.	23	15.0	24		24	12.9	2
Chelmsford, Bp	B	1930	Bp	18	11.8	2	1	1	1.1	2
+Chelmsford, V.	H	1931	Con.	6	5.4	3		3	1.7	
−Chelwood, L.	L	1917	Con.	32	53.3	8		8	27.6	28
Chesham, L.	H	1916	Con.	1	0.7					

Table C *(contd.)*

	Peerage type	Year of birth	Party	Attces	% attces	Total votes	Anti-Govt. votes	Pro-Govt. votes	% votes on Govt. bills	Interventions
Chester, Bp	B	1930	Bp	8	5.2	2	1	1	1.1	1
Chichester, Bp	B	1915	Bp	12	7.8					2
Chilston, V.	H	1946	Con.	2	1.3					1
Chitnis, L.	L	1936	X-B	23	15.0	3	3		1.6	
Cholmondeley, M.	H	1919	Oth.	13	8.5	6		6	3.2	
Chorley, L.	H	1930	X-B	27	17.6	8	3	5	4.3	3
Clancarty, E.	H	1911	X-B	10	6.5					
+Clanwilliam, E.	H	1919	Con.	19	70.4	19		19	36.5	
Cledwyn of Penrhos, L.	L	1916	Lab.	143	93.5	141	140		75.3	177
+Clifford of Chudleigh, L.	H	1948	X-B	3	3.1					
Clinton, L.	H	1934	Con.	16	10.5	21		21	11.3	2
Clitheroe, L.	H	1929	Con.	50	32.7	47		46	24.7	
Clwyd, L.	H	1935	X-B	9	5.9	1	1		0.5	
Clydesmuir, L.	H	1917	Con.	1	0.7					
Cobbold, L.	H	1937	Dem.	12	7.8	8	8		4.3	2
+Cockfield, L.	L	1916	Con.	82	60.3	38		38	20.4	8
Cocks of Hartcliffe, L.	L	1929	Lab.	148	96.7	134	133		71.5	12
Coleraine, L.	H	1931	Con.	140	91.5	72	1	71	38.7	17
Colgrain, L.	H	1920	X-B	4	2.6					
Colnbrook, L.	L	1922	Con.	96	62.7	68		68	36.6	8

Colville of Culross, V.	H	1933	Con.	34	22.2	8		8	4.3	1
Colwyn, L.	H	1942	Con.	139	90.8	64		61	32.8	15
Colyton, L.	C	1902	Oth	2	1.3	1		1	0.5	
Congleton, L.	H	1930	X-B	14	9.2	2	1	1	1.1	
Constantine of Stanmore, L.	L	1910	Con.	94	61.4	95		95	51.1	2
Cork and Orrery, E.	H	1910	Con.	84	54.9	67	1	66	36.0	3
Cornwallis, L.	H	1921	X-B	31	20.3	11	2	9	5.9	4
Cottenham, E.	H	1948	Con.	3	2.0	1		1	0.5	
Cottesloe, L.	H	1900	Con.	132	86.3	89	1	88	47.8	1
Cowley, E.	H	1934	Con.	28	18.3	16		14	7.5	
Cox, B.	L	1937	Con.	106	69.3	46		44	23.7	23
Craigavon, V.	H	1944	X-B	139	90.8	107	42	63	56.5	7
Craigmyle, L.	H	1923	Con.	73	47.7	62		62	33.3	1
Craigton, L.	L	1904	Con.	59	38.6	19	1	18	10.2	13
Cranbrook, E.	H	1933	Con.	39	25.5	37	1	36	19.9	13
Cranworth, L.	H	1940	Con.	6	3.9	1		1	0.5	
Crathorne, L.	H	1939	Con.	83	54.2	19		19	10.2	
Crawshaw, L.	H	1933	Con.	7	4.6	6		6	3.2	
Crickhowell, L.	L	1934	Con.	59	38.6	44		44	23.7	15
−Croft, L.	H	1916	Con.	15	11.9	15		15	11.2	
Croham, L.	L	1917	X-B	18	11.8	3		3	1.6	2
Cromartie, E.	H	1904	Con.	3	2.0					
+Crook, L.	H	1926	X-B	3	14.3	1	1		2.5	
Cross, V.	H	1920	Con.	79	51.6	35	1	34	18.8	2
Cudlipp, L.	L	1913	Dem.	27	17.6	10	10		5.4	

Table C *(contd.)*

	Peerage type	Year of birth	Party	Attces	% attces	Total votes	Anti-Govt. votes	Pro-Govt. votes	% votes on Govt. bills	Interventions
Cullen of Ashbourne, L.	H	1912	Con.	140	91.5	94	1	93	50.5	8
Cunliffe, L.	H	1932	X-B	3	2.0					
+Dacre, B.	H	1929	X-B	1	0.8					
Dacre of Glanton, L.	L	1914	Con.	50	32.7	46	7	39	24.7	5
Dainton, L.	L	1914	X-B	42	27.5	3	3		1.6	2
Darcy (de Knayth), B.	H	1938	X-B	49	32.0	23	15	8	12.4	5
Darnley, E.	H	1941	Con.	1	0.7					
Daventry, V.	H	1921	Con.	21	13.7	28		28	15.1	1
David, B.	L	1913	Lab.	132	86.3	137	136		73.1	82
Davidson, V.	H	1928	Con.	140	91.5	184		183	98.4	143
Davies, L.	H	1940	Dem.	6	3.9	2	2		1.1	
Davies of Penrhys, L.	L	1913	Lab.	114	74.5	78	77		41.4	1
De Freyne, L.	H	1927	Con.	117	76.5	28	2	26	15.1	1
De La Warr, E.	H	1948	Con.	4	2.6	3		3	1.6	
De L'Isle, V.	C	1909	Con.	27	17.6	11		10	5.4	1
Dean of Beswick, L.	L	1923	Lab.	152	99.3	143	142		76.3	95
Deedes, L.	L	1913	Con.	3	2.0	2		2	1.1	
Delacourt-Smith of Alteryn, B.	L	1916	Lab.	1	0.7	1	1		0.5	
Denham, L.	H	1927	Con.	143	93.5	170		169	90.9	89

Denington, B.	L	1907	Lab.	8	5.2	6	6		3.2	
Denman, L.	H	1916	Con.	5	3.3	2		2	1.1	
Denning, L.	A	1899	X-B	2	1.3					18
Derwent, L.	H	1930	Con.	45	29.4	25	1	24	13.4	2
Devonshire, D.	H	1920	SDP	13	8.5					
Diamond, L.	L	1907	SDP	25	16.3	8	7	1	4.3	9
Dickinson, L.	H	1926	X-B	6	3.9	1	1		0.5	
Digby, L.	H	1924	Con.	15	9.8	7		7	3.8	
Dilhorne, V.	H	1932	Con.	123	80.4	75		75	40.3	9
Donaldson of Kingsbridge, L.	L	1907	Dem.	85	55.6	43	41	2	23.1	21
Donaldson of Lymington, L.	L	1920	X-B	5	3.3					1
Donegall, M.	H	1916	Con.	18	11.8	13		13	7.0	
Donoughmore, E.	H	1927	Con.	4	2.6	3	1	2	1.6	
Donoughue, L.	L	1934	Lab.	79	51.6	22	22		11.8	3
Dormand of Easington, L.	L	1919	Lab.	151	98.7	163	162		87.1	67
Dormer, L.	H	1914	Con.	22	14.4	15	1	14	8.1	1
Dowding, L.	H	1919	X-B	1	0.7					
+Downshire, M.	H	1929	Con.	2	28.6					
Dudley, B.	H	1907	Con.	23	15.0	4		4	2.2	
Dudley, E.	H	1920	Con.	6	3.9	1		1	0.5	1
Dulverton, L.	H	1915	Con.	14	9.2	10		10	5.4	3
Dundee, E.	H	1949	Con.	111	72.5	140		137	73.7	55
Dunleath, L.	H	1933	X-B	13	8.5	2	2		1.1	10
Dunrossil, V.	H	1926	X-B	85	55.6	12	4	8	6.5	1

Table C *(contd.)*

	Peerage type	Year of birth	Party	Attces	% attces	Total votes	Anti-Govt. votes	Pro-Govt. votes	% votes on Govt. bills	Interventions
Durham, Bp	B	1925	Bp	1	0.7					
Ebbisham, L.	H	1912	Con.	4	2.6	1		1	0.5	
Eccles, V.	C	1904	Con.	73	47.7	25		25	13.4	10
Eden of Winton, L.	L	1925	Con.	66	43.1	75		75	40.3	14
Edinburgh, D.	C	1921	Oth	1	0.7					
Edmund-Davies, L.	A	1906	X-B	56	36.6					
Effingham, E.	H	1905	Con.	150	98.0	48		48	25.8	
Elibank, L.	H	1923	Con.	80	52.3	67		67	36.0	3
Ellenborough, L.	H	1926	Con.	116	75.8	74	4	70	39.8	
Elles, B.	L	1921	Con.	38	24.8	45		45	24.2	6
Elliot of Harwood, B.	L	1903	Con.	126	82.4	131	11	119	69.9	26
Elliott of Morpeth, L.	L	1920	Con.	130	85.0	100		100	53.8	14
Elphinstone, L.	H	1953	Con.	5	3.3	6		6	3.2	
Elton, L.	H	1930	Con.	62	40.5	39		39	21.0	26
Elwyn-Jones, L.	L	1909	Lab.	127	83.0	102	102		54.8	75
Ely, Bp	B	1919	Bp	19	12.4					
Ely, M.	H	1913	Oth.	22	14.4	2	1	1	1.1	
Emslie, L.	L	1919	X-B	1	0.7					
Ennals, L.	L	1922	Lab.	116	75.8	89	88		47.3	61
–Enniskillen, E.	H	1918	Con.	4	4.3	1		1	1.4	

Erne, E.	H	1937	Con.	50	32.7	23		23	12.4	
Erroll, E.	H	1948	X-B	16	10.5	5	1	4	2.7	1
Erroll of Hale, L.	C	1914	Con.	108	70.6	56		56	30.1	5
+Essex, E.	H	1920	Oth.	8	8.2					
Evans of Claughton, L.	L	1928	Dem.	17	11.1	15	15		8.1	4
Ewart-Biggs, B.	L	1929	Lab.	146	95.4	127	127		68.3	36
Exeter, M.	H	1935	X-B	1	0.7					
Ezra, L.	L	1919	Dem.	136	88.9	96	92	4	51.6	103
Fairfax of Cameron, L.	H	1956	Con.	4	2.6					1
Faithfull, B.	L	1910	Con.	124	81.0	94	9	85	50.5	52
Falkender, B.	L	1932	Lab.	37	24.2	45	45		24.2	
Falkland, V.	H	1935	Dem.	141	92.2	104	99	3	54.8	37
Falmouth, V.	H	1919	Con.	5	3.3	5		5	2.7	
Fanshawe of Richmond, L.	L	1927	Con.	106	69.3	39		39	21.0	12
Ferrers, E.	H	1929	Con.	120	78.4	135		134	72.0	252
Ferrier, L.	L	1900	Con.	32	20.9	13		13	7.0	12
Feversham, L.	H	1945	X-B	25	16.3	9	5	4	4.8	
Fisher, L.	H	1921	Con.	14	9.2	5		5	2.7	
Fisher of Rednal, B.	L	1919	Lab.	83	54.2	80	80		43.0	28
Fitt, L.	L	1926	Oth.	149	97.4	46	46		24.7	15
Fletcher, L.	L	1903	Lab.	55	35.9	1	1		0.5	
Flowers, L.	L	1924	SDP	20	13.1	7	7		3.8	2
Foley, L.	H	1923	Oth.	14	9.2	16		16	8.6	1
Foot, L.	L	1909	Dem.	83	54.2	65	65		34.9	2
Forbes, L.	H	1918	Con.	11	7.2	10		10	5.4	

Table C *(contd.)*

	Peerage type	Year of birth	Party	Attces	% attces	Total votes	Anti-Govt. votes	Pro-Govt. votes	% votes on Govt. bills	Interventions
Forester, L.	H	1938	Con.	12	7.8	13	3	10	7.0	
Forte, L.	L	1908	Con.	4	2.6	2		2	1.1	
Fortescue, E.	H	1922	Con.	95	62.1	72		71	38.2	6
+Fraser of Carmyllie, L.	L	1945	Con.	62	51.7	112		110	61.5	22
Fraser of Kilmorack, L.	L	1915	Con.	131	85.6	98		98	52.7	2
−Fraser of Tullybelton, L.	A	1911	X-B	5	13.5					
Gainford, L.	H	1921	Con.	151	98.7	76	1	75	40.9	26
Gainsborough, E.	H	1923	X-B	16	10.5	8	5	3	4.3	1
Gallacher, L.	L	1920	Lab.	128	83.7	125	125		67.2	43
Galpern, L.	L	1903	Lab.	149	97.4	132	131		70.4	1
Gardner of Parkes, B.	L	1927	Con.	142	92.8	75		75	40.3	58
Geddes, L.	H	1937	Con.	18	11.8	8		8	4.3	6
Gibson, L.	L	1916	X-B	38	24.8	8	4	4	4.3	6
Gibson-Watt, L.	L	1918	Con.	45	29.4	39		39	21.0	2
Gifford, L.	H	1940	Lab.	6	3.9	1	1		0.5	2
Gisborough, L.	H	1927	Con.	64	41.8	65	2	63	34.9	17
Gladwyn, L.	C	1900	Dem.	136	88.9	88	84	4	47.3	4
Glenamara, L.	L	1912	Lab.	92	60.1	35	35		18.8	35
Glenarthur, L.	H	1944	Con.	93	60.8	83		83	44.6	118
Gloucester, Bp	B	1925	B	1	0.7					

Gloucester, D.	H	1944	X-B	2	1.3					
Goff of Chieveley, L.	A	1926	X-B	16	10.5					3
Goodman, L.	L	1913	X-B	5	3.3					5
Goold, L.	L	1934	Con.	30	19.6	27		27	14.5	1
Gorell, L.	H	1927	X-B	7	4.6					1
Gormanston, V.	H	1939	Con.	4	2.6	3		3	1.6	
Goschen, V.	H	1965	Con.	3	2.0					
Gowrie, E.	H	1939	Con.	1	0.7	1		1	0.5	1
Graham of Edmonton, L.	L	1925	Lab.	145	94.8	166	164		88.2	125
Grantchester, L.	H	1921	X-B	89	58.2	31	5	26	16.7	13
Granville, E.	H	1918	Oth.	1	0.7					
Granville of Eye, L.	L	1899	X-B	144	94.1	1		1	0.5	
Gray, L.	H	1931	Con.	12	7.8	4		4	2.2	
Gray of Contin, L.	L	1927	Con.	117	76.5	77		76	40.9	13
Greene of Harrow Weald, L.	L	1910	Lab.	6	3.9					
Greenhill of Harrow, L.	L	1913	X-B	122	79.7	12	5	7	6.5	9
Greenway, L.	H	1941	X-B	147	96.1	80	12	68	43.0	11
Gregson, L.	L	1924	Lab.	116	75.8	30	29		15.6	3
Grenfell, L.	H	1935	Lab.	1	0.7					
Grey, E.	H	1939	Dem.	144	94.1	121	116	5	65.1	3
+Grey of Codnor, L.	L	1903	Oth.	1	4.2					
Gridley, L.	H	1906	Con.	126	82.4	93		93	50.0	6
Griffiths, L.	A	1923	X-B	19	12.4					4
Grimond, L.	L	1913	Dem.	141	92.2	43	40	3	23.1	63
Grimston of Westbury, L.	H	1925	Con.	49	32.0	38		38	20.4	

Table C *(contd.)*

	Peerage type	Year of birth	Party	Attces	% attces	Total votes	Anti-Govt. votes	Pro-Govt. votes	% votes on Govt. bills	Interventions
Grimthorpe, L.	H	1915	Con.	30	19.6	26		26	14.0	1
Guildford, Bp	B	1929	Bp	14	9.2	1	1		0.5	4
Hacking, L.	H	1938	X-B	70	45.8	20	12	5	9.1	16
Haddington, E.	H	1941	Con.	20	13.1	10	1	9	5.4	
Haig, E.	H	1918	Con.	26	17.0	31	1	30	16.7	3
Hailsham of Saint Marylebone, L.	L	1907	Con.	128	83.7	116		116	62.4	85
Halifax, E.	H	1944	Con.	1	0.7	1		1	0.5	
Halsbury, E.	H	1908	X-B	143	93.5	90	26	64	48.4	64
Hampden, V.	H	1937	X-B	3	2.0					
Hampton, L.	H	1925	Dem.	137	89.5	122	117	5	65.6	4
Hankey, L.	H	1905	X-B	34	22.2	3		3	1.6	4
Hanson, L.	L	1922	Con.	15	9.8	11		11	5.9	1
Hanworth, V.	H	1916	SDP/ Dem.	137	89.5	88	79	9	47.3	33
+Harding of Petherton, L.	H	1928	Oth.	2	4.2					
Hardinge, V.	H	1956	X-B	3	2.0					
Hardinge of Penshurst, L.	H	1921	Con.	56	36.6	42	3	39	22.6	
Harlech, L.	H	1954	Con.	9	5.9	12		12	6.5	
Harmar-Nicholls, L.	L	1912	Con.	137	89.5	89	1	87	47.3	78

Harmsworth, L.	H	1903	Dem.	1	0.7	1	1		0.5	
Harris of Greenwich, L.	L	1930	Dem.	147	96.1	109	101	6	57.5	61
Harris of High Cross, L.	L	1924	X-B	19	12.4	4		4	2.2	4
Harrowby, E.	H	1922	Con.	21	13.7	7	1	6	3.8	3
Hartwell, L.	L	1911	X-B	1	0.7					
Harvey of Prestbury, L.	L	1906	Con.	14	9.2	1		1	0.5	
Harvey of Tasburgh, L.	H	1921	Con.	2	1.3	1		1	0.5	
Harvington, L.	L	1907	Con.	81	52.9	66		66	35.5	2
Hastings, L.	H	1912	Con.	1	0.7	1		1	0.5	
Hatch of Lusby, L.	L	1917	Lab.	151	98.7	112	109		58.6	109
Havers, L.	L	1923	Con.	67	43.8	87		87	46.8	2
Hayter, L.	H	1911	X-B	144	94.1	64	51	13	34.4	12
Headfort, M.	H	1932	X-B	21	13.7	9	2	7	4.8	
Hemingford, L.	H	1934	X-B	8	5.2	5	5		2.7	5
Hemphill, L.	H	1928	Con.	32	20.9	22		21	11.3	
Henderson of Brompton, L.	L	1922	X-B	109	71.2	55	34	21	29.6	21
Henley, L.	H	1953	Con.	126	82.4	186		183	98.4	109
Henniker, L.	H	1916	Dem.	16	10.5	6	6		3.2	3
Hereford, Bp	B	1920	Bp	11	7.2	2		2	1.1	
Hertford, M.	H	1930	Con.	20	13.1	17		17	9.1	
Hesketh, L.	H	1950	Con.	126	82.4	175		174	93.5	207
Heycock, L.	L	1905	Lab.	31	20.3					
Hill-Norton, L.	L	1915	X-B	21	13.7	1	1		0.5	4
Hirshfield, L.	L	1913	Lab.	96	62.7	58	55	3	31.2	
Hives, L.	H	1913	Con.	126	82.4	171		171	91.9	

Table C *(contd.)*

	Peerage type	Year of birth	Party	Attces	% attces	Total votes	Anti-Govt. votes	Pro-Govt. votes	% votes on Govt. bills	Interventions
Holderness, L.	L	1920	Con.	85	55.6	73		73	39.2	
Home of the Hirsel, L.	L	1903	Con.	94	61.4	74		74	39.8	7
Hood, V.	H	1914	Con.	75	49.0	70	2	68	37.6	11
Hooper, B.	L	1939	Con.	128	83.7	160		160	86.0	92
Hooson, L.	L	1925	Dem.	102	66.7	38	37	1	20.4	22
Houghton of Sowerby, L.	L	1898	Lab.	149	97.4	90	90		48.4	18
Howe, E.	H	1951	Con.	9	5.9	3		3	1.6	
Howie of Troon, L.	L	1924	Lab.	107	69.9	55	55		29.6	18
Hughes, L.	L	1911	Lab.	101	66.0	57	57		30.6	9
Hunt, L.	L	1910	Dem.	64	41.8	40	38	2	21.5	23
Hunt of Tanworth, L.	L	1919	X-B	8	5.2					1
Hunter of Newington, L.	L	1915	X-B	72	47.1	28	6	22	15.1	13
Huntly, M.	H	1944	Con.	13	8.5	1		1	0.5	
Hutchinson of Lullington, L.	L	1915	Dem.	54	35.3	23	22	1	12.4	25
Hylton, L.	H	1932	X-B	67	43.8	35	34	1	18.8	103
Hylton-Foster, B.	L	1908	X-B	145	94.8	121	20	101	65.1	4
Iddesleigh, E.	H	1932	X-B	6	3.9	1		1	0.5	
Ilchester, E.	H	1920	X-B	60	39.2	13	7	6	7.0	2
Inchcape, E.	H	1917	Con.	7	4.6					

Ingleby, V.	H	1926	X-B	23	15.0					1
–Inglewood, L.	C	1909	Con.	1	1.0					
Ingrow, L.	L	1917	Con.	27	17.6	23		23	12.4	1
Ironside, L.	H	1924	Con.	118	77.1	21		21	11.3	10
Irvine of Lairg, L.	L	1940	Lab.	65	42.5	46	46		24.7	13
Irving of Dartford, L.	L	1918	Lab.	144	94.1	73	73		39.2	25
Jacques, L.	L	1905	Lab.	29	19.0	21	21		11.3	4
Jakobovits, L.	L	1921	X-B	3	2.0					1
Jauncey of Tullichettle, L.	A	1925	X-B	12	7.8					1
Jay, L.	L	1907	Lab.	66	43.1	67	67		36.0	31
Jeger, B.	L	1915	Lab.	132	86.3	120	120		64.5	42
Jellicoe, E.	H	1918	Con.	15	9.8	2		2	1.1	1
Jenkin of Roding, L.	L	1926	Con.	108	70.6	87		84	45.2	34
Jenkins of Hillhead, L.	L	1920	Dem.	112	73.2	72	67	4	38.2	26
Jenkins of Putney, L.	L	1908	Lab.	105	68.6	68	68		36.6	48
Jessel, L.	H	1904	Con.	35	22.9	5		5	2.7	
John-Mackie, L.	L	1909	Lab.	149	97.4	98	98		52.7	46
Johnston of Rockport, L.	L	1915	Con.	129	84.3	127		127	68.3	2
Joseph, L.	L	1918	Con.	102	66.7	84		84	45.2	4
Kaberry of Adel, L.	L	1907	Con.	95	62.1	66		66	35.5	
Kagan, L.	L	1915	Lab.	78	51.0	28	27		14.5	1
Kearton, L.	L	1911	X-B	66	43.1	25	24	1	13.4	5
Keith of Kinkel, L.	A	1922	X-B	14	9.2					
Kemsley, V.	H	1909	Con.	8	5.2	7		7	3.8	
Kenilworth, L.	H	1954	Con.	81	52.9	16	1	15	8.6	1
Kennet, L.	H	1923	SDP	142	92.8	42	40	2	22.6	196

Table C *(contd.)*

	Peerage type	Year of birth	Party	Attces	% attces	Total votes	Anti-Govt. votes	Pro-Govt. votes	% votes on Govt. bills	Interventions
Keyes, L.	H	1919	Con.	16	10.5	8		8	4.3	
Kilbracken, L.	H	1920	Lab.	147	96.1	87	87		46.8	25
–Kilbrandon, L.	A	1906	X-B	2	1.6					
Killanin, L.	H	1914	X-B	13	8.5	1	1		0.5	
Killearn, L.	H	1919	Con.	137	89.5	70		68	36.6	5
Kilmarnock, L.	H	1927	SDP	152	99.3	56	52	2	29.0	31
Kimball, L.	L	1928	Con.	104	68.0	85		84	45.2	8
Kimberley, E.	H	1924	Con.	43	28.1	8		8	4.3	21
King of Wartnaby, L.	L	1918	Con.	13	8.5	12		12	6.5	1
Kings Norton, L.	L	1902	X-B	41	26.8	4	3	1	2.2	
Kinloss, Ly	H	1922	X-B	133	86.9	75	35	40	40.3	23
Kinnaird, L.	H	1912	Con.	59	38.6	26	1	25	14.0	1
Kinnoull, E.	H	1935	Con.	119	77.8	22		22	11.8	4
–Kintore, E.	H	1908	Con.	1	0.8					
Kirkhill, L.	L	1930	Lab.	107	69.9	66	63		33.9	11
Kirkwood, L.	H	1931	Dem.	11	7.2	7	7		3.8	1
Kissin, L.	L	1912	X-B	2	1.3					
Kitchener, E.	H	1919	Con.	37	24.2	25	1	24	13.4	
Knights, L.	L	1920	X-B	11	7.2	9	1	8	4.8	5
Knollys, V.	H	1931	Con.	12	7.8	9		9	4.8	

Knutsford, V.	H	1926	Con.	26	17.0	38	1	37	20.4	1
Lane, L.	A	1918	X-B	2	1.3					2
Lauderdale, E.	H	1911	Con.	142	92.8	115	9	103	60.2	42
Lawrence, L.	H	1937	X-B	144	94.1	56	31	25	30.1	
+Layton, L.	H	1947	Con.	59	52.7	57		57	32.6	
Leatherland, L.	L	1898	Lab.	138	90.2	57	57		30.6	10
Leathers, V.	H	1908	X-B	30	19.6	1		1	0.5	
Leicester, Bp	B	1925	Bp	5	3.3	1	1		0.5	
Lewin, L.	L	1920	X-B	15	9.8					1
+Lewis of Newnham, L.	L	1928	X-B	9	7.4					1
Lichfield, Bp	B	1934	Bp	7	4.6					
Limerick, E.	H	1930	Con.	8	5.2	2		2	1.1	3
−Lindsay, E.	H	1926	Con.	10	7.8					1
Lindsey and Abingdon, E.	H	1931	Con.	75	49.0	44		44	23.7	1
Listowel, E.	H	1906	Lab.	84	54.9	79	78		41.9	8
Liverpool, Bp	B	1929	Bp	11	7.2	3	2	1	1.6	1
Liverpool, E.	H	1944	Con.	46	30.1	16	1	15	8.6	2
Llewelyn-Davies of Hastoe, B.	L	1915	Lab.	125	81.7	89	87		46.8	2
Lloyd of Hampstead, L.	L	1915	X-B	87	56.9	29	9	20	15.6	3
Lloyd of Kilgerran, L.	L	1907	Dem.	140	91.5	98	94	4	52.7	51
Lloyd-George of Dwyfor, E.	H	1924	X-B	28	18.3	4	1	3	2.2	
Loch, L.	H	1920	Con.	2	1.3	1		1	0.5	
Lockwood, B.	L	1924	Lab.	102	66.7	118	118		63.4	36
London, Bp	B	1921	Bp	6	3.9					2

Table C *(contd.)*

	Peerage type	Year of birth	Party	Attces	% attces	Total votes	Anti-Govt. votes	Pro-Govt. votes	% votes on Govt. bills	Interventions
Long, V.	H	1929	Con.	145	94.8	181		178	95.7	29
Longford, E.	C	1905	Lab.	151	98.7	104	103		55.4	24
Lonsdale, E.	H	1922	Con.	3	2.0	3		3	1.6	
Lothian, M.	H	1922	Con.	31	20.3	10		10	5.4	
Loudoun, C.	H	1919	X-B	2	1.3	2		2	1.1	
Lovat, L.	H	1933	Con.	56	36.6	10		10	5.4	
Lovell-Davis, L.	L	1924	Lab.	81	52.9	86	86		46.2	2
Lowry, L.	L	1919	X-B	13	8.5					
Lucas of Chilworth, L.	H	1926	Con.	133	86.9	82	2	78	43.0	30
Luke, L.	H	1905	Con.	38	24.8	24		24	12.9	
Lurgan, L.	H	1911	Con.	22	14.4	12		12	6.5	
Lyell, L.	H	1939	Con.	81	52.9	102		102	54.8	46
Lytton, E.	H	1950	X-B	23	15.0	5	1	4	2.7	2
McAlpine of Moffat, L.	L	1907	Con.	37	24.2	34		34	18.3	
McAlpine of West Green, L.	L	1942	Con.	26	17.0	16		16	8.6	1
+Macaulay of Bragar, L.	L	1933	Lab.	49	36.0	42	40		21.5	26
McCarthy, L.	L	1925	Lab.	59	38.6	51	51		27.4	32
McCluskey, L.	L	1929	X-B	8	5.2					3
+McColl of Dulwich L.	L	1933	Con.	24	88.9	23		23	44.2	

McFadzean, L.	L	1903	Con.	51	33.	34		34	18.3	
McFadzean of Kelvinside, L.	L	1915	X-B	5	3.3					
McFarlane of Llandaff, B.	L	1926	X-B	18	11.8	1	1		0.5	2
McGregor of Durris, L.	L	1921	Dem.	105	68.6	32	32		17.2	4
McIntosh of Haringey, L.	L	1933	Lab.	139	90.8	129	128		68.8	84
Mackay of Clashfern, L.	L	1927	Con.	136	88.9	132		132	71.0	98
Mackenzie-Stuart, L.	L	1924	X-B	2	1.3					
Mackie of Benshie, L.	L	1919	Dem.	52	34.0	45	45		24.2	38
Mackintosh of Halifax, V.	H	1958	Con.	7	4.6	1		1	0.5	
Maclean, L.	L	1916	Oth.	17	11.1					
MacLehose of Beoch, L.	L	1917	X-B	65	42.5	5	1	4	2.7	10
Macleod of Borve, B.	L	1915	Con.	118	77.1	119	1	118	64.0	40
–McNair, L.	H	1915	Dem.	123	95.3	114	108	5	83.1	19
Macpherson of Drumochter, L.	H	1924	Con.	13	8.5	4		4	2.2	
Mais, L.	L	1911	Dem.	77	50.3	33	32	1	17.7	
Malmesbury, E.	H	1907	Con.	56	36.6	62	1	61	33.3	
Manchester, Bp	B	1924	Bp	22	14.4	2	2		1.1	13
Manchester, D.	H	1938	X-B	35	22.9	7	1	6	3.8	
Mancroft, L.	H	1957	Con.	70	45.8	45		44	23.7	5
Mansfield, E.	H	1930	Con.	5	3.3	1		1	0.5	
Manton, L.	H	1924	Con.	35	22.9	36		36	19.4	
Mar, C.	H	1940	X-B	36	23.5	3	2	1	1.6	30
Marchwood, V.	H	1936	Con.	1	0.7	3		3	1.6	

Table C *(contd.)*

	Peerage type	Year of birth	Party	Attces	% attces	Total votes	Anti-Govt. votes	Pro-Govt. votes	% votes on Govt. bills	Interventions
Margadale, L.	C	1906	Con.	116	75.8	126		126	67.7	
Marlborough, D.	H	1926	Con.	1	0.7					
Marley, L.	H	1913	Con.	148	96.7	132		130	69.9	5
Marsh, L.	L	1928	X-B	30	19.6	2		2	1.1	1
Marshall of Goring, L.	L	1932	X-B	1	0.7					
Marshall of Leeds, L.	L	1915	Con.	134	87.6	51		51	27.4	4
Masham of Ilton, B.	L	1935	X-B	98	64.1	33	20	13	17.7	26
Mason of Barnsley, L.	L	1924	Lab.	121	79.1	103	102		54.8	61
Massereene and Ferrard, V.	H	1914	Con.	59	38.6	32		32	17.2	23
Maude of Stratford-upon-Avon, L.	L	1912	Con.	54	35.3	47		47	25.3	2
Mayhew, L.	L	1915	Dem.	91	59.5	64	58	3	32.8	49
Melchett, L.	H	1948	Lab.	0	0.0					2
Mellish, L.	L	1913	Oth.	145	94.8	15	15		8.1	70
Melville, V.	H	1937	Con.	19	12.4	5		5	2.7	
Merrivale, L.	H	1917	Con.	146	95.4	147	1	144	78.0	9
Mersey, V.	H	1934	Con.	130	85.0	121	3	115	63.4	17
Meston, L.	H	1950	Dem.	61	39.9	22	22		11.8	17
Middleton, L.	H	1921	Con.	58	37.9	65	1	64	34.9	9

Milford, L.	H	1902	X-B	2	1.3					
Milne, L.	H	1909	X-B	5	3.3	2		2	1.1	2
Milner of Leeds, L.	H	1923	Lab.	63	41.2	62	62		33.3	
Milverton, L.	H	1930	Con.	76	49.7	54	11	43	29.0	3
Minto, E.	H	1928	X-B	1	0.7					
Mishcon, L.	L	1915	Lab.	117	76.5	61	61		32.8	69
Molloy, L.	L	1918	Lab.	146	95.4	76	76		40.9	133
Molson, L.	L	1903	Con.	1	0.7					
Monckton of Brenchley, V.	H	1915	X-B	7	4.6	2		2	1.1	1
Monk Bretton, L.	H	1924	Con.	51	33.3	87	4	83	46.8	12
Monkswell, L.	H	1947	Lab.	9	5.9	4	4		2.2	8
Monson, L.	H	1932	X-B	109	71.2	90	75	13	47.3	64
Montagu of Beaulieu, L.	H	1926	Con.	112	73.2	6		6	3.2	9
+Monteagle of Brandon, L.	H	1926	Con.	26	18.6	31		31	16.7	
Montgomery of Alamein, V.	H	1928	Con.	69	45.1	49		49	26.3	27
Moore of Wolvercote, L.	L	1921	X-B	37	24.2					1
Moran, L.	H	1924	X-B	124	81.0	18	11	7	9.7	26
Morris, L.	H	1937	Con.	137	89.5	102	4	98	54.8	53
Morris of Kenwood, L.	H	1928	SDP	5	3.3	8	8		4.3	
Morton of Shuna, L.	L	1930	X-B	23	15.0	1	1		0.5	3
Mostyn, L.	H	1920	Con.	18	11.8	10		10	5.4	
Mottistone, L.	H	1920	Con.	130	85.0	108	4	103	57.5	58
Mountbatten of Burma, C.	H	1924	X-B	2	1.3					

Table C *(contd.)*

	Peerage type	Year of birth	Party	Attces	% attces	Total votes	Anti-Govt. votes	Pro-Govt. votes	% votes on Govt. bills	Interventions
Mountevans, L.	H	1943	X-B	147	96.1	90	41	49	48.4	16
Mountgarret, V.	H	1936	Con.	39	25.5	28	2	26	15.1	8
Mowbray and Stourton, L.	H	1923	Con.	108	70.6	81	1	80	43.5	12
Moyne, L.	H	1905	Con.	68	44.4	27	7	20	14.5	9
Moyola, L.	L	1923	Con.	3	2.0					
Mulley, L.	L	1918	Lab.	149	97.4	71	71		38.2	13
Munster, E.	H	1926	Con.	144	94.1	139		137	73.7	3
Murray of Epping Forest, L.	L	1922	Lab.	51	33.3	46	46		24.7	10
Murton of Lindisfarne, L.	L	1914	Con.	93	60.8	106		104	55.9	16
Napier and Ettrick, L.	H	1930	X-B	136	88.9	30		30	16.1	1
Napier of Magdala, L.	H	1940	X-B	4	2.6					
Nathan, L.	L	1922	X-B	43	28.1	8	7	1	4.3	2
Nelson, E.	H	1941	Con.	137	89.5	133	4	128	71.0	
Nelson of Stafford, L.	H	1917	Con.	50	32.7	31		30	16.1	6
Newall, L.	H	1930	Con.	74	48.4	34		34	18.3	2
Newcastle, Bp	B	1929	Bp	17	11.1	3		3	1.6	
Nicol, B.	L	1923	Lab.	133	86.9	147	146		78.5	50
Norfolk, D.	H	1915	Con.	91	59.5	72		72	38.7	7

Norrie, L.	H	1936	Con.	119	77.8	86	2	83	45.7	18
Northbourne, L.	H	1926	X-B	41	26.8	6	3	3	3.2	3
Northesk, E.	H	1926	Con.	11	7.2	11		11	5.9	
Northfield, L.	L	1923	Lab.	113	73.9	90	89		47.8	50
Nugent of Guildford, L.	L	1907	Con.	138	90.2	112	1	111	60.2	70
O'Brien of Lothbury, L.	L	1908	X-B	45	29.4	12		12	6.5	
Ogmore, L.	H	1931	Dem.	86	56.2	72	69	3	38.7	
O'Hagan, L.	H	1945	Con.	9	5.9	4	1	3	2.2	15
Oliver of Aylmerton, L.	A	1921	X-B	16	10.5					3
O'Neill of the Maine, L.	L	1914	X-B	143	93.5	35	35		18.8	1
Onslow, E.	H	1938	Con.	87	56.9	77	2	75	41.4	31
+Oppenheim-Barnes, B.	L	1930	Con.	47	38.8	63	2	61	35.2	11
Oram, L.	L	1913	Lab.	57	37.3	31	31		16.7	2
Orkney, E.	H	1919	Con.	141	92.2	144		143	76.9	
Orr-Ewing, L.	L	1912	Con.	126	82.4	86		86	46.2	40
Oxford and Asquith, E.	H	1916	X-B	5	3.3					
Oxfuird, V.	H	1934	Con.	136	88.9	126		126	67.7	27
Paget of Northampton, L.	L	1908	Lab.	116	75.8	13	13		7.0	24
Parry, L.	L	1925	Lab.	28	18.3	23	23		12.4	11
Peel, E.	H	1947	Con.	16	10.5	3		3	1.6	2
Pender, L.	H	1933	Con.	121	79.1	117	1	115	62.4	1
Pennock, L.	L	1920	Con.	53	34.6	18	1	17	9.7	1
Penrhyn, L.	H	1908	Con.	41	26.8	61		61	32.8	
Perry of Walton, L.	L	1921	SDP	47	30.7	15	13	2	8.1	1
Perth, E.	H	1907	X-B	35	22.9	5		5	2.7	13
Peston, L.	L	1931	Lab.	146	95.4	106	103		55.4	109

Table C *(contd.)*

	Peerage type	Year of birth	Party	Attces	% attces	Total votes	Anti-Govt. votes	Pro-Govt. votes	% votes on Govt. bills	Interventions
+Peterborough, Bp	B	1925	Bp	2	6.9					
+Petre, L.	H	1942	X-B	1	2.6					
Peyton of Yeovil, L.	L	1919	Con.	89	58.2	74	7	67	39.8	27
Phillips, B.	L	1910	Lab.	131	85.6	105	103		55.4	69
Pitt of Hampstead, L.	L	1913	Lab.	147	96.1	117	115		61.8	18
Platt of Writtle, B.	L	1923	Con.	81	52.9	52		52	28.0	12
Plowden, L.	L	1907	X-B	2	1.3					1
Plumb, L.	L	1925	Con.	1	0.7	1		1	0.5	
Plummer of St Marylebone, L.	L	1914	Con.	53	34.6	30		30	16.1	1
Plunket, L.	H	1925	Con.	2	1.3					1
Poltimore, L.	H	1957	Con.	1	0.7					
Polwarth, L.	H	1916	Con.	6	3.9	3		3	1.6	
Ponsonby of Shulbrede, L.	H	1930	Lab.	151	98.7	162	159		85.5	14
Porritt, L.	L	1900	X-B	134	87.6	54	11	43	29.0	1
Portland, D.	H	1897	Con.	42	27.5	14		14	7.5	
Portman, V.	H	1934	Con.	8	5.2	3		3	1.6	
Portsmouth, E.	H	1954	Con.	13	8.5	13		13	7.0	3
Prior, L.	L	1927	Con.	53	34.6	14		14	7.5	1

Prys-Davies, L.	L	1923	Lab.	136	88.9	90	90		48.4	49
Pym, L.	L	1922	Con.	89	58.2	48	1	47	25.8	5
Quinton, L.	L	1925	Con.	59	38.6	43		43	23.1	1
Radnor, E.	H	1927	Con.	36	23.5	53	2	51	28.5	15
Raglan, L.	H	1927	SDP	46	30.1	18	15	2	9.1	2
Rankeillour, L.	H	1935	Con.	101	66.0	89		87	46.8	1
Rathcreedan, L.	H	1905	Dem.	62	40.5	30	28	2	16.1	
Rawlinson of Ewell, L.	L	1919	Con.	25	16.3	4		4	2.2	9
Rayleigh, L.	H	1960	Con.	4	2.6	2		2	1.1	
Rea, L.	H	1928	Lab.	143	93.5	62	62		33.3	22
Reading, M.	H	1942	Con.	6	3.9	1		1	0.5	1
Reay, L.	H	1937	Con.	135	88.2	127		126	67.7	29
Redesdale, L.	H	1932	Con.	21	13.7	20		19	10.2	2
Rees, L.	L	1926	Con.	83	54.2	36		35	18.8	9
Rees-Mogg, L.	L	1928	X-B	7	4.6	1		1	0.5	1
Reigate, L.	L	1905	Con.	44	28.8	32		32	17.2	
Reilly, L.	L	1912	X-B	120	78.4	23	20	3	12.4	2
Remnant, L.	H	1930	Con.	1	0.7	1		1	0.5	
Renton, L.	L	1908	Con.	124	81.0	119	7	112	64.0	99
Renwick, L.	H	1935	Con.	123	80.4	72		72	38.7	3
Richardson, L.	L	1910	X-B	37	24.2	12		12	6.5	3
Richardson of Duntisbourne, L.	L	1915	X-B	2	1.3					
Ridley, V.	H	1925	Con.	23	15.0					3
Ripon, Bp	B	1931	Bp	16	10.5	5	4	1	2.7	2
Rippon of Hexham, L.	L	1924	Con.	101	66.0	37	4	33	19.9	37

Table C *(contd.)*

	Peerage type	Year of birth	Party	Attces	% attces	Total votes	Anti-Govt. votes	Pro-Govt. votes	% votes on Govt. bills	Interventions
Ritchie of Dundee, L.	H	1919	Dem.	86	56.2	69	67	2	37.1	11
Robertson of Oakridge, L.	H	1930	X-B	43	28.1	2		2	1.1	3
Robson of Kiddington, B.	L	1919	Dem.	56	36.6	37	36	1	19.9	17
Rochdale, V.	C	1906	Con.	47	30.7	55		55	29.6	
Rochester, L.	H	1916	Dem.	121	79.1	118	112	6	63.4	49
Rockley, L.	H	1934	Con.	2	1.3	1		1	0.5	
Rodney, L.	H	1920	Con.	107	69.9	79		78	41.9	14
Roll of Ipsden, L.	L	1907	X-B	13	8.5	1	1		0.5	3
Rollo, L.	H	1915	Con.	4	2.6	5		5	2.7	
Romney, E.	H	1910	Con.	56	36.6	54	4	50	29.0	1
Rootes, L.	H	1917	Con.	7	4.6	6		6	3.2	
Roskill, L.	A	1911	X-B	40	26.1	5	1	4	2.7	3
Ross of Newport, L.	L	1926	Dem.	47	30.7	80	79	1	43.0	36
Rotherwick, L.	H	1912	Con.	2	1.3	2		2	1.1	
Rugby, L.	H	1913	X-B	101	66.0	46	23	22	24.2	8
Russell, E.	H	1937	Dem.	56	36.6	63	63		33.9	57
Russell of Liverpool, L.	H	1952	X-B	128	83.7	21	13	8	11.3	
Ryder of Eaton Hastings, L.	L	1916	X-B	2	1.3					

Ryder of Warsaw, B.	L	1923	X-B	31	20.3	2	1	1	1.1	2
Sackville, L.	H	1913	Con.	4	2.6	7		7	3.8	
Sainsbury, L.	L	1902	SDP	147	96.1	69	64	5	37.1	
+Sainsbury of Preston Candover, L.	L	1927	Con.	6	4.7	3		3	1.6	
St Albans, Bp	B	1929	Bp	20	13.1	1		1	0.5	3
Saint Albans, D.	H	1939	Con.	80	52.3	18		18	9.7	
St Aldwyn, E.	H	1912	Con.	26	17.0	12		12	6.5	
Saint Brides, L.	L	1916	X-B	43	28.1	16	9	7	8.6	2
St Davids, V.	H	1917	X-B	139	90.8	74	1	72	39.2	28
St Germans, E.	H	1941	Con.	24	15.7	9		9	4.8	
St John of Bletso, L.	H	1957	X-B	116	75.8	24	3	19	11.8	4
St John of Fawsley, L.	L	1929	Con.	150	98.0	31		31	16.7	31
Saint Levan, L.	H	1919	Con.	9	5.9	6		6	3.2	
Saint Oswald, L.	H	1919	Con.	23	15.0	13		13	7.0	
Salisbury, Bp	B	1928	Bp	12	7.8	6	6		3.2	1
Salisbury, M	H	1916	Con.	3	2.0	3		3	1.6	1
Saltoun of Abernethy, Ly	H	1930	X-B	118	77.1	112	17	93	59.1	40
Sanderson of Bowden, L.	L	1933	Con.	94	61.4	144		142	76.3	66
Sandys, L.	H	1931	Con.	34	22.2	3		3	1.6	3
Savile, L.	H	1919	Con.	26	17.0	35		35	18.8	
Scanlon, L.	L	1913	Lab.	45	29.4	29	29		15.6	2
Scarbrough, E.	H	1932	Con.	2	1.3	1		1	0.5	
Scarman, L.	A	1911	X-B	4	2.6					
Schon, L.	L	1912	X-B	126	82.4					
Seafield, E.	H	1939	Con.	8	5.2					

Table C *(contd.)*

	Peerage type	Year of birth	Party	Attces	% attces	Total votes	Anti-Govt. votes	Pro-Govt. votes	% votes on Govt. bills	Interventions
Seear, B.	L	1913	Dem.	135	88.2	131	124	4	68.8	123
Seebohm, L.	L	1909	X-B	127	83.0	73	26	47	39.2	24
Sefton of Garston, L.	L	1915	Lab.	102	66.7	63	63		33.9	32
Selborne, E.	H	1940	Con.	39	25.5	26		26	14.0	1
Selkirk, E.	H	1906	Con.	69	45.1	30		30	16.1	29
Selsdon, L.	H	1937	Con.	5	3.3	1		1	0.5	
Sempill, Ly	H	1920	Con.	69	45.1	32		32	17.2	
Serota, B.	L	1919	Lab.	135	88.2	102	102		54.8	7
Shackleton, L.	L	1911	Lab.	106	69.3	62	61	1	33.3	5
Shannon, E.	H	1924	X-B	153	100.0	85	18	67	45.7	7
+Sharp of Grimsdyke, L.	L	1916	Con.	1	3.4					
Sharples, B.	L	1923	Con.	77	50.3	91	3	88	48.9	16
Shaughnessy, L.	H	1922	X-B	128	83.7	39	16	23	21.0	3
Shawcross, L.	L	1902	SDP	2	1.3					
Sheffield, Bp	B	1930	Bp	15	9.8	2		2	1.1	3
Shepherd, L.	H	1918	Lab.	100	65.4	88	88		47.3	10
Sherfield, L.	C	1904	X-B	93	60.8	4	3	1	2.2	6
Shrewsbury, E.	H	1952	Con.	38	24.8	22	1	21	11.8	10
Shuttleworth, L.	H	1948	Con.	2	1.3	1		1	0.5	
Sidmouth, V.	H	1914	X-B	4	2.6					1

Simon, V.	H	1902	Dem.	34	22.2	23	23		12.4	
Simon of Glaisdale, L.	L	1911	X-B	96	62.7	12	6	6	6.5	19
Skelmersdale, L.	H	1945	Con.	117	76.5	154		154	82.8	91
Slim, V.	H	1927	X-B	103	67.3	30	1	29	16.1	1
Smith, L.	L	1914	X-B	40	26.1					
Somers, L.	H	1907	X-B	103	67.3	59	18	39	30.6	18
Somerset, D.	H	1952	X-B	20	13.1	15	8	7	8.1	
Soper, L.	L	1903	Lab.	145	94.8	21	21		11.3	5
Soulbury, V.	H	1915	X-B	3	2.0					
Southborough, L.	H	1922	Con.	14	9.2	30		30	16.1	
Southwark, Bp	B	1926	Bp	22	14.4	1	1		0.5	6
Stafford, L.	H	1954	Con.	5	3.3	1		1	0.5	
Stallard, L.	L	1921	Lab.	150	98.0	90	88		47.3	45
Stanley of Alderley, L.	H	1927	Con.	49	32.0	66	6	60	35.5	33
Stedman, B.	L	1916	SDP	133	86.9	104	102	2	55.9	10
Stevens of Ludgate, L.	L	1936	Con.	17	11.1	8		8	4.3	3
Stewart of Fulham, L.	L	1906	Lab.	56	36.6	52	52		28.0	4
Stockton, E.	H	1943	Con.	31	20.3	22	1	20	11.3	3
Stodart of Leaston, L.	L	1916	Con.	63	41.2	43	1	42	23.1	9
Stoddart of Swindon, L.	L	1926	Lab.	139	90.8	143	143		76.9	105
Stokes, L.	L	1914	X-B	7	4.6					
Strabolgi, L.	H	1914	Lab.	148	96.7	112	110		59.1	32
Strafford, E.	H	1936	X-B	4	2.6					
Strange, B.	H	1928	Con.	111	72.5	107	4	103	57.5	51
Strathcarron, L.	H	1924	Con.	93	60.8	49		49	26.3	4
Strathclyde, L.	H	1960	Con.	141	92.2	168		167	89.8	76

Table C *(contd.)*

	Peerage type	Year of birth	Party	Attces	% attces	Total votes	Anti-Govt. votes	Pro-Govt. votes	% votes on Govt. bills	Interventions
Strathcona and Mount Royal, L.	H	1923	Con.	76	49.7	40		40	21.5	1
Strathmore and Kinghorne, E.	H	1957	Con.	27	17.6	45		45	24.2	5
Strathspey, L.	H	1912	Con.	85	55.6	58		58	31.2	
Strauss, L.	L	1901	Lab.	8	5.2					
Sudeley, L.	H	1939	Con.	99	64.7	73		72	38.7	4
Suffield, L.	H	1922	Con.	29	19.0	22		22	11.8	1
Swann, L.	L	1920	X-B	19	12.4	6	6		3.2	3
Swansea, L.	H	1925	Con.	120	78.4	50		50	26.9	7
Swinfen, L.	H	1938	Con.	143	93.5	75	3	71	39.8	19
Swinton, E.	H	1937	Con.	44	28.8	35	1	34	18.8	16
Tanlaw, L.	L	1934	X-B	2	1.3					1
Taylor of Blackburn, L.	L	1929	Lab.	146	95.4	97	97		52.2	28
Taylor of Gryfe, L.	L	1912	SDP	98	64.1	69	68	1	37.1	63
Taylor of Hadfield, L.	L	1905	Con.	18	11.8	2		2	1.1	1
Taylor of Mansfield, L.	L	1895	Lab.	132	86.3	99	98		52.7	
Tedder, L.	H	1926	SDP	1	0.7					
Templeman, L.	A	1920	X-B	36	23.5					3
Tenby, V.	H	1927	X-B	28	18.3					1

Terrington, L.	H	1915	X-B	133	86.9	59		59	31.7	
Teviot, L.	H	1934	Con.	145	94.8	83	1	82	44.6	18
Teynham, L.	H	1928	Con.	106	69.3	21		21	11.3	
Thomas of Gwydir, L.	L	1920	Con.	134	87.6	164		163	87.6	6
Thomas of Swynnerton, L.	L	1931	Con.	49	32.0	45	2	43	24.2	4
Thomson of Monifieth, L.	L	1921	X-B/ Dem.	16	10.5	21	21		11.3	
Thorneycroft, L.	L	1909	Con.	74	48.4	30		30	16.1	9
Thurlow, L.	H	1912	X-B	96	62.7	44	13	31	23.7	3
Thurso, V.	H	1922	Dem.	24	15.7	9	9		4.8	3
Todd, L.	L	1907	X-B	10	6.5	3	2	1	1.6	
Tollemache, L.	H	1939	Con.	2	1.3	1		1	0.5	
Tonypandy, V.	C	1909	X-B	18	11.8	1	1		0.5	1
Tordoff, L.	L	1928	Dem.	128	83.7	132	126	5	70.4	90
Torphichen, L.	H	1946	Con.	6	3.9	8		8	4.3	
Torrington, V.	H	1943	Con.	39	25.5	21		21	11.3	4
Townshend, M.	H	1916	Con.	2	1.3	3		3	1.6	
–Trafford, L.	L	1932	Con.	87	67.4	124	1	123	91.2	48
Tranmire, L.	L	1903	Con.	61	39.9	46		46	24.7	1
Trefgarne, L.	H	1941	Con.	119	77.8	118		118	63.4	156
Trenchard, V.	H	1951	Con.	13	8.5	10		9	4.8	1
Trevethin and Oaksey, L.	H	1929	Con.	2	1.3					
Trevor, L.	H	1928	Oth.	1	0.7					
Trumpington, B.	L	1922	Con.	101	66.0	160		160	86.0	146
Truro, Bp	B	1922	Bp	16	10.5	2	1	1	1.1	3

Table C *(contd.)*

	Peerage type	Year of birth	Party	Attces	% attces	Total votes	Anti-Govt. votes	Pro-Govt. votes	% votes on Govt. bills	Interventions
Tryon, L.	H	1940	X-B	46	30.1	23	1	22	12.4	
Turner of Camden, B.	L	1923	Lab.	145	94.8	139	139		74.7	88
Tweeddale, M.	H	1947	X-B	30	19.6	2	2		1.1	
Tweedsmuir, L.	H	1911	Con.	5	3.3	2		2	1.1	
Ullswater, V.	H	1942	Con.	84	54.9	85		85	45.7	24
Underhill, L.	L	1914	Lab.	142	92.8	165	164		88.2	112
Vaux of Harrowden, L.	H	1915	Con.	141	92.2	141	1	140	75.8	
Vernon, L.	H	1923	Dem.	26	17.0	14	13	1	7.5	1
Vinson, L.	L	1931	Con.	45	29.4	24	1	22	12.4	8
Waldegrave, E.	H	1905	Con.	23	15.0	23		23	12.4	1
Wallace of Campsie, L.	L	1915	Lab.	1	0.7					
Wallace of Coslany, L.	L	1906	Lab.	103	67.3	98	98		52.7	19
+Walpole, L.	H	1938	X-B	8	33.3	3		3	6.0	
Walston, L.	L	1912	SDP	93	60.8	83	81	2	44.6	18
+Walton of Detchant, L.	L	1922	X-B	6	21.4	1		1	1.5	
Wardington, L.	H	1924	Con.	3	2.0					
Warnock, B.	L	1924	X-B	20	13.1	8	7	1	4.3	4
Watkinson, V.	C	1910	Con.	9	5.9	4		4	2.2	
Wedderburn of Charlton, L.	L	1927	Lab.	46	30.1	34	34		18.3	8

Wedgwood, L.	H	1954	Con.	8	5.2	5		5	2.7	
Weidenfeld, L.	L	1919	SDP	4	2.6					2
Weir, V.	H	1933	Con.	15	9.8	13	2	11	7.0	3
Wells-Pestell, L.	L	1910	Lab.	8	5.2					
Westbury, L.	H	1922	Con.	138	90.2	52		52	28.0	8
Westmorland, E.	H	1924	Oth.	1	0.7					
Whaddon, L.	L	1927	Dem.	140	91.5	77	71	5	40.9	11
White, B.	L	1909	Lab.	121	79.1	145	142		76.3	29
Whitelaw, V.	C	1918	Con.	70	45.8	44		44	23.7	4
Wigoder, L.	L	1921	Dem.	56	36.6	20	20		10.8	5
Wigram, L.	H	1915	Con.	12	7.8	7		7	3.8	
Wilberforce, L.	A	1907	X-B	108	70.6	5	3	2	2.7	4
Williams of Elvel, L.	L	1933	Lab.	153	100.0	144	141		75.8	105
Willis, L.	L	1918	Lab.	71	46.4	38	38		20.4	2
Willoughby de Broke, L.	H	1938	Con.	11	7.2	6		6	3.2	1
Wilson of Langside, L.	L	1916	SDP	25	16.3	10	9	1	5.4	4
Wilson of Rievaulx, L.	L	1916	Lab.	130	85.0	22	22		11.8	
Winchester, Bp	B	1926	Bp	3	2.0					1
Winchilsea and Nottingham, E.	H	1936	Dem.	83	54.2	57	52	5	30.6	1
Windlesham, L.	H	1932	Con.	59	38.6	47		47	25.3	3
Winstanley, L.	L	1918	Dem.	120	78.4	79	74	5	42.5	58
Winterbottom, L.	L	1913	SDP	127	83.0	42	42		22.6	
Wise, L.	H	1923	Con.	152	99.3	88	7	81	47.3	6
Wolfson, L.	L	1927	Con.	45	29.4	34		34	18.3	8
Woolton, E.	H	1958	X-B	1	0.7					

Table C *(contd.)*

	Peerage type	Year of birth	Party	Attces	% attces	Total votes	Anti-Govt. votes	Pro-Govt. votes	% votes on Govt. bills	Interventions
Worcester, Bp	B	1929	Bp	15	9.8	3	2	1	1.6	3
Wrenbury, L.	H	1927	X-B	2	1.3	1	1		0.5	
Wyatt of Weeford, L.	L	1918	X-B	123	80.4	52	1	51	28.0	12
Wynford, L.	H	1917	Con.	46	30.1	111	1	110	59.7	2
Yarborough, E.	H	1920	Con.	8	5.2	15		15	8.1	
Young, B.	L	1926	Con.	90	58.8	65		63	33.9	13
Young of Dartington, L.	L	1915	SDP/ Lab.	23	15.0	22	19		10.2	2
Young of Graffham, L.	L	1932	Con.	66	43.1	58		58	31.2	133
Zouche of Haryngworth, L.	H	1943	Con.	50	32.7	21	1	20	11.3	
Zuckerman, L.	L	1904	X-B	55	35.9	3	3		1.6	6

INDEX

Notes: The Appendices are not indexed; bills are from the 1988–9 session unless otherwise indicated; holders of hereditary peerages are identified as such by the inclusion of a number ('1st', '2nd', etc.).